MW00986408

DEFA
East German Cinema, 1946–1992

DEFA

EAST GERMAN CINEMA, 1946–1992

edited by

Seán Allan and John Sandford

Berghahn Books

NEW YORK · OXFORD

First published in 1999 by
Berghahn Books

www.berghahnbooks.com

Reprinted in 2001, 2002, and 2003.

© 1999, 2001, 2002, 2003 Seán Allan and John Sandford

Library of Congress Cataloging-in-Publication Data

DEFA: East German cinema / edited by Seán Allan and John Sandford
Includes bibliographical references and index.
ISBN 1-57181-943-6 (cl.: alk. paper)
ISBN 1-57181-753-0 (pbk.: alk. paper)
1. DEFA—History. 2. Motion picture industry—Germany (East)—
History. 3. Motion Pictures—Germany (East)—History I. Allan,
Seán. II. Sandford, John, 1944- .

PN1999.D4D34 1999

384' .8'09431—dc21   97-41567

British Library Cataloguing in Publication Data

A CIP catalogue record for this book is available from
the British Library.

Printed in the United States on acid-free paper

CONTENTS

Abbreviations   vii

List of Illustrations   viii

Preface   ix

1.   DEFA: AN HISTORICAL OVERVIEW   1
     Seán Allan

2.   DEFA AND THE TRADITIONS OF INTERNATIONAL CINEMA   22
     Barton Byg

3.   'LETTING THE GENIE OUT OF THE BOTTLE':
     DEFA FILM-MAKERS AND *FILM UND FERNSEHEN*   42
     Rosemary Stott

4.   THE ANTI-FASCIST PAST IN DEFA FILMS   58
     Christiane Mückenberger

5.   DISCUSSION WITH KURT MAETZIG   77
     Martin Brady

6.   REBELS WITH A CAUSE: THE DEVELOPMENT OF THE
     '*BERLIN-FILME*' BY GERHARD KLEIN AND WOLFGANG KOHLHAASE   93
     Horst Claus

7.   DEFA: A PERSONAL VIEW   117
     Wolfgang Kohlhaase

8.   REPRESENTATIONS OF WORK IN THE FORBIDDEN DEFA FILMS
     OF 1965   131
     Karen Ruoff Kramer

9.   CENSORSHIP AND THE LAW: THE CASE OF *DAS KANINCHEN
     BIN ICH (I AM THE RABBIT)*   146
     Stefan Soldovieri

10. PATHS OF DISCOVERY: THE FILMS OF KONRAD WOLF   164
     Anthony S. Coulson

11. FROM MODELS TO MISFITS: WOMEN IN DEFA FILMS OF THE
    1970S AND 1980S   183
    Andrea Rinke

12. THE CONCEPT OF 'HEIMAT-GDR' IN DEFA FEATURE FILMS   204
    Harry Blunk

13. THE RE-EVALUATION OF GOETHE AND THE CLASSICAL TRADITION
    IN THE FILMS OF EGON GÜNTHER AND SIEGFRIED KÜHN   222
    Daniela Berghahn

14. IDEALISM TAKES ON THE ESTABLISHMENT: SOCIAL CRITICISM
    IN ROLAND GRÄF'S FILM ADAPTATIONS OF *MÄRKISCHE
    FORSCHUNGEN (EXPLORING THE BRANDENBURG MARCHES)*
    AND *DER TANGOSPIELER (THE TANGO PLAYER)*   245
    Detlef Gwosc

15. THE DOCUMENTARY WORK OF JÜRGEN BÖTTCHER:
    A RETROSPECTIVE   267
    Richard Kilborn

16. DOCUMENTING THE *WENDE*: THE FILMS OF ANDREAS VOIGT   283
    Helen Hughes

About the Contributors   302

Appendix: Research Sources for East German Cinema   305

Select Bibliography   309

Index   320

ABBREVIATIONS

BAP	Bundesarchiv Potsdam
BRD	Bundesrepublik Deutschland (FRG)
DDR	Deutsche Demokratische Republik (GDR)
DEFA	Deutsche Film-AG
FDJ	Freie Deutsche Jugend
FRG	Federal Republic of Germany
GDR	German Democratic Republic
GST	Gesellschaft für Sport und Technik
KPD	Kommunistische Partei Deutschlands
MDR	Mitteldeutscher Rundfunk
NÖSPL	Neues Ökonomisches System der Planung und Leitung der Volkswirtschaft
NSDAP	Nationalsozialistische Deutsche Arbeiterpartei
NVA	Nationale Volksarmee
PDS	Partei des Demokratischen Sozialismus
RIAS	Rundfunk im amerikanischen Sektor
SAG	Sowjetische Aktiengesellschaft
SAPMO	Stiftung Archiv der Parteien und Massenorganisationen der DDR im Bundesarchiv
SED	Sozialistische Einheitspartei Deutschlands
SFB	Sender Freies Berlin
SMAD	Sowjetische Militäradministration in Deutschland
Stasi	Staatssicherheitsdienst
Ufa	Universum-Film AG
VEB	Volkseigener Betrieb
WPA	Work Projects Administration
ZDF	Zweites Deutsches Fernsehen
ZK	Zentralkomitee

LIST OF ILLUSTRATIONS

The first DEFA film, *Die Mörder sind unter uns* (*The Murderers Are Among Us*, 1946)

Hildegard Knef and Ernst Wilhelm Borchert in *Die Mörder sind unter uns*

Jaecki Schwarz in *Ich war neunzehn* (*I Was Nineteen*), released in 1968

Aleksei Eibozhenko and Jaecki Schwarz in *Ich war neunzehn*

Berlin – Ecke Schönhauser (*Berlin – Schönhauser Corner*), released in 1957

SOLO SUNNY (1980), one of DEFA's most popular films

Manfred Krug in *Spur der Steine* (*Traces of the Stones*, 1966)

Kurt Maetzig's film *Das Kaninchen bin ich* (*I am the Rabbit*), suppressed in 1965

Hilmar Thate and Wolfgang Heinz in *Professor Mamlock* (1961)

Anke Friedrich and Heidemarie Schneider in *Das Fahrrad* (*The Bicycle*, 1982)

Heidemarie Schneider in *Das Fahrrad*

Hilmar Baumann, Katharina Thalbach and Jutta Hoffmann in *Lotte in Weimar* (1975)

Hans-Jürgen Wolf and Irmhild Wagner in *Die Leiden des jungen Werthers* (*The Sorrows of Young Werther*, 1976)

Roland Gräf's *Märkische Forschungen* (*Exploring the Brandenburg Marches*, 1982)

PREFACE

In stark contrast to its West German counterpart, East German cinema remains a largely unknown phenomenon in the English-speaking world and one which has received relatively little attention in the academic press. This volume seeks to redress this imbalance by introducing the reader to some of the key figures and themes from the cinema of the former GDR. To this end, the majority of the chapters have been arranged in roughly chronological order. The initial chapter of the volume attempts to provide a contextual framework for the reader unfamiliar with East German cinema by linking developments in film aesthetics to some of the key historical, political and cultural developments in the GDR. Needless to say, any attempt at such periodisation is bound to be flawed and subject to revision – and it is the hope of the editors that this volume will help stimulate such debates in the future.

During the preparation of this volume, it was far from easy to decide what should and should not be included. It was felt that the tradition of documentary film-making in the GDR was such an important phenomenon – and one which exerted such considerable influence on the makers of feature-films – that it could not be ignored. There are, however, inevitably omissions, perhaps the most serious being the absence of any detailed discussion of DEFA children's films, a genre for which East German cinema was held in particularly high esteem. This genre is in itself so extensive and complex that it was felt that it would not be possible to do justice to it in a volume of this size.

The essays published in this volume are, for most part, based on papers delivered at a conference on East German cinema staged by The Centre for East German Studies at the University of Reading. This conference – the first of its kind outside Germany – was made possible by financial assistance from the Goethe-Institut, London and the British Academy. In particular we would like to thank Margaret Deriaz of the Goethe-Institut, London and Hiltrud Schulz of Progress Film-Verleih GmbH, Berlin for their support of the project.

A great many people offered their assistance during the preparation of this volume. We are particularly grateful to Margaret Vallance for translating a number of articles from the German and to Birgit Röder for transcribing Wolfgang Kohlhaase's verbal address and preparing the bibliography for the volume. We would also like to acknowledge the generosity of the Research Endowment Trust Fund at the University of Reading who provided financial assistance towards the preparation of the volume. We are also very grateful to Barbara Newson of Berghahn Books for her editorial support.

It was with great sadness that the editors learned of the death of Harry Blunk as this volume was being compiled. Harry Blunk was a pioneer in the field of DEFA studies and it seems wholly appropriate that this volume should be dedicated to his memory.

The first DEFA film, *Die Mörder sind unter uns* (*The Murderers Are Among Us*, 1946) was directed by Wolfgang Staudte (left) and starred Hildegard Knef (right)

Hildegard Knef (left) and Ernst Wilhelm Borchert (right) in *Die Mörder sind unter uns*

The performance of Jaecki Schwarz (left) was a major factor in the success of Konrad Wolf's anti-fascist film *Ich war neunzehn* (*I Was Nineteen*), released in 1968

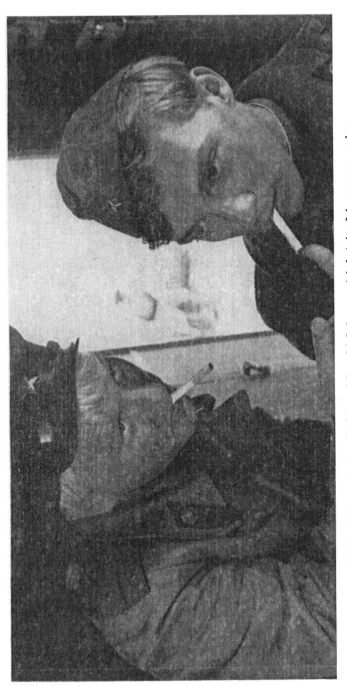

Aleksei Eibozhenko (left) and Jaecki Schwarz (right) in *Ich war neunzehn*

Berlin – Ecke Schönhauser (*Berlin – Schönhauser Corner*), released in 1957, was one of a series of films by Gerhard Klein and Wolfgang Kohlhaase focusing on young people in East Berlin during the 1950s

SOLO SUNNY (1980), directed by Konrad Wolf and Wolfgang Kohlhaase and starring Renate Krößner in the title role, became one of DEFA's most popular films

Manfred Krug (centre) as Hannes Balla in Frank Beyer's *Spur der Steine* (*Traces of the Stones*, 1966)

Kurt Maetzig's film *Das Kaninchen bin ich* (*I am the Rabbit*) was among the films to be suppressed in the wake of the Eleventh Plenum in December 1965

Hilmar Thate (left) and Wolfgang Heinz (right) in Konrad Wolf's *Professor Mamlock* (1961)

Anke Friedrich (left) and Heidemarie Schneider (right) in Evelyn Schmidt's *Das Fahrrad* (*The Bicycle*, 1982)

Heidemarie Schneider as Susanne in *Das Fahrrad*

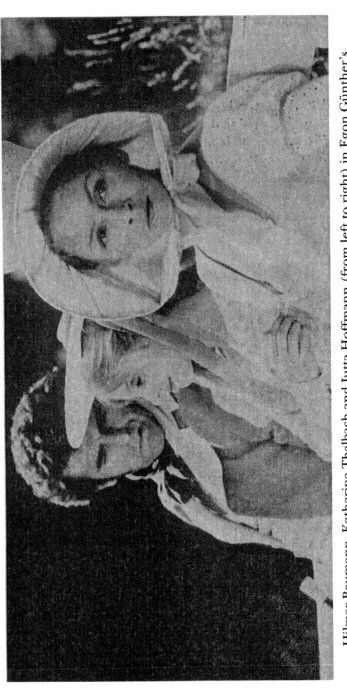

Hilmar Baumann, Katharina Thalbach and Jutta Hoffmann (from left to right) in Egon Günther's *Lotte in Weimar* (1975)

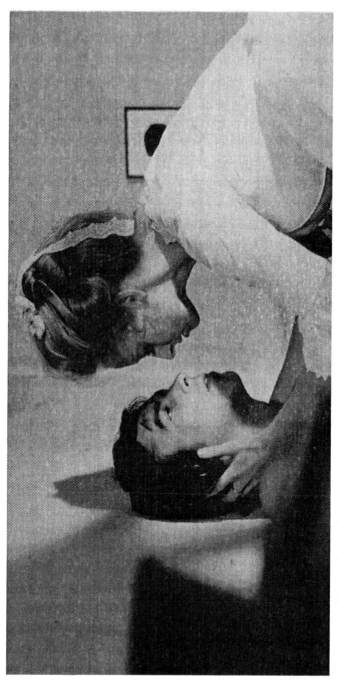

Hans-Jürgen Wolf and Irmhild Wagner in Egon Günther's *Die Leiden des jungen Werthers* (*The Sorrows of Young Werther*, 1976)

Roland Gräf's *Märkische Forschungen* (*Exploring the Brandenburg Marches*, 1982) based on the novel by Günter de Bruyn

DEFA: AN HISTORICAL OVERVIEW

Seán Allan

Some months before the sale of the DEFA studios to the French Conglomerate, the Compagnie Générale des Eaux (CGE) in December 1992, the name DEFA (Deutsche Film AG) was expunged from the official register of German companies. During the forty-five years of its existence, DEFA, the state-owned film company of the GDR, produced some 750 films. Although fourteen of these featured in a recent list of the hundred best German films of all time, few who did not grow up in the former GDR are familiar with more than a handful of them. This was not always the case. The first post-war German film to be shown outside Germany was a DEFA film, Wolfgang Staudte's *Die Mörder sind unter uns* (*The Murderers Are Among Us*, 1946). In the 1950s and 1960s, DEFA films were regularly screened at international festivals. But a number of factors resulted in East German cinema being confined to relative obscurity, among them the impact of the Cold War and the sense of betrayal felt by left-wing intellectuals following the Soviet intervention in the Prague Spring of 1968. In addition, unlike the national cinemas of other Eastern Bloc states, the development of East German cinema was hampered by an adherence to an increasingly outmoded realist aesthetic, a shortcoming which was to become increasingly apparent when set against the rise of the New German Cinema in the Federal Republic during the late 1960s, 1970s and early 1980s. In the light of these and other factors, it is tempting to dismiss East German cinema as dull and propagandistic, as merely an appendage of the state ideological apparatus. To do so, however, is to ignore the often considerable tensions that existed between the film-makers and their political masters and to overlook the excellence and originality of a number of films produced by DEFA at very different periods of the company's existence.

The origins of DEFA date back to the final stages of World War II. After the liberation of Berlin, the main centres of the German film-industry – located in and around the capital – fell into Soviet hands. Among these was the vast studio complex in Potsdam-Babelsberg in which so many of the classic pre-war German films had been produced and which belonged to the Ufa company (Universum-Film AG) – an organisation closely associated in German minds with the cultivation of that melodramatic pathos so evident in numerous films of the Nazi era. But even before the end of the war, negotiations were taking place aimed at normalising cultural production in Germany and making use of the cinema to counter years of Nazi indoctrination. To this end, the first cinemas in Berlin were reopened on 28 April 1945 showing dubbed versions of Soviet films that had been banned by the Hitler regime. The Soviets had little doubt about the educational potential of the cinema in Germany and whilst the Western Allies viewed film with a considerable degree of suspicion, the Soviet Military Administration in Germany (SMAD) wasted no time in attempting to re-establish film-production in their zone of occupation. In this they were well served by two men blessed with an intimate knowledge and understanding of German culture, Colonel Sergei Tulpanov and Major Alexander Dymschitz. Indeed so successful were they in their efforts that by the end of 1946, the first DEFA films had been released almost three years before the founding of the GDR in October 1949.

DEFA: The Early Years

On 25 August 1945, the Soviet Military Administration set up the *Zentralverwaltung für Volksbildung* ('Central Administration for Public Education') under Paul Wandel. Wandel in turn appointed Herbert Volkmann to head the section responsible for literature and the arts. In accordance with a Soviet directive issued on 4 September 1945 (No. 51), Volkmann started to compile a list of people with direct experience of film-making. Among those to approach Volkmann in the first instance were Carl Haacker, Willy Schiller, Kurt Maetzig, Alfred Lindemann,

Adolf Fischer and Hans Klering,[1] – all of whom became founder members of the *Filmaktiv*, a group established in October 1945 and entrusted with formulating a set of proposals for the revival of German cinema. On 22 November 1945 a historic meeting took place in the former Hotel Adlon in Berlin attended not only by the members of the *Filmaktiv*, but also by Friedrich Wolf, Gerhard Lamprecht, Wolfgang Staudte, Georg Klaren, and Peter Pewas among others.[2] In his closing remarks, the dramatist Friedrich Wolf appealed for a form of critical cinema that would address the problems of the transitional period and which would assist in bringing about a 'new and better Germany'.[3] In December, the proposals put forward by the *Filmaktiv* were officially approved and on 1 January 1946 Wolfgang Staudte started shooting the first sections of documentary footage in a railway tunnel under the River Spree with a view to incorporating them in a projected feature film, *Kolonne Strupp* (*The Strupp Convoy*).[4] Two weeks later, Kurt Maetzig started shooting the first edition of the news-reel *Der Augenzeuge* (*The Eyewitness*).

It was not until 13 May 1946, however, that the Soviet Military Administration granted DEFA a licence to produce films.[5] Despite this, work on the first feature film, Staudte's *Die Mörder sind unter uns*, had already started on 4 May. Speaking at the ceremony, Colonel Tulpanov remarked that 'DEFA faces a number of important tasks. Of these, the most crucial is the struggle to restore democracy in Germany and remove all traces of fascist and miltaristic ideology from the minds of every German, the struggle to re-educate the German people – especially the young – to a true understanding of genuine democracy and humanism, and in so doing, to promote a sense of respect for other people and other nations.'[6] On 13 August DEFA was officially registered as a joint stock company based in Berlin and with a starting capital of 20,000 marks supplied by *Zentrag*, a subsidiary organisation of the recently constituted Socialist Unity Party (SED). Hans Klering was appointed company secretary and the board of directors was made up of Alfred Lindemann, Karl Hans Bergmann and Herbert Volkmann. By the end of the year, DEFA could point proudly to three completed feature films: Staudte's *Die Mörder sind unter uns*, Milo Harbich's *Freies Land* (*A Free Country*) and Gerhard Lamprecht's *Irgendwo in Berlin* (*Somewhere in Berlin*).

Since the studios in Potsdam-Babelsberg were still being used by the Soviet Military Administration, the company's head office was initially situated in Berlin. Accordingly, one of the first tasks was the negotiation of lease agreements for the use of facilities in Berlin (the former Tobis studios) and Babelsberg (the former Althoff-Atelier). The following year, however, saw a number of far-reaching changes to the economic organisation in the Soviet zone. Those industrial plants which had not been dismantled and transported to the Soviet Union as part of the reparations agreement – some 200 in all – were converted to so-called *Sowjetische Aktiengesellschaften* ('Soviet Joint Stock Companies') or SAGs for short. As a result, on 14 July 1947 DEFA's head office was transferred to Potsdam and on 11 November the company became an SAG, its basic capital being increased to some ten million marks (once again by *Zentrag*). There was, however, considerable debate as to what form the internal reorganisation of the company should take.[7] Two proposals were put forward. Under the first, the Germans would control 55 percent of the company, with the Soviets controlling the remaining 45 percent. Under this scheme the Soviet influence within the company was to be quite transparent. Under the second scheme, it would be the Soviets who would control 55 percent of the company; however, in this case the degree of Soviet influence would remain concealed by appointing owners of Soviet capital who were German 'or who could be described as such'.[8] It was the latter proposal that was implemented on 3 November 1947. Thus Karl Hans Bergmann, Alfred Lindemann and Herbert Volkmann were to be joined by Ilja Trauberg and Alexander Wolkenstein on the board of directors.[9] In addition both the Soviet and German factions signed an additional agreement drawn up by the SED, whereby a select committee would be presented with an outline of the company's plans and would be shown rough cuts and completed versions of the films produced. And on 10 November, a further committee, the *Filmkommission* – or *DEFA-Kommission* as it became known – was set up to oversee matters arising out of the agreement of 3 November, a commision consisting of Anton Ackermann, Otto Meier, Erich Gniffke, Paul Wandel and Gustav von Wangenheim. Their duties consisted principally in liaising between the company and the Central Committee of the SED on matters relating to changes in personnel.

1947: The First Film-Makers' Conference and the Start of the Cold War

In 1947 the notion of a future unitary German state was still the guiding principle in formulating cultural policy in the Soviet Zone of Occupation. It was against this background that the *1. Film-Autoren-Kongreß* ('First Conference of Film-Makers') was held in Potsdam-Babelsberg on 6-9 June 1947, an event to which film-makers from all zones were invited. For as Alfred Lindemann put it – perhaps rather optimistically – in his address, 'It is our hope that this congress will provide the momentum for a broad exchange of views on how to build a secure basis for the revival of German cinema, an exchange of views which need not be hampered by the zonal divisions within Germany.'[10] Behind Lindemann's appeal for cooperation, other pressing concerns were clearly discernible. First, there was the very real threat that Germany would become a dumping ground for imported films that had been banned during the Nazi period. As Lindemann remarked:

> It will not be easy for us to make our mark. We must be quite clear that our ten-year isolation from the rest of the world has led to a backlog of foreign films which will be dumped on the German market in the near future. The dangers inherent in this are well exemplified by what has happened to film production in one particular country. For in 1946, after little more than a year, the American film industry acquired the rights to some 60 percent of films produced there with the result that its film industry cannot recoup its costs even on its home ground.[11]

If there was to be a revival in German cinema, it was imperative that Lindemann and his colleagues moved quickly. But whilst they had had relatively little difficulty assembling a new ensemble of actors, film technicians and directors, the lack of suitable scripts was becoming a serious problem. As Lindemann continued:

> In our efforts to build up a new generation of film-makers, one of the problems we have not yet overcome is that of finding script-writers. DEFA has succeeded in recruiting a number of talented writers; however, they do not find it easy to break with the style associated with the film companies of former times.[12]

Kurt Maetzig also referred to this tendency of even the new writers to lapse into the melodramatic pathos of the Ufa cinema in his conference address. Nonetheless, in urging writers to adopt a new approach 'not just in matters of form, but also in their choice of subject matter',[13] he showed that he understood full well – perhaps better than some of his colleagues – the popular appeal of this type of cinema for the average cinema-goer.

During the following year, however, it became increasingly clear that the zonal division of Germany could not be as easily ignored as Lindemann may have hoped. Developments in global politics had exacerbated the conflict between East and West, and in the Soviet Zone of Occupation the choice was between a 'German path to socialism' or a route following more closely that taken by the Soviet Union. In the event, it was the latter that was to prevail. At its First Party Congress, the SED opted to model itself on Stalin's Communist Party in the Soviet Union. On 23 May 1949, the Federal Republic was founded in the West, followed several months later by the founding of the German Democratic Republic on 7 October 1949.

Developments in the political sphere were also to have repercussions in the management structure of DEFA. In July 1948, Lindemann was dismissed on grounds of alleged financial irregularities, his place on the board being taken by Walter Janka.[14] On 6 October 1948, the SED strengthened its grip on the company when Janka, Volkmann and Maetzig were replaced on the board of directors by the loyal SED members Wilhelm Meißner, Alexander Lösche and Grete Keilson. Further changes were necessitated by the premature death of Ilja Trauberg in December 1948, his place on the board being taken by another Soviet director, Alexander Andriyevsky, and by the departure of Alexander Wolkenstein who in turn was replaced by another Soviet director, Leonid Antonov. However, perhaps the most important change was the arrival of Sepp Schwab, a hardline communist whose personal motto was, in the words of Albert Wilkening, 'better too little trust than too much'.[15]

DEFA in the 1950s

In his diary entry for 9 June 1949, Bertolt Brecht noted that 'DEFA … has all sorts of problems finding subjects, especially contemporary ones. Those at its head list significant themes: underground movement, distribution of land, two-year plan, the new man etc., etc.; then writers are supposed to devise stories that interpret the theme and its associated problems. This naturally often goes wrong.'[16] Hampered by a distinct lack of scripts capable of being exploited for the ideological offensive during the early phase of the Cold War, DEFA experienced acute difficulties in the early 1950s – only 30 films were released during the first four years of the decade. A number of these – Hans Deppe's *Die Kuckucks* (*The Cuckoos*, 1949) and Hans Müller's *Bürgermeister Anna* (*Mayoress Anna*, 1950) to name but two – had been singled out for criticism on the grounds that they were unsuited to the current ideological climate. In the light of this, Stefan Heymann, a member of the of the SED's executive committee wrote to the recently appointed Sepp Schwab in 23 June 1950, explaining that 'a decision has been taken that where films touch on certain topics ... not only the *DEFA-Kommission* but also the relevant members of the executive committee are to be consulted before the script is finalised'.[17] As a result there was often a striking discrepancy between what the board of directors wanted and what the freelance writers they engaged supplied. Indeed as Albert Wilkening – at that point production manager at the studio – noted:

> Whereas in the early days the process of putting an idea into production had been a relatively informal affair, increasingly the board of directors began to scrutinise these ideas on the basis of treatments, scripts and sometimes even the finished product itself. Often they demanded changes – both major and minor – without really offering an adequate constructive explanation. This led to scripts having to be radically rewritten several times over and demands for changes to the final versions of the films. Apart from the annoyance this caused to our freelancers, the whole thing ushered in a climate of uncertainty. Nobody was clear any more what it was that the board really wanted.[18]

In addition the efforts of film-makers and artists were also hampered in the early 1950s by the prevailing realist aesthetic. The extremes to which such an approach could be taken are well illustrated by a paper entitled 'Establishing a progressive German culture: the problem of formalist tendencies in art and literature' delivered by Hans Lauter at the Fifth

Conference of the SED's Central Committee in 1951: 'The task of art ... is to inspire the individual to achieve the targets set out in the Five-Year Plan'.[19] Such attacks were to have a detrimental effect on the aesthetic development of cinema in the GDR. Looking back some thirty years later, Albert Wilkening notes: 'All too often an unusual way of filming something or a strange lighting effect resulted in a film being accused of displaying formalistic tendencies. For years this led to our films having a rather ordinary, conventional look to them. In the absence of a socialist theory of aesthetics, the debates about formalist tendencies contributed to a feeling of uncertainty and a general lack of clarity, all of which held back the development of our cinema'.[20] Moreover, audience research suggested that cinema-goers in the GDR were not happy with a diet of films set in working-class milieus. For as one such respondent commented: 'I spend all day struggling with all sorts of problems at work; I don't want to experience that all over again when I go to the cinema in the evening'.[21]

In an attempt to counter the flagging production figures a number of changes were proposed. On 14 October 1950 a meeting was organised by DEFA's board of directors which led to a number of writing teams being set up with the aim of recruiting new authors and developing already existing material, teams that would allow new talent to develop at the side of more experienced film-makers. On 1 November 1952, Hans Rodenberg – a former member of the *DEFA-Kommission* – was appointed as general director of the studio, Sepp Schwab having been promoted to the position of chairman of the *Staatliches Komitee für Filmwesen* ('State Committee for Film'), an organisation which, however, only lasted until 1954. In 1953, DEFA officially became a VEB ('Volkseigener Betrieb'), the company having been split up into three constituent studios, each specialising in the production of feature films, educational films and news and documentary features respectively. In addition, from 1953 onwards, measures were taken to phase out the contracts of those company workers who continued to live in the West and whose presence in the studio had been a bone of contention for some time.

Needless to say, changes in the management structure of the company did not bring about an immediate solution to the studio's embarrassingly low output. The turning-point was to come in June 1953, prompted by the workers' uprisings in the

GDR in protest against proposed increases in the work norms. Having successfully convinced the studio's employees not to abandon their trust in the party, Hans Rodenberg exploited the prevailing climate of compromise to win for himself a greater degree of autonomy for the studio. In a letter written to Walter Ulbricht he unleashed a stinging condemnation of Sepp Schwab's role in the administrative hierarchy. Six months later Schwab was appointed to a post in the diplomatic service.[22] Gradually the tide was beginning to turn, so much so indeed, that at a meeting in the GDR's Academy of Arts in February 1954, Kurt Maetzig felt confident enough to state publicly that 'It is essential to have free and unrestricted debates about artistic matters. Such debates are valuable if they lead to more and better films. They are pointless when they are exploited to talk a potential film project out of existence.' [23]

The years following Stalin's death in 1953 were a relatively productive period for DEFA. Indeed one of the problems with which DEFA film-makers were faced was that of how the former leader of the Soviet Union should be represented, a problem which Kurt Maetzig had to resolve during his work on the two-part epic film about the life of the communist leader Ernst Thälmann: *Ernst Thälmann – Sohn seiner Klasse* (*Ernst Thälmann – Son of the Working Class*, 1954) and *Ernst Thälmann – Führer seiner Klasse* (*Ernst Thälmann – Leader of the Working Class*, 1955). Despite Maetzig's misgivings about the project, both films were exhibited to a wide audience in the GDR and considerably boosted the standing of both Hans Rodenberg and the DEFA studio in the process. With Khrushchev's denunciation of Stalin's policies in 1956, a more liberal climate was discernible, with the result that studio output picked up. With the emergence of a new generation of DEFA directors, amongst them Konrad Wolf, Gerhard Klein, Heiner Carow, Frank Beyer, Ralf Kirsten and Konrad Petzold, the prospects for the future seemed distinctly bright. Born between 1920 and 1932, they were – with the exception of Wolf who had returned from exile in the Soviet Union – all men in their prime when the GDR was founded in 1949.

The late mid-1950s saw the release of some of DEFA's best-known films, the Berlin films of Gerhard Klein and Wolfgang Kohlhaase, *Alarm im Zirkus* (*Circus Alarm*, 1954), *Eine Berliner Romanze* (*A Berlin Romance*, 1956) and *Berlin Ecke Schönhauser* (*Berlin – Schönhauser Corner*, 1957), films which revealed the growing influence of Italian neo-realism and challenged the traditional paradigms of cinematic realism in the GDR. Despite serious misgivings on the part of the *Hauptverwaltung Film* (a sub-department of the GDR Ministry of Culture set up to control all aspects of the film industry), *Berlin Ecke Schönhauser* was released on 30 August 1957 attracting large audiences. The debate over *Berlin Ecke Schönhauser* concerned the film's hard-hitting – though far from negative – portrayal of a group of adolescents in East Berlin. Nonetheless, the debates that were provoked by the making of the film were to signal another shift in attitudes in GDR film policy.

During the Film Conference staged by the Ministry of Culture on 3–5 July 1958 in Berlin, it became clear that the more liberal climate that had been ushered in following the death of Stalin had given way to a return to the ideological dogmatism of 1952. Without question, international developments in the Eastern Bloc played a key role: the Hungarian uprising of October 1956 and events in Poland all pointed to the threat of revisionism, a threat from which the GDR itself was not safe. Gradually the dissatisfaction of the SED leadership with the DEFA studios became increasingly public. This reached a climax at the conference itself when, in his address to the assembled delegates, Alexander Abusch berated recent DEFA productions, saying 'Some film-makers ... have offered an absurdly exaggerated critique of a number of isolated instances of dogmatic and inflexible aspects of everyday life and in the process convinced themselves that they have discovered the key to making marvellous films'.[24] What was at stake was the appropriate means of analysing individual alienation in a non-capitalist society, a point on which Abusch was quite explicit: 'It must be clear to film-makers in the GDR that the aesthetics of the Italian neorealists – intended as they are to expose the irresolvable antagonisms of capitalist society and encourage the members of that society to rebel against it – are not appropriate for films set in a Workers' and Peasants' State ... The use of "critical realism" cannot but leave us with a pseudo-representation of the new reality in which we live.'[25] Abusch's intervention marked the beginning of a new period of stagnation and a stark decline in the popularity of DEFA films, a decline that was to be exacerbated by the influence of television. For audiences and film-makers alike it was a period of acute frustration that was made even worse when DEFA productions were compared with those from other Eastern Bloc countries.

DEFA in the 1960s: The Impact of the Eleventh Plenum

In an article published in *Neues Deutschland* on 30 March 1961, Slatan Dudow remarked: 'We are years behind in the development of our cinema.' Although this may have been true for the bulk of films produced in the immediate aftermath of the Film Conference of 1958, there were a number which stood out from the rest, notably Frank Beyer's *Fünf Patronenhülsen* (*Five Cartridges*, 1960), Gerhard Klein's *Der Fall Gleiwitz* (*The Gleiwitz Affair*, 1961) and Konrad Wolf's *Professor Mamlock* (1961). It is striking that by returning to 'safe' ground – the genre of the anti-fascist film – these directors were able to acquire a degree of freedom for formal experimentation.

It is one of the paradoxes of the GDR's historical development that with the building of the Berlin Wall in August 1961 artists and writers felt that they would enjoy a greater degree of autonomy than hitherto. This mood is perhaps most aptly summed up by Klaus Wischnewski – at that time *Dramaturg* ('script editor') with DEFA – in an article written some years later in *Neues Deutschland* in which he noted: 'Now that that border has been made secure, at last we can get down to the business of intensifying the critical aspect of our cinema'.[26] Although the wall itself was eventually to become a taboo subject, the first film to deal with it, Frank Vogel's *Und deine Liebe auch* (*And Your Love Too*) – a film in which the female protagonist Eva decides in favour of the East – appeared as early as 1962. Frank Beyer's comedy *Karbid und Sauerampfer* (*Carbide and Sorrel*, 1963) which took a deceptively light-hearted look at the division of Germany was another milestone in DEFA's history. Likewise, Konrad Wolf's film adaptation of Christa Wolf's novel *Der geteilte Himmel* (*The Divided Heaven*, 1964) was another film that sought to test out the limits of what would be tolerated.

Increasingly the films of the 1960s tackled subject matter that was both controversial and contemporary. That this occurred was in part a reflection of a more liberal working climate, in part a reflection of the emergence of a new generation of directors, writers and cameramen such as Herrmann Zschoche, Egon Günther, Günter Stahnke, Helga Schütz, Ulrich Plenzdorf, Roland Gräf and Günter Ost. Kurt Maetzig's suggestion of setting up a number of production ensembles within the company – a way of working which had already been established in Czechoslovakia and Poland – was beginning to bear fruit. Under the liberal line adopted by the new head of the studio, Jochen Mückenberger, these groups enjoyed a considerable degree of autonomy. This new sense of freedom was further enhanced by remarks made in public by the then film minister Günter Witt criticising the purchase of apolitical entertainment films from the West and insisting on the need to produce serious critical works of art in the GDR.[27] Looking back on the period from 1961 up until the notorious Eleventh Plenum in 1965, Klaus Wischnewski comments: 'My memory of the years from 1961 to 1965 are characterised by a sense of energy, self-confidence and a willingness to take risks.'[28]

This climate of tolerance was not to last, however. Two films – Kurt Maetzig's *Das Kaninchen bin ich* (*I am the Rabbit*, 1965) and Frank Vogel's *Denk bloß nicht, ich heule* (*Just Don't Think I'm Crying*, 1965) – tackled issues about which the SED leadership was particularly sensitive, namely the GDR's system of criminal justice and the emergence of a youth culture which demanded to be taken seriously. Nonetheless, it is not easy to understand the reasons for the vehemence with which the writers and filmmakers were attacked at the Eleventh Plenum of the Central Committee of the SED in December 1965. The most widely accepted interpretation is that it was intended to deflect attention away from the acute economic problems that the New System of Economic Planning and Management (NÖSPL) – a programme of economic decentralisation – had run into the previous year. However, whatever reasons lay behind the reprisals, the film-makers had to listen to a stinging criticism of their work delivered by Erich Honecker:

> The German Democratic Republic in which we live is an honest, upright state. Within its borders there are clear-cut notions of ethics, morality, and decent behaviour [...]. Appealing to some abstract notion of truth, these artists have concentrated their attention on alleged deficiencies and shortcomings in the GDR. Some artists and writers seem to believe that the process of a socialist education can only be successful if it represents all these deficiencies and shortcomings in their entirety.

They fail to realise that the effect of these works of art is to retard that process and to hinder the development of a socialist consciousness on the part of the working classes [...]. The matter is quite straightforward. If we are to increase productivity – and thereby raise our standard of living still further – we cannot afford to propagate nihilistic, defeatist and immoral philosophies in literature, film, drama and television. Scepticism and a rising standard of living are ... mutually incompatible. In a number of films produced in the past few months – *Das Kaninchen bin ich* and *Denk bloß nicht, ich heule* – certain views and tendencies both alien and damaging to socialism are represented ... Often the relationship between the individual on the one hand and the Party leaders and collective on the other is portrayed as cold and detached. The reality of our society is portrayed as a difficult road – and one which requires many sacrifices along the way – to a beautiful, but illusory future.[29]

Against this assault, Günter Witt's apologia, in which he refers to his 'error' in granting *Das Kaninchen bin ich* a licence and assuming that 'we could leave it up to the audience to reflect on a solution to the contradictions and conflicts shown in it',[30] stood no chance. And even when, some weeks later, Kurt Maetzig attempted to defuse the situation by conceding that some of the criticisms of *Das Kaninchen bin ich* were justified, Walter Ulbricht responded with an open letter that was no less damning than Honecker's speech at the Plenum and accused Maetzig of pandering to 'counter-revolutionary' tendencies from the Federal Republic.[31]

In 1965 and 1966, some eleven films were banned. Indeed the Eleventh Plenum effectively ended the careers of several directors whose work was suppressed. Amongst those to suffer were Günter Stahnke, the director of *Der Frühling braucht Zeit* (*Spring Takes its Time*, 1965), a film which touched too closely on the contradictions inherent in implementing the NÖSPL. Jürgen Böttcher – whose *Jahrgang 45* (*Born in 1945*, 1966) with its experimental documentary style might have heralded an aesthetic revolution in GDR cinema – never made another feature film for DEFA, opting to devote himself to documentary work instead. After the furore surrounding *Spur der Steine* (*The Trace of Stones*, 1966), Frank Beyer, the director, was banned from working for DEFA and 'banished' for several years to the Staatstheater in Dresden: he did not make another film with DEFA until *Jakob der Lügner* (*Jacob the Liar*) in 1974. The directors were not the only ones to suffer. Hans Bentzien, the Minister for Culture, Günter Witt, the Deputy Minister for

Culture and director of the *Hauptverwaltung Film,* Jochen
Mückenberger, the director of the DEFA studio, and Klaus
Wischnewski, the *Chefdramaturg* ('senior script editor') were
amongst those relieved of their official duties at the end of
1965 and beginning of 1966.[32] When *Das Kaninchen bin ich* was
finally shown some 24 years later in 1990, Kurt Maetzig
commented: 'I keep returning to the thought: how different
and how much better things might have been for our country if
at that point in time, the artists, writers, film-makers and people
from the theatre had succeeded in getting rid of Stalinism.'[33]

Not surprisingly, the years following the Eleventh Plenum
were years of considerable uncertainty. In place of those films
banned, a variety of light-weight comedies, such as Wolfgang
Luderer's *Meine Freundin Sybille* (*My Friend Sybille,* 1967) and
historical costume dramas, such as Werner Wallroth's *Hauptmann Florian von der Mühle* (*Captain Florian of the Mill,* 1968)
were screened. At the same time DEFA intensified its efforts to
establish itself as a maker of genre films, in particular westerns,
building on the success of Josef Mach's *Die Söhne der großen
Bärin* (*The Sons of the Great She-Bear,* 1966) and extending this
genre with great success into the late 1970s. However, two films
in particular stand out amongst the somewhat bland
productions of the late 1960s: Konrad Wolf's remarkable semi-
autobiographical work, *Ich war neunzehn* (*I was Nineteen,* 1968),
a film which did much to restore Wolf's credibility after the
débâcle of the Eleventh Plenum, and Egon Günther's *Abschied*
(*Farewell,* 1968), a film which experiments with the possibilities
of form in its exploration of a young man's rebellion against
patriarchal authority in the years leading up to World War I.

1971: No Taboos?

When seen against the political background of the crushing of
the Prague Spring, the caution displayed by film-makers in the
late sixties is perhaps understandable. However, the launch of
Willy Brandt's *Ostpolitik* in 1969 (which led to the Basic Treaty
between the two German states and the offical recognition of
the GDR), together with the replacement of Walter Ulbricht by
Erich Honecker as First Secretary of the SED, appeared – at
least at first sight – to herald the start of a yet another new era
of openness for artists and intellectuals. In a speech in

December 1971, Honecker proclaimed that 'Providing one starts from an established socialist standpoint, there cannot, in my opinion, be any taboo subjects for art and literature.'[34] This new attempt to establish a more liberal climate also coincided with the arrival of the next generation of directors, amongst them Lothar Warneke, Rainer Simon, Roland Gräf and Ingrid Reschke, DEFA's first woman director. Taking their inspiration from the documentary style of Jürgen Böttcher's *Jahrgang 45* these film-makers developed a style of film-making based on case studies of individuals with specific problems, a style which Warneke was to term 'documentary narrative films ('Der dokumentare Spielfilm')[35] and which he was to employ in such films as *Dr. med Sommer II* (*Dr Sommer II*, 1970) and *Leben mit Uwe* (*Living with Uwe*, 1974).

The early 1970s were one of the most interesting periods in the history of DEFA film cinema, a period which saw the release of such films as Egon Günther's *Der Dritte* (*Her Third*, 1972) and *Die Schlüssel* (*The Keys*, 1974), Heiner Carow's phenomenal success *Die Legende von Paul und Paula* (*The Legend of Paul and Paula*, 1973), Frank Beyer's *Jakob der Lügner* (1975) – the first and only DEFA film to be nominated for an Oscar – as well as Konrad Wolf's hitherto banned *Sonnensucher* (*Sun-Seekers*, 1958). However, it was the popular success that these and other films enjoyed that alarmed the SED leadership, insofar as it put them beyond the control of the *Hauptverwaltung Film*, and already by the mid 1970s a process of ideological retrenchment was discernible. Following sharp criticism in 1973 of the writers Ulrich Plenzdorf (who had written several screen plays for DEFA) and the dramatist Volker Braun, matters came to a head in 1976 with the expatriatiation of the singer Wolf Biermann following his criticism of the GDR during a concert tour in the Federal Republic. The 'Biermann Affair', as it became known, prompted a wave of protest amongst writers, artists and intellectuals in the GDR, a number of whom signed an open letter expressing their disapproval. The consequences for DEFA were catastrophic as a large number of prominent actors and actresses were to leave the GDR in the late 1970s and early 1980s – among them Manfred Krug, Jutta Hoffmann, Angelica Domröse, Hilmar Thate, Armin Müller-Stahl, and the emerging star Katharina Thalbach – a drain of talent which was to hinder film production in the years to come. Indeed it seems hardly coincidental that one of the dominant themes in the DEFA films of those years is the role of the artist in society as portrayed in such films as Horst Seemann's *Beethoven – Tage aus einem Leben* (*Beethoven – Days in a Life*, 1976), Egon Günther's *Lotte in Weimar* (1975) and Lothar Warnekes's film about Georg Büchner, *Addio, piccola mia* (1979). This film genre — the origins of which go back to such films such as Konrad Wolf's *Goya* (1971) and *Der nackte Mann auf dem Sportplatz* (*The Naked Man on the Playing Field*, 1974) increasingly assumes a degree of poignancy insofar as such 'artist films' set out to explore the alienation of the individual, a theme which was to be extended in a number of film versions of classic literary works such as Egon Günther's adaptation of *Die Leiden des jungen Werthers* (*The Sorrows of Young Werther*, 1976). In a further attempt to present an oblique commentary on conditions in the GDR, film-makers turned their attention to another group of 'outsiders': women. Although very few women directors were employed by DEFA, a great many of the films made in the late 1970s and early 1980s have a female character as their central protagonist: Erwin Stranka's *Sabine Wulff* (1978), Heiner Carow's *Bis daß der Tod euch scheidet* (*Until Death Do Us Part*, 1979), Lothar Warnekes's *Unser kurzes Leben* (*Our Short Life*, 1981) – an adaptation of Brigitte Reimann's novel *Franziska Linkerhand* – not to mention two films by women directors, namely Evelyn Schmidt's *Seitensprung* (*Escapade*, 1980) and Iris Gusner's *Alle meine Mädchen* (*All My Girls*, 1980). Indeed in what was undoubtedly one of the most popular DEFA films of all time – Konrad Wolf's *SOLO SUNNY* (1980) – both the 'artist' and 'woman' genres were combined in the same film.

1980s: The Last Years

With the premature death of Konrad Wolf in 1982 – a man revered both by the SED leadership and the DEFA film-makers themselves – DEFA was to lose the man who perhaps more than any other might have guided it through the troubled last decade of the GDR's existence. And as the 1980s unfolded, developments in Eastern Europe – above all the declaration in Poland on 16 September 1980 of the first independent trade union in a socialist country – were beginning to alarm the SED leadership. Significantly, whereas at the begining of the 1970s, citizens of the GDR had been able to watch the latest films from Poland and Hungary, in the 1980s they were increasingly presented with a diet of bland entertainment features imported from America. Indeed the significant role played by West German television in conditioning East German audiences to prefer such entertainment features to films from their own country and from Eastern Europe generally cannot be overlooked.

At the same time the approval or non-approval of films produced in the GDR in this period seems disconcertingly arbitrary. It is not easy to see why, given the immense problems encountered by Rainer Simon with *Jadup und Boel* (1980) – a film which was banned until 1988 – Roland Gräf's *Märkische Forschungen* (*Exploring the Brandenburg Marches*, 1982) should be so readily accepted and receive an official prize as the best DEFA film of 1982. Similarly, Ulrich Weiß's film about the anti-fascist resistance *Dein unbekannter Bruder* (*Your Unknown Brother*, 1982) had been fêted in *Neues Deutschland* on the grounds that it been selected for screening at the Cannes Film Festival. However, after the intervention of members of the *Hauptverwaltung Film*, the film was withdrawn.

The 1980s also witnessed the emergence of a new generation of film directors, amongst them Maxim Dessau, Michael Kann, Jörg Foth, Lothar Großmann, Dietmar Hochmuth, Peter Kahane and Karl Heinz Lotz, a group of film-makers who had graduated from the Babelsberg Film School and who were becoming increasingly frustrated by the lack of opportunities for young directors within DEFA. On 28 October 1982, a number of them took part in a meeting to plan a subsequent meeting in December with Kurt Hager, the member of the Politbüro reponsible for cultural affairs. A panel of 18 representatives was elected to present Hager with a dossier of suggestions as to how working conditions for young directors might be improved. However, their suggestions fell on deaf ears. Looking back on events, Jörg Foth, the chairman of the elected panel, reflected: 'A thorough, honest and constructive attempt to analyse the situation was simply ignored.'[36] When the same group planned to read out a manifesto at the Fifth Congress of Film and Television in 1988, they were dissuaded from doing so by the-then head of the studio, Hans Dieter Mäde, on the grounds that this would only result in the studio being subjected to yet closer scrutiny.[37] However, time was running out for such rearguard action as political developments were moving too quickly to be stopped. Following Gorbachev's accession to power in 1985, the demand for *perestroika* and *glasnost* in the GDR increasingly gathered momentum. In 1988, Hans Dieter Mäde stepped down as the head of the studios, Rudolf Jürschik taking over as artistic director with Gerd Golde assuming responsibility for financial matters. By then the climate had changed markedly as can be seen by the release of such films as Lothar Warneke's portrait of church-state relations *Einer trage des anderen Last* (*Bear Ye One Another's Burdens*, 1988), Heiner Carow's film about a homosexual teacher, *Coming Out* (1989), and by the approval of a number of projects dealing with hitherto problematic subjects such as disability in Karl Heinz Lotz's *Rückwärts laufen kann ich auch* (*I Can Run Backwards As Well*,1990) and environmental issues in Jörg Foth's *Biologie* (*Biology*, 1990), together with the approval of a number of projects previously held up, such as Peter Kahane's *Die Architekten* (*The Architects*, 1990), Evelyn Schmidt's film *Der Hut* (*The Hat*, 1990), and Andreas Höntsch's *Der Straß* (*Synthetic Ice*, 1991). Needless to say, by the time the majority of these films were released, they were overshadowed by events on the political stage.

By 1989, with the opening of Hungary's borders on 11 September, the rapid growth of the regular Monday-night demonstrations in Leipzig from mid-September, the visit of Gorbachev on 7 October, Egon Krenz's take-over from Honecker on 18 October and finally the fall of the Berlin wall itself on 9 November, events were happening so fast that the cinema – in common with perhaps all the arts in the GDR – was simply unable to keep pace. On 18 October 1989, a commission was set up to review the situation of those films which had been banned in the past, many of which were restored and eventually screened in 1990. At the same time, a group of young film-makers set up an independent organisation – the first of its kind – which became known as the 'Gruppe DaDaeR'. Egon Günther returned from the Federal Republic to shoot *Stein* (1991) and Herwig Kipping – who, ever since his highly critical outburst at the meeting of 28 October 1982 had been a *persona non grata* within DEFA – directed *Das Land hinter dem Regenbogen* (*The Land Over the Rainbow*, 1992). However, many of the films produced at this time suffered from the defect that they were so packed with oblique ironic references to the former GDR as to be almost totally inaccessible to anyone not intimately versed in the cultural rhetoric of that state. Now that DEFA's directors had a free hand to produce whatever films they wanted, there was no longer an audience who wished to see them, a problem that was exacerbated in the early part of 1991 by the privatisation of the cinemas in what had now become the former GDR and the inevitable arrival of a wave of American entertainment films.

Notes

1. Adolf Fischer had appeared in Slatan Dudow's *Kuhle Wampe* (1932), a film on which Carl Haacker – the former chief designer for the film production company, Prometheus – had also worked as co-designer. Willy Schiller had worked as a designer on a number of films including *Der Golem, wie er in die Welt kam* (*The Golem*, 1920). Alfred Lindemann had been one of the founder members of Erwin Piscator's proletarian theatre. Kurt Maetzig was a qualified chemist, who – because of his Jewish origins – had been prevented from making films and had worked primarily in film-copying laboratories. Hans Klering was an actor who had appeared in a number of Soviet films.
2. For a full list of those who attended – as well as a wealth of detail relating to the early years of DEFA – see Christiane Mückenberger and Günter Jordan, '*Sie sehen selbst, Sie hören selbst … ': Die DEFA von ihren Anfängen bis 1949*, Marburg, 1994, p. 25.
3. See the report in the *Deutsche Volkszeitung*, 6 December 1945. This is reproduced in Albert Wilkening, *Geschichte der DEFA von 1945–1950: Betriebsgeschichte des VEB DEFA Studio für Spielfilme*, Potsdam, 1981, vol. 1, pp. 32–3.
4. The film was never completed.
5. The Soviets ensured that distribution of films remained in their control.
6. *Tägliche Rundschau*, 18 May 1946.
7. See Mückenberger, '*Sie sehen selbst*', pp. 187–93 for further details.
8. SAPMO (Stiftung Archiv der Parteien und Massenorganisationen der DDR im Bundesarchiv) IV/2/22/61, Bl. 96–7.
9. In the event Bergmann left the board to run the publishing outlet *Deutscher Filmverlag*, itself a subsidiary of DEFA. His place on the board was taken by Kurt Maetzig.
10. See Wilkening, *Geschichte der DEFA*; vol. 1, pp. 74–8 (p. 78).
11. Ibid., p. 75.
12. Ibid., p. 77.

13. Ibid., p. 79.

14. Walter Janka was eventually to become the chief of the *Aufbau Verlag*, the principal publishing house in the GDR, only to be imprisoned for alleged subversion in 1957.

15. Wilkening, *Geschichte der DEFA*: vol. 1, p. 128.

16. Bertolt Brecht, *Journals 1934–1955* (trans. Hugh Rorrison, ed. John Willett), London, 1993, p. 421.

17. SAPMO IV 2/906/203.

18. Albert Wilkening, *Die DEFA in der Etappe 1950–1953: Betriebsgeschichte des VEB DEFA Studio für Spielfilme*, vol. 2, Babelsberg, 1984, p. 22.

19. Wilkening, *Geschichte der DEFA*: vol. 2, p. 47.

20. Ibid., p. 48.

21. Ibid., p. 53.

22. See Ralf Schenk, 'Mitten im Kalten Krieg: 1950 bis 1960' in *Das zweite Leben der Filmstadt Babelsberg: DEFA Spielfilme 1946–1992*, ed. Ralf Schenk, Berlin, 1994, pp. 50–157 (p. 83). This work is an invaluable source for information on the history of DEFA and contains a detailed index of all DEFA films produced.

23. Günter Agde (ed.), *Kurt Maetzig – Filmarbeit: Gespräche, Reden, Schriften*, Berlin, 1987, p. 249.

24. Alexander Abusch, 'Aktuelle Probleme und Aufgaben unserer sozialistischen Filmkunst: Referat der Konferenz des VEB DEFA Studio für Spielfilme und des Ministeriums für Kultur der DDR', *Deutsche Filmkunst* 6, 1958, no. 9: 261–70 (267).

25. Ibid.

26. *Neues Deutschland*, 6 January 1966.

27. See Günter Witt, 'Von der höheren Verantwortung hängt alles ab', *Filmwissenschaftliche Mitteilungen* 5, no. 2, 1964: 251–63 (261).

28. Wieland Becker, '"Hoffnungen, Illusionen, Einsichten": Klaus Wischnewski im Gespräch mit Wieland Becker', *Film und Fernsehen* 18, no. 6, 1990: 35–9.

29. Erich Honecker, *Bericht des Politbüros an die 11. Tagung des Zentralkomitees der Sozialistischen Einheitspartei Deutschlands, 15–18 December 1965*, Berlin 1965, p. 56.

30. Extracts from Günter Witt's speech – together with a wealth of material relating to the bans following the Eleventh Plenum – can be found in *Prädikat: besonders schädlich: 'Das Kaninchen bin ich' und 'Denk bloß nicht ich heule'*, ed. Christiane Mückenberger, Berlin, 1990, p. 349.

31. *Neues Deutschland*, 23 January 1966.

32. Mückenberger, *Prädikat*, pp. 355–6.

33. Ibid., p. 317.

34. *Neues Deutschland*, 18 December 1971.

35. Lothar Warneke, 'Der dokumentare Spielfilm' in *Lothar Warneke: Film ist eine Art zu leben. Eine Dokumentation*, ed. Hermann Herlinghaus (= *Aus Theorie und Praxis des Films*; 1982, no. 3),10–35.

36. Jörg Foth, 'Forever Young' in *Filmland DDR: ein Reader zu Geschichte, Funktion und Wirkung der DEFA*, ed. Harry Blunk and Dirk Jungnickel, Cologne, 1990, pp. 95–106 (p. 101).

37. Ibid., p. 103.

Chapter 2

DEFA AND THE TRADITIONS OF INTERNATIONAL CINEMA

Barton Byg

At the height of the Cold War, shortly before the landmark conference on Kafka at Liblice near Prague, Jean-Paul Sartre compared Kafka to a railway carriage loaded with dynamite which each Cold War camp kept trying to push to the other side.[1] Now that the Cold War era is over, the cultural legacies of socialist states may well serve a similarly stimulating if unwelcome function. Indeed GDR culture has long been the repressed 'other' within the culture of the Federal Republic; since unification, this is now also true in a geographical sense. In the East, its critical, creative potential constantly had to be tamed, as Deleuze and Guattari said of Kafka in the West.[2] The potential now is for another Liblice, in which this productive and problematic legacy – no less contradictory than Kafka's identity as a canonical, German author – can be discovered by new audiences.

In the West so far, the reception of DEFA has generally been blocked by ignorance about the films and lack of access to them. Such a starting point, however, is not unusual in the context of popular culture. Many generally educated Americans have never seen *Citizen Kane* (1940) or a John Ford Western or a Douglas Sirk melodrama. As each generation has to create its own relation to film history, then, a rediscovery of DEFA can belong to the next generation. The method of taking this new look at DEFA might also parallel the development of women's history out of the women's movement. Just as feminism has not merely consisted in adding the 'great women' to the histories of 'great men', it is also not enough now to add DEFA to the books already written on German film that excluded this aspect. The subject must also address the question why these books were written to exclude DEFA in the first place.

1945: Rupture or Continuity?

A starting-point in the discussion of DEFA is the question, 'What significance does it have that DEFA happened to be located in the German Democratic Republic?' One particularity is that there was less of a rupture in cultural identity in 1945 in the East than in the West, despite the socialist rhetoric of the 'New Germany'. As Christiane Mückenberger and Günter Jordan's book has made clear, to a great degree both the facilities and the personnel were the same.[3] The popular front policy of the German Communist Party (KPD), Socialist Unity Party (SED) and the Soviet Union meant that for a long period, extending into the 1960s, DEFA was meant to be a German studio, and not just the East German studio. The number of people who kept their jobs after Nazi Germany may even have exceeded the number who have kept their jobs since 1989. And the mode of production, which has only recently given way to more emphasis on project-based subsidy, was also more continuous with the rather centralised studio system that had developed since World War I.

The official anti-fascism of the GDR played a role in this tolerance for continuity with Nazi institutions. Regardless of the degree of complicity of its citizens with Nazism, the official self-definition of the GDR as an anti-fascist state freed them from many of the conflicts regarding German cultural symbols and practices that otherwise may have been tainted by Nazi Germany. Appeals to such concepts as folk, nation, *Heimat* and even the term *Kultur*, could eventually be given socialist content. The GDR thus could preserve some institutions and forms from earlier states without the admission that the form of these institutions necessarily was tainted by National Socialist content. A prominent example would be the Free German Youth (FDJ), a national youth organisation developed out of the Communist youth groups of the 1920s and 1930s. In the West, such a group is unthinkable due to its similarity to the Hitler Youth; in the socialist context, it was logically the victorious, and thus justified, alternative. Other examples could be named here, from the uniform of the National

People's Army (NVA) to the word *Reichsbahn,* an 'Imperial Railway' operated by a little people's republic.

This feeling of guiltlessness for the crimes of German culture, whether justified or not, supports the assertion that GDR cinema was almost always more of a 'national cinema' than the cinema of the West. Philip Rosen has defined a 'national cinema' as arising at the intersection of multiple narrative discourses of nationhood. Referring to the famous films banned by the SED in 1965, the GDR critic, Hannes Schmidt, has observed that they represent just such a constellation of national narratives, reflecting – even when censored – a negotiated public space between government and citizens.[4]

The cinema of the GDR was also more 'German' and 'National' than that in the West partly because it did not feel the need to make such a radical break with the past. Along with the lack of a guilt-driven break there is the fact of the more 'foreign' occupation by the Soviets, not the Western allies dominated by the USA. Thus the debate over American popular culture that plagued the West from the late 1940s on and became one of the defining qualities of the national cinema called the 'New German Cinema', was not the same issue in the East. Whereas in the West, identification with the occupiers became fundamental to identity, in the East, to the extent that the USSR influenced the cinema of the GDR, it did not – or could not – successfully represent an alternative, popular-culture identity.[5] The 'popular culture' forms that did develop in GDR film thus mediate in a unique way between Western, Eastern European and Soviet models. The historian Uta Poiger has demonstrated how central the cinema was to struggles over youth culture in the early phases of the Cold War, and study of youth film from an Eastern point of view demonstrates its importance to GDR film culture generally.[6] The deservedly paradigmatic banned films of 1965 are thus not an exception, but the culmination of a least a decade of creative development.

Beyond the influence of Western popular culture in the East, however, a rather unproblematic acceptance of 'Germanness' still allowed for cultural continuities that were much more controversial or even taboo in the West. One genre that benefited from this dispensation of innocence was comedy, which in the West has almost always had either a regional or slapstick quality, or has referred to American forms such as the screwball comedies of Doris Dörrie. The DEFA comedies, however, were relaxed enough to laugh to a degree at their own Germanness – with such examples as Wolfgang Staudte's *Der Untertan* (*The Kaiser's Lackey*, 1951) and Frank Beyer's *Karbid und Sauerampfer* (*Carbide and Sorrel*, 1963) most prominent. A particularly 'national' use of the genre is also represented in the *Aufbau* comedies *Anton der Zauberer* (*Anton, the Magician*, 1977) directed by Günter Reisch, *Die besten Jahre* (*The Best Years*, 1965) directed by Günther Rücker, and aspects of Frank Beyer's *Spur der Steine* (*Traces of the Stones*, 1966) and Slatan Dudow's Cold War comedy, *Der Hauptmann von Köln* (*The Captain of Cologne*, 1956).

Cinema and National Identity

What is 'German cinema' is an old question, like Adorno's 'What is German?'.[7] With the opportunity to ask the question anew in regard to DEFA and the cinema of the GDR comes the obligation to ask questions in regard to West Germany too, lest we perpetuate the common assumption that the Federal Republic is synonymous with 'Deutschland'.

Future study of the cinema of the GDR, which is already not synonymous with the cinema of DEFA, could profit from a continuation of the work already begun by Cultural Studies. In doing so, the subject is not only DEFA or the GDR, but how the Cold War has structured an entire apparatus of intellectual history. Anna Szemere has written about this challenge, noting that Cultural Studies has mainly concentrated on advanced capitalist society or the Third World, i.e., 'the dominated or colonised "Other"'. 'Yet,' she goes on, 'those societies which until quite recently have been the site of "existing socialism" have been left virtually unexplored by cultural studies'.[8]

In considering the various cultural contexts of DEFA and DEFA scholarship, then, the kind of social history of cinema pioneered by Thomas Elsaesser in regard to New German Cinema provides an excellent model. This approach does not treat history as a narrative, but examines the intersection of various cultural realms, from politics and cultural policy to technical, financing and reception conditions to literary, artistic creativity and personal fantasies and desires. All this is at work in the cinema of DEFA, and has often been neglected by the polarities of Cold War concepts.

The following will thus look at some of the films of DEFA in contexts other than the linear historical narrative of the GDR, and interrogate their Germanness, their Europeanness and their resonances with international film history from a 'third point of view', to borrow Peter Weiss's phrase. After all, it is more liberating to think of Germany not as synonymous with the Federal Republic or either state that existed before 1990 but as that entity described by Hans Koning in a 1987 article, 'Where money has little currency'. Koning writes that 'the Red Michelin Guide titled "Germany" does not even mention the existence of East Germany. My Webster's *New World Dictionary* quite properly says under "Germany": "Former Country in North Central Europe, divided ...".' [9]

The challenge is to look at the history of DEFA without forcing it into a narrative that merely leads to the outcome we now know since 1989. It is unlikely that any system of government has either succeeded or failed because of the films that were made under its auspices. But looking at the cinema of DEFA can tell us some things we cannot learn anywhere else – about the possibilities and limitations of both cinema and socialism, about particular German practices in regard to European film traditions, and about the interrelations of East and West German cinemas which now make up what presently confronts us as 'The German Cinema'.

Expanding the view of DEFA from the national narrative of the GDR to the wider context of German culture of the past one hundred years is an example of the fascinating work that can begin with the observance of the fiftieth anniversary of the foundation of DEFA. The years following 1946 opened exciting possibilities for starting something new and for pursuing lines of film tradition that had been interrupted or co-opted under National Socialism. Accordingly, this essay will consider DEFA not primarily as an expression of GDR national culture, but as a space where film styles, movements and traditions were or could have been pursued.

The Expressionist Legacy

If one thinks of the situation of 1945–6, with film artists returning from exile, some as members of occupying forces, and joining with others who had worked in the Nazi cinema, one asks what would have been the most likely traditions to pursue. The first strain that comes to mind is Expressionism, and it would be interesting to trace the Expressionist traditions in post-war German cinema both East and West up to the present. One legacy of this German tradition took the form of *film noir*, gangster and horror films – especially in the United States. Horror films seem to have been virtually eliminated from the German tradition by the real horrors of Nazism and the state's wish to deny the existence of monstrous or evil forces in society, for fear of turning them loose in political form once again. But Expressionist styles were indeed used in early DEFA films to look backward at the horrors of the past, in a rather *noir* style in Staudte's *Die Mörder sind unter uns* (*The Murderers Are Among Us*, 1946) and in the gangster genre of Erich Engel's *Affaire Blum* (*The Blum Affair*, 1948). The tactic of using the Expressionist-gangster genre as a popular way to depict the Nazi enemy of course goes back at least to Fritz Lang's 1943 Hollywood film *Hangmen also Die* (with a script by Lang, John Wexley and Bertolt Brecht). The formalism debates of the early 1950s, led by SED cultural functionaries such as Alexander Abusch and Alfred Kurella, attempted to bring such stylised film-making to an end. This aversion to Expressionist film in official GDR cultural policy must also be understood in the context of the problematic relation of the GDR to German Romanticism. Romanticism's implication in the irrational seductiveness of Nazi imagery (indirectly by way of Expressionist film) has made many film people averse to this German tradition of meretricious spectacle (if not narrative pleasure), and not only in the East. This also accounts in part for the relative reticence of West German cinema where spectacle and narrative are concerned.[10]

Looking at a film such as *Die Mörder sind unter uns* in the context of *film noir*, we see both the common post-war theme of threatened masculinity and a strong woman. But in the socialist context, the woman is not and cannot be seen as the threat to masculinity but instead must offer a civilising solution to the crisis. It is telling that Staudte at first wanted his male lead to murder the villain in a final scene, and removing the murder was the only change insisted on by the Soviet film officer Alexander Dymschitz. In a *film noir*, the revenge might as often as not have included the murder of the emasculating, aggressive woman (as in George Marshall's *The Blue Dahlia* (1946),

– 27 –

written by Raymond Chandler, or John Huston's *The Maltese Falcon* (1941)). The rather indirect relation to the true horrors of the Nazis' destruction of the Jews in GDR anti-fascist films could also be productively contrasted with American films of the era. The realist drama *Gentleman's Agreement* (directed by Elia Kazan in 1947), for instance, ostensibly attacks anti-Semitism head-on, but manages to avoid all mention of either Nazism or World War II. Edward Dmytryk's *Crossfire*, a *film noir* from the year 1947, similarly limits anti-Semitism to a personal villainy, but manages to find a *noir* compromise to the dilemma of *Die Mörder sind unter uns*: like the voice of Susanne Wallner at the end of the Staudte film, Robert Young's fatherly civilian authority figure tames the unruly soldiers among whom the murder of a Jew has been committed; here, however, the murderer is not brought to trial, but is gunned down in 'satisfying' *noir* fashion as he tries to escape down a dark city street.

Another strain of Expressionism's legacy can be found, however, in the stylised socialist realism that replaced the gangster or *noir* thriller in the GDR. Here the most apt Hollywood comparison may be the Western. The socialist realist epics produced by DEFA in the 1950s share with their earlier Soviet counterparts a grand scale, a stark dramatic conflict between good and evil, the visual pleasure of spectacular and stylised cinematic qualities, and a viscerally engaging narrative characterised by suspense as well as a satisfying climax and resolution. Maya Turovskaya has pointed out the international resonance of this film style, by comparing the 1930s 'production' films of the USA and the USSR, such as Sergei Gerassimov's *Komsomolsk* (1938) and Cecil B. de Mille's *Union Pacific* (1939). In the late 1940s, the political context of this socialist response to the 'Western' genre was rather simple, as in Mikhail Chiaureli's *Padeniye Berlina* (*The Fall of Berlin*, 1950) and in the heroic Soviet films of the 1930s. And in Chiaureli's film we do indeed see clear traces of German Expressionism: the evocation of Fritz Lang's *Metropolis* (1926) in the flood scene: Hitler as both Nosferatu and the raving Renfield.

In the GDR of the 1950s, some of these qualities of the Western action drama are found in Kurt Maetzig's Thälmann films,[11] aspects of *Schlösser and Katen* (*Castles and Cottages*, 1957), and Slatan Dudow's *Stärker als die Nacht* (*Stronger than the Night*, 1954). There is even a stylised blending of socialist realist and Western Expressionism in some of the more differentiated and nuanced socialist realist films: Konrad Wolf's gold-rush town transported to the GDR Wismut uranium mines in *Sonnensucher* (*Sun-Seekers*, 1957), complete with saloon fight scene but minus the six-shooters; the drama of the concentration camp liberation in *Leute mit Flügeln* (*People with Wings*, 1960); or the negotiations at the Spandau Citadel in *Ich War 19* (*I Was Nineteen*, 1968). It is equally irresistible to see Frank Beyer's *Spur der Steine* as a 'Bitterfeld Western', and certainly the adventure of his Spanish Civil War drama *Fünf Patronenhülsen* (*Five Cartridges*, 1960) is the Expressionist one of lonely heroes against an inhuman landscape and an invisible enemy. The subgenre of actual Westerns made in the GDR, the so-called 'Indianerfilme', also seem to mediate between the progressive messages of socialist realism and a mythical depiction of 'man' and 'nature'. The working class as subject of history in Marxist terms is here invited to identify with the Indians in their struggle against the imperialist invader.[12]

Both *Sonnensucher* and *Fünf Patronenhülsen* bear remarkable similarities to John Ford's western myths of nation-building, such as *Stagecoach* (1937), *The Searchers* (1956) or *The Man Who Shot Liberty Valance* (1962). The illusion for which the men have fought (and which keeps them going) in the Beyer film is very close to the message of myth-making voiced by the newspaper man at the conclusion of *Liberty Valance*. If you have to choose between the truth and the legend, print the legend. And like the John Wayne character in *Liberty Valance* and a number of other Ford films, the mine foreman with an SS past in *Sonnensucher* is both the flawed hero of the film and the one who has to die in order for a more orderly (socialist) civilisation to be established.

Melodrama

The other great tradition of Weimar cinema seen in the early years after the war, along with the Expressionist legacy, is the melodrama. Here, too, like the gangster style, it was necessary in the early GDR context to confine melodrama largely to the fascist/anti-fascist problematic. This is no doubt related to the connection often made in German culture of this century between women, consumer pleasures, and fascism.[13] The 1920s equation between the cinema itself as sensual commodity and a female prostitute has perhaps never been completely absent from views of melodrama, and may account for its general absence as a separate genre from DEFA production. Like the myth-making Western, however, such a 'pleasurable' form could not be totally eliminated from a film industry, but was also partly replaced by a particularly socialist form, the anti-fascist film.

Seeing DEFA's anti-fascist films as melodramas may be one among many explanations for the fact that so many such films have female protagonists and are structured around a hetero-sexual love affair. The drama of the Wielands in Kurt Maetzig's *Ehe im Schatten* (*Marriage in the Shadow*, 1947), with the love triangle almost grotesquely juxtaposed with the rise of Nazism, is the clearest, and perhaps trend-setting, example. Others have already pointed out the many stylistic and biographical conti-nuities between this film and Nazi-era melodramas. Its suicide scene is an almost exact quotation from the euthanasia drama *Ich klage an* (*J'accuse*, 1941) directed by Wolfgang Liebeneiner.

Other anti-fascist films could also be seen as melodramatic love stories, however, from Wolf's *Lissy* (1957) to Günther Rücker and Günter Reisch's *Die Verlobte* (*The Fiancée*, 1980) and even one of the latest DEFA films, Siegfried Kühn's *Die Schauspielerin* (*The Actress*, 1988). The protagonists of these films suffer for the man they love, and in the case of Lissy, Wolf makes explicit the link between female desire (both for her Nazi husband and the commodities he provides) and the seductions of Nazi Germany. A woman seduced by pleasure is a theme consistent with melodramas from Hollywood in the same period (those by Douglas Sirk have been most exhaus-tively studied in this respect).[14] Wolf's Lissy, however, takes an explicit stand against the evil represented by these seductive Nazi commodity pleasures, but, in a manner not unlike that of the morally upright Hollywood, this at the same time allows the audience to briefly revel in them in the form of spectacular film production values.

The message of Western melodramas regarding gender roles seems to have been consistent with the urging of post-war women to abandon their war-time 'masculinised' roles as inde-pendent workers and return to the role of house-wife and consumer. Although this sacrifice of independence is one form of renunciation, it is compensated by both the pleasure of the film and the commodities offered to women in the marketplace. In the DEFA version, the renunciation is more complete and is seldom compensated by the heroine ending up with the good man after all. On the contrary, her compensation for renouncing the seductions of commodities and fascism is mainly the role of producer/worker and socialist citizen. For that reason, a woman alone (partly due to her confidence in the support of socialism) is the final image of numerous DEFA films – including the Konrad Wolf films *Lissy*, *Sonnensucher* and even *Der geteilte Himmel* (*The Divided Heaven*, 1964) – anything but a melodrama in formal terms, but less clearly so in regard to its love story.[15]

Thus there is a connection deserving study between the melodrama and the strong tradition of 'women's films' in the GDR. Whether the term 'women's film' applies or not, strong female characters stand at the centre of DEFA dramas from Maetzig's *Die Buntkarierten* (*The Girls in Gingham*, 1946) and *Schlösser und Katen* to *Das Kaninchen bin ich* (*I Am the Rabbit*, 1965). In the 1970s and 1980s there are many examples (as Andrea Rinke's contribution to this volume illustrates), including Heiner Carow's *Die Legende von Paul und Paula* (*The Legend of Paul and Paula*, 1973), Erwin Stranka's *Sabine Wulff* (1978), Konrad Wolf's *SOLO SUNNY* (1980), and Egon Günter and Helga Schütz's *Die Schlüssel* (*The Keys*, 1974) and *Der Dritte* (*Her Third*, 1972). The links to melodrama and to the problematic connection between women's identity and the state or civilisation certainly deserve investigation, especially in comparison with Fassbinder's work, for instance.

DEFA and Modernism   New Sobriety

Less visible after 1946 are the pre-war traditions of the leftist avant-garde and the New Sobriety ('Neue Sachlichkeit'). After Stalinism rejected the left avant-garde tradition about 1929 and the Nazis destroyed the rest in 1933, its presence in German cinema and in DEFA has been submerged but never entirely absent. This could not be the case for biographical reasons alone, since many artists who were important for 1920s modernism – Slatan Dudow and Hanns Eisler, for example – were involved with DEFA as well. Even the logo of the DEFA studio has its origins in the graphic arts innovations of the Weimar Republic. The word modernism alone suggests that virtually all aspects of

DEFA cinema, except perhaps for certain nineteenth-century narrative styles, belong to European modernism. As such, they grew out of the movements responding to the social realities and material possibilities presented by urban, mass, industrial society. DEFA in particular participates in this modernism in part merely by its location in Babelsberg, with its industrial studio tradition and its proximity to Berlin, a city virtually synonymous with modernity. Modernism is quite evident in the consistent support for documentary film as a cultural product, and in the role that cinema played in GDR society, whatever its political significance. Even the stylised socialist realism of the Stalin era and after has to be classified as a form of modernism, functionalised as it may have been. There is no other term to describe it.

But the strongest modernist legacy in feature films of DEFA is a submerged one – the hidden and embattled influence of the leftist avant-gardes that had so much influence between the wars. If we look at the legacy of those leftist movements internationally, we see both that DEFA was not exceptional, and also that it represents a specific interaction with that portion of film history. Doubtless the most significant and sustained dialogue with another modernist, leftist film tradition was DEFA's relation to Italian neo-realism. It should not be forgotten, first of all, that DEFA provided production facilities for one of the landmarks of Italian neo-realism in Germany, Roberto Rossellini's *Germania anno zero* (1947). It is no surprise that the first DEFA film, and the first 'rubble-film' ('Trümmerfilm'), also has at times a neo-realist look – Staudte's *Die Mörder sind unter uns*. The neo-realists had an impact on a few other films of the post-war years, but, as Klaus Kreimeier has argued, their direct influence at the time was relatively limited.[16]

The relation of DEFA to neo-realism does not stop there, however. Neo-realist films remained central to discussions among DEFA artists throughout the 1950s, ranging from both Friedrich Wolf and Konrad Wolf to Heiner Carow, Wolfgang Kohlhaase, and Gerhard Klein. Even if Kreimeier is right about the shifting of emphasis away from neo-realism soon after 1946, it was not much later, in 1953, that Klein and Kohlhaase explicitly returned to the neo-realist approach for their children-as-detectives film *Alarm im Zirkus* (*Circus Alarm*). They use street children as protagonists, dense black-and-white film stock as medium, and present a tale reminiscent of *Emil und die Detektive* (*Emil and the Detectives*). Directed by Gerhard Lamprecht in 1931, with a script by Billy Wilder from Erich Kästner's story, *Emil und die Detektive* is a classic Weimar film that also became a cinematic victim of Nazism. Both Rossellini's film and Lamprecht's own *Irgendwo in Berlin* (*Somewhere in Berlin*, 1947) thus form a neo-realist bridge between Weimar cinema and Klein's early 'Berlin-Film'. The same can be said of all the Berlin films that followed: Carow's *Sheriff Teddy* (1957) and *Sie nannten ihn Amigo* (*They Called Him Amigo*, 1959) and Kohlhaase and Klein's *Berlin – Ecke Schönhauser* (*Berlin – Schönhauser Corner*, 1957) and *Berliner Romanze* (*A Berlin Romance*, 1956).

The popular front politics and youthful modernism of these films led them to be attacked by doctrinaire Stalinists in the late 1950s but also led the series to be revived when youth culture was briefly in vogue again in the early 1960s, especially in the form of Kohlhaase and Klein's *Berlin um die Ecke* (*Berlin Round the Corner*, 1965). That this approach to both youthful style and issues of alienation in socialism resonated deeply with the audience is confirmed by the resounding success of the latter-day 'Berlin-Film' – a self-conscious seventies exploitation of the type – *SOLO SUNNY*.

A politically and chronologically parallel development in cinema to neo-realism, perhaps the dominant type among all of DEFA productions, is what has been called the 'social-realist' film. Although usually linked to the 1970s cultural liberalisation in the GDR, this type arises from *Neue Sachlichkeit* in the 1920s and the social problem films that include the worker milieu films *Kuhle Wampe* (1932) directed by Slatan Dudow and *Cyankali* (1929) directed by Hans Tintner (and based on Friedrich Wolf's play), Piel Jutzi's *Mutter Krausens Fahrt ins Glück* (*Mother Krause's Journey to Happiness*, 1929) and aspects of such films as G.W. Pabst's *Kameradschaft* (*Comradeship*, 1931).

Social realism was also found in Hollywood, as a recent video-tape called *Red Hollywood* (1995), by Noël Burch and Thom Andersen, so clearly documents. A social-realist approach is found not only in Herbert Biberman's independent film *Salt of the Earth* (1954), but in realist dramas with social themes such as Kazan's *Gentleman's Agreement* and *On the Waterfront* (1954) and William Wyler's *The Best Years of Our Lives* (1946). Even *noir* films such as *Crossfire* dealt with anti-Semitism (but not Nazism or the Holocaust). From the left-wing, Stanislavsky and WPA-

influenced work of the 1930s and 1940s it is only a small step to
the youth films of the 1950s, even in the face of the McCarthyist
purges and blacklisting.

Stylistically, the early DEFA 'social dramas' such as Slatan
Dudow's *Unser täglich Brot* (*Our Daily Bread,* 1949) fit into this
international phenomenon quite easily, and DEFA films repeatedly pick up this aesthetic and youth emphasis: Beyer's *Nackt
unter Wölfen* (*Naked among Wolves,* 1963) and *Jakob der Lügner*
(*Jacob the Liar,* 1975), the films of Helmut Dziuba, Rainer
Simon's *Jadup und Boel* (1981), Carow's *Die Russen kommen* (*The
Russians Are Coming,* 1968), and much of the new social cinema
of the 1970s,[17] e.g. Carow's *Bis daß der Tod euch scheidet* (*Until
Death Do Us Part,* 1978) and Erwin Stranka's *Sabine Wulff.* It
would certainly make sense to compare the stylistic and polit-
ical concerns of these GDR directors to the work of Martin Ritt,
Elia Kazan, John Sales, Terence Davies and many others.

Reminiscent of the battles over Lewis Milestone's *All Quiet on
the Western Front* in 1932, the 1950s cultural scene in much of
Europe was dominated by controversy over American youth
culture, especially in such films as *The Wild One* (1954),
produced by Stanley Kramer and directed by Laslo Benedek,
Nicholas Ray's *Rebel without a Cause* (1955), and Richard
Brooks's *Blackboard Jungle* (1955). Although GDR film criticism
was not open to seeing the Western in socialist realism as the
cineastes of France saw auteurism in Budd Boettcher or Sam
Spiegel, film clubs in both East and West resisted censorship or
lack of access to films from Italy, France and the USA that were
considered morally or politically suspect. Although the work of
historians such as Uta Poiger and Heidi Fehrenbach[18] have
made major contributions here, Western film history still has
much to learn about the connection between these youth
culture debates and the Cold War, and thus the Cold War influence on the ensuing new waves, both East and West.

An example discussed elsewhere in this context is Alain
Resnais's *Hiroshima mon amour* (1959) and its influence on
Konrad Wolf's *Der geteilte Himmel.*[19] Paving the way for *Hiroshima
mon amour* was Resnais's first contribution to the French New
Wave, the modernist classic *Nuit et brouillard* (*Night and Fog,*
1957). But it is easily forgotten that this modernism was partly
made possible by resistance to the Cold War – and thanks to
Polish co-sponsorship and Hanns Eisler's musical score. This
adds to the evidence supplied by the Berlin-films, the banned

films of 1965, and modernist works such as Gerhard Klein's *Der Fall Gleiwitz* (*The Gleiwitz Affair*, 1961), that a number of GDR film-makers thought of themselves as participating in the European New Waves that extended from Italy to Moscow. Cinematographer Werner Bergmann, Konrad Wolf's longtime collaborator, even pointed with pride to the fact that *Lissy* anticipates some of the famous camera innovations of Mikhail Kalatozov's *Letyat zhuravli* (*The Cranes Are Flying*, 1957).

Erbe-Diskussion

Film and Literature

Another international aspect of film culture relevant to GDR film studies is the relation of films to literature. In many countries, especially those with subsidy systems, literature makes film bureaucratically possible. But, as Karsten Witte has pointed out, canonical works of German literature are often criticised by GDR films.[20] This again is part of the GDR's unique *Erbe-Diskussion* – the debate over its relation to the German cultural heritage. Also specific to the GDR, and perhaps another example of continuity with pre-1945 studios, is the prominent status of the screenwriter. Many GDR writers are first, or even mainly, authors of film: Christa Wolf wrote for the films from the start of her career, and film influenced her development in narrative experimentation.[21] Other such writers are Helga Schütz, Helga Schubert, Ulrich Plenzdorf, Günther Rücker and especially Wolfgang Kohlhaase. The role of literature and the writer in DEFA also could be productively studied in the context both of German Romantic views of the artist and the bureaucratic structures of subsidised culture, as Thomas Elsaesser has done for West Germany. Elsaesser writes, 'The subsidised artist, I have argued, has thrust upon him his role of representative: a middle ground where originality is compromised by speaking on behalf of others. The label of author thus becomes a dubious value. Conferred by committees, in advance filled with social meaning, his status is, by an ironic twist, a subtle form of revenge society extracts for his privilege.'[22] The controversy around Christa Wolf in the early 1990s is certainly one example of this revenge.

Barton Byg

DEFA beyond the GDR

A final assumption to be challenged is that DEFA was completely confined by the border represented by the Berlin Wall. DEFA does not belong to the GDR alone, and cannot bear sole 'blame' for the GDR, if for no other reason than its continuous relationship with FRG cinema. In the beginning this was true in practical terms, since it was not until 1961 and the Berlin Wall that DEFA had an exclusively Eastern identity. And from a Western point of view, where convenient, early DEFA films are even treated as simply German. Later there was an explicit campaign to keep Western talent out of DEFA and keep DEFA films out of the West. But DEFA contributions exist in many Western films, including Roberto Rossellini's *Germania anno zero* (1947), Straub/Huillet's *Chronik der Anna Magdalena Bach* (*The Chronicle of Anna Magdalena Bach*, 1967), Wenders's *Der Himmel über Berlin* (*Wings of Desire*, 1987) or documentaries such as Helga Reidemeister's *DrehOrt Berlin* (*Location Berlin*, 1987) or *Aufrecht Gehen* (*Walking Tall*, 1988), a film on the life of Rudi Dutschke. Co-productions became more and more common after the 1970s, such as Peter Schamoni's *Frühlingssinfonie* (*Spring Symphony*, 1982/3), Bernhard Wicki's *Die Grünstein-Variante* (*The Grünstein Variation*, 1984), based on a script by Kohlhaase, and Frank Beyer's work for West German television.[23] International co-productions beyond West Germany, although seldom practical, were also undertaken with French, British and other partners, especially in Eastern Europe. The failure of continuous collaboration among socialist countries despite official slogans of solidarity also deserves study in regard to the interconnections between film history and nation-building. But from the West German point of view, the GDR remained a phantom in the national imaginary – as evidenced by Helke Sander's *ReDuPers* (*The All-round Reduced Personality*, 1978), Alexander Kluge's *Abschied von Gestern* (*Yesterday Girl*, 1966), and films by Thomas Brasch.[24]

Further refutation of a hermetic definition of DEFA is the long list of beloved and admired screen stars and stage actors of West Germany who began their careers in GDR films. Most prominent among these are international figures such as Armin Mueller Stahl and Katharina Thalbach, Jutta Hoffmann, Hilmar Thate, Angelika Domröse, Jörg Gudzuhn and the very popular Manfred Krug.[25] Directors were a somewhat rarer

– 36 –

occurrence, but were able to work in the West as well, and technicians were always, like actors, quite well respected for their skill and good training, despite the commonplace about the technical backwardness of the GDR.

Mapping the metaphorical journeys of these actors would provide an interesting intertextual account of DEFA's place in the imaginary geography of contemporary Germany: Hilmar Thate from the troubled youth of the 1950s to the reliable factory director of *Der geteilte Himmel* to the troubled newspaperman in Fassbinder's *Veronika Voss* (1981); Manfred Krug from the irrepressible worker heroes of *Spur der Steine* or *Fünf Patronenhülsen* to *Liebling – Kreuzberg*; Armin Mueller Stahl from the blind violinist in *Der Dritte* to the comic taxi-driver in Jim Jarmusch's *Night on Earth*. This kind of intertextuality has recently been studied in regard to Marlene Dietrich and allusions to her persona by Hanna Schygulla, Marianne Sägebrecht, Barbara Sukowa and even Madonna, for instance in an article entitled 'The Marshall Plan at the movies'.[26] The 'Stalin Plan' has yet to be chronicled.

DEFA's location among a complex and shifting network of state institutions, film movements, historical and aesthetic periods, and production arrangements beyond the GDR could be exemplified by the career of the composer Hanns Eisler.[27] In 1923 Eisler composed music for Walter Ruttmann's *Opus III*, a part of the international avant-garde extending across Europe. From this rather abstract and formalist beginning, Eisler's film work moved to Alexis Granowsky's working-class film *Das Lied vom Leben* (*The Song of Life*, 1931), with songs sung by Ernst Busch. On the other hand, one of Eisler's collaborators on that film was Friedrich Hollaender, author of several of Marlene Dietrich's most famous siren songs. After the pathbreaking work *Kuhle Wampe*, Eisler worked on leftist documentaries such as those by Joris Ivens, and eventually ended up in the USA, writing music for a Joseph Losey film commissioned by the oil industry, *Pete Roleum and His Cousins* (1939). Hollywood also gave Eisler the chance to work with John Ford on *The Grapes of Wrath* (1940) and Fritz Lang on *Hangmen also Die* (1943), on leftist works by Harold Clurman and Clifford Odets as well as films by Douglas Sirk, Jean Renoir, and Edward Dmytryk. In Hollywood he also wrote the important book *Composing for the Films* with T.W. Adorno, an author not usually associated with the GDR. And lest the Cold War be forgotten, in the light of

McCarthyist attacks on Eisler and others, Adorno concealed his co-authorship of that book until the 1960s.

Thus Eisler's career – like many at DEFA – begins in the Weimar cinema and touches the leftist avant-garde as well as socially-engaged Hollywood. For DEFA he worked on Dudow's *Frauenschicksale* (*Fates of Women*, 1952) and *Unser täglich Brot* (1949), Maetzig's *Der Rat der Götter* (*Council of the Gods*, 1950) and Andrew Thorndike's *Wilhelm Pieck* (1950). His modernism was banned as decadent and formalistic in the form of the opera *Johann Faustus*, but was part of the French New Wave in the form of *Nuit et brouillard.*[28] He ended his career writing for DEFA and GDR television, in such productions as Erich Engel's *Geschwader Fledermaus* (*Bat Squadron*, 1958) and Walter Heynowski's *Aktion J* (*Operation J*, 1961). Clearly, on the basis of one example, the historical, political and aesthetic boundaries are very fluid, and deserve a renewed reception and study.

Part of the excitement of this time is to anticipate a rediscovery by young Europeans of such aspects of their cultural heritage the Cold War either hid from them or presented in an oversimplified and unproductive view. Again, one can compare this rediscovery of tradition with the New German Cinema's search for models – and not finding them, except perhaps in Hollywood. Christian Ziewer touched on the West Germans' lack of connection to film history in his eulogy for Wolfgang Staudte – for him, along with Konrad Wolf, the most significant director of postwar Germany. Ziewer wrote:

The protest against the 'fathers' makes one blind toward one's friends. The fact that Staudte, with his resolute insistence on 'an active part in public life', was our forerunner, left in us, if we recognised anything at all, no feeling of affinity which might carry and stimulate us.

It seems to me that the unfinished and problematic element in our relationship to Staudte has a lot to do with our broken relation to the German past in general. We young directors who wanted so much to come to grips with this past have in fact completely and neurotically cut ourselves off from it, so much so that we have destroyed the necessary connections to it […] Staudte's great DEFA films? They remained something talked about in film societies and in no way a part of our present. At the time when I made my first films, ones that Staudte liked a lot, I explained to him with a smile and a certain smugness: there weren't any German influences, no Dudow, no Jutzi, no Pabst (I didn't need to say 'no Staudte', that was understood!), but rather English, Italian … and my own experiences. The latter in particular: we had to

discover everything for ourselves, to reinvent, to formulate filmically, because the past was garbage – or ideology. The romanticised search for a German Hollywood and its directors is only the flip side of the same coin, and Staudte hardly makes a good cult figure: someone who possesses the ability to depict social inequity under such a harsh light does not lend himself easily to transfiguration [...]
To judge film art according to its economic potential at the box office — this is the one, still living tradition in our country. The other, related to it like Scylla to Charybdis, is the demand to avoid any political controversy and to try to please mass tastes. Remembering Wolfgang Staudte and his films should help strengthen us in our fight against these traditions.[29]

One of the truisms of the German cinema has it that to be carefree is to be dull. To be tormented is to be interesting.[30] The torment of DEFA's history is a tradition to be explored and built on, and a tradition to be resisted. For these reasons, DEFA will always be interesting.

Notes

1. See Paul Reimann (ed.), *Kafka aus Prager Sicht 1963*, Prague, 1965 and Jean-Paul Sartre, 'Die Abrüstung der Kultur: Rede auf dem Weltfriedenskongreß in Moskau' (trans. Stephan Hermlin), *Sinn und Form* 14, 1962: 805–15.
2. See Gilles Deleuze and Félix Guattari, *Franz Kafka: Toward a Minor Literature* (Trans. Dana Polan), Minneapolis, 1986.
3. Christiane Mückenberger and Günter Jordan, '*Sie sehen selbst, Sie hören selbst ...*': *Die DEFA von ihren Anfängen bis 1949*, Marburg, 1994.
4. See Philip Rosen, 'History, Textuality, Nation: Kracauer, Burch, and Some Problems in the Study of National Cinemas', *Iris* 2, no. 2, 1984: 69–84; Hannes Schmidt, 'Kollision mit der Umwelt: zu G. Kleins Spielfilm *Berlin um die Ecke* (DEFA 1965)', *Medium* 18, no. 2, 1988: 69–70 (69).
5. Wolf Biermann underscores this difference in 'Reden über das eigene Land: Deutschland', *Klartexte im Getümmel: 13 Jahre im Westen. Von der Ausbürgerung bis zur November-Revolution*, Cologne, 1990, pp. 235–257 (p. 247).
6. Uta Poiger, *Taming the Wild West: American Popular Culture and the Cold War Battles over East and West German Identities, 1949–1961* (PhD Diss., Brown University, 1995). See also Hannelore König, Dieter Wiedemann and Lothar Wolf (eds), *Zwischen Bluejeans und Blauhemden: Jugendfilm in Ost und West*, Berlin, 1995.
7. Theodor W. Adorno, 'On the question "What is German?"', *New German Critique* 36, 1985: 121–31.

– 39 –

8. Szemere goes on to place the question in the context of Western leftist intellectuals' Cold War situation: 'I have wondered whether this apparent lack of interest might be due to Western leftists' ambivalence towards these societies: are they perceived as sites of a compromised, abused, and now defeated utopia? Could there have been a fear that a critical stance towards these political systems (while they were still socialist) would threaten the distinctive political edge of cultural studies and Western leftism *vis-à-vis* the dominant discourse on socialism in their own society?' See Anna Szemere, 'Bandits, Heroes, the Honest, and the Misled: Exploring the Politics of Representation in the Hungarian Uprising of 1956', in *Cultural Studies*, ed. Lawrence Grossberg, Cary Nelson, Paula Treichler, New York, 1992, pp. 623–39 (p. 623).

9. Hans Koning, 'Where Money Has Little Currency: Travels in East Germany', *Harper's Magazine*, November 1987: 71.

10. See Anton Kaes, *From Hitler to Heimat: The Return of History as Film*, Cambridge MA, 1989, p. 8.

11. *Ernst Thälmann – Sohn seiner Klasse (Ernst Thälmann – Son of the Working Class*, 1954) and; *Ernst Thälmann – Führer seiner Klasse, (Ernst Thälmann – Leader of the Working Class*, 1955).

12. The most prominent examples of this group are Josef Mach's *Die Söhne der großen Bärin (The Sons of the Great She-Bear*, 1966), Richard Groschopp's *Chingachgook, die Grosse Schlange (Chingachgook, the Great Snake*, 1967), and two films by Gottfried Kolditz, *Spur des Falken (The Falcon's Trail*, 1968) and *Apachen* (1973). All featured the Yugoslavian actor Gojko Mitic as the native American lead.

13. See Poiger, *Taming the Wild West*, p. 5 and p. 11.

14. On Hollywood melodrama see Christine Gledhill (ed.), *Home Is where the Heart Is: Studies in Melodrama and the Women's Film*, London, 1987.

15. On Konrad Wolf's female characters, see Marc Silberman, 'Remembering History: the Film-maker Konrad Wolf', *New German Critique* 49, 1990: 163–91.

16. Klaus Kreimeier, '*Germania, anno zero*: eine Momentaufnahme', *epd film* 12, no. 6, 1995: 17–25 (22).

17. See Sigrun Leonhardt, 'Testing the Borders: East German Film Between Individualism and Social Commitment', in *Post New Wave Cinema in the Soviet Union and Eastern Europe*, ed. Daniel J. Goulding, Bloomington, 1989, pp. 51–101.

18. See Poiger, *Taming the Wild West* and Heidi Fehrenbach, *Cinema and Democratizing Germany: Reconstructing National Identity after Hitler*, Durham NC, 1995.

19. Barton Byg, 'Geschichte, Trauer und weibliche Identität im Film: *Hiroshima mon amour* und *Der geteilte Himmel*', (trans. Thomas Nolden) in *Zwischen gestern und morgen: Schriftstellerinnen der DDR aus amerikanischer Sicht*, ed. Ute Brandes, Berlin, 1992, pp. 95–112.

20. See Karsten Witte, 'Geteilte Filme: einige Erfahrungen mit Literatur

und Politik im DEFA-Film', *Film und Fernsehen* 23, no. 1, 1995: 17–19.

21. See Alexander Stephan, *Christa Wolf*, Munich, 1976, p. 58.

22. Thomas Elsaesser, *New German Cinema: A History*. New Brunswick, NJ, 1989, p. 74.

23. See Ralf Schenk (ed.), *Regie: Frank Beyer*, Potsdam, 1995.

24. Although he emigrated to the West in the 1970s, Brasch continued to treat GDR experience in his work, especially *Domino* (1981/82), *Engel aus Eisen* (*Iron Angel*, 1980/81) and *Vor den Vätern sterben die Söhne* (*Sons Die before their Fathers*, 1981). His *Der Passagier – Welcome to Germany* (*The Passenger – Welcome to Germany*, 1988) was a collaboration with the GDR novelist Jurek Becker, who authored both Beyer's *Jakob der Lügner* and the Western television series *Liebling – Kreuzberg*.

25. A recent article in *The Economist* speaks of Jörg Gudzuhn as 'a leading actor on the German stage and television', leaving out his DEFA career. DEFA, for its part, is dismissed as 'being stuck for half a century turning out communist romps to please its East German political masters'. See 'Schmaltzy Days Are Here Again', *The Economist*, 30 November 1996.*

26. Joseph Loewenstein and Lynne Tatlock, 'The Marshall Plan at the Movies: Marlene Dietrich and Her Incarnations', *The German Quarterly* 65, nos. 3-4, 1992: 429–42.

27. This information relies on the entry on Eisler in Hans-Michael Bock (ed.), *Cinegraph: Lexikon zum deutschsprachigen Film*, Hamburg, Munich, 1984.

28. Tellingly, the cover of the video version of *Night and Fog* distributed in the USA makes no mention of Eisler's music.

29. Christian Ziewer, 'Last Words for Wolfgang Staudte (1984)', in *West German Film-makers on Film: Visions and Voices*, ed. Eric Rentschler, New York, London, 1988, pp. 118–20.

30. Vlado Kristl: 'German films are by far the most accurate reflections of the Europe of our time. For film history they are more important as failures than where they were successful ...' Cited in: Elsaesser, *New German Cinema*, p. 79.

❖ *Chapter 3* ❖

'LETTING THE GENIE OUT OF THE BOTTLE': DEFA FILM-MAKERS AND *FILM UND FERNSEHEN*

Rosemary Stott

The aim of this essay is to consider the nature of film criticism and discussion by DEFA feature film-makers published in the journal *Film und Fernsehen* (*Film and TV*) from its inception in 1973 to 1988, a period that corresponds almost exactly to the Honecker era, and how this related to developments in cultural policy with regard to the feature film. I shall analyse to what extent film-makers writing in *Film und Fernsehen* addressed the contradictions and constraints they faced in film-production and thus reveal how far the journal could be said to have presented a complete and critical picture of the role of the DEFA film in the lives of GDR citizens. First an outline of the journal's history and profile in the context of the print media will be given, followed by a brief analysis of the nature of its reviews in comparison with other GDR publications.

Film und Fernsehen was the major film journal in the country and as such represents an important historical document of film-making in the GDR, indeed of film-making in the whole of the former Soviet Bloc. It was set up as the organ of the *Verband der Film- und Fernsehschaffenden der DDR* ('Film and Television Association of the GDR'). The association itself was founded in 1967 to provide a forum for all those working within the spheres of film and television in the GDR.[1] The idea of a new film magazine was conceived in 1973 by the Ministry of Culture's Film Bureau, the *Hauptverwaltung Film.*[2]

All new magazines had to be officially sanctioned by the press board, which also determined the number of copies published.

Film und Fernsehen received its licence from the Press Board on 10 May 1973, initially for 4,000 copies.[3] The magazine was funded entirely by the State. It was published by the Henschel publishing company, a company with an academic profile, and the editorial office was situated at Henschel's main complex in Oranienburger Straße in East Berlin. The editor and editorial board, all members of the Association, were responsible for its contents.

Kurt Hager, the Minister for Culture, had ultimate responsibility for the journal because the spheres of film and publishing fell within the jurisdiction of his ministry. This meant that unlike most print journalism – the bulk of which was controlled by the Minister for Agitation and Propaganda, Joachim Herrmann – *Film und Fernsehen* was answerable to a different branch of the ministerial hierarchy. Although ministers possessed the ultimate power of veto, the extent to which they could maintain personal oversight of individual periodicals was inevitably limited. It was the editors of newspapers and periodicals – Günter Netzeband in the case of *Film und Fernsehen* – who determined their profile and content. Would-be editors of print journalism in the GDR all underwent a five-year degree course in journalism, and only after many years of journalistic experience were they selected by the appropriate ministry for a post as editor. Editors attended weekly meetings at the ministry where they were informed about the party line on current issues.[4] Netzeband was no exception, although it appears that the pressure to adhere to party lines was less severe for *Film und Fernsehen* than it was for those publications supervised by the Ministry for Agitation and Propaganda. In those instances where Netzeband failed to publish contentious articles, it has been suggested that he did not want to risk jeopardising the release and distribution of controversial films and that he did not want to offend or incriminate his colleagues in the Association.[5]

Netzeband remained the editor of *Film und Fernsehen* from its inception until 1991, when the Association was dissolved. There were two full-time editorial staff in addition to the editor when the journal was established, and three full-time editorial staff from 1978. Although the editorial personnel changed over the years, there were a number of long-standing members. In addition there was an editorial board of ten, which consisted of members of the Association who had other full-time jobs, for example, Lothar Bisky, who was principal of the film school in Potsdam before becoming a deputy for the PDS (Party of Democratic Socialism) in the *Bundestag* after unification. Some members of the board – Heinz Grote, for example – served during the whole period covered by this study. Articles were contributed by editorial staff, by members of the editorial board and by a variety of other film critics. A number of well-known and respected film directors wrote for the journal and it is these articles which I shall discuss here.

Although it was not cheap by GDR standards, *Film und Fernsehen* sold well and circulation gradually increased to a maximum of 10,700 in 1988.[6] Subscriptions accounted for some 20% of sales, the bulk of which were, however, foreign subscriptions; within the GDR itself, subscriptions were notoriously difficult to come by.

Film und Fernsehen dealt above all with national film and television production. It also ran regular features on film in the Soviet Union and other Eastern Bloc countries, as well as on film in the developing world. There was relatively little reporting of film and television in capitalist countries. The format consisted of reviews of individual films, articles of a more general nature, for example about a particular film genre, reports from festivals, workshop discussions, interviews with film actors and a review section. Twice a year on average *Film und Fernsehen* appeared in the form of a special number; in September 1984, for example, one such issue was devoted to the thirty-fifth anniversary of the GDR.

The feature film received the widest coverage in the journal, with reviews of individual films as well as summative articles of a more theoretical nature. Television received considerably less coverage and was restricted to articles on GDR productions, with little material on television abroad and few reviews of individual programmes. This was possibly due to the four-month production delay the journal suffered from throughout its history. Such a time-lag deterred writers from attempting to review material which would no longer be topical by the time the journal had appeared. Coverage of East German documentary production was thorough, perhaps because of the high standard of documentary film-making in the country and the annual documentary film festivals in Leipzig and Neubrandenburg, which had an international reputation and which received detailed analysis in *Film und Fernsehen*.

The only other film periodical in the GDR targeted at an essentially non-academic audience was the *Filmspiegel*, a journal which was set up in 1953. *Film und Fernsehen* was a monthly journal, whereas *Filmspiegel* appeared every fortnight and had greater mass appeal, largely as a result of its cinema listings and colourful format. The circulation of *Filmspiegel* was around 400,000 and only two percent of its sales were by subscription. The two were thus hardly competitors. *Filmspiegel* was a magazine people bought in a kiosk to find out about the latest film releases whereas *Film und Fernsehen* was for readers who wanted to inform themselves about wider issues relating to film. The editors and staff were different, but were subject to the same constraints referred to above. Both journals were published by Henschel and occupied neighbouring offices.

Daily newspapers such as *Neues Deutschland* and *Junge Welt*, as well as weeklies such as *Sonntag* and *Eulenspiegel*, regularly contained film reviews and comment. The reviews in these papers and magazines were more up-to-date, though usually shorter and more superficial than those in *Film und Fernsehen*. What all the newspapers and magazines had in common was that their film reviews corresponded closely to the publication's character and target audience and thus the film reviewer's response to any particular film tended to be rather predictable. For example, the SED's newspaper, *Neues Deutschland*, ran reviews heavily criticising DEFA films which presented a less than favourable view of everyday reality in the GDR. In a review of Herrmann Zschoche's film *Insel der Schwäne* (*Swan Island*, 1983) published on 4 May 1983 and headed 'A Distorted View of Life Here' ('Verstellte Sicht auf unsere Wirklichkeit'), the paper's regular film critic, Horst Knietsch, attacked the film for drawing on ideologies inherent in the bourgeois cinema, pointing to what he saw as an analogy between the teenage hero in the film and the heroes of the Hollywood Westerns. In addition, he criticised the way in which the film-makers had departed from the original novel on which the film was based, simplifying it in the process and portraying the high-rise suburb as soulless and alienating.

Picking up in particular on the final criticism, *Junge Welt*, the newspaper of the East German Youth movement, the 'Freie Deutsche Jugend' or 'FDJ', used a stock device in its critique of the film: the 'reader's letter'. Although apparently from a wide variety of sources – they were ostensibly written by soldiers, car mechanics and apprentices in the building industry – these letters all criticised the film for not taking a more favourable view of society. Thus they attempted to deflect from the fact that such disillusionment was present amongst some, though admittedly not all, young people in the GDR.

By comparison, *Film und Fernsehen* was more sophisticated in its criticism. Although it often ran general articles attacking the Western media – a number of which were written by Horst Knietsch himself – the film reviews it contained were a good deal more subtle than the average newspaper review. In a page-long review of *Insel der Schwäne* written in May 1983, the critic provides a sensitive analysis that takes full account of the film's complexity and ironic dimension. The author of the review highlighted the real motive of the film-makers, namely the wish to engender discussion concerning the problems of GDR life, to analyse their causes, and suggest ways of solving them: 'In order to live together in a meaningful way, we have to acknowledge the existence of intolerance, negligence and indifference.' [7]

Film und Fernsehen often ran leading articles written by film-makers themselves or interviews with them. These articles dealt almost exclusively with the role of film in GDR society and rarely touched upon debates about international film theory and aesthetics. Nonetheless, they often reflect the turning-points in the development of East German cinema, and highlight attempts to introduce new themes and develop new styles – as well as the frustrations experienced by the film-makers. In an issue of *Film und Fernsehen* written after the *Wende*, Heiner Carow was to reflect on the events of the Eleventh Plenum of 1965, noting that: 'The icy winds which kept returning every decade have not been forgotten. New initiatives froze and died and promising developments were nipped in the bud.' [8]

In addition to being a source of entertainment, cinema played an important pedagogical role in the GDR. In common with the other arts, it was seen as a means of propagating socialist values and integrating GDR citizens into a socialist society. The dominant aesthetic was that of socialist realism, although under Erich Honecker's leadership – a period lasting from 1972 up until the *Wende* in 1989 – there were moments characterised by a greater degree of tolerance for artistic works which did not conform rigidly to this aesthetic.

As the Honecker era unfolded, the realities of a more pragmatic (though not officially sanctioned) film policy increasingly gained the upper hand, a policy of not only tolerating – but even propagating – Western television and films. This new agenda, which was only tacitly acknowledged in journals such as *Film und Fernsehen*, was effectively an admission on the part of the SED leadership that the traditional socialist view of culture – the view that high-brow art should and could be made accessible to all sections of society – was simply impractical. As a result, the GDR began to witness the emergence of a more differentiated film culture. Holidaymakers, for example, could visit large tent cinemas erected in the summer at resorts to show entertainment films, often Western imports. These cinemas had extended screenings of popular films which thus reached large audiences. At the opposite end of the spectrum, the *Camera* programmes in city cinemas showed art-house imports from the West as well as film classics from around the world and from DEFA's own archives. Clearly aimed at the small, well-informed intellectual audience, most of the screenings were one-off or late-night performances. DEFA film-production too was increasingly geared towards serving smaller target groups.

From the early 1970s onwards, film-makers clearly welcomed the opportunities to depart from the strict socialist realist model which had been their strait-jacket in the early days of DEFA. At the same time, like most artists and intellectuals in the GDR, the majority of them were committed to socialism and strove to produce films that were both artistic and politically committed.[9] They did not want to overthrow the system; nonetheless they were intent on raising controversial issues and ridding DEFA of the obsolete and heavy-handed socialist realist aesthetic.

Heiner Carow was a frequent contributor to *Film und Fernsehen* and in the second issue of 1976 he took up the debate surrounding the appropriateness of the socialist realist model. He discussed, in particular, the audience's annoyance and disillusionment with DEFA productions, and attributed their dissatisfaction to a rejection of DEFA's didactic approach and the tendency to present an idealised version of reality. He cited the specific example of the audience who were presented with an image on screen of a collective whose achievements were exemplary together with an unequivocal message that they too should be achieving such targets at work. Carow rejected this patronising and overly didactic approach – so typical of the worst examples of socialist realism – and demanded greater respect for an audience who knew only too well the complexities and ambiguities of working life under socialism. He found it objectionable that the audience should be told what to think in the cinema and called for a truly Leninist film art which really could claim to address the people. Effectively, Carow was urging a thorough renewal of socialist film art: 'Lenin speaks of film as the most important art form because of its revolutionary function. It is this function that contemporary film art is failing to fulfil in our cinemas.' [10]

There is no doubt that his article in *Film und Fernsehen* reflected the feelings of intellectuals at the time who were beginning to challenge the form of socialism prevailing in the GDR. Rudolf Bahro's book *Die Alternative* (*The Alternative*) was representative of their feelings that the GDR could not genuinely call itself a socialist state.[11] However, these challenges went too far for the authorities and the consequence was the 'Biermann affair'. Like Biermann, Bahro was forced to settle in the Federal Republic and left the GDR in 1978 after serving one year of an eight-year prison sentence.

Film-makers clearly supported the democratisation of the system. However, in contrast to such well-known writers as Christa Wolf and Stefan Heym, relatively few film-makers spoke out publicly in support of Biermann[12] and none of the well-known directors chose to leave the country as a consequence. *Film und Fernsehen* revealed some evidence of the film-makers' feelings concerning the controversy. Thus in April 1977, it published another contribution from Carow, this time an interview by Hermann Herlinghaus, in which there were veiled references to the rift between Party and artists which had developed as a consequence of the Biermann affair. Preparations were under way for the Conference of the Film and TV Association and Carow stated that it was vital to continue discussion and clarification of the issues facing film-makers. In this context he quoted Dudow: 'Above all we must not shy away from disagreement.' [13] There were no direct references to the Biermann affair, but it is clear that Carow was siding with the Biermann sympathisers.

The article indicated that film-makers did not want to jeopardise the considerable gains made in the film-making industry during the early 1970s. The continued production of films tackling controversial issues during the latter part of the 1970s – films which put the realism back into socialist realism – underlines how successful film-makers such as Carow were in averting a backlash during this time. Indeed this period – which saw the release of such films as Roland Gräf's *PS* (1978), Konrad Wolf's *SOLO SUNNY* (1980) and Lothar Warneke's *Unser kurzes Leben* (*Our Short Life,* 1980) – is widely seen as heralding a renaissance in East German film-making. Films like these were given extensive coverage in *Film und Fernsehen* in the form of detailed reviews, sometimes by more than one critic. They were discussed in terms of their departure from the prevailing model of socialist realism – although the more covert criticism contained within the films tended to be ignored. Thus *Unser kurzes Leben,* for example, raised a number of feminist issues. The SED was proud – in part justifiably – of the measures they had introduced to provide equal opportunities for women at work, but the film questioned the degree to which these measures were empowering, rather than further disadvantaging, women in the workplace. The journal ignored such issues altogether, praising it instead for its sense of realism, subtle characterisation and cinematography.[14]

The continued commitment to departing from the socialist realist model is clearly reflected in the articles written by film-makers in *Film und Fernsehen* during this period. In the October 1980 issue, Kurt Maetzig referred to the first years of DEFA's existence, a time when the DEFA film was the leading art form in the Soviet-occupied zone of Germany. He did not need to mention that this was the period before socialist realism became so firmly established within the cultural ideology of the GDR. Since then, he maintained DEFA's reputation had waned, but declared that at the time of writing 'the weak period has been overcome, or to be more precise, we are in the process of overcoming it'.[15] In this article, the main justification for moving away from the socialist realist model was once again its overt didacticism. Maetzig ascribed the increase in quality in the DEFA film to the recent rejection of obsolete dramaturgical models which had been formulated with the view of educating the audience.

The models to which he was alluding were clearly those of socialist realism though, typically for the magazine, they were not specifically referred to and official Party policy was not mentioned. He did not go as far as to suggest abandoning a didactic thrust altogether, but considered that the 'message' of the film should not be the overriding element, just as he did not dismiss the exemplary hero out of hand but felt that this need not be the only type of protagonist – a shortcoming often associated with films in the past. Like Carow, Maetzig stressed the need for an active rather than a passive audience, an audience which entered into a discursive relationship with the film rather than being instructed by it. He believed that the filmmakers' aim should be 'to make the audience more aware of how they live, and in this way to help them understand their own situation and their own point of view more clearly.' [16]

East German film-making in the 1980s continued to be almost entirely within the socialist tradition. A large proportion of films dealt with contemporary life in the GDR. They continued to raise controversial issues, but following the suppression of a number of films – amongst them Rainer Simon's *Jadup und Boel* (1981) – they did so in an oblique and ambiguous manner. A typical example of such a film is Lothar Warneke's *Eine sonderbare Liebe* (*A Strange Kind of Love*, 1984), a film which showed the realities of the socialist collective at work whilst at the same time dealing with personal disillusionment and withdrawal into the private sphere. Such films received wide coverage in *Film und Fernsehen* and were reviewed enthusiastically by critics. However, there was still a certain reticence in discussing the contentious issues raised.

A topic of major concern to film-makers in the GDR was the development of film policy. The issues of how DEFA could compete with the Western media, with West German television in the 1970s and with the competition from commercial Western imports in the 1980s, were debated frequently in *Film und Fernsehen.* Needless to say, the question of how any national film culture could resist the hegemony of the American film industry was one which dominated the whole of Europe at the time, but it had an added twist in the Eastern Bloc states. The term used in the journal to refer to such debates was 'audience appeal' ('Publikumswirksamkeit'). These debates, like those about the acceptance or rejection of the socialist-realist aesthetic, were at their most vigorous in the 1970s. Indeed, some of the issues overlapped: many film-makers believed that the feature film in the GDR could only compete with the increased competition from Western television and the film imports from Western countries by dispensing with the socialist-realist aesthetic.

Some authors of articles in the journal went as far as specifying the criteria by which they judged a film to be effective. By and large, however, articles published in *Film und Fernsehen* in the 1970s tended to emphasise educational criteria in the socialist-realist sense: the film was 'effective' if it educated or inspired the audience as socialist citizens. It is in these terms that the issue is couched in a report from the the third conference of editors of film publications in socialist countries published in the February edition of 1976. At this stage in the cultural history of the GDR, television (in particular West German television) and the increasing dominance of films imported from the West were already posing a serious threat to the socialist ideology propagated in the DEFA film. The solution to the problem was seen to lie in educating young people to be more discriminating in their selection of viewing. During this period there was clearly an awareness of difficulties and an optimism that they could be overcome with increased ideological commitment.

In the same issue Carow continued the debate. He saw the main task as being that of improving the quality of the films themselves. In addition, he argued for more openness in film criticism, better quality cinemas, more technical improvements and better advertising, adding that these would improve automatically if the films produced a greater mass-appeal ('Massenwirksamkeit'). Bearing in mind the gulf between the SED leadership and the majority of artists which had developed by the eighties, Carow's final comments – he talked of the advantage that the GDR had in terms of its unified cultural policy – acquire retrospectively a degree of irony. The sound basis of unified principles linking the television and the film industry in the GDR meant that they could collaborate to achieve 'the greatest possible audience-appeal'.[17]

In a follow-up to this interview in May 1977, Carow talked more pointedly about what the DEFA film-makers had to compete with. He referred to audiences' preferences for television as opposed to cinema and stated that their taste for 'pure entertainment' had to be accepted. It was catered to, he believed, by the 'not insignificant amount of Western imports on TV and in the cinemas'.[18] Nonetheless, he went on to claim that the same audiences also had a taste for entertainment of a

Rosemary Stott

more demanding and interesting kind in the form of feature
films which provided 'a socialist response to the issues they
faced in their own society'.[19] Despite the optimistic tone, it is
hard to ignore the subtext of Carow's remarks, namely a tacit
acceptance that DEFA films occupied a 'niche' role alongside
the Western import. Even more significant is the fact that the
precedence enjoyed by commercial imports from the West is
neither challenged nor discussed. As to the real cause of the
problem – the double standards regarding film distribution –
Film und Fernsehen was largely silent. For the first time Carow
also specified in this article what he understood by the term
'mass-appeal' ('Massenwirksamkeit'): not only the number of
tickets sold, but the depth of the cinematic experience and the
degree to which the film promoted discussion and controversy.
He concluded that this was something which was rarely experienced in the films at that time. These comments, like many of
the leading articles in *Film und Fernsehen*, were a reflection of
discussions held by the Film and TV Association.

By the end of the 1970s, the optimism of such articles
appeared to have been confirmed by the renaissance of the
GDR film. But this was not to last. No doubt affected by the
backlash against experimentation in the early 1980s and an
increasing readiness on the part of the SED leadership to
tolerate Western culture and values, DEFA film-makers failed to
continue producing films of a consistently high quality in the
1980s. Various writers after the *Wende* have apportioned a
degree of blame to the film-makers themselves for this
phenomenon. They argue that DEFA film-makers were handi-
capped by a significant degree of self-censorship and were
gradually worn down by the air of disillusionment and dissatisfaction with GDR society as a whole.[20] Given the increasing
prominence of Western imports and the inevitable under-
mining of national film-production that this entailed, it seems
hardly surprising that film-makers found it difficult to stage an
effective socialist challenge to the advance of the Western
media. It was as if the front of the Cold War battle of conflicting
ideologies had moved from between East and West Germany to
within East Germany itself. In the face of an inconsistent
cultural policy – at times blatantly hypocritical – it began to
seem as if only the intellectuals and artists were on the side of
socialist ideology.

The decreasing desire to assert socialist principles and the lack of interest in finding new ways to make the DEFA film more effective is evident in *Film und Fernsehen*. One such indication was the disappearance of the debate about the audience-appeal of DEFA films, which coincided with the demise of the debate concerning the socialist-realist aesthetic. Indeed the amount of coverage devoted to DEFA films changed quite considerably between 1982 and 1988. It became limited almost exclusively to reviews of particular films; the leading articles of the type so common in the 1970s had disappeared. Now the term 'audience-appeal' ('Wirksamkeit') was more likely to be used in the context of American films screened in the GDR.

The only occasion during this six-year period when the debate about 'audience-appeal' returned to something like the intensity it enjoyed in the 1970s was in 1984, after the release of Horst Seemann's film *Ärztinnen* (*Women Doctors*, 1984). This film was set in West Germany and concerned the corrupt practices of the pharmaceutical industry. It was a fast-paced drama laden with heightened emotional effects, a film which borrowed much from the Hollywood melodrama and little from the conventional DEFA film. In June 1984 the film was discussed in *Film und Fernsehen* by a panel of GDR critics. Criticism of the film was surprisingly restrained. The number of reviewers who wrote positively about it was greater than those who did not. Amongst its admirers was Renate Holland-Moritz, the regular film critic of the GDR satirical magazine *Eulenspiegel*. She described it as a very effective ('effektvoll') film.[21] It is clear, however, that the criteria she used to judge the film were not those that Carow highlighted in 1977, but those which increasingly had come to dominate film policy in the GDR, namely: box-office takings.

Rarely did the journal *Film und Fernsehen* solicit audience opinion when it investigated the appeal of certain films. Whereas newspapers and other film magazines at least published readers' letters – albeit letters that had been carefully selected or indeed faked – the whole issue of audience reception was largely absent in *Film und Fernsehen*. An article in *Film und Fernsehen* recording audience reactions to Konrad Wolf's film *Mama, ich lebe* (*Mother, I'm Alive*, 1976), offers a rare insight of audience reactions to the conventional DEFA film – something Wolf's film quite clearly was *not* – and the alternatives to it. The article was written by Konrad Wolf himself, one of the first film-makers in the mid-1970s to call for renewed efforts to improve the quality of DEFA films. *Film und Fernsehen* did not publish these comments – which Wolf summarised and assessed at the Third Congress of the Film and TV Association in 1977 – until 1982. What is more, this was in an issue devoted exclusively to Wolf, since he had died the same year. The delayed publication could only be an indication of the controversial nature of the speech. It was also typical of the journal that controversial subject matter was suppressed until time had rendered it safe again.

The controversy surrounding the speech was due to the fact that in it Wolf had summarised letters he had received from audiences who had watched the film. Here was a rare example where audience reaction had not been subjected to a process of prior scrutiny. In common with his colleagues Carow and Maetzig, Wolf felt that for too long the SED leadership and the writers and artists in the GDR had shied away from a genuine dialogue with the people. In these letters it was the audience themselves who rejected the crude socialist-realist aesthetic, thereby lending support to the film-makers' shared convictions. Instead the audience demanded 'films which clearly portray conditions in our state without idealising them'.[22] In addition, the letters told of how they were pleasantly surprised by the film's lack of schematic socialist-realist formulas, formulas with which they were only too well acquainted and which they had come to expect in DEFA films.

Wolf seems to have clearly perceived the danger of the film-makers and, above all, the political leaders in the GDR losing touch with their public. How frustrating it must have been for him and others like him that their words were not heeded: 'What sort of person is it who goes to see our films today? Certainly not someone we need to be afraid of, somebody concealing a truncheon behind his back. The person who goes to see our films today is our ally.'[23] The equation of spectator ('Zuschauer') with ally ('Verbündeter') broadened the statement from an artistic to a political one.

In retrospect, the most pertinent and prophetic words concerning audience reception in the GDR came once again from Konrad Wolf. In January 1981 in an article entitled 'Letting the Genie out of the Bottle' ('Der Geist aus der Flasche'),[24] he warned his fellow film-makers of the dangers of being lulled into a false sense of security by the recent wave of DEFA successes, the most prominent of which was his own film, *SOLO SUNNY*. In this article Wolf referred, in rather veiled terms, to his fear that film alone was not able to satisfy the audiences' need to raise issues relating to their own lives, hopes and frustrations. He demonstrated an acute awareness of the crisis in GDR society, the gulf between the people and their political masters, as well as a sense of the profound frustration on the part of the citizens which in turn led to the desire to abandon the GDR. He did not address these issues directly, but referred to them using the metaphor of a genie being let out of a bottle. The bottle referred to the limited capacity of cinema to raise controversial issues, the huge all-enveloping genie, the enormity of the expectations and needs of the audience to enter a dialogue about the realities of their society. He warned that if this challenge were not taken up, the genie would take its revenge – and with some justification. And so it did – one might argue – in 1989. In the sphere of film, the blame surely rests with those responsible for the formulation of cultural policy – who rather than risk the fall-out from a film such as *Jadup und Boel* preferred to put their trust in the palliative effects of Western imports – and not with the film-makers, who consistently demonstrated a genuine commitment to improving film output in the GDR and indeed society as a whole.

The articles written by film-makers in the GDR in *Film und Fernsehen* represented some of the most critical writing in the country. However they still only hinted at the contradictions film-makers faced. A contemporary reading of the journal requires us to try and approach the text as a GDR reader might have done, disregarding the usual formulaic references to the 'class enemy', and searching for a possible hidden agenda. Reading the journal for a full and critical analysis of the DEFA film, however, can often be a frustrating endeavour since what this – and other journals – from the period tell us today is as much about the nature of the print media in the GDR as about film-making there.

Rosemary Stott

Notes

1. See Peter Ludz et al. (eds), *DDR Handbuch*, Cologne, 1985, p. 1043.
2. Information from an informal interview with Axel Geiss, GDR film critic and editor of *Film und Fernsehen* 1990–1.
3. *Film und Fernsehen* 16, no. 4, 1988: 36.
4. Annette Leo, 'Der hippokratische Eid auf die Wahrheit oder Der Traum vom wirklichen Journalismus', in *Aufbruch in eine andere DDR*, ed.: Hubertus Knabe, Hamburg, 1989, pp. 83–89 (p. 86).
5. Margit Voss (a film critic for GDR radio) suggested the first reason with respect to GDR film critics in Bettina Hindemith, 'Der DEFA-Spielfilm und seine Kritik, Probleme und Tendenzen', in *Filmland DDR: ein Reader zu Geschichte, Funktion und Wirkung der DEFA*, ed. Harry Blunk and Dirk Jungnickel, Cologne, 1990, pp. 27–46 (p. 43).
6. 'In eigener und in anderer Sache: Rechenschaftsbericht der Zeitschrift Film und Fernsehen', *Film und Fernsehen* 16, no. 4, 1988: 36–41 (36).
7. H.D., 'Eine Insel im Häusermeer', *Film und Fernsehen* 11, no. 5, 1983: 5–6 (6).
8. Fred Gehler, 'Machen und Machen lassen: Auskünfte von Heiner Carow. Notiert von Fred Gehler nach Gesprächen mit Heiner Carow', *Film und Fernsehen* 18, no. 2, 1990: 7–8 (7).
9. Graham Bartram and Anthony Waine (eds), *Culture and Society in the GDR* (GDR Monitor Special Series, no. 2), Dundee, 1984, 17, state that criticism on the part of artists was not about overthrowing the socialist system but rather confronting the realities of GDR society.
10. Heiner Carow, 'Es ist Zeit, über das Kino nachzudenken', *Film und Fernsehen* 4, no. 2, 1976: 12–16 and 48 (15).
11. Rudolf Bahro, *Die Alternative*, Cologne, 1977.
12. Alexander Stephan, 'Cultural politics in the GDR under Erich Honecker' in *The GDR under Honecker*, (GDR Monitor Special Series, no. 1), ed. Ian Wallace, Dundee, 1981, pp. 31–42.
13. Heiner Carow, 'Zwischenbilanz', *Film und Fernsehen* 5, no. 4, 1977: 5–9 (5).
14. Dieter Schiller, '*Unser kurzes Leben*', *Film und Fernsehen* 9, no. 3, 1981: 40–1 (41).
15. Kurt Maetzig, 'Kino für mündige Zuschauer', *Film und Fernsehen* 8, no. 10, 1980: 4–7 (4).
16. Ibid., 6.
17. Carow, 'Es ist Zeit': 16.
18. Heiner Carow, 'Zwischenbilanz' *Film und Fernsehen* 5, no. 5, 1977: 10–13 (11).
19. Ibid.
20. See for example, Sibylle Schönemann, 'Stoffentwicklung im DEFA-Studio für Spielfilme', in Blunk and Jungnickel, *Filmland DDR*, pp.

71–82 (p. 80), who refers to the internalised forms of self-censorship on the part of the film-makers.

21. See 'Aus Rezensionen', *Film und Fernsehen* 14, no. 6, 1984: 18.
22. *Film und Fernsehen* 10, no. 10, 1982, [Special number on Konrad Wolf]: 67–9 (68).
23. Ibid., 69.
24. Konrad Wolf, 'Der Geist aus der Flasche', *Film und Fernsehen* 9, no. 1, 1981: xi–xii.

✣ Chapter 4 ✣

THE ANTI-FASCIST PAST IN DEFA FILMS

Christiane Mückenberger

Many of the DEFA films dealing with fascism are regarded as the most artistically interesting films produced in the GDR and, a fact which should not be overlooked, they are some of the most enduring in the minds of contemporary cinema-goers. Indeed it would be no exaggeration to say that some of these films are among the best films ever made in Germany. Given that what they portrayed was hardly flattering to their viewers, how was it that they managed to affect people so deeply? It was because people felt that the film-makers were genuinely concerned with their subject matter and that their approach was fundamentally honest. In the early years of DEFA the directors and script writers were people who had returned from exile, men like Gustav von Wangenheim, Friedrich Wolf and his son Konrad, or those who had been liberated from prison such as the actor Erwin Geschonneck, or had managed to survive 'in freedom' but in danger of their lives, such as Kurt Maetzig (who, according to Nazi terminology, was a 'half-Jew') or those who had survived 'illegally', such as the actor Alfred Balthoff, or who had been active in the resistance, like the director Falk Harnack. There were also those who had lived through the Nazi years with a measure of opportunism and who now wished to give an honest account of their collaboration with the system.

Here were films made by directors of their own free will. Nobody needed to commission them. These were 'confessional films', as one contemporary director put it. They achieved this by dint of their power to convince and because of the emotional climate of the time, a time in which those who had fought in the resistance expressed a readiness to understand those who had reached a compromise with the regime (providing they had not actually committed any crimes). The writer and political émigré Johannes R. Becher (later to become Minister of Culture in the GDR) said in one of his first speeches: 'We have brought guilt upon ourselves.'[1] Significantly he did not say 'you'.

Nonetheless, despite an understandable desire not to deprive German people of all sense of self-respect but to shake them out of their lethargy and encourage them to get on with their lives and work, it was not long before a more critical approach to the past was discernible. The first weekly newsreel, *Der Augenzeuge* (*The Eyewitness*) presented a series of ongoing reports on the Nuremberg War Crimes Tribunal all of which were preceded by the slogan: 'Never forget – they are guilty!' as the camera panned along the faces of the main defendants. The clear emphasis on the word 'they' contained the seeds of a premature moral exoneration of those who were not sitting in the dock and who had, it might be supposed, not committed any 'great crimes' themselves.

The feature films of the 1940s did not take this line. Their main protagonists were the opportunists, the minor spies and careerists, and those few – all too few – brave individuals who struggled to preserve their human dignity, even if this consisted merely of attempting to act normally, to do the kinds of things that one takes for granted in a civilised society. Accordingly, the main subject of these films was everyday fascism, a subject familiar enough to most Germans.

The first German post-war film, DEFA's *Die Mörder sind unter uns* (*The Murderers Are among Us*, 1946) directed by Wolfgang Staudte, represents a prototype of these films. Staudte had written the outline of the film together with his friend, the cameraman Friedel Behn-Grund, whose leg had been removed by a grenade shortly before the end of the war. 'In the midst of the horror during the last days of the war it was in itself an act of coming to terms with oneself, a kind of intellectual settling of accounts with fascism and its ideology.'[2] However, working on this subject matter meant subjecting one's own behaviour during this time to critical scrutiny: 'At that time I was very proud of the fact that I had never fired a shot in my life. Today I would not regard it as something to be particularly proud of. It would have been better to have fired a few shots in the right direction'.[3]

The long struggle to get the script accepted by a production company began after the capitulation of the German forces. At this time Staudte was living in the British sector of Berlin: 'So of course I took my script first to the British, then to the Americans and finally to the French. Nobody wanted the material. Peter van Eyck was the Cultural Officer for the Americans and he gave me to understand, in broken German, but wearing an amazingly well-cut uniform, "that we Germans could forget about films for the next twenty years".'[4] Staudte added, 'Only the Russian Cultural Officer was interested in my project. ... I can still remember it quite vividly. I was summoned to him one night. There was no electricity. We negotiated by candlelight. He congratulated me and knew almost every part of the script by heart.'[5]

These different experiences of the Allied institutions were indicative of diverging political notions regarding the role of film in political re-education. The Americans saw Germany – which at the time was twelve years behind the rest of the world – as a lucrative market for their own film industry and wanted to assume complete responsibility for political re-education themselves. By contrast, the Soviets relied on working together with German partners (above all those who had been émigrés in the Soviet Union or who had been in prison or concentration camps), not least because such partnerships had been established for a number of years. For instance, the Head of the Propaganda and Information Department of the Soviet Military Administration in Germany (SMAD), Colonel Tulpanov, had, in his civilian days, been a lecturer at the University of Leningrad; Major Dymschitz, the officer directly responsible for matters relating to film, was well acquainted with the German cultural scene and was later appointed to a Chair in German at the University of Moscow. And both men had worked at the front with German émigrés, artists and politicians engaged in the political education of the enemy. Both parties – artists and politicians – were united by one overriding concern, namely that of overcoming fascism, and those early years are characterised by a natural alliance between artists and politicians – a phenomenon that was never to be experienced again. This was important since it created a special climate in which artists could develop their ideas without fear of censorship and in which they could feel confident that they were both wanted and needed.

Cultural agitation

In the Lux Hotel in Moscow, émigré politicians and artists had laid plans as early as November 1944 for cultural agitation in the Soviet Zone of Occupation and their aims are clearly reflected in the following statement: 'Confronting the phenomenon of fascism cannot just begin with 1933, but must involve a reappraisal of the entire history of Germany.' [6] It would, however, be a mistake to assume that the films they produced – which do indeed have the appearance of an excursion through a hundred years of German history – were the result of an official decree. For they had a quite different type of structure. Often based on material which had lain hidden away in a drawer since the time of the Weimar Republic or Third Reich, the motivation of the film-makers was, in virtually every case, an entirely personal one drawing on their own experiences.

For his film *Die Mörder sind unter uns,* Staudte invented the story of an army doctor who tries in vain to stop the captain of his platoon from ordering the shooting of Polish hostages, women and children. He encounters him again after the war, now a successful entrepreneur, manufacturing saucepans out of steel helmets, and passes judgement over the captain. He chose Hildegard Knef (at that time totally unknown) to play the title role, thus launching her screen career. The film – a story of guilt and atonement, of revenge and catharsis – was based on a real incident that Staudte had himself witnessed during the last days of the war. The expressive gestures, the way in which objects are endowed with emotive significance, the details and the locations – themselves often representing cryptic metaphors – are highly reminiscent of the German studio films, of the spirit of the anti-war film of the early 1930s with its pacifist message. It was, of course, pure coincidence that the review of *Die Mörder sind unter uns* appeared in the same number of *Sonntag,* the weekly periodical of the *Kulturbund zur demokratischen Erneuerung Deutschlands* ('Cultural Alliance for the Democratic Renewal of Germany'), as the leading article on the carrying out of the sentences passed at the Nuremberg War Crimes Tribunal, but an editorial rightly pointed out an inherent link between the two items.

Ehe im Schatten (*Marriage in the Shadow,* 1947) was the first German film to tackle the subject of the persecution of the Jews in Germany, the first to 'touch the guilty conscience, the suppressed memories, the most vulnerable point, of millions of

Germans'.[7] The story is based on the fate of the popular actor,
Joachim Gottschalk, who had worked in the theatre and starred
in a number of Ufa film productions. In 1942 he committed
suicide, together with his twelve-year-old son and his Jewish
wife, whom he could no longer save from being deported. As
contemporary critics noted, it is a film which focuses on the
everyday manifestations of fascism – not the murderers and
executioners ... Nobody is by nature an out-and-out Nazi. All
the people in the film think of themselves as respectable.[8]
Commenting on the film, the director, Kurt Maetzig, said:
'Almost everything in the film is based on what I myself, or my
family and friends, have experienced.'[9] Indeed Maetzig's
mother had taken her own life to escape being arrested by the
Gestapo. And the Jewish actor, Alfred Balthoff, is practically
playing his own life in this film.

The film looks back to the Weimar Republic, to the eve of
Hitler's take-over of power, and confronts the failure of large
sections of the German intelligentsia – its suicidal lack of
concern with regard to political and social events – and does
not exclude the victims themselves. The film is small in scale
and adheres to the basic structure of melodrama – in the best
sense of the term. Its aesthetic format is also in keeping with
traditional visual expectations and this reliance on conventional forms was a significant factor in the film's powerful effect
on audiences. It was the only German film to have its première
in all four sectors of Berlin simultaneously. Audiences sat in
silence for several minutes after the end of the film before
applauding. *Ehe im Schatten* was designated the most successful
German post-war film of the year and received the Bambi
award, a prize awarded annually by the magazine *Bild und Funk*
for the German film with the greatest audience appeal. Within
a short time ten million people had seen the film.

Affaire Blum (*The Blum Affair*, 1948) went back yet another
decade into Germany's past. It was the first attempt to show one
particular aspect of National Socialism – anti-Semitism – as the
consequence of something that had been gradually developing
over a long period of time. It is a true story, based on an incident – robbery and murder – that took place in 1926 in
Magdeburg. In the film, the murderer – a former member of
the Reichswehr, who has the sympathy of his former regimental
comrades on the bench – has little difficulty in pinning the
blame on a Jewish industrialist. Blinded to the truth by their

anti-Semitic tendencies, the judges are only just prevented from carrying out a judicial murder themselves. The director, Erich Engel, who followed the dramatic events in court at the time, tells a gripping story – a genuine thriller – which even today ranks as one of the most remarkable German post-war films. He sought out new faces for the film, such as Hans-Christian Blech, who was later to become one of the stars of the West German film and theatre world .

In *Die Buntkarierten* (*The Girls In Gingham*, 1949) Kurt Maetzig was to pose the question: 'How did it all really begin?'. He searches through German history, going back to the time of the Kaiser, to find the social and political causes for the failure of, amongst other groups, large sections of the German working class. It was the first attempt in a post-war German film to portray developments in Germany from the 1880s onwards from the perspective of a working-class woman. The film presents a family saga with the dramatic structure of an *Entwicklungsroman* ('novel of individual development'). Critics dubbed it admiringly 'the proletarian *Cavalcade*', a reference to Lloyd Frank's film of Noel Coward's play, a film which became highly popular with German audiences in the early post-war years.

Guste, the main character in the film, starts life as a serving girl in an officer's family during the reign of Kaiser Wilhelm; during the First World War she works assembling hand grenades; during the Nazi period she loses her husband; during World War II she loses her son in a bombing raid. From the brightly coloured bed covers that she had been given by 'Her Ladyship' as a wedding present, she sews a dress for her granddaughter – the only member of her family to survive the war – to wear at her graduation ceremony at the Humboldt University. For the first time in her life Guste, a working-class woman, no longer feels socially inferior; now she feels that she belongs, and has no fears for the future.

Even material such as Georg Büchner's unfinished drama *Woyzeck*, the first socially critical drama in German literature and one which though written in 1837 was not publicly performed until 1913 – 'on the eve of a turning-point in world history', as renowned theatre and film critic, Herbert Ihering put it[10] – was used as a vehicle to explore the causes and tendencies that had led to Germany's recent past. Georg C. Klaren (who both adapted the text and directed the film) was the *Chefdramaturg* ('senior script editor') at DEFA at the time and had been deeply moved since the 1920s by Büchner's tragic depiction of a life destroyed in a militarised society. In the 1920s, such material was not looked upon favourably and under the Nazis it was, of course, totally out of the question. From an aesthetic point of view, Klaren was, with *Woyzeck* (1947), consciously exploiting the success of the classic German films of the Expressionist era, and as a result became embroiled in the formalism debate of the 1950s, when he was cited as an example of a negative tendency. The sets were designed by one of the designers who had worked on *Das Cabinet des Doktor Caligari* (*The Cabinet of Dr Caligari*, 1919), Hermann Warm, and the costumes by Walter Schulze-Mittendorf, who had worked on Fritz Lang's *Metropolis* (1926). In terms of form and content the film conjured up associations with the deformation of human beings during the Third Reich.

With Staudte's *Rotation* (1949), the story of a man who mistakenly believes that he can live in a society that is corrupt and yet preserve his individual integrity, DEFA films had returned to the Nazi period, and for the time being the excursion into German history was abandoned. At this point there occurred the first instance of a collision between this type of film and the exigencies of contemporary politics. The hero of the film says to his son who has just returned from a prisoner-of-war camp in the Soviet Union: 'That was the last uniform you'll ever wear', and burns it. Staudte had to cut this sequence from the film since the GDR was embarking upon a recruitment drive for the *Volkspolizei* (the East German police force), and the total rejection of uniforms of any sort did not fit in with the government's plans. The pacifist sentiments expressed by the films of the 1940s were no longer officially desirable.

On an aethetic level, it is hard to point to revolutionary innovations, as there had been, for instance, in the neo-realistic tendencies of Italian cinema and the techniques of filmic montage deployed in the Russian films of the 1920s. The early DEFA films sought inspiration – either consciously or subconsciously – from the German film classics, and found it in the small-scale studio films, in the legacy of the Expressionist movement and in the anti-war films of the early 1930s. Film-makers were well aware that the new subject matter required new forms. However, the only point on which there was general agreement concerned what was not wanted: the discredited

Ufa-style of the Nazi period. They also wanted to make a clean break with the conventional Ufa-style of the allegedly unpolitical 'B movies'. But in this respect their achievements fell short of their aspirations. Nonetheless, it is important to bear in mind that even directors who had had nothing whatsoever in common with the tendencies of Ufa cinema had been deeply affected by this visual aesthetic (the influence of which was not solely confined to the production of film classics) whether they were conscious of this influence or not. Amongst the cameramen working on DEFA productions in the early years of the company there was not a single one who had emigrated during the Nazi period or who had been banned from working by the Nazis. Indeed they had worked on dozens of films during this period. Since there was a general consensus that their influence would be mainly in terms of form and technique, rather than content, less attention was paid to their political past than to that of their fellow directors and script writers. Thus there was nothing odd about the fact that Bruno Mondi – the cameraman in all of Veit Harlan's films – was in great demand on account of his outstanding technical ability with the camera, when it came to making the important anti-fascist films.

This was even more the case with soundtrack composers whose political sympathies were clearly regarded as irrelevant when it came to the ideological aspect of film-making. Nobody bothered to ask questions about their earlier activities. Thus it came about that the same man who composed the music for Harlan's *Jud Süß* (*Jew Süss*, 1940) also wrote the music for *Ehe im Schatten* – a career path that was by no means untypical for German film composers of this time. As a result, the musical soundtrack is perhaps the most conservative aspect of the films of the late 1940s and early 1950s. Despite all this, however, these concerns relating to the aesthetic dimension of the films in no way diminished their intended effect on contemporary audiences.

The films made in the 1940s were concerned with the history and guilt of an undivided Germany. It was a theme which concerned Germany as a whole, or at least it should have done. With the changing political situation in the 1950s, a new element emerged in the treatment of this theme. Ever since the end of the 1940s relations between the two military blocs had been deeply affected by the Cold War. Along the border

Nuremburg documents

between them the two German states confronted each other with growing hostility. Priorities had changed. In July 1950, the Third Party Congress of the Socialist Unity Party (SED) took place, at which the political function of film as an instrument of propaganda in the service of current political activities was clearly formulated. The emphasis of films was now to be on the present time. Of course, the theme of anti-fascism still had an important part to play, but its function was altogether different. The assignment of guilt and the relationship between the guilty and those who had resisted became an increasingly important component in the overall political message. And thus in the majority of the films made in the 1950s, the enemies of socialism are shown to have had a Nazi past, whilst those representing the new socialist order are shown to have an anti-fascist background. There is no denying that both statements often contained elements of truth: what these films did was to present the issue in terms of moral absolutes. Nonetheless, even here there are clearly discernible differences of quality.

Schwer?

The prelude to this development was marked by Kurt Maetzig's *Rat der Götter* (*Council of the Gods*) made in 1950. The film is based on authentic material found in documents relating to the follow-up to the Nuremberg trials involving those who had committed economic crimes, as well as on the remarkable book by the American writer, Richard Sasuly, head of the Finance Department of the American military administration and also chairman the committee investigating the activities of the chemical industry. The documents provide proof that the German company, IG-Farben, helped Hitler to seize power and that the company made huge profits from the war, particularly in the East. What was new was the critical view of the neighbouring Federal Republic which the film articulates by tracing the development of company traditions – not least the attitudes of its owners to questions of ethics and management – a development which the film shows as continuing unbroken from the Nazi period up to the present.

A graphic example of the continuity to which the film alludes was provided by an event which took place while the film was being shot. There was an explosion at a West German branch of the company in Ludwigshafen, which caused quite a stir in the press at the time because it revealed what was being produced at the plant, namely chemical weapons, which had been outlawed under the Potsdam Agreement. In Maetzig's film, we see how the conscientious employee involved in the development of Zyklon B – though quite unaware of the purposes it was to serve – is influenced by one of the workers and manages to distance himself from the company and helps to uncover its intrigues. Variations of this basic plot were used in a number of later films but they were mostly of very poor artistic quality.

One such film was *Der Auftrag Höglers* (*Högler's Task*) directed by Gustav von Wangenheim, which also had its première in 1950. In the film a West German parent company uses criminal methods to get its hands on a new invention which has been developed in its subsidiary company located in the East, with the intention of thus sabotaging production. The plan is foiled by the joint efforts of a trade unionist from Bavaria and a female trade union functionary from the GDR, who had worked together in the anti-fascist resistance. Thus the story represents the hand of friendship extended to fellow comrades in the West and the attack on the company which threatens them both.

The basic construction of *Geheimakten Solvay* (*The Secret Files of Solvay*, 1953), directed by Martin Hellberg two years later, is very similar. The film is based on a real case. By using ledgers, proof is provided that the Solvay works, which are under trust administration in the East, actually belong to IG Farben; according to the Potsdam Agreement this would have meant the expropiation of the works. The owners of the company attempt, via middlemen, to purloin the incriminating documents. The opening sequence of the film clearly hints at the political orientation of the factory owner. He is shown in a luxurious prison guarded by Americans where he is doing time as a war criminal. The Americans release him early because they are interested in continuing certain business relationships which were never broken off, even during the war. The factory owner's secretary in Frankfurt am Main, who has taken on work as a courier, decides to opt out when she discovers the brutal methods they are using and saves the life of the worker from the East, whose life is threatened by the unscrupulous activities of the West German owners. Although films of this kind were ostensibly concerned with economic sabotage, the real case against the defendants is one of complicity in war crimes. It was this charge which provided the discursive thrust of the films and which was used to justify the actions of the GDR's security forces. The film-makers relied so strongly on the persuasive power of these arguments that they showed – in a manner seldom to be seen on screen – the course of the trial and the passing of the draconian sentences.

People's attitude to fascism was even shown as a crucial factor in love relationships and in marriages. Films set in Berlin were particularly well-suited to this purpose, showing the confrontation between the two states and two social systems. Characteristic of films of this kind was Kurt Maetzig's *Roman einer jungen Ehe* (*Story of a Marriage*, 1952). The marriage between two actors threatens to break up because the young husband allows himself to be taken in by the ostensible artistic freedom in West Berlin, not realising that on stage and in films he is being used to further the cause of the Cold War warriors. When his wife, who is already disgusted by this abuse of art, then sees the director of *Jud Süß*, Veit Harlan, celebrating his come-back in the Federal Republic, she decides in favour of the GDR, where she sees the ethical standards of her profession upheld, and performs in front of the building workers in the Stalinallee.

Conflict and war led to a decline in both ethical and aesthetic standards. The artistic deterioration during these years was horrifying. Audiences stayed away from the cinemas and the seemingly endless stream of stories about saboteurs and secret agents were dubbed *Sabogentenfilme*, a term that is both ironic and disparaging. In August 1950, however, another film went into production which, both in terms of form and content, resisted this tendency and it provoked DEFA's first great censorship scandal. It concerned the filming of Arnold Zweig's novel, *Das Beil von Wandsbek* (*The Axe of Wandsbek*, 1951). The story is set in the Nazi period and concerns a butcher who, when faced with economic ruin, accepts a lucrative offer of employment, namely to take over the job of the public executioner, who has fallen ill, and behead four anti-fascists with his axe. As a result, he is shunned by his neighbours and boycotted by his customers. His wife takes her own life and he also ends up committing suicide. The official complaint was that the film did not 'promote a hatred of fascism, but elicited a degree of sympathy with the murderers instead'.[11] The author of the literary text, the German-Jewish writer Arnold Zweig, had written the novel in 1943 in Hebrew whilst in exile in Palestine, and it was published in the Soviet

Occupation Zone in 1947. At the time of the filming Zweig was president of the GDR's *Akademie der Künste* (Academy of Arts) and a deputy in the parliament ('Volkskammer') of the GDR. The director, Falk Harnack, brother of Arvid Harnack, who was executed for his part in organising the largest German resistance group, had himself been a member of the *Weiße Rose* (the White Rose resistance group) and from 1943 had fought with a Greek resistance group. The main actor was Erwin Geschonneck, who, because he was a communist, had been in danger when Hitler came to power in 1933. He had fled to Prague, but later fell into the hands of the Nazis and had survived the concentration camps of Sachsenhausen, Dachau and Neuengamme. Thus the objections to the film were malicious and patently absurd. Nonetheless, the film was banned. The real cause of the controversy was the fact that the film had offended against the prevailing canon of East-West polarisation and had tackled a theme that had been avoided up until then, namely the complex relationship between the victims of fascism and those responsible.

In many of the films praised by the authorities during these years, the treatment of the German Nazi past simply became the means to an end, a means of portraying new developments in inter-German politics. In the 1940s the strategic aim of party politics was a united Germany. After the founding of the two German states it still remained as a long-term goal, but the actual tactics had changed. In the struggle to prove which was the better Germany, emphasis was laid not on what the two states had in common, but on the differences between them. According to Georgi Dimitroff's famous definition of fascism, a definition articulated in 1935 at the Seventh Congress of the Comintern, of which he was General Secretary, fascism was the 'blatant, terrorist dictatorship by the most reactionary, most chauvinist, most imperialist elements of finance capital'.[12] That is to say, fascism was characterised as a consequence of monopoly capitalism. Here we see the origins of the accusation which was often to be levelled at the GDR, namely its tendency to create the impression that all the anti-fascists were to be found in the GDR, whereas the Federal Republic embodied the Nazi past. Films with this kind of argumentation aimed at portraying political structures, demonstrating on the one side the old entrenched structures of power, and on the other, a society which had overthrown these outmoded traditions. In the light of this, apportioning blame seemed a straightforward matter.

A whole host of documentary films made during these years seemed to prove this thesis by providing authentic cases which exposed the Nazi past of leading figures in West German public life such as Globke, Oberländer, Speidel, Reinefahrt and others. The arguments were not without a certain cogency. At the same time, a number of films were produced which made it quite explicit to which political tradition the GDR saw itself as belonging. Thus the two-part political biography of Ernst Thälmann, *Ernst Thälmann – Sohn seiner Klasse* (*Ernst Thälmann – Son of the Working Class*, 1954) and *Ernst Thälmann – Führer seiner Klasse* (*Ernst Thälmann – Leader of the Working Class*, 1955) were commissioned, as was Carl Balhaus's film *Der Teufelskreis* (*The Vicious Circle*, 1956), a film about Georgi Dimitroff, the leader of the Bulgarian Communists, who inflicted the first defeat on fascist propaganda in the Reichstag fire trial in 1933, and Karl Paryla's film *Mich dürstet* (*I'm Thirsty*, 1956), a film about German communists fighting against Franco in the International Brigades during the Spanish Civil War.

In the Thälmann films, both of which were directed by Kurt Maetzig, for the first time the recent past was interpreted from the official party-political angle. Here fact was combined with elements of the officially endorsed distortion of history concerning the disastrous in-fighting between Communists and the Social Democrats on the eve of Hitler's coming to power. In the films, the blame is laid solely on the Social Democrats, thus providing retrospective justification for the Stalinist line of the Communist party, which was to fight the Social Democrats as its arch-enemy. Thus the historical line propagated by the Stalinist leadership of the SED, a line that took a narrow and highly selective view of the role played by the resistance movement, dominates the narrative. In this way recent history increasingly came to be portrayed as an extension of party ideology.

It was also at this time that a sinister development began to take place, namely the exploitation of the anti-fascist past of the older generation as a means of legitimising a form of political power that was no longer in keeping with the spirit of anti-fascism. Accordingly, the events of 17 June 1953, which should have led the authorities to some self-critical reflection, were dismissed as an attempted fascist putsch. Another instance of this blinkered mentality was later the official description of the Berlin Wall as a 'protective barrier against fascistic elements'. Here we have an example of a positive term being used to distort historical and political reality. It is an irony of history that those film-makers in the 1960s who were critical of the system actually exploited this euphemistic nomenclature as an argument for speaking more openly about the shortcomings in GDR society, on the grounds that now one was 'protected' against 'the enemy'. Drawing on this line of argument, almost an entire year's film production was completed, only to be banned in a spectacular fashion in 1965 by the Central Committee of the SED at its Eleventh Plenum, which accused the film-makers of expressing views which were hostile to Party and State. All of these films dealt with contemporary themes. It was no accident that most of them touched upon a theme which until then had been treated as taboo – the generation conflict, a conflict which, in official terminology, could not actually exist. This group of highly provocative films explored the theme from many different angles: conflicts between teachers and pupils, between young teachers and their superiors, between children and parents, between young factory workers and old party functionaries.

The theme of youthful rebellion was one that dominated the cinema in many countries at this time. In the Federal Republic it was to be found in Georg Tressler's film *Die Halbstarken* (*The Hooligans*, 1956); in France in André Cayatte's *Avant le Déluge* (1955); in the United States in Richard Brooks's *Blackboard Jungle* (1955) to name but some of the many examples. But although all these films have certain elements in common, there are also certain characteristics which are quite specific to those films made in the GDR and which are bound up with the treatment of the theme of anti-fascism. An important feature in almost all the films referred to above is the breakdown in communication between the generations, the impossibility of finding a common language, and the resort to violence, frequently of a self-destructive kind. The DEFA films dealing with this theme are the only ones in which the link between the generations is never completely severed. When relations have all but reached breaking point, the innate respect of the younger generation for the anti-fascist past of their elders prevents total rupture. This is the constellation presented in *Berlin um die Ecke* (*Berlin Around the Corner*, 1965), directed by

Gerhard Klein, for whom Wolfgang Kohlhaase wrote the script, a film which was also banned in the wake of the Eleventh Plenum. In it, a young foreman is berated for having massaged the production figures. His response is to point out that this small piece of retouching is nothing in comparison with the manipulation of the figures which goes on every day at a higher level in the organisation, and that he is only trying to correct the unjust wage system. Representing the older generation is a functionary, the editor of the works newspaper, and a merciless accuser, who criminalises the young people by accusing them of crimes against the socialist state and state-owned property. He is portrayed as a fossil, as an intolerant zealot. The audience is provoked into feeling sympathy for the boy who lies in wait for the editor in the entrance hall of his house and knocks him down. The attack takes place in the dark. When the light comes on, the older man does not defend himself, nor does he reproach the boy, or make dramatic accusations or threats. He wipes the blood from his nose and goes up the stairs. The boy follows him into his flat where he is told: 'The last person to hit me like that was a guard in the concentration camp. He was a young chap like you.' The boy feels ashamed and listens to the older man. Thus a dialogue begins in which the older man learns about the boy's world, and begins to realise that the young are, in their own way, trying to stand up for justice and honesty and trying to save and uphold some of the moral beliefs of the older generation.

In Herrmann Zschoche's film, *Karla* (*Carla*, 1965) – the story of a young female teacher who battles against rigid, old-fashioned teaching methods, which are based on mistrust and which underestimate pupils' intellectual abilities – the key role is played by the headteacher. He has a sneaking regard for the young woman and her unconventional methods of teaching and also has a feeling for how young people should be treated. His own teaching is dogmatic and authoritarian and the pupils do not like him. They are triumphant when one day they chance upon a photo showing him in SA uniform, and they organise a revolt. However, it turns out that the photo is of him acting the part of a Nazi in Brecht's play *Fear and Misery in the Third Reich*, a part he played well because he was familiar with the reality of the situation, having himself been a prisoner in a concentration camp. The pupils are thunderstruck, the starting point for a cautious process of rapprochement.

The film which tackled this taboo most boldly was Frank Vogel's *Denk bloß nicht, ich heule* (*Just Don't Think I'm Crying*, 1965). Its hero is a rebellious six-former who sees through the shortcomings of the teaching system and refuses to cooperate with it. As he says: 'It's no use trying to talk to you. You are always in the right.' The girl who is in love with this rebel is the daughter of a man who has survived internment in a concentration camp. His distrust of someone who has been expelled from school, whom he regards as an enemy, is motivated by his extreme insecurity due to his past experiences. The girl becomes a mediator between her father, whom she loves and respects, and her boyfriend, for whose sake she stands up to her father for the first time in her life. Complete understanding between the generations is not reached, but a degree of acceptance is achieved. In this film, which was banned even before its première, there was one scene in particular which provoked the censors' displeasure. This is where the young couple walk through the grounds of Buchenwald, the former concentration camp, which is kept as a memorial to the victims. But the couple do not experience it as a special, sacred place to be treated with reverence, as the authorities intend. For them it is just a natural part of their living space. It is here that Anne recites a poem about love, and it is here that they become aware of their own expectations of life. Here, as in other films of this kind, the character of the anti-fascist has a regulating function. The relationship between the generations is based on respect for the achievements of these exemplary figures from the older generation and cannot be broken just like that. But the exemplary function of such figures is no longer accepted in all spheres of life. Here then were films which might have constituted the beginning of a dialogue, a dialogue which only a few years later was no longer possible.

Throughout the entire history of DEFA, from its beginnings up until the last few years, there was a remarkable continuity and thoroughness in the treatment of anti-fascist themes, which was not typical of German cinema as a whole. In the 1950s there were Konrad Wolf's *Lissy* (1957), the tragedy of a lowly individual seduced by the social rhetoric of the Nazis, and *Sterne* (*Stars*, 1959), the love story between a German soldier and a Greek Jewess, a film which won an award in Cannes; works such as Frank Beyer's *Nackt unter Wölfen* (*Naked among Wolves*, 1962) based on the autobiographical novel by Bruno

Wolf in Red Army
→ Ich war Neunzehn

Apitz about the saving of a Jewish child by the underground committee in Buchenwald, and *Ich war neunzehn* (*I was Nineteen*, 1968) in which the director, Konrad Wolf, himself a lieutenant in the Red Army, tells the story of his return to the country of his childhood; there was *Die Verlobte* (*The Fiancée*, 1980), directed by Günther Rücker and Günter Reisch, based on the true story of a young woman who endures the torment of imprisonment because of her deep feeling for her lover, who does not survive the Nazi period; and there was the tragicomedy of the life-saving lie of a Jew in the ghetto, based on an experience which was recounted to the author of the film, Jurek Becker, by his father and which was filmed by Frank Beyer. This film, *Jakob der Lügner* (*Jacob the Liar*, 1974) was nominated for an Oscar.

Frequently fears were expressed that this theme had been exhausted along with the public's interest. Such fears were never borne out. For in telling the stories of people who had risked their lives in fighting against an inhuman system, these films succeeded in conveying the vision of a different, better world. The belief that such a world was to be found in a socialist country lived on, not only in the films themselves, but also in the example set by those individuals who consciously decided in favour of the GDR. For it was they, above all, who affirmed the belief in the future articulated in these films, whether it was the Red Army lieutenant, Konrad Wolf, the Buchenwald prisoner, Bruno Apitz, Eva Lippold, the 'fiancée', who spent ten years in prison, or the Jewish Polish child rescued by the selfless behaviour of the concentration camp inmates, who, at the time the film was being shot, was himself studying at the GDR's film school in Potsdam-Babelsberg.

Indeed the anti-fascist approach was so closely bound up with a conscious decision to embrace socialism – in this instance the decision to pledge oneself to the GDR – that when that vision, in which so many had believed, began to lose credibility, so too the idealised status of the dominant images also began to wane. This became increasingly clear in the 1980s. Herrmann Zschoche's film *Insel der Schwäne* (*Swan Island*, 1983), a film which questions the officially praised quality of life in a new housing estate, is symptomatic of this tendency and at the time was sharply censured for attacking the sacred cow of the Honecker era, the housing programme. One seemingly small detail was significant. The hero who creates a living space between the concrete blocks is a twelve-year-old boy. His most dangerous opponent, brutal, cunning, repulsive – today he would surely be portrayed as a young right-wing extremist – has been brought up by his grandparents who had been active in the anti-fascist resistance.

This depiction of the protagonists led to the scriptwriter, Ulrich Plenzdorf, being accused of denigrating the anti-fascist past. Plenzdorf had added these ideal figures from the past – who do not feature in the novel on which the film is based – to see if they still had relevance for the present time, and found that they had none. His conclusions had been understood only too well. The criticism in the press – inspired by official prompting – claimed that the film had dug trenches where no battle-fronts existed. In truth, bitter fighting was already being waged in those trenches. The ideal image of anti-fascist behaviour that had been propagated for decades had now become something so remote that it was now no longer adequate to the needs of a new generation. In conclusion then, we may say that the treatment of anti-fascist themes in DEFA cinema reflects the deformation and dissolution of GDR society, a society, however, whose vital contribution to the process of understanding the National Socialist past in Germany is indisputable.

(Translated from the German by Margaret Vallance)

Notes

1. Johannes R. Becher, *Deutsches Bekenntnis: drei Reden zur deutschen Erneuerung*, Berlin, 1945, p. 2.
2. 'Wolfgang Staudte zu dem Film *Die Mörder sind unter uns*', in *Vier Filmerzählungen nach bekannten DEFA-Filmen: 'Die Mörder sind unter uns', 'Ehe im Schatten', 'Die Buntkarierten', 'Rotation'*, ed. Ellen Blauert, Berlin, 1969, pp. 1–4.
3. Margit Voß, 'Interview mit Wolfgang Staudte für den Berliner Rundfunk, 1966' in *Zur DEFA-Geschichte: Spielfilme 1946–1949: eine Dokumentation. Studienarbeiten des I. Studienjahres der Fachrichtung Film- und Fernsehwissenschaft* (Hochschule für Film und Fernsehen der DDR: Reihe Information, nos. 3/4/5/6), ed. Christiane Mückenberger, Potsdam, 1976, pp. 92–105 (p. 94).
4. Ibid., 96–8. Peter van Eyck was later to become a very well-known actor in the Federal Republic.
5. Blauert, *Vier Filmerzählungen*, p. 74.

6. SAPMO (Stiftung Archiv der Parteien und Massenorganisationen der DDR im Bundesarchiv), [formerly, IML. ZPA, NL 36/499], quoted in *Exil in der UdSSR*, ed. Klaus Jarmatz, Simone Barck, Peter Dietzel, Leipzig, 1979, p. 131.

7. See W. Lenning, 'Ein filmisches Bekenntnis: Ehe im Schatten in allen Sektoren in Berlin gleichzeitig aufgeführt', *Berliner Zeitung*, 5 November 1947.

8. See H. U. Eylau, '*Ehe im Schatten*: ein Film aus Deutschlands dunkelster Zeit', *Tägliche Rundschau*, 5 October 1947.

9. See Fred Gehler and Ulrich Kasten, '"Wir hätten auch Aurora heißen können": mit Kurt Maetzig sprachen Fred Gehler und Ulrich Kasten', *Film und Fernsehen* 2, no. 8, 1974: 10–14.

10. Herbert Ihering, *Theater der produktiven Widersprüche*, Berlin and Weimar, 1967, p. 39.

11. See 'Für den Aufschwung der fortschrittlichen deutschen Filmkunst: Resolution des Politbüros des ZK der SED', *Neues Deutschland*, 27 July 1952.

12. Georgi Dimitroff, *Ausgewählte Werke*, 3 vols, Sofia, 1976, vol 2, p. 6.

Chapter 5

DISCUSSION WITH KURT MAETZIG

Martin Brady

The following discussion took place at the Goethe-Institut London on 11 March 1996 following a screening of Kurt Maetzig's film Der Rat der Götter (The Council of the Gods, *1950). Before the screening, the director said a few words about the film.*

Kurt Maetzig: Ladies and Gentlemen, I don't like introductions to films, but in this case please allow me to tell you a few things which I think you should know before the screening of the film. This film was made in 1949. It is true that the première of the film was only in 1950, but it was already finished by 1949. The film introduced a new genre in film-making, the so-called documentary feature film. This means that the story surrounding the family of the chemist Dr Scholz in the film is purely invention, but that everything concerning the relations between the German chemical industry and American industry is based on official sources. One of the most important of these sources is a book entitled *IG-Farben* by Richard Sasuly, published in New York in 1947. In this book, Sasuly was not writing simply as an author or journalist, but had a very important official position: he was the Chief of Finance, Intelligence and Liaison of the Finance Division of the United States Military Government. He was one of the investigators who analysed the files and prepared the case against IG-Farben. In his book he disclosed the most astonishing and overwhelming facts about the cooperation between the Nazi chemical industry and American industry. In his book he reports that the cartel which was set up a short time before the outbreak of the Second World War covered Europe as well as America, and that the Second World War took place within the framework of this cartel. This means that he proved that neither Nazi Germany nor the United

States of America would have been able to lead a modern war with huge mobile armies and thousands of aircraft without this cartel between IG-Farben and Standard Oil of New Jersey. This can be proved, and the proof is not only provided by the book by Richard Sasuly, but also by a second interesting and important source: the files and records of the trial against IG-Farben in Nuremberg under the flag of the United States of America. This is the second point I wanted to make. On occasion I have read that this is a film which could offend, or was directed against, the Federal Republic of Germany. This is impossible, because the action of the film takes place between the years 1932 and 1948, i.e., at a time when the Federal Republic of Germany did not even exist. The film was made between 1948 and 1949, and the première was at the beginning of the fifties. And a final word: I have sometimes heard it said that this was a film made in and for the Cold War. I want to defend myself against this accusation, because the film was not only based precisely on the book of Richard Sasuly and other sources, but was also made in his spirit and was true to his intention. He was a very strong supporter of the anti-Hitler coalition and fought against those who destroyed this coalition in order to replace it with the politics of 'Rollback', which led into the Cold War. I have always regarded my film as a contribution *against* the Cold War and *for* the world peace movement. That was my position at the time when I made the film. And now I hope you will have two pleasant hours with the film, and after the screening I will, of course, be entirely at your disposal. Thank you very much.

Discussion Following the Screening

Martin Brady: It is both extremely appropriate and exciting that at the beginning of a season of DEFA films leading up to a four-day conference on East German cinema in Reading we should have a co-founder of DEFA (the Deutsche Film-Aktiengesellschaft) and, I think, its most versatile director, with us this evening to discuss one of the most important and controversial films in the early years of East German Cinema.

In 1992 Kurt Maetzig summed up his life as follows, and I hope he will forgive me for quoting it back to him: 'I lived under the Kaiser and experienced the First World War, went to school in the Weimar Republic and had my first political experiences during that period. Miraculously I survived fascism and the Second World War and in 1945 went to the place where I felt I could be most actively involved in fighting the root causes of fascism and saw my own future in a state struggling to achieve socialism. I saw its mistakes early on and stayed because I thought it could be reformed. I experienced its disintegration and rightful collapse and now I'm living in a capitalist society again. So my future is behind me and I'm moving forward into what I've already been through, namely the past. In the interests of all of us, I sincerely hope that I will be spared a revival of fascism.'

Herr Maetzig had been actively involved in the film industry for around fifteen years before he made *Der Rat der Götter*, having first worked as an assistant director in 1933, then in animation film, worked as a chemist in a photochemical laboratory during the war and as a documentary film-maker immediately after it, shooting footage of the ruined Berlin in the winter of 1945–6.

Early in 1946 he co-founded the influential East German newsreel *Der Augenzeuge* (*The Eyewitness*), with its famous motto 'See for yourself, hear for yourself, judge for yourself!' ('Sie sehen selbst, Sie hören selbst, urteilen Sie selbst!'), a slogan coined by Kurt Maetzig. He made his first feature film, *Ehe im Schatten* (*Marriage in the Shadows*), in 1947, shortly after the founding of DEFA. This film, shown here at the Goethe-Institut last May, is based on the life and death of the actor Joachim Gottschalk and his Jewish wife, who committed suicide together in November 1941. This landmark film was the most successful German film of this early period, seen by an audience of well over ten million.

The films which followed over the next three decades are characterised by an astonishing range, marking out their director as an innovator and pioneer of enormous versatility. As he himself put it in 1977, three years after the première of his twenty-third and last film, *Mann gegen Mann* (*Man against Man*): 'I have never been a specialist for one particular genre, I have always been keen to open a window and see what happens. I think that I set a lot of things in motion without ever really bringing them to fruition.' His films range from the epic two-part state-commissioned biography of Ernst Thälmann produced in the early fifties, through to the famous 'forbidden film' *Das Kaninchen bin ich* (*I am the Rabbit*) of 1965, which was promptly banned and only finally seen in public, to great acclaim, at the end of 1989 and then here in London in 1994. Perhaps less well-known over here are films such as the comedy *Vergeß mir meine Traudel nicht* (*Don't Forget my Traudel*) of 1957, historical dramas including *Das Lied der Matrosen* (*The Sailors' Song*) to celebrate the fortieth anniversary in 1958 of the German November revolution, spy thrillers, a portrait of a crisis in the life of a young sportswoman, *Das Mädchen auf dem Brett* (*The Girl on the Springboard*) of 1967 – which demonstrates Herr Maetzig's acknowledged talent for portraying female protagonists – and, perhaps most intriguingly, DEFA's first sci-fi film, *Der schweigende Stern* (*The Silent Star*) of 1960, based on a novel by Stanislav Lem and set on Venus in 1970.

Finally, I would like to pick out one film which, along with *Der Rat der Götter*, has been a real discovery for me whilst preparing for this evening – *Schlösser und Katen* (*Castles and Cottages*) of 1957, a two-part portrait of the upheavals and land reforms in a rural community between 1945 and 17 June 1953. This wonderfully rich chronicle of village life, hardship and political struggle is one of the most striking DEFA films I have seen, and a valuable corrective to Edgar Reitz's *Heimat*.

As well as working as a director, Herr Maetzig has also been very active in supporting young film-makers and encouraging the growth of film clubs both in the GDR and world-wide as vice-president of the FICC, the International Federation of Film Clubs, in which capacity he indeed visited London in the early seventies – not, I have heard, for the first time, because I believe you visited London in the 1920s with your father.

Kurt Maetzig: Yes.

Martin Brady: As I mentioned, you shot a number of documentary films and founded *Der Augenzeuge* newsreel in East Germany before making your first feature. What was it that made you decide to turn to feature film-making in 1947?

Kurt Maetzig: During my work for the newsreel – *Der Augenzeuge* – I received a letter one day from Hans Schweikart, who at that time was the director of the Münchner Kammerspiele, and he sent me a few sheets of paper on which he had written down the tragic story of his friend Joachim Gottschalk, who was married to a Jewish actress and who had committed suicide during the Nazi period. These few pages shocked me very deeply because I had seen in my own circles many such tragedies. My mother had died fleeing from the Gestapo and I had many friends who I had seen persecuted and who had lost their lives during the Nazi period. And so, in spite of the fact that I had never directed a film, I thought that no one else could make it, and I sat down in the terribly cold winter of 1946 to 1947 and wrote my first scenario, *Ehe im Schatten*, and made the film soon afterwards. And it turned out that this film was in fact a key which opened up people's hearts after those terrible years of fascism. About sixteen million people were living in the small territory which was later to become the GDR, and amongst them the film had ten million spectators during its first run, which meant that everyone who was of an age to go to the cinema saw the film several times. That gave me the hope, and perhaps the illusion, that through art I could have a great influence on the feelings and on the hearts and minds of people. I think that I overestimated this possibility, which led me to many illusions.

Martin Brady: One of the things that is obviously most striking about this film is the use of documentary material. You mentioned the Sasuly book about IG-Farben and the Nuremberg trial protocols, but of course there is also the archive footage. Moreover, there is a strong documentary dimension to *Schlösser und Katen*. Were you deliberately aiming at this period to create a synthesis of fiction and documentary, a documentary fiction film?

Kurt Maetzig: Yes, and I don't think that I would be able to point you to any other contemporary examples of this style. But at that time I thought it would be necessary to add documentary material because the revelations in *Der Rat der Götter* were so overwhelming and so unbelievable. I hoped to strengthen them by adding it. That is how it came about. But I did not repeat this procedure. Afterwards I felt that the film was over-loaded with facts, and that it was too much to expect of the audience that they should understand all these details and so on. In the films that followed I tried to speak more to the heart than to the intellect of the public as I had done in this film.

Martin Brady: It is of course the facts which are particularly shocking in this film, isn't it?

Kurt Maetzig: Yes.

Martin Brady: It seems to me that the use of the documentary material is particularly striking in the scenes with the launching of the battleship and the building up of the armaments industry. And one of the things that underlines the message is the remarkable music of Hanns Eisler, the electronic music, which he himself described as being deliberately dialectical. I wondered in that respect, given that Eisler had worked with Brecht a lot, and that you yourself had a number of encounters with him, whether Brecht was to some extent a model in your mind for this use of documentary material, this type of realism.

Kurt Maetzig: No, I don't think so. I admired Brecht very much, but our artistic paths were very different. For instance, when Brecht saw my first film *Ehe im Schatten* – he had just returned from emigration and people told him that there was a film which was a great success, and we immediately arranged a screening of the film for him – when the screening was over he said 'what terrible kitsch!'. That's what he said. But the next day he sent me his book *A Short Organon for the Theatre*, which was not yet printed at that time, and I read it and understood better what he wanted me to do! Afterwards we were on very friendly terms, but my artistic path was very different from his, and I thought that his method in particular was a purely theatrical one, purely made for the theatre. It could not easily be applied to film.

Martin Brady: What strikes me as fascinating about this film, is that one reads everywhere in the books about the difficulties that DEFA film-makers had moving from the anti-fascist film of the early years to the *Gegenwartsfilm* – films about contemporary issues, the topical film – which became much more important at the end of the fifties and in the sixties. But it seems to me that really from the start – in *Die Buntkarierten* (*The Girls in Gingham*, 1949), in tonight's film – you were already bringing together the anti-fascist theme and the genre of the contemporary film or *Gegenwartsfilm*. Was this a deliberate strategy from the outset?

Kurt Maetzig: Yes. I think in some ways my first film, *Ehe im Schatten*, had also been a topical film. We regarded it as a *Gegenwartsfilm* because the subject matter was so close to us. But I have to say that this only really holds true for the first period, which today I still think was a wonderful period – the years from 1945 until say 1949 – and then a lot changed. In the first years we were very free and could make the films we wanted to make. Staudte made his films, Erich Engel made his films, I made my films and there was almost no interference. There was not yet any German censorship. Censorship was in the hands of the cultural division of the Soviet Military Government, and there we met officials of a very high standard of education – they were all university professors and so on, and they gave us an enormous amount of freedom. This was possible because at that time the theory was officially approved that there should not be an imitation of the Soviet system in Germany, but rather a specifically German road to socialism. And I think today – having had many discussions with these Soviet officials responsible for culture – that they hoped that they could help Germany to a better system than the one they had left behind them at home. But this wonderful first period lasted only three or four years, then everything changed with the creation of the GDR and censorship passed into the hands of the new state authorities. I would say that at around the same time that the row broke out between the Soviet Union and Yugoslavia everything changed. A Stalinist cultural policy was applied to us as well, and as a result many things changed, and not for the better. We lost the sympathy of a large part of the public, and it was to take a very long time for us to regain the position we had once had.

Martin Brady: I wonder what effect this had on your own film-making, because if you compare your two major films of the 1950s – *Ernst Thälmann* and *Schlösser und Katen* – one is struck by the enormous differences in their aesthetic and in their whole approach. Would it be fair to describe *Ernst Thälmann* as a public, an official film, on the one hand, and *Schlösser und Katen* as your own personal response to it, so that you were in some sense moving between these two positions?

Kurt Maetzig: Yes, I'm glad that you mention the great difference between these films. I have to say that the film about Ernst

Thälmann was the only film I made on demand. I proposed all
my other films myself, but one day I was asked whether I would
be willing and able to make a film about the life of Ernst
Thälmann. I didn't know him personally, and I felt it would
be a difficult task, but I also thought it was an honour to make
a film about a worker's politician who, unlike all the other
politicians, had alerted everyone so clearly to the danger of
fascism. Already at the time when Hindenburg was elected as
President he had said 'anyone who votes for Hindenburg votes
for Hitler, anyone who votes for Hitler votes for war'. He was
a victim, a martyr killed by the Nazis, and so I thought it would
be an honour to make a film about him. But after I had
accepted I discovered very soon that they didn't want the sort
of film I had in mind, a film of a worker who despite great difficulties finds his personal path in political life. The leaders
of the GDR wanted something totally different. They had
young people in mind who during the fascist period had not
heard anything about Thälmann, except the worst possible
things – that he was a criminal and so on. And so they wanted to
build a kind of monument for these young people. Accordingly
they put this sympathetic and simple man Thälmann on a
pedestal and corrected the scenario all the time. They eliminated everything that was personal and not affirmative in the
obvious sense of the word; they wanted a film of an idealised
person. It is a film which you can no longer watch today. It is
terrible. When I saw it once again I had red ears and was
ashamed. Not because of the things that are said, the way in
which the history is painted, but because of the form, which
was my own responsibility. The content of the film is okay, but
the form – which is the responsibility of any film-maker – is
terrible. Absolutely terrible. Of course I was already aware of
this during the making of the film. In the process of directing it
I was aware that I was on the wrong track; I can prove this by the
film *Schlösser und Katen*, which followed immediately after the
films about Thälmann, and in which the style and everything is
totally different. I had learnt my lesson during the making of
the Thälmann films.

Martin Brady: I wondered if after making the Thälmann films
you were surprised that when you came to make *Das Kaninchen
bin ich* in 1965, in what appeared to be a period of opening up,
where it was possible to say things that hadn't been possible

before, that the film should be banned so suddenly. Did it come as a shock?

Kurt Maetzig: No, I was not so very surprised that it was banned, but the really surprising thing was that the film could be made at all. But I must say a few words about the situation after the erection of that terrible wall across Berlin. After the closing of the frontier we thought it was now a good moment to deal with the internal problems of the GDR because, before, we were always being told 'it is a very difficult and dangerous situation at present, you must act in a disciplined manner, it's not the moment to criticise everything'. But now we felt it was necessary, because it was evident that the whole system was inefficient. It was not only artists who had this impression – it was shared by others as well. For instance, Ulbricht's economic adviser made a proposal for a new economic structure to abolish the super-centralised system and give more responsibility from top to bottom, i.e., to make the whole system more efficient. This corresponded with the wishes of the artists for more freedom and liberty for their work, for more responsibility and for more freedom of speech regarding the problems of the country and so on. All of this occurred during the first three or four years of the 1960s, which was the time when in the Soviet Union Khrushchev was at work. He made some very timid, but nevertheless very visible steps toward democratisation. And this encouraged us immediately – we felt it was the right moment for reform of the whole system. During this period there were many films in production including my own film *Das Kaninchen bin ich*. The film dealt with criminal justice in the GDR: at the beginning you see a trial carried out along thoroughly Stalinist lines, whilst at the end you see a second trial, which is conducted according to democratic principles. It was a film which formulated a hope that the course could be set towards democratic socialism in the GDR. But it was a vain hope because Khrushchev was brought down, and was followed by the terrible Brezhnev. He undertook a secret visit to those in power in the GDR and told them that all attempts to implement any sort of liberalisation must be stopped immediately and that they must all return to the old course. And Ulbricht's economic adviser, Erich Apel, who had already drawn up the new system, committed suicide, he shot himself. The central committee which had already been called together to work on the new economic system stopped doing so and turned instead to directing harsh criticism at artists. More or less by chance it was my film which was at the forefront of these condemned films. It was described as counter-revolutionary, as hostile to the state, as an economic crime, as an insult to the entire Republic. Those were terrible days, and along with this film many other works of art were also banned, and more or less the whole annual production of DEFA could not be completed. It was not until the beginning of the seventies that art in the GDR was able to recover from this blow.

Martin Brady: I'd like to open up the discussion at this point and take questions from you – reactions to the film you've seen and any questions you have about it.

Question: I have a question not about the film, but about the film directors you personally admired. Which film-makers had an influence on your own work? What were the films that you saw as a young man and which influenced your subsequent film-making?

Kurt Maetzig: I can still remember very clearly the first film I saw, and which affected me very deeply. At the time I was a young boy – about ten years old. My grandmother said, we're going to the the cinema today, we're going to see a film. We saw *The Kid* (1921) by Charlie Chaplin with Jackie Coogan, and I was very moved by the figure of the vagabond, played by Chaplin, who as a social outcast himself looks after this little boy. It gave me a very childlike moral desire to be on the side of the weak in life.

Question: I have two questions for the director: first, how, in his opinion, did Hitler come to power and, second, what is his position on the Nuremberg trials?

Kurt Maetzig: I have brought with me a couple of extracts from the book I mentioned at the beginning, *IG-Farben* by Richard Sasuly. In these extracts you can read about all of the incredible things which are depicted in *Der Rat der Götter*. If you wish I can give them to you to look at. In another section of the book, which I haven't brought with me, there is a very clear analysis of the situation which led to Hitler's accession to power. At the final election the Nazi party lost one million votes, and in the wake of this result the leaders of German industry met Hitler and promised to help him to power, which is what then happened very soon afterwards. This is not something to which I can bear personal witness as I was, of course, not there, but Mr Sasuly, whose authority I acknowledge as the man who did the preparatory research for the Nuremberg trials, believes this to be the case.

I think that the first trial, the proceedings against the principal war criminals, was good and just. In the case of the second trial, against the war criminals from the chemical industry, it has to be noted with regret that the proceedings were no longer conducted under the four flags of the anti-Hitler coalition, but only under the banner of the United States. I think it was even more regrettable that the Chief Prosecutor was replaced mid-trial; for me this marks the transition point from the anti-Hitler coalition to the Cold War. I felt at the time that it was a turning-point, and I tried to depict it as such in *Der Rat der Götter*.

I certainly think that things would have turned out better in Germany if the anti-Hitler coalition had survived. But, as you know, this was unfortunately not to be the case because Adenauer decided in favour of dividing Germany, saying that he would rather have a whole share of Germany than the whole of Germany shared.

Question: Where was the film shown apart from in Germany? Was it shown elsewhere, for example in America at the time? And what was the reaction?

Kurt Maetzig: The film was shown in many countries, although not in the United States or in West Germany.

Martin Brady: Were you told why the film couldn't be shown in the Federal Republic?

Kurt Maetzig: No, no one told me why. Of course I did read that people cast doubt on the facts which are presented in the film, calling it communist propaganda. But it was no such thing, it was an accurate reflection of the conclusions drawn by Sasuly in his book. I really must show you these extracts afterwards, because they contain the most extraordinary revelations, especially concerning the formation of this enormous cartel, into which IG-Farben put two thousand patents and Standard Oil also. They were deposited in a joint holding company called Jasco, in which they held 50:50 shares – 50% to Standard Oil, 50% to IG-Farben. The extracts explain precisely what the *modus vivendi* was to be during the war. All the possible variations were carefully considered in advance: a war in which the United States would participate, and a war in which they wouldn't. It was decided that even if the United States did enter the war the cartel would continue to operate throughout.

Question: I was curious when you referred movingly to the early years of idealism which you enjoyed after the war, whether you ever considered leaving the GDR when things quite clearly changed. What made you decide to remain as a film-maker in the GDR?

Kurt Maetzig: No, I never considered leaving the German Democratic Republic, because I felt that I could only fight for the kind of democratic socialism I was hoping for from within the system and not from outside it. I retained until the very last the hope and the illusion that the system could be reformed from top to bottom. I know today that it was a mere illusion, but I clung to it until the end.

Question: Did the explosion of the chemical factory at the end of the film have a factual basis?

Kurt Maetzig: Yes, the explosion occurred in 1948 in a factory in Ludwigshafen, and several kilometres' length of factory were destroyed. What happened was as follows: the screenplay had been written by Friedrich Wolf, the famous author. It was already complete and I wanted to start shooting the film when this explosion took place in Ludwigshafen. As a result the film was given a new ending.

Question: I wondered, to go back to the early years, whether you were influenced in the immediate post-war period by Anton Ackermann?

Kurt Maetzig: Yes, Ackermann did influence me, especially through his theory of a unique German road to socialism. This made a big impression on me.

Question: Could you tell us something about what happened in your work after *Das Kaninchen bin ich*?

Kurt Maetzig: Immediately after the Plenary Session of the Central Committee all those responsible were thrown out of office: the *Chefdramaturg* of DEFA was sacked, the General Director of DEFA was sacked, the Deputy Culture Minister was sacked and the Culture Minister was sacked. I was the only one who remained, waiting to see what would happen. Then I was summoned to a discussion with Politburo member Kurt Hager and I had a four-and-a-half-hour discussion with him, during the course of which he repeated the accusations and added a few more for good measure. In particular he accused me of two further things: first of all he said that West German intellectuals were not well pleased with their government, because Minister Erhard had cursed them for being people who didn't understand anything about politics and who should mind their own business and so on – even Böll felt insulted. As a result there was a bad atmosphere, and Hager accused me of building a bridge to the West German intellectuals on the basis that we didn't like our government, they didn't like theirs, and therefore we could get on pretty well. And second, he reproached me with having a completely false grasp of history. He said that I always distinguished between what happened before the revelations about Stalin's crimes and what happened afterwards, i.e., that for me the decisive turning-point was the Twentieth Party Congress of the Communist Party of the Soviet Union, at which Stalin's crimes were exposed. But that is misguided, Hager told me, the turning-point was 1945 – fascism and what followed it. As far as he was concerned it was this false historical categorisation which had led me down the wrong path. But throughout the conversation I had the distinct impression that the leaders of the GDR themselves were in a weak and defensive position, and today historians have confirmed that this impression was correct. Honecker exploited Brezhnev's visit in order to weaken Ulbricht, who was prepared to take on more decentralisation and liberalisation. I have to say that throughout the conversation I rejected all the accusations and defended my position.

Finally he said that I should think it all over once more and that if I wished I should write a sort of self-criticism and publish it. I understood that the battle we had fought was well and truly lost, and I consulted the author of the screenplay, because the only options open to us now were to leave the GDR or take a step backwards and write the self-criticism. The scriptwriter, Bieler, decided to go, he left the Republic, and I decided to undertake a limited self-criticism, i.e., I didn't accept the four accusations, I declared my good intentions and merely regretted that these good intentions had not met with a correspondingly positive response. In the wake of this letter an open letter was published in *Neues Deutschland* from Walter Ulbricht to Kurt Maetzig; it took up half a page of the newspaper and toned down the accusations. Today we know that this was because Walter Ulbricht had to extricate himself from the situation, but the positive outcome of the letter was that none of those who were dismissed was actually put on trial and no one ended up in prison; everybody was able to continue working, albeit in other capacities, everyone was consigned to a different function but they were all able to stay in work. And so I felt that a certain compromise had been reached.

Question: Your film *Schlösser und Katen* ends in June 1953. I wonder what your attitude was to the events of June 1953 at the time, and what it is now.

Kurt Maetzig: *Schlösser und Katen* offered an interpretation of the events of June 1953 which differed from the official line in East and West. Of course the evaluations of these events in East and West were diametrically opposed, but the interpretation provided in *Schlösser und Katen* was my own, and it diverged substantially from both of them. Thus, on the one hand, the big mistakes that had been made during collectivisation and the founding of the agricultural collectives were named by name – excessive acceleration of the changes and the use of unnecessary force. On the other hand, however, there was the influence exerted on the whole process from across the border during the Cold War. I still think today that this was an accurate interpretation.

Question: To what extent was your relationship, your positive relationship to the regime, in its early years at least, related to its anti-fascism and the role that the political regime had played in the destruction of fascism, and to what extent was it actually based on a belief in the construction of socialism?

Kurt Maetzig: Both. Both. I was, of course, as a result of everything that I had experienced and suffered in my life, an opponent of fascism, and not just as a political system. I also tried to lay bare the origins and roots of fascism in my films, and *Der Rat der Götter* is a contribution to this end. But of course if you clear something away you also make space for something new, the two are intimately connected, and both led me into a good deal of conflict and many difficult battles. I am still striving for democratic socialism because I can see quite clearly that the world as it is today is never going to be in a position to defeat the three great evils which are confronting humanity: hunger, war and the destruction of the environment. Of course history doesn't repeat itself, of course I don't want a return to something which has proved itself to be incapable of surviving, but I'm absolutely sure that mankind will make further attempts to change the structure of society. I don't believe for a minute that the situation as it exists today represents the end of history, on the contrary, mankind is confronted with crucial decisions, and it must find the strength to make a new start without repeating past mistakes.

Martin Brady: I think that would be an excellent point to finish on, because of course it confirms the contemporary relevance of the film we have just seen – we don't need 'Arms to Iraq' or such like to prove that to us! And I could perhaps add to what Herr Maetzig has said, that he very tantalisingly suggested to me while we were talking before this discussion that he might well now have an idea for a new film, so I think happily that the chapter is still open. I'm sure you will now want to join me in thanking Herr Maetzig sincerely for coming to London – it's been a wonderful and exciting evening – and for giving us so many insights not only into DEFA, but above all into his own work as one of the main contributors to East German Cinema. Thank you very much indeed.

[Applause]

Kurt Maetzig: Thank you very much for your interest.

Note

The discussion was conducted in both English and German with Ann Pearce acting as interpreter where necessary. The discussion was transcribed and translated by Martin Brady. Thanks to the concision and lucidity of Professor Maetzig's responses it has been possible to reproduce them here without any cuts.

Chapter 6

Rebels with a Cause: The Development of the *'Berlin-Filme'* by Gerhard Klein and Wolfgang Kohlhaase

Horst Claus

'What sort of men do you fancy?', asks Dieter shortly after midnight at the front door of a block of flats in the Dimitroff Straße just around the corner from Schönhauser Allee in East Berlin. 'Doctors and boxers', replies Angela, as she opens the door. 'Nonsense, I mean, what do they have to look like?', retorts Dieter. The girl with the pony-tail turns to him – 'Like Marlon Brando' – and, with a hint of a provocative smile, disappears, locking the door behind her.

Neither *The Wild One* (1953), nor *On the Waterfront* (1954) – the films which established the American actor as a rebel star and teenage-idol of the fifties on both sides of the Atlantic – were ever released in East Germany. For many who tried to make socialism work in the Soviet Zone of Occupation after World War II, Hollywood films represented capitalism and all that was wrong with the Western way of life. The scene above is not to be found in earlier drafts of the script of *Berlin – Ecke Schönhauser* (*Berlin – Schönhauser Corner*, 1957) when the film still had the abstract, but – from an East German perspective – politically correct working title, 'Where we are not …', a title which invited the audience to supply the missing rejoinder, '… there are our enemies', and which implied that social, economic and political positions not under socialist control would be taken over by Western capitalists.

The reference to Marlon Brando (without a hint of criticism) and the change of title from an overt political statement to the more neutral name of a street corner in East Berlin, highlights an important aspect of the intentions of Gerhard Klein (the film's director) and Wolfgang Kohlhaase (the scriptwriter) – namely their desire to promote their ideal of socialism through film without submitting to the pressures of ideologues for whom art is simply another means to advance political doctrines.

Berliner Romanze (*A Berlin Romance*, 1956), *Berlin – Ecke Schönhauser* (1957), *Berlin um die Ecke* (*Berlin around the Corner*, 1965) together with *Alarm im Zirkus* (*Circus Alarm*, 1953), established them as creators of the so-called 'Berlin-Filme' – films set in Berlin during the first two decades after World War II which focus on the personal experiences of working-class people under twenty-five in the divided city. Though rooted in fiction, these films are generally regarded as the most authentic portraits of a generation which was expected to realise the dream of a fair and equal German society in the East. They also bear witness to their creators' insistence on remaining critical voices within the context of the GDR's changing political and cultural policies. Between 1953 and 1965, the optimistic hopes for a better future which characterise the idealistic commitment to socialism of the early films by Klein and Kohlhaase give way to a sceptical portrayal of the realities of life in a socialist state. Dramaturgically, it is a shift from action to analysis, from black-and-white stereotypes to complex characters. While the early films interpret human behaviour and living conditions in Berlin from a strictly East German perspective and a communist assessment of Cold War politics, the later films aim to explain their characters' motives and actions with references to the wider context of Germany's history. At the same time, the films' emphasis shifts from the private spheres of the main characters to the social milieu in which they are situated with increasing attention being directed to the importance of the workplace.

The transformation from overt anti-Western propaganda to criticism and analysis of the GDR's social and political system parallels Klein and Kohlhaase's growing competence and confidence in handling the technical and dramaturgical skills of their profession. More significantly, it reflects their reluctance to adjust to every twist and turn of the SED's directives in respect of a medium which – following Lenin – GDR officials regarded as the most important of the arts. Film content was severely affected by debates about the function of art within socialist society which in turn were prompted by changes in the country's political climate. Whenever the GDR went through a period of entrenchment, doctrinaire socialist realism was the order of the day. This approach regards film as a propaganda tool, demands set patterns of plot, stereotypical characters, and rejects experiments in aesthetic form. Focusing on positive heroes who achieve self-realisation within a socialist collective, socialist-realist films are expected to make substantial contributions towards the building of a socialist society. Individuality, contradictions, or subtle hints at cracks in the socialist system are unacceptable, and are consigned to the realm of critical realism. Critical realism is an aesthetic which identifies controversial issues, opens them up for critical debate, and allows formal experiments which enhance and deepen the understanding of reality. The most prominent and influential examples of critical realist films are the films of Italian neo-realist directors such as Vittorio de Sica or Roberto Rossellini (who, in 1948, made his own 'Berlin-Film' with a young protagonist – *Germania Anno Zero*). Having raised their own awareness of the filmic potential of ordinary everyday events, this style of cinema was fully endorsed by Klein and Kohlhaase. And not just by them: it surfaced whenever GDR politics seemed to steer a more liberal course – only to be attacked by doctrinaire party ideologues. Since film production was guided by political rather than artistic considerations, sensitive issues – such as the existence of a youth culture not interested in, or even opposed to, official youth policies – had to be handled with care. Frequently, their representation (or just the reference to them) was subliminal and coded in such a way that Western audiences missed it completely. It is one of the achievements of the 'Berlin-Filme' – and a reason for their immense popularity – that Klein and Kohlhaase did not resort to such underhand tactics and always remained outspoken.

By the time both men began their collaboration in the early fifties, the relative artistic and creative freedom which had been the hallmark of DEFA's production policy during the immediate post-war years was disappearing. Company management had passed from Russian into German hands, i.e., into the control of the SED. Confrontational Cold War politics resulted in a call for *Gegenwartsfilme* – films set in the present – which supported the struggle to build up a socialist society. DEFA's director Sepp Schwab, a Moscow-trained *apparatchik*, deliberately replaced the mainly bourgeois personnel from the Western sectors of Berlin with socialists. This severe drain of talent offered newcomers like Klein and Kohlhaase the chance of a lifetime.

Their first joint venture, *Alarm im Zirkus*, is a crime thriller for children with a political message. Its simple, linear plot focuses on two boys, Max and Klaus, from a working-class district in West Berlin whose favourite sport is boxing. Their parents are too poor to pay for higher education, and both face unemployment after leaving school. In an attempt to get enough money to buy real boxing gloves they unwittingly become involved in a plot to steal valuable horses from the eastern sector of the city. The mastermind behind the plan is Klott who has just threatened Klaus's mother with eviction because she cannot pay the rent. Klott also owns a bar frequented by American soldiers which is the meeting place of the young thugs who are to carry out the crime. When Max and Klaus attend a performance of the East Berlin Circus Barlay they become acquainted with the girl Helli, a member of the communist youth organisation, the *Junge Pioniere*, who informs them that in the East being poor is no obstacle to a university education – indeed, she herself wants to become a vet. Following a visit to the circus stables during which he recognises one of the stable hands as a man he has seen in Klott's bar it dawns on Klaus that the horses to be stolen are those of the Circus Barlay. Max does not believe Klaus's suspicions and unwittingly joins the criminals because they promise him money for his help. After the West Berlin police refuse to act on his warnings, Klaus, with the help of Helli's father, informs the East German police who, in a shoot-out and subsequent chase through the ruins of Berlin, apprehend the culprits and prevent the horses from being taken across the border. Furious, an American officer leaves the spot at which the horses should have crossed into the Western Sector and where a large number of journalists and cameramen had gathered, hoping to witness an escape from communist atrocities. The final sequence shows Klaus, Max and their families as guests of honour at the Circus Barlay where an elephant presents the boys with boxing gloves.

The film's leading characters are not yet teenagers or adolescent drop-outs, but children. Though the spectator does not learn much about the lives and concerns of those who grew up in East Berlin in the early fifties, the film captures the distinct atmosphere of the divided city. The Western attitude towards the East is summed up succinctly in two lines. When Jimmy offers Max and Klaus tickets for the Circus Barley, Klaus reacts sceptically: 'That's in the Eastern Sector.' And Jimmy replies: 'So what?! Circus is the only thing over there which is still okay.' The children could come from either East or West Berlin. Their portrayal rings true and conveys a sense of authenticity. The opening sequence which shows Max and Klaus as they try to sell a knife to other children reveals a sharp eye for character movement and behaviour. Their bartering and arguments about trash novels could have taken place on any street anywhere in Germany.

The film's anti-Western stance has to be seen in the context of the propaganda war in which East and West bombarded each other with hostile accusations and abuse. According to Kohlhaase it was Margot Honecker, then head of the *Junge Pioniere* (the section for the six to thirteen-year-olds of the country's youth organisation, the Free German Youth), who suggested basing the film on a real-life cloak-and-dagger operation which took place during the night of 21 April 1953. The practice of adapting a real-life incident for propaganda purposes in a children's film with the encouragement of the state's youth organisation can be traced back to *Hitlerjunge Quex* (*Hitler Youth Quex*, 1933), Ufa's opportunistic, commercial response to the National Socialists' seizure of power in 1933. As with *Hitlerjunge Quex*, *Alarm im Zirkus* could be seen as an attempt to reach adults through their children. But its approach to, and representation of the state youth organisation is radically different and suggests that director and author tried to maintain their independence. Unlike the Hitler Youth in *Hitlerjunge Quex*, the *Junge Pioniere* are never referred to in the film. They are only seen as members of the circus audience when they can be identified by their white shirts and scarves. Helli, the female lead, always wears a coat which more often than not conceals her membership. Though committed to socialism, Klein and Kohlhaase were not interested in producing propaganda for the FDJ. They were eager to make their first film.

The East German authorities, however, fully exploited the propaganda potential of *Alarm im Zirkus*. Advance publicity stressed the faithful rendering of the crime on which it was based. Press material issued by *Progress*, DEFA's distributor, contained a section entitled 'Points for discussion' which advised children to take a leaf out of Klaus's book by being vigilant, helping the police to prevent crime and defending their Socialist Republic against its enemies.[1] A leaflet issued to cinema managers, schools, cultural authorities, and officials of the FDJ contained an introduction to be read out prior to every performance for children outside Berlin. It concluded that: 'Klaus knows that honest convictions have nothing to with political borders, that evil will always be evil. You should always remember this, dear children. Help us to get the borders within Berlin removed, so that we may have a united and beautiful Berlin in which the children of West Berlin may enjoy your happy way of life.'[2]

Though Klein and Kohlhaase were surprised when they were awarded the *Nationalpreis*, the state's highest accolade, they were also aware it had come their way not just for artistic achievements, but as an encouragement of a new generation and a specific kind of film.[3] The prize enabled them to develop the ideas and principles which had governed their work on *Alarm im Zirkus* further, without undue worries about either getting their next project accepted or the time it would take to develop it.

Berliner Romanze originated from the desire to make another film about the young generation. The climate of the period, the special circumstances of Berlin, where people were able to move between two different worlds for the price of a tram ticket, suggested an East-West love story between Uschi, a trainee sales girl in a department store near Alexanderplatz, and Hans, an unemployed youth from West Berlin. Following her participation as an amateur model in one of her store's fashion shows, a picture of her wearing a glamorous evening dress appears on the cover of a magazine, the *Berliner Illustrierte*. As a consequence, she wants to break out of her working-class environment and dreams of a career in modelling. During a stroll along West Berlin's Kurfürstendamm she meets Hans, whose single-parent mother constantly reprimands him for not contributing enough to the family budget. Hans pursues Uschi with such persistence that she overcomes her initial aversion and falls in love with him. Hearing of her hopes to become a model, he decides to finance her training at an expensive mannequin school – despite the fact that he earns very little money by occasionally washing cars in a garage at night. To raise the cash Hans becomes a bouncer in a bar during the night and an unskilled labourer on a demolition site during the day. When he gets injured as a result of the inadequate safety precautions on the site, he loses both positions and is even thrown out of the night-club after attacking one of the customers, whom he identified as the unscrupulous owner of the demolition company. For Uschi there is also a bitter awakening. First, she is confronted with the modelling school's horrendous fees, and then, having run away from home, finds out that the flat where she and Hans spent their first night together does not belong to him. Realising the folly of her dreams she ruefully returns home. After a serious talk, her mother allows her to invite her boyfriend home. Uschi fetches Hans and brings him to East Berlin, where he will have a chance to realise his ambition to become a motor mechanic, and where both of them will live happily ever after.

Berliner Romanze is an unspectacular, quiet film. In many ways it comes closest to the Italian neo-realist model, even if Kohlhaase has dismissed it as the 'Berlin-Film' least likely to stand the test of time.[4] Its simple, linear plot is unexciting, almost unnoticeable. Emphasis is not on action, but on the two main characters, the development of their relationship, on their feelings and emotions. Though sweet, attractive, and pretty, Uschi is not the tempting seductress or sex kitten found in Western films about adolescent dropouts, such as Karin Baal in *Die Halbstarken* (*The Hooligans*, 1956) or Natalie Wood in *Rebel Without a Cause* (1956). Boys turn round when she goes by, but it does not need fist-fights or dare-devil challenges to win her favours. Uschi has all the usual illusions and teenage dreams about glamour and fame, but she is happy enough when a young man buys her a 'Napo' (a popular sweet at the time), takes her to the fair or just follows her with his eyes. She is the girl next door who struggles with the same problems as most teenagers whose parents are reluctant to allow them the freedom to which they feel they are entitled. Having briefly tasted the thrills of public admiration and applause, she objects to her family treating her like a child. However, as she is guided mainly by impulse and emotion, her parents are fully justified in reprimanding her: 'For once, accept your mother's advice: always think before you act.' Kohlhaase and Klein's movement away from stereotypes towards individualisation becomes even more apparent when comparing the male protagonists of *Alarm im Zirkus* and *Berliner Romanze*. Hans has nothing in common with the painfully well-behaved and obedient Klaus in *Alarm im Zirkus*, whose preoccupation with the pursuit of his widowed mother's peace of mind and happiness reveals him as a descendant of Emil Tischbein in Gerhard Lamprecht's adaptation of Erich Kästner's *Emil und die Detektive* (*Emil and the Detectives*, 1931). Hans tells us that he already argued with his mother at the age of eleven (i.e., when he was about three or four years younger than Klaus). He resents that she prevented him from attending training sessions for boxing. Hans's fascination with the sport and the naïveté with which he hopes to earn the money for Uschi's modelling course link him with Max, the one mildly differentiated character in *Alarm im Zirkus*. Both are naïve when it comes to financial matters, and when they are finally forced to face reality Max has to be rescued by Klaus, while in Hans's case the decision about their joint future is left to Uschi. In *Alarm im Zirkus* the happy ending is brought about by the state, first through the arrest of the criminals by the East German police and then in the form of the boxing gloves given to the boys by the circus (which – it is emphasised – is owned by the state). A similar solution is suggested at the end of *Berliner Romanze*. The final shot shows the two lovers walking down a street beside an elevated rail track in East Berlin while the voice of the film's off-screen narrator describes their future prospects: 'Now they are really a couple, one of thousands living in Berlin. Or as we say: They are going out together. Uschi and Hans – together they'll find their place, right in the middle of our lives, where there is work, struggle, and love'. The film's plot and images, however, tell a different story: the happy ending of *Berliner Romanze* is not brought about by a socialist community, but by Uschi's parents who allow their daughter to invite Hans home. It is not – as the artificially imposed commentary claims – the East German state which clears the path for the young lovers' happiness, but the security of a home with strictly maintained, traditional family values. In contrast to *Alarm im Zirkus* there is no *Volkspolizist* (GDR policeman), no father of a *Jungpionier* or any other representative of an East German state organisation who contributes to the solution of the problems confronting the protagonists. Neither is there an equivalent to the girl Helli. Indeed, the voice-over text, which contributes nothing at all to the film, seems to have been added mainly for fear that the political message might not be clear enough. The scenes showing the brightly lit Kurfürstendamm with its display cases offering luxury goods fully justify Uschi's desire to live in the West. On the other hand, the representation of her family's cramped living conditions even led to complaints from East German audiences that such flats were a relic of the past and did not do any justice at all to the advances made in raising the East German standard of living.[5]

The trend towards a more balanced portrait of Berlin can also be seen in the representation of the teenagers from West Berlin. They are no longer criminals, but victims of an economic system epitomised by ruthless employers. In addition, the film does not just talk about unemployment in the West: it actually shows it. In scenes clearly inspired by the first part of *Kuhle Wampe* (1931), Hans races on his bike from employer to employer only to be told there are no vacancies. Just like the parents of the unemployed youth in the film by Slatan Dudow and Bertolt Brecht, Hans's mother contributes to her son's frustration because she is unable to identify the real reasons for his desperate situation – a fact which the film conveys not just through words, but also through images.

While much of the success of *Alarm im Zirkus* has been attributed to its visual impact, Wolf Göthe's black-and-white cinematography in *Berliner Romanze* with its carefully composed chiaroscuro is even more striking and convincing. The dominance of wide-angle lenses, the use of high-speed film stock and extensive location work convey a sense of authenticity. Even the smell of Berlin seems to have been captured in scenes such as those of the fair or the visit to the cinema. This is not the dispassionate look through the camera with which the neorealist Roberto Rossellini waited for the truth to reveal itself in his 'Berlin-Film' *Germania Anno Zero* in 1948. This is a lovingly designed, carefully reconstructed representation of working class-life in Berlin based on in-depth knowledge, extensive research and thorough familiarity with the milieu and its people. The impression of 'coincidence' which permeates the 'Berlin-Filme' is deliberately forged.[6]

Despite distinct traces of Cold-War sentiments, in *Berliner Romanze* Klein and Kohlhaase signal their independence from their political masters and begin to formulate the difference of their work from that of other film-makers. They reveal themselves to be committed socialists whose roots reach back to the proletarian cinema of the Weimar Republic. Their representation of Uschi's tough, stern, but fair mother who holds her family – including her husband – together with an iron fist is a salute to working-class women. On the other hand, in presenting Uschi's call for personal independence only in the context of her spontaneous desire to become a model, and interpreting it simply as an immature teenage pipedream, they are not yet seriously analysing the youth culture of their time. Nor do they show it in a differentiated social context. They could even be accused of hypocrisy, since the lengthy, nation-wide search for the unknown amateur, who would represent and play the typical 'Berlin girl' stimulated precisely those false expectations which the film dismisses as immature: 14,000 hopefuls reportedly turned up in Babelsberg for the first preliminary selection. When the right one was not amongst them, the bandwagon rolled through other parts of the country, accompanied by the obligatory press reports. With a capitalist-style publicity campaign, toned-down anti-Western propaganda, a trend towards a balanced portrait of Berlin, and the suggestion that the young should accept their position and are best cared for within the fold of a traditional family, it is hardly surprising that the portrayal of the attitudes, dreams and desires of the film's characters does not differ from that on the other side of the German-German border. Most reviews and reader's letters to the editors of the newspapers confirm that Klein and Kohlhaase were fully in tune with the emotional wavelength of the teenagers of their time.

Critical reaction, however, also foreshadowed the debate which, from now on, accompanied all subsequent 'Berlin-Filme'. The popular East Berlin newspaper, *BZ am Abend,* pats Klein and Kohlhaase on the back for having pointed out the direction future *Gegenwartsfilme* should take but reprimands them for not being positive enough about the achievements of socialism GDR-style.[7] Horst Knietzsch, critic of the official party organ *Neues Deutschland,* notes that the representation of issues affecting 'vital matters of the divided city' could have been dealt with in a 'more accentuated' way, and criticises Klein and Kohlhaase for not always having captured the positive and negative aspects of Berlin. He singles out Annekathrin Bürger who plays Uschi for special criticism:

'She has a sweet, attractive face and a sexy figure (accentuated by tight dresses), but as an amateur she is only convincing as long as she plays herself.'[8] *Junge Welt* took up the gauntlet thrown down by the establishment and printed an enthusiastic letter by teenager Gerda Sonnenberg of Berlin-Treptow. Hoping to see another film starring Annekathrin Bürger in the near future, she declares *Berliner Romanze* to be the love story which presents young Berliners as they really are.[9] Two days later the FDJ newspaper openly defended the actress with whose appearance and feelings young GDR citizens clearly identified. Mocking Knietzsch's disapproval of Uschi's sex appeal, the paper concedes with a wink that Uschi 'still has a lot to learn', only to conclude that the features she has been endowed with by nature are nevertheless preferable to Knietzsch's sour remarks.[10]

Repartee such as this is more than just a reflection of the generation gap. Critical remarks about the close relationship between Annekathrin Bürger and her role are prompted by the debate between socialist realism and neorealism, a debate which Erich Honecker was to try to end once and for all in his speech to the notorious Eleventh Plenum in December 1965. There he was to insist that neorealism is the appropriate means of revealing the deficiencies of capitalist society, but that it was quite inadequate for a critical analysis of socialism. Ten years earlier in 1955, however, debates about aesthetics were less intense. Following the film's first night in May 1956 as part of DEFA's tenth anniversary celebrations, the *Berliner Zeitung* heralded *Berliner Romanze* as a true reflection of the country's reality, which successfully managed to negotiate all the hurdles put up by the extensive apparatus of DEFA and the Film Committee.[11]

It is in this context that *Berlin – Ecke Schönhauser*, the most popular and, in the opinion of many, the best of the 'Berlin-Filme', came about. It is Klein and Kohlhaase's response to questions raised by teenagers about the contradictions of the world in which they are growing up. The film captures the flavour of Berlin so well that its title (which refers to a street corner in the working-class district of Prenzlauer Berg) acquired a life of its own and became a synonym for 'Heimat-Berlin'. In 1992, Bärbel Dalichow, director of the Potsdam Film Museum, selected it as one of two films which in her opinion best convey the feeling of 'Heimat-GDR'. Though based on fiction and relying on a narrative technique of cause and effect, for her *Berlin – Ecke Schönhauser* has a 'documentary feel' and represents the kind of honest *Gegenwartsfilme* GDR audiences really wanted to see, namely films addressing the socialist ideal, as well as the contradictions within GDR society.[12]

Berlin – Ecke Schönhauser is about four teenagers aged between 16 and 19 who belong to a group of youths whose regular meeting-place is underneath the elevated train-tracks at the corner of Schönhauser Allee and Dimitroffstraße. They provoke passers-by with rock-and-roll dancing and impertinent reactions to complaints about their outward appearance and behaviour. Angela, a seamstress, is the daughter of a single mother whose husband has been killed in the war. Twice a week she has to leave their cramped flat until midnight because her mother wants to be alone with her boss, a married man with whom she has an affair. Dieter, a building worker, has lost both parents and lives together with his older brother who belongs to the *Volkspolizei* and talks down to him rather than with him. Kohle is unemployed and receives regular thrashings from his widowed mother's lazy partner, a drunkard who shares their flat. Karl-Heinz, the son of a tax consultant, has dropped out of grammar school. Though opposed to the socialist system, his bourgeois family is reluctant to leave for fear of losing their property in East Berlin. The fifth central character is an unnamed *Volkspolizist* who represents a caring authority, intent on helping the young to find their place in society. It is to him that the story is told in a flash-back by Dieter, who has just run from West to East Berlin and informed him that Kohle is dead.

One day, when hanging out with their crowd at the corner of Schönhauser Allee, Karl-Heinz challenges Kohle to smash a street light for a West mark, but then refuses to pay up. Witnesses of the vandalism call the police, who take all the youngsters in. After checking their passports, the *Volkspolizist* reprimands them, promises to find an apprenticeship for Kohle, and sends everybody home. Outside the station Karl-Heinz asks Dieter to join him and steal East German passports which they could sell at a nice profit to West Berliners who would use them for buying goods in East Berlin at considerably lower prices than those charged in the West. Initially Dieter agrees, but when Karl-Heinz intends to take the passport of a friend of Angela's while dancing in a youth club, he refuses to go through with it because he is in love with Angela. Tempted by what he perceives as the good life in the West, Karl-Heinz becomes involved with a gang of illegal money traders and inadvertently kills a man during an attempted robbery. He returns to his parents and forces them with a pistol to hand over their Western savings account book. When he tries to leave the house, Kohle and Dieter challenge him to pay the one West mark he owes Kohle. In the attempt to stop him from shooting Dieter, Kohle knocks Karl-Heinz unconscious with a stone. Because they believe that Kohle has murdered Karl-Heinz, he and Dieter escape to West Berlin, where they register as political refugees. The staff of the reception camp are anything but friendly, particularly when Dieter displays the same kind of individuality and independence which brought him into conflict with the authorities in the East. When Kohle learns that Dieter will not be allowed to leave the camp, and that he will be flown to West Germany without him, he is desperate. To prevent his separation from Dieter he drinks a mixture of coffee and tobacco designed to make him ill by just giving him a fever. However, the cocktail turns out to be lethal. Dieter knocks down the bully who guards the exit of the camp and returns to East Berlin where the *Volkspolizist* informs him of Karl-Heinz's arrest and tells him to go and see Angela who is expecting his child.

Long before *Berlin – Ecke Schönhauser* went into production, *The Wild One, Blackboard Jungle* (1955), and *Rebel Without a Cause* – the three American films which made the biggest impact on Western youth films of the time – had been widely exhibited in West German cinemas, and there are similarities between characters and character constellations of *Berlin – Ecke Schönhauser* and *Rebel Without a Cause*. But though several members of the Berlin gang – including Karl-Heinz – imitate James Dean's posture and hair style, the reasons for their rebellious attitudes are different. Significantly, Ekkehard Schall, who plays Dieter, has none of the features which would make him a teenager idol; his deliberate movements, his restrained and wary facial expressions are the exact opposite of James Dean's charm. Dean's frustrations are rooted in his father's inability to be a 'real' man. When asked in *The Wild One* what he is rebelling against, Marlon Brando replies: 'What have you got?' By contrast, Ekkehard Schall knows precisely what it is he does not like about the world around him: 'Why can't I say what I want? Why do you have all those ready-made rules? Standing at a corner I'm a hooligan, dancing boogie-woogie I'm an American, and when I leave my shirt hanging out, I'm politically suspect.' In contrast to contemporary American and West German films about youth in the fifties such as Tressler's *Die Halbstarken* or von Baky's *Die Frühreifen* (*The Precocious Ones*, 1957), *Berlin – Ecke Schönhauser* tries to identify the causes of young people's disenchantment. It locates the source of such problems not just in the generation gap or in conflicts within individual families, but in a specific social and political environment resulting from a lost war, the division of Germany, and the politics of the Cold War. This disenchantment is reflected in broken homes, financial greed, lack of ideals, lack of direction and interference in, rather than genuine concern for, the life of the individual. It is not just political propaganda when, in one of the last shots, Dieter looks across a courtyard up to Angela's window and the voice of the *Volkspolizist* is heard saying: 'So it's my fault and it's your fault. Where we are not, there are our enemies. We've got to start all over again, right from the beginning!' It is also an idealistic appeal to accept responsibility for each other and develop a genuine concern for other human beings.

The advances made by Kohlhaase and Klein can best be seen through the characters of the film's four young protagonists. While in *Berliner Romanze* Uschi's disenchantment with her family is explained by means of her spontaneous, immature desire for glamour and fame, Angela has genuine reasons to rebel against her mother, because she sees through the contradictory behaviour of the adults and their double standards. Angela has to leave the house when her mother's boyfriend arrives. She has to eat a sandwich without anything on it, while he is served expensive ham. Her mother dresses up and puts on make-up for her boyfriend, but tells Angela off for doing the same. When the girl wants to go downstairs to join her gang, her mother orders her to stay in. Angela is always loyal to her friends. Her behaviour and attitudes demonstrate maturity and a sense of responsibility. She goes upstairs as soon as she thinks her mother's boyfriend has left. She flirts with Dieter, but also firmly closes the door in his face. (Indeed, the child she expects from him is nothing but a weak and unconvincing dramaturgical device, a *deus ex machina*, to bring the conflict with her mother to a head.) On the other hand, the film also explains and raises sympathies for her mother's situation.

Widowed at a young age, she has sexual needs and desires, and is a victim of the shortage of men as a result of the war. Her lover ruthlessly exploits her situation with promises of marriage that he has no intention of keeping. Indeed, when throwing him out she too has undergone a learning process.

Dieter's character appears more complex than Angela's. He lives with his brother and objects to being bossed about by him. He is said to be a good, reliable worker, and loyal to his friends to the point of making wrong decisions. He almost joins Karl-Heinz in stealing passports, but also considers the consequences for the victim of the theft. When the crime is reported, he does not betray Karl-Heinz to the police. His strong sense of justice causes him to threaten Karl-Heinz when the latter shows no intention of paying the one West mark he owes Kohle. He sums up his independence and self-reliance when he tells the *Volkspolizist*: 'I don't ask anyone for help, and I'm not going to help anyone either. Everybody learns best by his own experiences'. He insists on his individuality and resists any attempt to be controlled or just guided by the FDJ, the police or any other state organisation. When Karl-Heinz suggests that both of them should go to West Berlin, he simply tells him he has no intention of leaving because his brother lives in East Berlin, and that is also where he works.

Kohle is a further development of Max in *Alarm im Zirkus*. Naïve and trusting, he is played by the same actor who in real life grew up in circumstances similar to those of his environment in *Berlin – Ecke Schönhauser*.[13] The film gives a number of reasons for his insecurity and lack of confidence. Extremely weak at school, he is classified as stupid and has no chance of finding an apprenticeship. He grows up on his own because both his mother and sister go out to work. Though they love and try to protect him, they are unable to stop his mother's partner from beating him up. Kohle's only refuge are the cinema and his dreams in which he takes the kind of revenge against his 'stepfather' he has seen in hundreds of films in West Berlin.

Karl-Heinz represents the negative influences coming from the West and is the most stereotyped of the four characters. Nevertheless, his attitude and behaviour are not just the result of him being tempted or corrupted by Western luxuries. The film traces them to his parents' lack of principles and to the contradictions between what they say and what they do. On the one hand they have allowed their son to abandon school because they want to move to the West, on the other, they are not prepared to give up their houses in East Berlin despite their belief in the superiority of capitalism over socialism. Karl-Heinz's father is convinced that eventually the West will win – 'Psychologically the West has the edge' – and he anticipates the collapse of socialism: 'This entire system will collapse. Germany is not Asia.' As Karl-Heinz also conducts monetary transactions for them through their secret savings account in West Berlin, it does not surprise anyone that he lacks principles and loyalty, and tells his mother he has no friends.

Though minor aspects – such as the weak characterisation of the partner of Angela's mother – were criticised, the reaction of the press was, on the whole, enthusiastic. Critics pointed out that this was a film for young people as well as adults, they rated it one of the best DEFA productions of recent years,[14] and recommended schools and youth organisations to organise group visits.[15] When the film was revived twenty years later the critic of *Sonntag* recalled her response when she saw the film for the first time:

> *Berlin – Ecke Schönhauser* was my kind of movie. At sixteen I wore tight, black, three-quarter length trousers, danced rock'n'roll wherever there was a notice 'No dancing apart'... Then, in 1957, I saw the new DEFA film *Berlin – Ecke Schönhauser* which freaked me out, even though the leading man was not my type ... I had the feeling someone understood me. This was the world I lived in, and I cried when, in the transit camp, Kohle died from a mixture of tobacco leaves and tea.[16]

There was even approval from the other side of the Iron Curtain: West German matinee idol Dieter Borsche wholeheartedly endorsed *Berlin – Ecke Schönhauser*,[17] West Berlin's radio station RIAS (Radio in the American Sector) broadcasted a scene from it, and Anna Teut of the daily *Die Welt* (at that time not yet the mouthpiece of Axel Springer's personal politics) wrote that the film – despite indications to the contrary – displayed a critical stance towards the SED regime and should be released in the West.[18]

Some East German officials clearly agreed with Teut's observation. Indeed, Klein and Kohlhaase had had enormous problems getting the project accepted in the first place and progress on it was hindered throughout production. A comparison of the finished product with earlier versions of the script reveals that even during pre-production not everything was plain sailing. The film no longer contains a pedantic, doctrinaire FDJ secretary whose approach to Dieter is revealed as misguided. In the earlier versions of the script, Dieter is asked to join the East German army – the *Volksarmee* – but refuses. In the final version, Dieter refuses to join not the *Volksarmee* but the FDJ, thereby facilitating the removal of a number of Dieter's – at the time – highly provocative remarks, such as: 'I cannot stand uniforms' or 'As for me, I'm never going to touch a gun. And over the border there are also Germans who are never going take part in a war again.' In January 1956, the law regulating the establishment of the *Volksarmee* had been passed, and such anti-military sentiments did not suit the prevailing political climate, any more than Dieter's more general remark: 'I am also against capitalists ... But I don't like everything here either.' [19]

A hint of the trouble which lay ahead despite the film's popularity is found once more in a review by Horst Knietzsch. Alluding to the film's original title 'Where we are not ...' he advises Klein and Kohlhaase that:

> It would be a logical extension of the films created by this collective if their next one concentrated on those areas 'where we are'. To create such a film in an artistic way would be commendable not only for the development of cinema art in our country, but also for the advance of Wolfgang Kohlhaase, Gerhard Klein and Wolf Göthe to a higher level of creativity.[20]

The same criticism is voiced in a letter of 12 September 1957 to the editor of *Junge Welt* by a certain Klaus Hofstädter of Berlin which complains about 'an accumulation of negative aspects which may exist, but which in this concentrated form render a one-sided picture of our life'. 'Why', he asks, 'is there no job for Kohle? Why does the audience laugh at the FDJ? Why does the *Volkspolizist* not insist on discipline and order? Why does the film not give more space to Dieter's colleagues on the building site?'[21] The letter was almost certainly planted. For despite *Junge Welt's* earlier recommendation to arrange group visits,[22] an influential section of the FDJ was clearly unhappy about the film's representation of the youth organisation itself.

At the Second Film Conference in July 1958, this faction was represented by Rudi Raupach from the FDJ's Central

Committee. In his speech 'The growing demands on film production by the young', he suggested that a film be made about the conflicts faced by young people who secretly joined the FDJ against their parents' wishes[23] – a kind of *Hitlerjunge Quex* from a communist perspective. Raupach also emphatically endorsed the conference's key-note address by Alexander Abusch, at that time Deputy Minister for Culture, which quashed all hopes for a more liberal film policy. The 'Berlin-Filme' – particularly *Berlin – Ecke Schönhauser* – bore the full brunt of Abusch's attack. Citing them as examples of the negative influences of Italian neorealism on the development of progressive *Gegenwartsfilme* he insisted on the prerogative of the socialist realist aesthetic.[24]

Though the attack against their films was a severe blow, Klein and Kohlhaase did not renounce their basic principles. As a writer Kohlhaase agreed to pay more attention to the main protagonist's social position and environment, and to emphasise the positive aspects of society; but he also insisted on the need to point at contradictions and difficulties as long as these did not confuse the spectator. In a speech to the 1961 Writers' Congress he unmasked socialist realism as 'a crude, sociological approach to the representation of human beings' and declared that: 'The quality of a film cannot be determined solely with reference to questions of formal aesthetics: one has to look at the film's vision, thought, engagement and creativity as a unified whole.'[25] Nonetheless, in *Berlin um die Ecke*, which he and Klein envisaged as the last in their series of 'Berlin-Filme', the criticisms of *Berlin – Ecke Schönhauser* were taken on board. Klein and Kohlhaase paid close attention to the social environment in general, and the workplace in particular, and took account of the historical dimension of socialism. The film is further proof of their personal and artistic integrity as well as their desire to improve upon their previous work. The idea for it had been inspired by Kohlhaase's father, a metal worker in the factory which eventually was used for location shooting of *Berlin um die Ecke*. Their aim was to contrast the different experiences of the older generation who had been trained in the strict, authoritarian factory environment of the capitalist system with those of the younger workers who had grown up in the planned economy of a state-run industry. The central question posed by the film is: how can young people determine their place in the world?

With the Berlin Wall in place since August 1961 to restrict external influences on East Germany's internal affairs, Klein and Kohlhaase approached the project believing that the authorities would allow a greater degree of creative freedom and a more open debate about their country's domestic problems than before. In an interview given in October 1965 Kohlhaase states: 'My interest in the new film focuses particularly ... on the development in Berlin after 1961, on the increased stability of our social position and the new contradictions which have come about with these developments. ... [The film] aims to capture a specific moment in history and to verify it through the everyday lives of ordinary people.' [26] *Berlin um die Ecke* had two working titles: 'Berlin – Kapitel IV' ('Berlin – Part IV') and 'Berlin und um die Ecke' ('Berlin and around the Corner'). Its production dragged on over eight months because of poor weather conditions and illness. [27] Work was stopped during post-production when it fell victim to the Eleventh Plenum in 1965. It was confined to the storage vaults of the so-called 'forbidden films' until 1987 when a rough cut was shown without any publicity in East Berlin. It survives in an unfinished version, deliberately reconstructed as a fragment by Wolfgang Kohlhaase after the fall of the Wall for the Fortieth Berlin Film Festival in 1990 – long after Gerhard Klein's death.

Metal worker Olaf is the leader of the youth team in a factory in the Berlin district of Schöneweide. Because their wages are lower than than those of other workers doing the same job he records false, higher production figures. The discovery of the fraud leads to controversies with the other workers, and the youth team is dissolved. All its members resign in protest, except Olaf and his friend Horst who take their revenge by exceeding their quotas by up to three hundred percent, revealing the poor productivity of the others. Matters come to a head during an official workers' meeting when Olaf and Horst reject a medal awarded for their achievements. Their main opponent is Hütte, a radical party activist and editor of the factory's newsletter. Accused of having written the words 'We are all slaves' on a washroom wall, Horst denies the charge. Hütte's insistence that Horst did it leads to a physical attack on the old man by Olaf. When Horst privately admits to Olaf that he was responsible after all, their friendship comes to an end. Olaf realises that Hütte is a lonely man, full of idealism. His understanding of the older generation is further advanced through his friendship with the old worker Paul, whose frustrations over the disappearance of traditional work ethics and standards contribute to his death from a heart attack. At the same time, Olaf is in love with Karin, who is studying French and is in the process of divorcing her husband. To assert her independence, she works as a kitchen help, sings in youth clubs, and tries to gain acting experience as an extra in the hope of a future career in film. A large cast representing a cross-section of society supplements these characters. Though completed, many of their scenes regrettably have been cut from the reconstructed film reducing the panoramic character of the original script.

Once again, the point of departure, as in the previous films, is the friendship between two young men, into which a female character is introduced. In *Berlin um die Ecke* they are slightly older – about twenty, and on the verge of becoming adults. At the beginning Olaf and Horst are young trouble-makers who collect a sofa from a woman and dump it on the roof of their modern apartment block, to pocket the five marks she has given them for its proper disposal. The thoughtless prank leads to complaints, arguments, and a confrontation between parents and their younger children who have explored their sexual differences on the sofa. By the end of the film, Olaf has become an adult who accepts his responsibility in society and carries on the tradition of the conscious and efficient worker Paul. Following the old man's heart attack he switches off all the machines the others have left running. He then returns to his own machine, continues working, and, at Hütte's request, writes Paul's obituary for the factory's newsletter.

Unlike Dieter, Kohle and Angela in *Berlin – Ecke Schönhauser*, whose behaviour and attitudes are rooted in their private lives and family backgrounds, the development of Olaf, Horst and Karin in *Berlin um die Ecke* is located in a much wider social context. There are only two very brief scenes showing them with a parent: Olaf's mother simply worries about whether a modern language student is an appropriate partner for her working-class son, and Horst's mother is angry with her son because of his absenteeism from work. Having lived briefly in the West and praising Western life, Horst seems to be another Karl-Heinz, another youth led astray by the trappings of capitalism. But unlike Karl-Heinz's parents with their capitalist background and convictions, Horst's father (whom we never actually see) is a teacher at a technical college and a committed SED party activist who always insisted on his son being top of the class. Horst's disillusionment with the GDR is explained partly through his inability to live up to these expectations, and partly through what he perceives as unfair treatment at work. The total breakdown of the relationship between father and son has a parallel in the collapse of Karin's marriage.

Klein and Kohlhaase demonstrate a deep respect for the old generation of workers represented by Paul and Hütte with their idealism, integrity, and pride in their work; but they do not take sides in their presentation of the different factions and age groups. In contrast to the other 'Berlin-Filme' in which teenagers and their personal relationships dominate, *Berlin um die Ecke* devotes roughly equal space to the representation of young and old, of private life and the working environment – and shows how they are related. The young, skilled workers protest about their lower pay and are not prepared to consider the vast experience of their unskilled colleagues who have helped to found the factory before the war. While it is said that their own work is unreliable, Olaf and his friends complain to a policeman about motor mechanics who charge the earth without offering quality in return. The middle-aged generation which makes up the majority of the factory's workforce is angry about the unruly behaviour of the unreliable young, but forget their own low production figures brought about by their adherence to inefficient work patterns. The film castigates the inability of most individuals to look beyond their limited personal interests. An apprentice who goes to fetch Horst from home by taxi and justifiably complains about an unnecessary detour is told by the driver that this is the route he has taken all his life. In an earlier version of the script Karin has everything a young GDR citizen could dream of – fashionable dresses, a flat complete with all modern conveniences, a husband who claims to love and revere her. But she moves out and into an empty room with make-shift furniture because she wants to get away from a man who takes her by the hand and negotiates all the obstacles in life for her. It is a question of striking a balance between personal freedom and security. Paul's grandfather had saved what little he could to give his grandson a better future only to lose it through inflation. Paul's generation fought for better working conditions and a brighter future, only to discover that subsequent generations take their achievements for granted. Hütte's radicalism comes from his fear that the achievements of socialism might be lost again. But his intransigence is also the reason for Olaf's frustrations:

> Why doesn't anybody believe us? We are no different from others. We do our work. Admittedly, sometimes willingly, sometimes unwillingly. But I also think things over. What do I have to do if we build socialism; what can I ask for in return? I may talk a load of rubbish, as people do on occasion. But I can see what's happening around me. It's just that occasionally I realise that I am not quite as happy as I should be according to my newspaper.

At the root of the problem lies the lack of understanding between different groups of interest, the inability or unwillingness to take the needs of others into consideration, and the reluctance to listen and discuss issues of common concern.

Unlike in the West, GDR politicians paid close attention to what their country's artists were saying and writing, but – as the fate of *Berlin um die Ecke* demonstrates – they were not prepared to tackle criticism. In an earlier version of the script, Olaf justifies his forgery of the job report forms with the words: 'The state cheats us, too.' [28] This statement is not found in the final cut. Instead of addressing the charge the party hierarchy simply swept it under the carpet and, together with other critical films, banned *Berlin um die Ecke*. In the long run, this tactic led to the downfall of the East German regime and ultimately discredited and betrayed the ideals of the kind of socialism advocated by the rebel-characters in the 'Berlin-Filme' and their rebel-creators Gerhard Klein and Wolfgang Kohlhaase.

Notes

Author's note: Unpublished, earlier versions of the scripts of the 'Berlin-Filme' were consulted in the Library of the Hochschule für Film und Fernsehen 'Konrad Wolf' in Potsdam-Babelsberg. Special thanks are due to the Hochschule's library staff, Renate Göthe, Hannelore Grusser, and Lydia Wiehring von Wendrin, as well as to Peter Franzke of the Mediathek of the University of Oldenburg.

1. See Progress Film-Vertrieb, *Der Filmagitator – Alarm im Zirkus*, Berlin (Reprint 1987), p. 10.
2. Contained in the dossier to 'Alarm im Zirkus', Bundesarchiv, Berlin.
3. 'Interview with Wolfgang Kohlhaase' in *Werkstatterfahrungen mit Gerhard Klein – Gespräche*, ed. Hannes Schmidt (= *Aus Theorie und Praxis des Films*; 1984, no. 2), 6–44 (17).
4. Schmidt, *Werkstatterfahrungen*, 26.
5. Reader's letter in *BZ am Abend*, 6 June 1956
6. In the words of Wolfgang Kohlhaase: 'The feeling that we tried to get across in our films – that they were statements about those times generally – was something we put a great deal of thought into; the specific moment itself was unimportant.' See Angelika Mihan, 'Interview mit Wolfgang Kohlhaase' in *Stiluntersuchung der Berlin-Filme* (Diplomarbeit, Hochschule für Film und Fernsehen der Deutschen Demokratischen Republik, 1978), p. 58.
7. 'The critique of living conditions on the "other side" – a critique which is quite justified and which shatters any illusions one may have entertained – is dealt with in the film adequately; but Uschi's super-ficial attitude to the more down-to-earth and less glamorous way of life "here" is not really countered. The stark contrast between the impact of the new way of life here and the superficial appeal of goings-on played out in front of the 'shop-window of the West' is only hinted at.' See *BZ am Abend*, 23 May 1956.
8. *Neues Deutschland*, 20 May 1956
9. 'I thought she was really great; she was so true to life and we hope to see her again soon.
   In my view, DEFA took this love-story straight from everyday life in Berlin. When Uschi and Hans finally come together and he takes her in his arms at the fairground and kisses her tenderly and the group of young people watching cough and shout "Hey – the half-time whistle's gone", you just feel that's the way young people in Berlin really are.' See *Junge Welt*, 14 June 1956.
10. See Pike, 'Strammsitzendes', *Junge Welt*, 16 June 1956.
11. *Berliner Zeitung*, 20 May 1956.
12. Bärbel Dalichow, 'Heimat-Filme der DEFA?', *Film und Fernsehen* 20, no. 6, 1992: 55-61 (57).
13. Sigrid Smolka, 'Ran an's heiße Eisen', *Wochenpost*, 7 December 1957.
14. *Sonntag*, 8 September 1957.
15. *Neuer Tag* (Frankfurt an der Oder), 30 August 1957.
16. *Sonntag*, 15 October 1978.
17. *Junge Welt*, 13 September 1957.
18. *Die Welt*, 7 September 1957.
19. Wolfgang Kohlhaase, 'Wo wir nicht sind …', unpublished script, pp. 44–5.
20. *Neues Deutschland*, 3 September 1957.

21. *Junge Welt*, 12 September 1957.
22. *Junge Welt*, 26 July 1957.
23. Rudi Raupach, 'Wachsende Anforderungen der Jugend an die Film-produktion', *Deutsche Filmkunst* 6, no. 11, 1958: 350–51 (351).
24. Alexander Abusch, 'Aktuelle Probleme und Aufgaben unserer sozialistischen Filmkunst', *Deutsche Filmkunst* 6, no. 9, 1958: 261–70.
25. Wolfgang Kohlhaase, 'Filmqualifizierte Schriftsteller – nicht nur Stofflieferanten', *Deutsche Filmkunst* 9, no. 8, 1961: 273.
26. 'Menschen, die dir schon irgendwo begegnet sind': Interview with Wolfgang Kohlhaase, *Berliner Zeitung*, 17 October 1965.
27. Hannes Schmidt, 'Interview mit Wolfgang Kohlhaase', *20. Internationales Forum des jungen Films Berlin 1990–40. Internationale Film-festspiele* Berlin 1990, no. 18.
28. Wolfgang Kohlhaase, *Berlin und um die Ecke*, unpublished script, p. 31.

❖ *Chapter 7* ❖

DEFA: A PERSONAL VIEW

Wolfgang Kohlhaase

The following is an edited transcript of a verbal address originally made in German at the conference on East German Cinema held in March 1996 at the Centre for East German Studies, The University of Reading. At the end of his address, Wolfgang Kohlhaase responded to questions from the audience.

DEFA made about 600 films during the forty years of its existence. Which ones will survive? The better ones, of course. One day these films will also be used as a source of information to help people understand what the GDR was: whether it was an epoch, a footnote in history or just a misunderstanding. In this conference we have been talking mainly about the political or philosophical context in which these films were made. But these films also show us other things: hair-styles, skirt-lengths, the girls people thought were beautiful in any given year. Everyday life is preserved in films and this is what gives the medium a different kind of significance.

DEFA films were made by three, perhaps four generations of directors. Here I can only speak for myself, or for the people I worked with, that is, from the perspective of my generation. How people reacted to the GDR, how they responded to its achievements and its failures varied enormously depending on how old they were when they began to confront the political world. So let me start by saying a few words about myself, without telling you my whole life-story.

I was fourteen years old when the Russians came. I can remember the day when they reached the Berlin suburb where I lived, it was the 24 April. It was quiet, you could hear the sound of gun-fire far off, and the twittering of the birds. At the end of the street you could see columns of Russian soldiers moving into the city; you didn't know whether or not to go and have a closer look. It suddenly dawned on me – at any rate that's how it seemed to me later – that I was one day older than the Thousand-Year Reich, I had survived it. And although we had no idea of what was going to happen, by the third day we had grasped one thing at least: this wasn't an end, it was a beginning. This was an amazing discovery, for the Nazis had declared that our demise would mean the end of the world. After us there would be nothing, only oblivion.

I had never believed this, perhaps for purely biological reasons; I was just fourteen and couldn't accept that everything would stop here. But of course I couldn't produce any intellectual arguments to refute this claim, and so it was a liberation in the truest sense of the word to discover that the Nazis had been lying. Here something was beginning. The sense of life that is born in such moments lasts a long time. It is a matter of luck, of course, when puberty and world history happen to coincide, as they did here. This feeling endured and became a part of my hopes – and the disappointments – that were to come; my reactions to everything were different from what they would have been if I had been ten years younger or ten years older.

How did I come to be a writer? I was soon back at school again; my main recollections are of black-marketeering during break, of noise and confusion, classes with eighty pupils, constantly changing teachers, in short, a place of enjoyment. We didn't learn much, but then we didn't intend to. One day it happened. A boy who sat behind me in class had written a thriller. I was astonished to realise that it was possible not only to read thrillers but also to write them. That same afternoon I sat down and began writing a thriller of my own.

It was set in London, in the fog. By the time I had reached page forty there were two houses that had burned down, eight dead bodies and no plot. I hadn't thought about what was going to happen, I had simply sat down and begun to write. So I abandoned that project and turned my attention to something that seemed to me more worthwhile. I wrote about my experiences of the end of the war. Again when I had reached page forty – obviously a highly significant number for me – I found that I had got to the end of my experiences and was confronted by the question: can one write about something that one hasn't actually experienced at first hand, or is that lying? I had been writing in the first person, after all. Finally I came to the conclusion that it probably was lying, not because I was such a high-minded fellow, but because I thought someone might read it and then point out that it wasn't true, that I had made the whole thing up. I felt so ashamed at the very idea that I stopped at page forty. There was no one I could turn to for advice. And so it came about that at a very early stage in my life I was faced with the problem of reality and truth.

Now that my interest in writing had been aroused I turned to the newspapers. With no previous training I wrote various articles, including film reviews. I went to see lots of films. Above all I wanted to write, and I thought that perhaps I could be a film writer. For me the real inspiration was neorealism which produced stories about the real world, the world I knew. Up until then I had seen the cinema as something exotic, about other people, not my world, in costume, as it were. I had enjoyed watching films but had never thought that I could have something to do with making them.

Then there was another factor: those first years after the war were bright years for me, for they were accompanied by a vast expansion of our awareness. The war, which until then had been something dark and incomprehensible that had led to catastrophe, became something we could grasp. Suddenly it was possible to discuss it, there were angles from which we could approach it, there were explanations. We were no longer blind. People began to write literature. The German émigrés returned. I had the immodest feeling that everything was happening on my account, all I had to do was take what was offered.

It was a time when doors opened. A whole generation was missing, the generation of the soldiers. The soldiers were either dead or prisoners, or they were brain dead. Whole areas opened up to us. If you tell that to people who are even only five years younger, they can hardly believe it. All you had to do was knock and ask whether there was anything to do. There was always something that needed doing. So at the age of sixteen I became a journalist and at twenty-three I made my first film.

It was wonderful. This state of affairs induced in us a feeling of responsibility for the future. We believed that all sorts of things had to be changed, why not the world? All that was needed was the will to do it. Later, as our horizons broadened and we started to look at things from a Marxist standpoint, we began to notice that a certain narrowing of vision was taking place. Marxism was often being interpreted in a rigid and dogmatic way. It was supposed to explain everything, but it could not. However, this realisation only came later, not right at the beginning.

By then we had made our first films and had acquired a certain degree of self-confidence. We didn't feel we had to accept every criticism, particularly when a film was going down well with the public. And we had allies – some of whom were politicians. It would be a distortion of the truth to suggest that it was always the politicians who were responsible for over-simplifying things and that it was the artists who had the monopoly when it came to sensitivity and seeing the world in a multitude of different ways. There were some of each in both camps. There were politicians who loved art and who had no wish to subject it to crude demands. And amongst my fellow film-makers there were those who were quite happy to resort to clichés.

However, the cultural policy of the GDR was governed by a rather limited, narrow understanding of the nature of art. Many of those in political office had spent more time in prison than in libraries. Their concept of literature was often purely didactic and, in Germany, there had been a long tradition of this. In the 1930s, Upton Sinclair was a much-read author in the German workers' movement. Gorky's most popular work was *The Mother*, a work that took you straight into politics. This attitude is understandable but it leads to a narrow view of literature and of art in general. For example, in 1938, when Hitler's shadow had long since fallen across Europe, a bitter argument broke out amongst German émigrés concerning Expressionism. The debate started in the periodical *Das Wort* which was published in Moscow and you can follow the argument there. Lukács was involved as were Bertolt Brecht, Anna Seghers and many others. Expressionism was to be rejected because it represented an artistic position that was alien to real life and that was of no direct use in the political struggle. Brecht, who was not an Expressionist, was not alone when he put forward the view that it was more important to be united in the struggle against Hitler. One can understand people arguing about Expressionism, but it must be obvious to anyone that 1938 was not the ideal time in which to debate the matter through an exchange of letters in a periodical.

I mention this example just to show that certain misunderstandings, which had a long history behind them, were carried further in the GDR. However, Brecht, Seghers, Arnold Zweig, Heartfield, Eisler, Dessau, to mention but a few, also lived there. Because of these writers, who believed in socialism, we were not forced to adopt uncritically a theory which called itself 'socialist realism'. Many books have been written about this magic formula but I have only really encountered people who have tried to explain what it does not mean. They wanted to rescue a concept that had been conceived in Moscow in 1934 and which had immediately been taken over by the wrong people. For them it meant basically a kind of idyllic naturalism: true to life but more beautiful. Once the manager of a GDR enterprise was asked how he would like art to be, and he answered, quite correctly, full of conflicts, but enjoyable.

Views of this kind were not enough when, as a government, you are in charge of running the arts. Soon artistic debates were taking place but they all had a hidden political agenda. In the 1950s it was the so-called formalism debate, the offspring of a similar debate in Moscow. This affected not only people of my age, but also artists who had returned from exile abroad. They had to go through it all over again. Brecht's didactic plays, written in the 1930s, were now regarded as modernist. Now only the classics were accepted as suitable models. Nevertheless, despite all these arguments, we never lost sight of the belief that art, in all its multitude of different forms, should help us to understand the world. Nobody thought that after the end of the Nazi era there was nothing new to be learned.

Despite huge differences of opinions, there was, for many years, a kind of solidarity between art and politics. This applied to the film industry as well. So the damage that was done in the middle of the 1960s was all the greater when a rigid division of labour was introduced: there were those who made films, and there were those who banned them. Many things were destroyed at that time, including a common belief in the social relevance of our work. Film-making became a more solitary occupation. The history of the cinema shows us how productive it usually was when similarly motivated people were making films at the same time and reacting to each other's work. It was good for the cinema, the *Zeitgeist* was being explored. Film-making is a sociable affair, and the cinema is a place for communication, not for meditation.

DEFA was run on a budget. Every year it was allocated a certain sum, perhaps fifty million marks, and was expected in return to produce between fifteen and twenty films. The money would come the following year, even if the films had not proved to be successful in economic terms, that is, if they had not recouped the money spent on them. It was like the way an opera house is financed. So the film-makers had a degree of security. If a director was not successful, there was nothing to stop him carrying on making films, unless he had proved to be a complete dilettante.

You enjoyed a certain degree of security when you had a contract. Provided you didn't steal the silver, once you were employed, you were always given another chance. This caused some injustice. As hardly anyone was ever sacked, there was little room for new and young people. There were about thirty full-time directors and a production of about twenty films a year. They all got their money, though sometimes they weren't too happy about it. They wanted to work, not to be bribed. In the case of some of them we were glad when they just took the money, and didn't make a film. Looked at in hindsight this does seem rather strange.

The studio had a thematic agenda, with particular aims and projects for which certain writers and directors were needed. For instance it was decided that a film should be made about developments in agriculture or about the growing self-confidence of women at work. Material was collected, and *Dramaturgen* ('script editors') travelled around making recon-naissance trips. But in the end they usually made the film that the film people wanted, using the angle that fitted in with the studio's plan. So a film like *Alarm im Zirkus* (*Circus Alarm,* 1953) was supposed to be a film about how our young people's polit-ical ideas were shaped in the divided city of Berlin. And somehow that's how it turned out.

The importance given to work on the screenplay encouraged a certain division of labour in the artistic work. The type of film-maker which is so fashionable today, who does everything himself, was a rarity in those days. I'm still in favour of a certain division of labour, even today. There are only a few people who can do one thing well and even fewer who can do two. To write a book, to direct a film, perhaps even to drum up the finances for it, that is a lot to expect of one person. It takes time, it puts a massive pressure on him to succeed. If things go wrong, the greater the catastrophe is for him. When success, and failure, too, is shared, it creates a better atmosphere in both work and life. I was lucky with my partners: five films with Gerhard Klein, four with Konrad Wolf and things worked well with the others too. Billy Wilder once said that the problem between authors and directors was not that the directors couldn't write, but that they couldn't read. Mine could. In the long run you can only work successfully with people when everybody feels happy, not only yourself.

We had a saying: when there is a shortage of potatoes, there are sure to be some major discussions about art. The banning of ten films in 1965 was intended to impose some discipline on society when the country was going through a difficult time, politically and economically. The politicians used art as a medium for expressing concerns they did not dare to tackle directly. This had the effect of bestowing a greater importance on art. The lack of public discussion which increased over the years led the public to seek questions and answers in films and books or in the theatre. How otherwise are we to explain why the film *SOLO SUNNY* was a topic of conversation for many months? For the film wasn't just about how to survive as a singer when your singing isn't much good, it was about the individual and society, about the importance of having a dream, and it was about what Wolf called the creeping brutality of life. Without taking ourselves too seriously we did neverthe-less have the feeling of having done something useful, as well as achieving success at the box office. We had ambitions for society, romantic ones perhaps. Volker Braun came up with the phrase 'Haftung durch Reibung' – a phrase that means some-thing like 'people who rub each other up the wrong way stick together all the more'. Well we rubbed quite a few people up the wrong way. It was not comfortable but it seemed to make sense. Those in power expected a lot of art, but they feared it even more. In both respects they got it wrong. Our society was based on the principle of enlightenment; the search for knowl-edge was not forbidden and an understanding of history was encouraged. At the same time constraints were put on our thinking. In some areas people were supposed to think, in others they were expected merely to believe. This is enough to make people ill, it's enough to make an entire country ill. Thought is like light, it shines in every direction.

The politicians increasingly lost their sense of reality. By the time of the Eleventh Plenum, at which they banned, amongst

other things, virtually an entire year's film production, they
had cancelled reality. Political life suffered the worst damage. It
was not possible to destroy the cinema totally. Not because film
people are indestructible but because films arise out of actual
physical contact with real life. And real life cannot be adjusted
to be in tune with the demands of ideology. People experience
reality at first hand. In addition, there was a new generation of
people who experienced the country in a different way from
us. This also tells us something about the demise of the GDR. It
did not satisfy their needs in the way it had satisfied ours. These
young people had grown up in a state which already existed,
whereas we had the feeling that we had invented it and were
making something of it. With hindsight everything looks
inevitable. At the beginning it looked like, and was, a great
adventure.

So far the discussions at this conference have concentrated
on films in the context of contemporary history and cultural
policy. That is important, of course, but I would like add a few
words about the moral and aesthetic intentions that motivated
many of our films. It moves me when I look back at our
attempts to portray the reality of people's everyday lives. We
wanted to explore in film what occupied people for eight hours
a day and took up most of their lives: the world of work. Often
this was not what the public wanted to see. My father would
come home from the factory and say: 'When I put the television on, what do I see? Another helmet. And I've just taken
mine off.' And from his perspective he was right. No one goes
to the cinema just to see themselves. The girl next door and the
queen are both legitimate characters in films, representing the
world we are closest to and that which is furthest from us, familiarity and distance, the attainable and the dream. I would never
advocate leaving out the dream.

At home we had a photo of my grandmother in which she
looked just as she had always looked. We all loved this picture.
She had had eleven children, her health was not good, you
could see this in the photo, and you could see the destruction
life had wrought. We thought it beautiful. The one person who
did not like it was my grandmother. It showed her as she didn't
want to be. She had created a different picture of herself, a
more flattering one. She had had a hard life and she hadn't
had that many opportunities, apart from that of having a better
image of herself. What I am trying to say is that things are not

simple for the so-called ordinary people when they see films about themselves. Sometimes films showing poor pregnant girls without husbands are praised by the intellectuals: at last, they exclaim, a film showing the truth about poor pregnant unmarried girls. But the poor pregnant unmarried girls don't go to see these films, they don't need to buy a ticket to see this reality. They go to see quite different films. We should not try to compare different kinds of film-making, and their different possibilities. When we began to make these films, inspired by neorealism, we were convinced that this was the only way in which to portray the truth. Filming in the streets, close-ups, raw material, professional actors working together with amateurs. A little older and wiser, having worked longer in the profession, we now know that you can tell lies with a camera in the street and that, conversely, you can tell the truth filming in a studio.

We were interested in such things. And we weren't constantly at war with the authorities. There were times when we had a good laugh. Now, at a time when people tend to see things in black and white, I would like to emphasise that even with a wall around your country you could still think for yourself. Of course today you sometimes find there are other walls than the one you had experienced before. You can also have walls around your head.

Making a film is a collective affair, and you need other people's money for it. Whether it be state money, as it was then, or a mixture of private or public funding, as is now the case, you find yourself having the same discussions, only the substance of the discussion is different. You're trying to persuade someone that you want to make a beautiful film. You cite your earlier films – a real problem for someone just starting out – banking on the persuasive powers of your rhetoric. It is easier and more legitimate for money or politics to have their say in the making of a film than when it is just a work of art produced by an individual. Friends who paint pictures have all, at some time or other, settled for a frugal life and painted what they wanted, the Berliners, the people of Leipzig, the Dresden school, the German tradition.

When we talk about censorship – and a lot has been said on this subject already – I would like to add that there was also a subtle form of censorship which affected films in particular. I am referring to lack of courage. The initial idea is often pretty imprecise. You try to explain it to someone, they look at you for a long time, understanding nothing, and you go home again. How do you manage to get a project started in the case of a film which no one wants? Where there is censorship I think it is exacerbated by the process of self-censorship. When works are banned it is done in order to teach people lessons. The banning of films in 1965 did not just affect the people who made them. Everyone was affected. But people can lack courage today as well. We are not, after all, living in a totally different world. If we think about conformity I dare say we can all come up with a few examples. It wasn't just an East European invention, it is the way of the world, the pressure to conform. I have not yet found that wonderful country where, if you want to make a film, someone says: here's the money – don't tell me what you are going to do with it. If I could find it I'd go there.

Question: You have spoken about the lack of encouragement and I wonder whether the main actress in *SOLO SUNNY* represents a kind of alter ego, a *doppelgänger* for the film-maker, because Sunny herself suffers so much from this lack of encouragement, for instance when she is standing there on stage and nobody looks at her.

Kohlhaase: I didn't feel it as directly as that. A film often develops spontaneously, not theoretically. I knew a few people who lived rather in the way that Sunny did, and for years I did not have the feeling that it could be turned into a film. And then I did. I think you have a story when you are moved by someone's experiences, even if there is another dimension to it. This is what literature is about, the metaphorical element, where a story tells you more than the mere facts. *SOLO SUNNY* was also about loneliness, which you find everywhere. But what did it feel like in a society which constantly proclaimed that no one was lonely? What we were showing was the other side of the coin; we were alluding to the fact that life can be dangerous. Our material actually fitted into a cinematic pattern: the girl with a heart of gold who deserved better. We were not unhappy with this pattern – in fact it suited us quite well. Of course the film could be understood at various different levels, but the massive public response to it from the moment it went on release was something we hadn't bargained for, it really took us by surprise. I often think that cinema is a matter of luck. It was our luck to find an actress who could achieve that delicate balance between beauty and ugliness, between someone you like and someone who gets on your nerves, but it was her talent.

What interested us about the character was that she wasn't much good at making compromises, and as people in the GDR had to live with so many compromises this was what made her attractive. At that time there was a really denigrating term that was often applied to young people who wouldn't conform; they were dismissed as fringe elements. There were those who were at the centre of things, who told others that they were on the fringe. The self-righteousness of this attitude angered many people, including Wolf and myself. But we wanted to film the story because it was a bit sad and a bit funny. When one gets a story right, I think it often raises many more questions than the person who wrote it ever imagined.

Question: To what extent were you personally prepared, or even forced, to make compromises in order to reach a wider public?

Kohlhaase: We were used to trouble. Often films – which were by no means bad – were unpopular with the public because they were fed up with the way certain messages were being put across. Of course we always had the public in mind, although we often suspected that we were making a film for a minority. But we hoped to win the majority of this minority. Unlike books, films can't wait for long and they seldom come back. A film is for now and the next three weeks. Indeed, if it hasn't been successful in four days, it's finished. The distributors will withdraw it.

SOLO SUNNY worked, so did *Berlin – Ecke Schönhauser* (*Berlin – Schönhauser Corner*, 1957). I mention the titles because they are being shown at this conference. I have made my share of films which were not box-office successes. Some of them probably weren't very good, some of them were. I'm always happy to wait for the judgement of the audience out there in the darkness. If there are only six people sitting out there, you know you have done something wrong. It is no good running to the sociologists and listening to them going on about target groups and the media landscape.

Sometimes when I'm working I think of particular people, that he or she would like this. Or I imagine a neighbour and think, he'll be surprised by this, or, this will amuse him. But you have got to handle your material according to its own inherent rules. If it were easy, it wouldn't be well paid.

Question: It is often said that you and Gerhard Klein in particular were influenced by the Italian neo-realists, especially in the so-called 'Berlin films'. To what extent were you influenced by developments on the international film scene?

Kohlhaase: For us and some of our friends neo-realism was a revelation. We were fascinated by the themes and the methods, the social commentary, the way they relied on the poetry of everyday life, the sober tone which fitted well with the post-war era. We were beginners, sitting in our small rooms with our big questions, afraid of emotion, no matter where it came from. It was only later that I realised that the German cinema before Hitler had produced a few films which were similar to those of the neo-realists.

Until the Wall was built we could go to the cinema in West Berlin. After that we usually saw the most important Polish, Hungarian, Soviet and Czech films either in the cinema or at internal showings. Of a hundred films that were shown in the GDR about sixty would come from Western countries. Of course they weren't always the most important ones, from an artistic point of view. There were however so-called informational presentations in the studio or the film-makers-union, where some films were shown which were not bought.

Question: What were relations like with your West German colleagues? Did you have contact with each other and was it possible for you to see the odd film from the Federal Republic?

Kohlhaase: West German films were shown on television, ours and theirs, after the usual time lapse. Otherwise DEFA films, which were not part of mainstream cinema, were hardly shown anywhere else. They were received with some interest by our Western colleagues, at film clubs, at festivals or film weeks but they didn't reach a wide public. In the GDR more films from West Germany were shown than ours were shown in the West. Although in the 1980s West German television began showing DEFA films fairly regularly. We frequently invited colleagues from West Germany to our Academy of Arts. They enjoyed coming; we provided them with an alert, open-minded audience. It wasn't a normal situation in the sense of an ordinary, everyday working relationship, but there were a few co-productions.

Question: Could you tell us a bit more about your long period of collaboration with Gerhard Klein?

Kohlhaase: Klein had obviously been crazy about the cinema since he was a child. He always went to a cinema in Kreuzberg which was built on a corner. A narrow room in the right-hand corner of the cinema led into another narrow room. Beside the screen there was a mirror. For forty pfennigs you could see the film directly, for twenty you could see it in the mirror. That's where Klein sat.

To begin with, after he had survived the war as a soldier, he made documentary films. He was someone who directed through the camera. He sat behind the lens at least as often as the cameraman. He was a man obsessed by detail; he spent hours at the cutting desk. I came from the newspaper world and through Klein I began to realise that film is not just literature, photographed. We spent a long time discussing the following problem: a door bangs shut and the cut comes at the moment the door bangs. Or should the cut be made before it bangs? Or it bangs and we still see the door? We got quite intoxicated at the idea that with each variant we would be making a different film. And it's true. If you are not prepared to search for the right image and the exact cut with the same dedication that a writer devotes to finding the right word, then you might as well forget it. For Klein it was just as important to get the social details right. There is probably nothing in the world as difficult to reproduce as the social nuance. You can always go on learning, but one thing you can't learn is what the view from your window looked like during the first ten years of your life. Klein grew up in the streets where we made our films. So did I, but it was more important that he did, because it was he who made the pictures.

Question: Can you describe the practical side of your work once you had decided to write a screenplay?

Kohlhaase: Let's take *SOLO SUNNY*. I know that I'm not writing prose. I'm writing for the director and the cameraman, above all for the actors. I try to get in touch with the basic feel of the story, through language; it's not a synopsis. A certain sound should begin to resonate, the action has not been fully worked out yet. The next thing that we have to find and build on is the most important element, the story, what actually happens. First of all you have space and stillness, then comes movement, and only then come words, what people actually say. I usually found it helpful to think of this sequence. Once the action is clear the screenplay will virtually write itself. Writing a screenplay can be a pleasure, but it can become a torment when you realise too late that the action isn't right.

Wolf got involved as director very early on, after all, we were making our fourth film together. Then came the cameraman and then the set-designer. We looked at various possible locations, for example, backyards of tenement blocks, trying to imagine how long the sun would shine into them, for that determined how long we could film. If we knew a location already I just reproduced it for the screenplay. It was supposed to be practical. My screenplays gradually became shorter and shorter, or perhaps I should say, more laconic.

I repeat, the artistic direction is the most important factor; this goes both for the whole film and the individual scene. The actor's chances of success depend on the artistic direction. At any one moment the scene can not belong to an indefinite number of people; mostly it can only belong to one character, and at the next moment to another, and then to a third. The interaction depends on sequencing. I learned that from Klein, who knew something like that instinctively. None of us had studied. The audience loves the artistic element in production and so do the actors, because they need it.

I work on the basis that a screenplay is not in fact a form of literature at all, but actually the noting down of a story for the purpose of filming it.

(Transcribed by Birgit Röder
and translated from the German
by Margaret Vallance)

Chapter 8

REPRESENTATIONS OF WORK IN THE FORBIDDEN DEFA FILMS OF 1965

Karen Ruoff Kramer

One of those laconic GDR jokes of yesteryear, the sort one no longer hears, went like this: a man seeks the help of a psychiatrist because he has hallucinations that he's being followed; when the psychiatrist asks him to be more specific, the man explains: he went to see a DEFA film and had the distinct impression that someone was sitting in the seat behind him.

DEFA films did not tend to be box-office hits. This was not due to poor cinematography, acting or technical expertise – and it certainly was not the price of the ticket. The company itself was aware that the GDR populace generally viewed it sceptically; indeed, DEFA's poor reputation is explicitly referred to in two of the films I shall discuss here. In *Spur der Steine* (*The Trace of Stones*, 1966), Balla invites Kati to the movies: 'For a date with you', he says, 'I'd even be willing to watch a DEFA film.' Horst, the young rowdy in *Berlin um die Ecke* (*Berlin around the Corner*, 1965), disparagingly characterises a typical DEFA scenario as 'Lovers exercise self-criticism.' The shears of censorship (be they the scissors in the mind, the verdicts of boards which passed judgement on proposed scenarios and scripts, or the cutting table) and the public awareness of the ever-watchful eye of GDR censorship inhibited GDR filmmakers' attempts to engage the minds and win the hearts of the population. The dead weight of official approval rendered DEFA films, in the public mind, underwhelming by definition – just one of many self-defeating mechanisms that flourished in 'the First Workers' and Peasants' State on German soil'.

The GDR suffered from a kind of auto-immune disorder. Party doctrine posited an abstract identity of interest between the people and the State, but in fact the relationship was one of mutual mistrust, a fact driven caustically home in Brecht's bitter poem, 'Die Lösung' ('The Solution').[1] To build socialism required tapping the formative energy of the populace whose interests legitimised the project. But populaces are volatile entities, they may define their interests differently from the way their ruling élite does; under 'real socialism' this disparity led to the paradoxical condition that citizens of the GDR were, from the standpoint of the leadership, both the alpha and omega of the socialist project and the potential enemy within. The massive allocation of national resources to surveillance would indicate that the latter perception weighed more heavily than the sundry tautological truisms on the identity of interest between the State and a populace whose creative energies it could not simultaneously unleash and control: in *Denk bloß nicht, ich heule* (*Just Don't Think I'm Crying*, 1965) we are told 'the enemy lies not before us, but within us'. In the case of artists and intellectuals this proved a severe double-bind, their very métier being that unstable quantity, consciousness. They were granted a certain artistic space, but were constrained by relatively short tethers.

In the brief thaw which ensued in the early sixties between the Twentieth Party Congress in the Soviet Union and the beginning of the Brezhnev era, DEFA artists detected a window of critical opportunity, and opened it. The window had the precise dimensions of the aspect ratio. It was not a window to the West; with the erection of the Berlin Wall, that window had been replaced by the window to the West's self-illusions, the TV screen (*via* illicit antennae). Ironically, it was – in the view of most of the film-makers whose works will be discussed here – precisely the walling off of the West which set the precondition for the opening of a new window, a window one did not look out of, but *into*. It was a window between rooms of the domestic space of the GDR, between official spaces and real ones – an artistic atrium. In this brief, aborted attempt at internal transparency, DEFA artists hoped to make good on promises that the 'securing' of the state boundary between East and West would create the preconditions for a freer, more candid discourse within. When interviewed upon the release of their films in 1989 and 1990, many of the makers of the forbidden films of the mid-sixties cited the building of the Wall as the signal that they would now, finally, enjoy a protected discursive space in which critical works of art would no longer be lambasted for playing into the hands of the West.[2]

The great majority of DEFA films produced in 1965 were shot through this window: *Das Kaninchen bin ich* (*I am the Rabbit*), directed by Kurt Maetzig; *Spur der Steine,* by Frank Beyer; *Denk bloß nicht, ich heule,* by Frank Vogel; *Berlin um die Ecke* by Gerhard Klein; *Der Frühling braucht Zeit* (*Spring Takes Its Time*) by Günter Stahnke; *Karla* (*Carla*), by Herrmann Zschoche; *Jahrgang 45* (*Born in 1945*), by Jürgen Böttcher; and *Wenn Du groß bist, lieber Adam* (*When You're Grown Up, Dear Adam*) by Egon Günther. But before these films could be completed and released, the window slammed shut; those few which had been released were recalled, others were never completed. A few of the films were screened decades later, in the last days of the GDR, but the full corpus was not premièred until the Berlin Film Festival in February 1990. This belated première was, for many of those involved in the films' production, the first time they had seen the finished (or reconstructed) product. After the films were confiscated in 1965-6, rumour had it that they had been sent to the 'comb-factory', i.e., recycled as plastic in a perverse (and rare) act of ecological stewardship. It is one of the mercies of history that they were, instead, locked in the basement of the Politbüro, where they were retrieved, and, to the extent possible, reconstructed, the moment the SED lost control.

Had these films enjoyed a wide public screening in the period in which they were produced, things would have turned out differently. Not that the GDR would have survived, as some have suggested;[3] the contradictions in which the 'first workers' and farmers' state on German soil' was mired were too fundamental to be resolved by increased artistic freedom or by subjecting the society to a protracted debate about its problems. It is true that a vicious circle plagued development in the GDR: pervasive paranoia in the political leadership inhibited the development of a consensual national consciousness whose lack fuelled the paranoia. But the primary stalemate lay in the structure of the economy; the distribution of the forbidden DEFA films would by no means have eradicated the fundamental problems of real socialism in the GDR. But the history of the DEFA itself – its popularity and effectiveness within GDR society, its artistic position in international cinema – would most definitely have been written very differently, had these films been distributed. Their banning and the constraints placed upon their makers sent out a shrill warning. As Frank Beyer put it, some good DEFA films were produced in the following years, but they were never again 'openly political and embedded in the panorama of the times'.[4]

The Problem of Retarded Reception

Having been released twenty-five years late, these films are, like Kurt Vonnegut's anti-hero Billy Pilgrim, 'unstuck in time'; unification has rendered them also unstuck in space. The society in and for which they were produced lingers on in the form of fading memories and as the object of sundry mopping-up operations of the new Federal Republic. The challenge to contemporary analysts, looking at these films six years after the society from and for which they were created was swept into the dustbin of history, is not only to decide in what contexts and from what perspectives they can most productively be viewed, but indeed what 'productively' can mean in the post-communist context.

One can, and one should, underscore the courage of their makers; I hereby do so. That done, what remains? There are many conceivable approaches to the material. One can approach these films as documents of political history, for example; the politics of the Eleventh Plenary Session of the Central Committee, the forum which banned the films, were symptomatic of a deep systemic crisis. Indeed, the Plenary Session had originally been convened to discuss the disastrous results of the New Economic System; the head of the state planning committee had committed suicide after the statistics came in, and the mood was very tense. The film tribunal stood proxy for a serious confrontation with non-resolvable problems of the socialist economy.

The films can be examined in the context of cinematic history; one can analyse their technical qualities, their generic affinities, and trace influences in the context of international film-making trends of the period. Nothing really speaks against this approach except that little really speaks for it beyond filling in some of the blanks in film history. Most of these films are technically interesting in their own right, but their significance lies elsewhere, namely in the subtle and not-so-subtle ways in which they sought to intervene in the public sphere they were attempting to create.

These films dare the viewer to probe the nature and status of their representations, a challenge for which we – as late, after-the-fact viewers – lack essential instruments. They pose a considerable challenge. Do their critical representations *reflect* real social interchanges and expressed concerns of their time and society, or are they *proposing* that such interchanges take place and that such concerns find expression? In attempting to answer such questions, the analyst is doubly impeded, by too little memory and too much – the lack of a contemporary reception record (except for the death-knell sounded by the Party), on the one hand, and the extra baggage our minds schlep forward, laden with differences of history and interest on a united German terrain where something is always at stake.

There is yet another inhibitor. Is it possible fully to resist an intrusive fascination with the very forbiddenness of these films, to cut through the hubris of their 'Dissidentenbonus' – the status they acquire precisely by virtue of having been banned – to avoid positioning oneself as a somewhat patronising judge, bestowing late laurels to compensate for the films' erstwhile underacknowledgment? Only by bracketing out those Cold War games can one become cognisant of their real achievements. It is significant that these films did not make it through the critical gauntlet of their times; that tells us something about differences between the gauntlet and those running through it. But with respect to the films as texts, an informed preknowledge of the tense context of their production can distort and constrain the viewing act rather than enrich it.

It is more significant that the films were produced than that they were forbidden. I have attempted to bracket out, to the extent possible, their highly charged historical environment in the hope of becoming more receptive to their internal coding, have attempted to resist the temptation to confirm educated hunches about socialism-as-was. To return to my original metaphor: I have first tried to wash the window as best I could, then sought to detect through that cleaner window elements which, in the differently conflicted context of united Germany, have demonstrated longer-term relevance, resonating in those paradigms of memory and recollection which those Germans from the former western *Länder* tend – incorrectly – to dismiss as 'Ostalgia.' Although few East Germans dispute the fact that they gained much in 1989-90, they have also experienced losses and do not hesitate to say so. Recurrently, the sense of loss and disappointment concern the problematics of work (i.e., its absence), women (i.e., their disempowerment), and the West (as an 'unheimliche Heimat', an 'uncanny homeland'). Whereas films are representations, not the stuff of life, the contribution of these DEFA films to what Joshua Feinstein called the 'civic imaginary' of the erstwhile GDR is likely, as memory fades, to increase.[5] Filmic images, more durable than the memories of mortals, will replace and transform the traces of real experience, playing a formative role in what real socialism *will have been.* I would posit (in a gesture which provides at least an organising principle for interpretation, whether or not history bears me out) that these films are likely to influence collective memory most strongly at the pressure points which have built since unification – namely the triptych of work, women and the West. And it is to an analysis of the representations of work in the critical DEFA films of 1965 that I shall confine the rest of my argument.

The Future of the Past

The future GDR, as retroactively elicited by these films, will be black-and-white. The choice of film stock may have been economically motivated in part (colour stock was expensive and hard to come by in the GDR), but black-and-white was also an apt medium for the stark contradictions and confrontations which characterise these films. Only one of the films under discussion – *Wenn du groß bist, lieber Adam* – was in colour. This film, the only comedy in the corpus, is inferior to – and has little in common with – the other films, and is worthy of mention here only because Manfred Krug, in the role of a Lutheran Priest, wears what – after his role as Balla in *Spur der Steine* – seems suspiciously close to being a cowboy hat. Granted: it is in actuality a clerical hat. And Balla's hat in *Spur der Steine* is in reality the traditional, broad-rimmed carpenter's hat. And Olaf's hat in *Berlin um die Ecke*, if it is a cowboy hat, is rolled up so tightly at the brim on both sides that Roy Rogers would not have touched it with a ten-foot pole. Be that as it may, affinities with the genre of the Western are unmistakable in the latter two films. Indeed, in *Spur der Steine* – in which the hat-bearers are rebellious heroes, honcho macho men – the genre reference is not only unmistakable, it is explicit; a party functionary refers to Brigadier Balla disparagingly as 'the Texas King'.[6] Fists play a role, as do brawn and physical domination. The similarities to the cowboy genre are most interesting because they draw our attention to the differences, thematized in the films. Cowboy films are not about the work of riding the range, but its mythic freedom; Westerns are paradigmatically Western. *Spur der Steine* and *Berlin um die Ecke* are 'Easterns', indeed consciously so. The construction sites and industrial plants in socialism-as-was were constricted, denaturalised environments diametrically opposed to Marlboro country. Although the association with the American cowboy genre undoubtedly lent the heroes a certain charisma in these films, the thrust of this comparison was not to expose the socialist workplace as lacking in romance and excitement, but rather to invest it with a populist manliness.

Spur der Steine and *Berlin um die Ecke* provide interesting takes on associations in the workplace and the organisation of production. The ethos of hard work is validated in both of these films, but in neither case is the work motivated by socialist consciousness. The range which Balla and his crew ride in *Spur der Steine* is a construction site in Schkona. The brigade dons traditional carpenter-cowboy garb; they are unruly, quick with their fists, hard drinking. They work hard because men are manly and because they want to beat the other brigades. In fact, they work *too* hard – harder than the supply of raw materials permits. They strong-arm their way to the raw materials they need to exceed their quotas, hijacking them if necessary, not because the plan must be met but because without exceeding it they can't earn their bonuses.

In the paradigm of building socialism in these films, hard work is more important than working hard for the right reason. As a worker asks, in *Berlin um die Ecke:* 'What's more important: that I'm politically suspect, but work hard; or that I'm politically a true party-liner but work like a rat?' But there are limits to how far this value-free work-ethic can go; Balla's collective walks a thin line between being a somewhat disorderly posse and a band of partially domesticated outlaws, as becomes apparent when they strike – a forbidden act in the GDR, where the antagonistic contradiction between capital and labour had been defined away. The strike scene is rendered swiftly and at night –

the viewer can hardly see the figures; the quasi-conspiratorial dialogue is spoken almost inaudibly. They strike because there are no raw materials. In effect, they are striking not against but for socialism, against system-immanent inhibitions. Ironically, they are commanded back to work by Party functionaries who drive onto the scene – though of course they cannot go back to work without the delivery of the wood whose failure to arrive had sparked the strike. The sheriff at the Schkona plant is Werner Horrath. The show-down between hero Balla and his foil Horrath happens not at the OK Corral, but in the shed where the workers take their break; it takes the form of an ever more aggressive fist-and-knee-slapping drinking game they call the Carpenter's Dance; Balla shows the Party Secretary how to play the game, and knocks him off his stool when the lovely young damsel, engineer Kati Klee – for whose affection the two have been competing – enters the room.

In *Berlin um die Ecke*, two young machinists, the motorcycle-riding protagonist Olaf and his buddy Horst, momentously over-fulfil the plan by roughly 300 percent – not to endorse the system, but to expose it. Having been censured for having falsi-fied his production output (an act Olaf later concedes was foolish, adding that it would not have been necessary had the low wages of the young workers not violated the principle of 'equal pay for equal work'), Olaf and Horst put in a record-breaking week and blow the output statistics off the charts. When they are publicly decorated for this 'positive exceeding of the norm' Olaf explains cockily that he and his buddy only did it to expose the fact that output falsification is the rule, not the exception, refuses to accept his medal, and proclaims his resignation (an empty threat, as it turns out since he and Horst continue working at the plant without the viewer's ever learning why).

Workplace woes lie at the core of *Der Frühling braucht Zeit* as well. The film begins with a family crisis: engineer Solter, the film's protagonist, has been fired. The crisis in which he is involved at the power plant at which he works is first played out in the context of its implications for his family. The film begins with Solter and his wife discussing how they are going to make ends meet, followed by an angry confrontation with their daughter, who has had to break off her engagement to one of her father's adversaries at the plant, an opportunistic comrade, in the wake of the dismissal. Unlike Balla and Olaf, Solter is not a worker but a member of the technical intelligentsia. He too insists on good work – not to build socialism, nor to earn a *Prämie*, nor to expose the system's built-in incentive to cheat, nor to prove he's a man – but because he endorses a work environment appropriate to the scientific ethos and to the effective implementation of technology. He had been forced by his foil, plant Director and Party member Faber, to approve substandard electrical power lines to the plant because to have brought them up to standard would supposedly have caused a two-week production slowdown; later, during a winter freeze, the substandard line breaks down, jeopardising the energy supply to the northern areas of the GDR. The emergency repair is costly and risky and an employee is injured. Faber asks Solter to write the report for the investigating committee on the causes of the accident. In that report, Solter criticises Faber for mismanaging the power plant. Later accused of covering up the fact that he had himself approved the electrical lines, Solter punches the official who is questioning him and is fired. The counter-report on the accident investigation, written by the ex-fiancé of Solter's daughter, discloses twenty-five instances of substandard construction. The testimony of a respected ex-employee of the firm and the persistence of an unbiased district attorney establish the truth, namely that Faber had forced Solter to approve the substandard lines. At the behest of the ageing party secretary, Solter is rehired and appointed technical director of the plant. Faber is held responsible for the cover-up and – more importantly – of overworking and endangering employees, not to mention the energy supply of the GDR. Here we have a fifth possible (and in this case unacceptable) motive for hard work: personal ambition.

The only figures in these films who expressly endorse hard work because hard work builds socialism are party functionaries (who demand work of others), or old Communists and class-conscious workers (who demand it also of themselves). The struggle of old worker Paul in *Berlin um die Ecke* takes the form of trying to use 16-millimetre bolts without the appropriate nuts, an image which torments him constantly: at the workplace, in the delirium he suffers after a heart attack, and even beyond the grave. Young Olaf writes the eulogy for Paul, the integrating figure in his work life, lovingly linking the longevity of Paul's memory with the persistence of the shortages which plagued his work-life: 'When electricity is abundant and there are as many 16-millimetre nuts as sand at the seaside, Paul, you will still be with us' – the implication being that that will be a very long time indeed. The old communist father of Anne, the female protagonist in *Denk bloß nicht, ich heule,* demands hard work of himself and of all the agricultural workers on the collective farm he runs, the lot of them young ingrates who, in his estimation, can neither work nor struggle. When the young rowdy, Peter (his daughter's unemployed suitor, who was thrown out of school for writing what he really felt about the GDR) does not thank Anne's father for the half bar of chocolate he'd gruffly tossed him, the father barks 'Never heard of saying thank you? Don't suppose you've ever heard of fighting for what you believe in either!' When Anne's father discovers Peter pent up in a shepherd's hut on the farm, studying for exams he will not be allowed to take, his only words are: 'Can you drive a tractor?'

The old-generation Communists and workers generally come off well in these films. They act as positive foils to younger Party functionaries, who have neither their historical legitimation in the anti-fascist struggle nor their proletarian experience, and their narratives of life in pre-socialist times – the class oppression of Weimar capitalism and the persecutions of the Nazi period – establish a comparative backdrop for reiterating the relative advantages of real-socialism. In *Berlin um die Ecke* Paul recalls poignantly that his dying grandfather had bequeathed him his lifetime savings of three thousand marks, painstakingly eked out of wages of ten marks a week, noting that he didn't have the heart to tell him that the great inflation had long ago rendered it worthless. Anne's father tells her of his persecution as a Communist in the Nazi period; Hütte, the editor of the plant newspaper, having been slugged by Olaf, whom he had turned in to the police, shames him by pointing out that the last time he was beaten, it was at a concentration camp. In the film *Karla*, an incident occurs which leads the viewer to believe that the figure of the honourable old Communist is actually going to be debunked in a DEFA film; the old Communist in this film is the director of the school where Karla, fresh out of college, has her first teaching job. He is a sympathetic character, fatherly in his support of Karla, though uneasy about her unrelenting insistence that the purpose of education is to teach young people to think for

themselves. The obstinately free-thinking student Schimmelpfennig unearths an old photo of the director in Nazi uniform,
and scribbles a swastika on the director's desk to draw him out.
When accused of pro-fascist agitation, Schimmelpfennig
reveals the photo. But the director has no skeleton in his closet
after all: he proves that it was not a Nazi uniform, but rather a
costume he wore in a post-war production of Brecht's play, *Fear
and Misery in the Third Reich.*

Although the old Communists' narratives of the dark pasts
they experienced underscore certain benefits of socialism, the
films debunk the figure of the old Communist in at least one
significant respect. With the exception of Paul, they are across
the board incapable of understanding the concerns of youth
and are thus powerless in their attempt to engage their energies for the socialist project. In *Berlin um die Ecke* the old
Communist Hütte asks Olaf why his generation refuses to
understand that socialism has given them mastery over their
lives. Olaf responds that he is tired of forever hearing how it
was in the bad old days and adds that it sometimes strikes him
that he is simply not as happy as the newspapers say he is. In
Denk bloß nicht ich heule, Anne's father is callous about matters of
the heart and wholly misunderstands Peter, considering him to
be lazy, rude, ungrateful, and no good. In *Karla*, the head-
master warns Karla on several occasions that she must see
reason; instead of responding to the issues she addresses, he
repeatedly cuts off their conversations with an emphatic 'That's
all I have to say on the matter!' Instead of entering into a
dialogue with the successor generation, the Party brandishes its
weapons.

Although the historical legitimacy and comparative advantages of socialism find spokespersons in these films, their positions tend to be undermined by the deficits of those
spokespersons and by the endemic problems of daily experience on which the films aggressively focus. These films are not
heavily vested in the truisms of historical legitimacy; they grant
it in passing – and contrast it with the flawed experience of
daily life in real socialism. Hindsight reveals the films to have
been utopian in thrust – not because they assert the grand
design of a flourishing future, which they do not, but because
they express a yearning for a certain quality in human relations
and communal life which real socialism was incapable of
enabling. The anti-fascist past and a future which seemed ever

farther away were the legitimising poles of a problematic, real-socialist present. The Party cliché – 'Let's not get bogged down in problems, comrades, let's look to the future!' – parroted by Party members on two occasions in *Spur der Steine*, entirely brackets the present, the only temporal register ever experienced by humans. The films are utopian not because they spin grand, unlikely designs, but because the changes in daily, intersubjective relations they call for are as non-implementable in the transitional phase of real socialism as they are fundamental to the evolution of a humane socialism. Instead of holding a wrong-headed populace responsible for failing to grasp the symbiosis of individual and social interest, these films indict the Party as incapable of developing a system whose fruits would make tangible that posited identity of interest and engage the energy and intelligence of younger generations.

The work process is a split process. Given the complex division of labour in advanced industrial societies, alienation does not necessarily dissolve when property relations are formally altered. Marx saw the commodity-fetish as rooted in the failure of producing labourers to recognise social wealth as the product of their own activity. The modern twist: from the standpoint of use-value production, the fetish character of the commodity disguises the origin of the product; from the standpoint of exchange-value, however, it reflects the distribution of power and wealth in the society accurately. This is not the place to discuss to what extent there may or may not have been an identity of 'objective' interest between individual labour and the productive apparatus in real socialism; *subjective* experience, in any event, did not bear it out. In *Denk bloß nicht ich heule*, Peter hits the nail on the head in a testy, common-sense syllogism: 'Being determines consciousness. I've always lived under socialism: So how come I'm not a socialist?' Representation of really existing problems in the socialist work-world in these films lends credence to the fact that the officially propounded identity of interest did not ring true to the workforce. Attempts at self-determination in the workplace do sometimes carry the day in abrupt happy endings – Solter is promoted, reformer Horrath is not expelled from the Party, and Balla is effectively won for the socialist project – but it is the problems, not these quick-and-clean resolutions, which dominate the lasting impression. The intended audience was expert in reading the reality barometer, a fact of which the film-makers and their censors were well aware. Ten years later, during his ill-fated concert in Cologne, Wolf Biermann formulated the central paradox of alienated socialist work – also in the form of a mock syllogism: 'The exploiters have been expelled. The people are hard at work in the factories. The people own the factories. But who owns the people?'

How do these films depict the more *subjective* experience of the workplace – beyond the structural issues of poor planning, lack of materials, the tedious presence of idealists and conformists as Balla describes the dual problem of bracketing out the really existing present and surveillance? Noise pollution is high. When Peter visits his mother at the factory where she works (clearly for the first time in his life), it is so loud that the viewer cannot hear what is said until Peter and his mother move outside the building. Her face is grimy. Somewhat embarrassed that her drop-out son (who wants to borrow part of her hard-earned wages) sees her in this state, she hurriedly points out that the new machine at which she stands eight hours a day is really great.

Olaf's workplace is loud as well, and chaotically organised; heavy metal – not the musical variety – is the dominant image. The point in the film in which Olaf, at the workplace, is most at peace is when he takes an extended break outside, snoozing in the sun with his cowboy hat tilted over his eyes, still languishing in the memory of his first night with Karin. This is the very moment at which his friend, the old worker Paul, dies of a heart attack inside the plant, a result of work-related stress. Olaf's lovely girl-friend, an amateur jazz singer and actress, is in real life a cook. She seems singularly ill-placed schlepping crates in a kitchen. Her older female co-worker figures in the film for a few seconds only, just long enough to utter one thing: 'My back is killing me.' In *Der Frühling braucht Zeit*, an avoidable industrial accident costs Rudi his toe. In *Das Kaninchen bin ich*, Maria's work in the dance bar is exhausting, the hours are long, she is forever being accosted by annoying males who want to pick her up, and she finally collapses with a back ailment.

If the experience of work in these films is anything but romanticised, it is not wholly negative, either. A certain low-key and very personal solidarity characterise some of them. In *Jahrgang 45*, young Al, who has taken a vacation to work through his divorce, shows up at work during his vacation and asks whether they do not have something for him to do because he is being driven up the wall at home. His estranged wife Lisa is shown in warm personal interactions with a nurse colleague, and she clearly enjoys presenting new-borns to joyous families peering through the glass. There are many depictions of extended social relations of colleagues outside the institutional confines of the workplace. Peoples' institutional and private lives are linked in sometimes pleasurable ways. There are dance scenes in every one of these films; the recurrent trope of the dance sometimes takes the form of firm-organized after-work entertainment. In *Der Frühling braucht Zeit*, dancing couples provide a degree of comic relief in parallel cuts spliced between plant crisis sequences; a short, pudgy but generally sympathetic Party official, for example, buries his face deliciously in the bosom of a taller female comrade, digging it – and in – to the hilt. The relation between members of Balla's collective is one of strong camaraderie, disturbed only by the reactionary trouble-maker Bolbig, who attempts to organise a mutiny in the brigade by accusing Balla of selling out to Party interests. After some hesitation, the crew sticks with Balla. In *Spur der Steine* work is generally fulfilling at the intersubjective level; the 'Ballas' are buddies who drink together, challenge authority together, work together, interact frankly and pleasurably. The socialist workplace is by no means being criticised here *per se*; the entire narrative interweave of the film underscores the workplace as the primary locus of interpersonal life. Critique is levelled at the organisation of production and the related incompetence of the planners and policers (in Balla's terms, the conformists), not the quality of personal interaction or of individual output.

However frustrating the productive process and however inadequate the output may have been, it appears to be the workplace that Germans of the new *Länder* most sorely miss in a unified, market-based Germany. This has partly to do with the fact that to have no job at all is worse than having a problematic one. Certainly, the inefficiencies of production, the ineptness of planners, and the slogan-slinging of functionaries – recurrent themes in these films – will be part of the lasting memory of socialism-as-was to which these films will contribute. But the workplace-based, interpersonal solidarity which they also underwrite to some degree undercuts the negative thrust of that critique. Whether or not such solidarity generally characterised workplaces in the GDR is a question for social historians; but its representation in the daring DEFA films of 1965 will tend, against the bitter backdrop of the discontinued or de-personalised workplaces of the new *Länder*, to brighten what remains of the GDR as memory.

Notes

1. After the uprising of the 17th June
    The secretary of the Writers' Union
    Had leaflets distributed in the Stalinallee
    Stating that the people
    Had forfeited the confidence of the government
    And could win it back only
    By redoubled efforts. Would it not be easier
    In that case for the government
    To dissolve the people
    And elect another?

    Bertolt Brecht, *Poems: 1913–1956* (edited by John Willett and Ralph Manheim with the co-operation of Erich Fried), London, 1976, p. 440.
2. See Christa Maerker and Peter Jansen, *Verbannte Bilder: die Verbotsfilme der DDR* (documentary film), Südwestfunk, April 1991. The author has access to the typescripts of the uncut interview footage.
3. Ibid.
4. 'Afterwards there simply weren't any more films like these, films which were politically frank and which told stories firmly rooted in the panorama of that time. The new generation looked to stories set in a more intimate milieu. They knew what was allowed and what wasn't and, of course, they took DEFA films off in a new direction'. See Axel Geiss, 'Frank Beyer – Menschen in ihrer Zeit: Interview mit Axel Geiss', *Film und Fernsehen* 18, no. 8, 1990: 10–13 (10)
5. Joshua Feinstein, *The Triumph of the Ordinary: Depictions of Daily Life in the East German Cinema, 1956–1966*, (PhD Diss., Stanford University, 1995) p. 10.
6. Frank Vogel openly admits to experimenting with the genre of the Western in this film. See Maerker and Jansen, *Verbannte Bilder.*

Chapter 9

CENSORSHIP AND THE LAW: THE CASE OF *DAS KANINCHEN BIN ICH* (*I AM THE RABBIT*)

Stefan Soldovieri

Of the group of films banned in the context of the Eleventh Plenary of the SED in December 1965, Kurt Maetzig's *Das Kaninchen bin ich*, based on the novel of the same name by Manfred Bieler, is one of the best known. Relating the story of the relationship between a young woman and the judge who has sentenced her brother to a severe prison term, the film was charged with grossly misrepresenting the administration of justice in the GDR. In fact the film had drawn on the judiciary's own rhetoric of reform as it had been articulated in a series of policy statements beginning with the 1961 *Rechtspflegebeschluß* ('Resolution on Jurisprudence'). Unfortunately for the filmmakers, by the time the first screenplay had been completed in December 1964, legal discourse was once again entering a period of flux as the State's continuing problems with managing the GDR judicial system reached crisis level. At odds with these developments, the DEFA Studio and a few sympathetic film officials struggled to negotiate the minimum script revisions that would be acceptable to the Central Committee, the Ministry of Justice, and the Attorney General's Office.

The *Rechtspflegebeschluß* and the Rhetoric of Reform in the Early 1960s

The early 1960s are commonly regarded as the beginning of a period of relative stabilisation in GDR society in which the State turned to practical matters of government and the economy.[1] On the level of political rhetoric, the new pragmatism and the attempt to implement more flexible administrative methods enabled a wary ideological redress that permitted SED policy-makers to strike less strident chords as they set out to project the image of a mature state and a new stage in GDR history.

Issued on 30 January 1961, the first *Rechtspflegebeschluß* was an indication that the rhetoric of stabilisation had begun to take hold in the judiciary.[2] Grounding its reformist mandate in the 'increasing solidification of our socialist society,'[3] the *Rechtspflegebeschluß* exhorted moderation and leniency in procedures of prosecution and sentencing. The resolution further directed that a share of judicial authority be delegated to public 'conflict committees' for refereeing petty crimes and certain first offences.[4] SED functionaries hoped that the resolution would help to improve the public image of the legal system which had suffered as a consequence of the repressive and largely unsuccessful measures that had been implemented to cope with the continued emigration of GDR citizens, difficulties in enforcing the collectivisation of the agricultural sector, and 'political crimes'.[5] Efforts to popularize the *Rechtspflegebeschluß* and the impression of a fairer, more impartial judiciary included newspaper publicity, forums (see Werkentin, p. 244), and an informational pamphlet aimed in part at a West German audience.[6]

A notable feature of the party's modified rhetoric in the judicial sphere was the expanded role assumed by the notion of contradictions in the historical development of a socialist system of justice. While the language of class struggle and anti-imperialism continued to form the frame of judicial rhetoric, at the beginning of the 1960s references to internal incongruities accompanying the development of socialist jurisprudence began to appear with increased frequency. Seeking to recast the language of the administration of justice in a fashion that would be compatible with the SED's new policy of appeasement, judicial professionals were compelled to find rhetorical strategies to account for crime in East German society that went beyond mere finger-pointing at the West.

One of these tactics entailed a partial displacement of the rigidly class-determined view of the roots of crime in the GDR that had been previously dominant in legal discourse (cf. Werkentin, pp. 244 f.). In its stead the *Rechtspflegebeschluß* and subsequent glosses of it conceded the existence of incongruities in the development of socialist society – contradictions which were attributed to the challenges posed to individuals grappling with rapidly changing technological and historical forces. According to the resolution, the development of socialist consciousness '... transpires with difficulties and contradictions. The personal conduct of individuals does not always conform to the norms of the socialist community, because consciousness develops neither uniformly, linearly, nor at a continuous rate' (p. 4).

In the same spirit, an article published in June 1962 urged a continuation of the initiative of the 1961 *Rechtspflegebeschluß* and demanded that legal professionals expose such contradictions in a way that would benefit the development of GDR society.[7] The article denounced the 'schematic,' in the sense of 'undifferentiated,' and formalistic concepts of law and justice among legal professionals that its author claimed were hampering the proper formation of a system of socialist justice: 'Schematic thinking and the insufficient differentiation between [true] enemy activity and [mere] ideological incertitude, the failure to pursue the real circumstances, causes, motives, and methods of crimes, on the other hand, have led to the circumstance that real criminals do not receive the appropriate punishment'.[8] The revision of the language of jurisprudence crested in July 1962 with the publication of a polemic in *Neue Justiz*, the official journal of the Ministry of Justice.[9] Entitled 'Overcome dogmatic convictions in the theory and practice of penal law!', the article radicalised the rhetorical impetus of the first *Rechtspflegebeschluß* and the critique it had launched on narrowly class-based accounts of crime. The article took legal scholars to task for neglecting the role of the political and moral consciousness of GDR citizens in the development of society.[10] The authors – the unnamed members of the journal's editorial board – went on to cite particularly egregious examples of 'dogmatic' and 'abstract' views in a variety of legal publications. A number of these texts on judicial policy had appeared in the journal's own pages.

Two things need to be emphasised regarding the *Rechtspflegebeschluß* and the rhetoric of judicial reform that it helped to initiate in the first half of the 1960s. First, the judicial revision facilitated by the *Rechtspflegebeschluß* entailed an expansion and differentiation of legal discourse and not a wholesale break with past policy. One of the primary tasks for GDR administrators was to find ways of mediating the language of new Politbüro and Central Committee directives in a fashion that would not jeopardise the narrative of GDR society's continuous development. The representation of socialist development in the judicial sphere and elsewhere could accommodate a rhetoric of contradictions, but not ruptures. This would in fact surface as a major critique of the way in which *Das Kaninchen bin ich* thematised the critique of dogmatism. Official opponents of the film rejected a portrayal of the *Rechtspflegebeschluß* as an abrupt change of course, insisting that the resolution had to be seen as a stage in the continuous development of GDR society as a whole. A statement issued by the *Abteilung Kultur* ('Department of Cultural Affairs') on the film, for instance, charged the film-makers with focusing too narrowly on negative aspects of the legal system. The author wrote that 'the *Rechtspflegebeschluß* can thus only appear as the correction of dogmatic errors in the administration of justice and not as a continuous and logical development of socialist justice'.[11] Like other policy administrators, the authors of legal agenda were under continuous pressure to properly negotiate this grey area of admissible socialist self-critique.

Second, the rhetoric of reform characterising judicial discourse in the early 1960s was neither completely homogenous nor uncontested. The serious problems that the state continued to have in managing a disgruntled population made the interpretation of the *Rechtspflegebeschluß* a complicated affair in which the balance between those advising a return to stricter policies and those pushing for even more fundamental judicial reform proved to be quite precarious. This became apparent once again in November 1965 when the Central Committee recognised that current policies designed to inspire trust in the system of justice had failed. The consequence was a departure from the rhetoric of the 1961 *Rechtspflegebeschluß* that would contribute to the banning of *Das Kaninchen bin ich.*

The Judiciary and the Production of
Das Kaninchen bin ich

As was the case in other areas of state administration, the judiciary in the GDR was a highly redundant apparatus. Nominally headed by the Ministry of Justice and the Attorney-General's Office, the judiciary was subject in significant degree to the supervision of the Central Committee's *Abteilung Staats- und Rechtsfragen* ('Department of State and Legal Affairs'). While none of these agencies designated staff posts exclusively for film matters, the Ministry of Justice and the Attorney-General's Office at least monitored the representation of legal issues outside of the judicial sphere proper. The Press Office performed this function at the Attorney-General's Office, which kept tabs on DEFA documentaries and features and reviewed scripts for the law-and-order-related television series *Der Staatsanwalt hat das Wort* (*The Public Prosecutor Has the Floor*) and *Polizeiruf 110* (*Emergency 110*).[12] At the Ministry of Justice aides were frequently sent to the DEFA studios to represent the interests of the judiciary,[13] whereas the *Abteilung Staats- und Rechtsfragen* seems to have served primarily as an adviser to the Central Committee's 'Abteilung Kultur'.[14]

The early involvement of the judiciary and the *Hauptverwaltung Film* (the Ministry of Culture's Film Bureau) in the *Das Kaninchen bin ich* project was a result of the circumstance that the novel upon which the script was based had recently been denied a publication licence or 'Druckgenehmigung' by the *Hauptverwaltung Verlage und Buchhandel* ('Publishing Bureau'), the *Hauptverwaltung Film's* counterpart in the book trade.[15] As a consequence the script quickly became the object of intense official scrutiny.[16] This was unusual since the requirement that individual scripts be approved by the *Hauptverwaltung Film* had been rescinded in the late 1950s as a part of reforms in the system of film regulation. In the light of the problematic nature of Bieler's novel, high-level discussions of the screenplay adaptation began shortly on the heels of the completion of the 12 December 1964 script draft.[17] Both the Attorney-General and the Ministry of Culture were already in possession of the script by mid-January.[18]

Once informed about the plans for a film bearing so directly on pressing judicial issues, the Ministry of Justice acted quickly to contact the studio. In a note addressed to the DEFA Studio, Ullmann, an aide at the Ministry, reported that his office had heard of the film project dealing with the life of a GDR judge and was eager to participate in the film's production in an advisory function. Somewhat more bluntly, the letter also requested that the Ministry of Justice be included in the proceedings when the film came up for state certification.[19] Additional memos stemming from Ullmann show that the Ministry of Justice saw the film project as an opportunity to set a precedent for influencing future film projects.[20]

An initial meeting between judicial officials and the DEFA Studio to discuss the 12 December 1964 script version was held in late January 1965. Although Maetzig had requested that either the Minister of Justice, Hilde Benjamin, or her deputy attend, in the end neither Benjamin, the Deputy-Minister, nor Maetzig himself participated. Instead Ullmann and a colleague met with film team producer, Günter Karl, in the hopes of turning their grave reservations about the script's treatment of legal issues into concrete alterations.[21] In his summary of the meeting Ullmann reported:

> We made it clear to Comrade Dr Karl that in our view the basic premise and thematic proportions of the script at hand are unsuited for the making of a realistic film. We told Comrade Dr Karl that a film of this kind would communicate a politically false picture of our judges and our administration of justice in the area of punitive law. We explained to Comrade Dr Karl that in our opinion such a film would simply be grist for the mill of the enemy.[22]

According to Ullmann, the film team producer defended the script, maintaining that in his opinion there was no denying that there had been cases of excessively severe sentencing in the past and that such situations were indispensable from a dramaturgical point of view. Ullmann further reported that Karl had suggested continuing the discussion with the rest of the film team, but that he had not committed his office to do so. Later attempts by producer Karl to schedule another meeting with the Ministry of Justice and the Attorney-General's Office appear to have been frustrated by the Deputy-Minister, who informed Ullmann that the matter would be pursued on the Party level.[23] Nevertheless Ullmann diligently drafted a position paper on the December script version for his office's files.

In his report, dated 19 May 1965, the aide targeted those aspects of the film pertaining to the legal system that he considered to be in need of revision. These included the portrayal of the judge, Paul Deister. Ullmann wrote: 'The judge is depicted as a ladder-climber, a well-off petit bourgeois (well-off Wartburg, sailboat, weekend cottage) who is only concerned with outdoing the prosecutor by pronouncing even more severe sentences than those appealed for.' In addition, the aide recorded the precise setting of the plot in the history of GDR jurisprudence and expressly addressed the script's interpretation of the *Rechtspflegebeschluß* of 1961: 'The script communicates the idea that before the first *Rechtspflegebeschluß* the administration of penal law was completely false. The dialogues and monologues reveal a judge who is out of touch with our social order.' [24]

The *Abteilung Staats- und Rechtsfragen* in the Central Committee took a similar view of the *Das Kaninchen bin ich* project. On 21 May 1965, Tord Riemann, an official in the section, directed a letter to Siegfried Wagner, director of the *Abteilung Kultur* and a notoriously dogged ideologue, complaining that a meeting between his Section, *Hauptverwaltung Film director* Günter Witt, Deputy Attorney-General Wendland, and Karl and Maetzig from the DEFA Studio had not resulted in the script alterations that had been demanded. At the meeting, the legal officials had reiterated their criticisms of the script and charged the film-makers with 'reworking the issue of jurisprudence in particular'.[25]

Riemann later documented his reasons for rejecting the script at this meeting in some detail in an internal position paper. Filed on 15 December 1965 – a full six months after the meeting in question – the timing of the paper places it suspiciously close to the Eleventh Plenary of the Central Committee and after the *Hauptverwaltung Film*'s repeal of the film's licence.[26] This was the climax of the attack on the film, suggesting that Riemann may have been trying to protect himself and his Section for having failed to successfully intervene at the script stage. As it stands, Riemann's report is probably a better indicator of the critique being aimed at the film at the time of the Plenary than when the meeting took place the previous summer. This being as it may, the Central Committee official's four-page report offers insight into what was at stake for the *Abteilung Staats- und Rechtsfragen* in the film's treatment of the *Rechtspflegebeschluß*. Riemann wrote: 'The *Rechtspflegebeschluß* plays an essential role [in the film]. Maria recognises judge Deister's true (base) character only because the *Rechtspflegebeschluß* appears as a 'new course' – a swerve from a 'hard' to a 'soft course,' as a 'liberal policy'. This is precisely the false and harmful interpretation that we have repeatedly resisted.' [27]

The fact that the Ministry of Justice, the Central Committee, and the Attorney-General's Office were having such difficulties in motivating the *Hauptverwaltung Film* to accommodate the interests of the judiciary in the production of *Das Kaninchen bin ich* illustrates the complicated nature of film management in the cinema industry. While the *Hauptverwaltung Film* was in part responsible for negotiating just the kind of changes that the judiciary was demanding, film administrators seemed determined to prove that they could fend for themselves in managing the production of ideologically acceptable and attractive films.

Having acquiesced to the studio early on in permitting the adaptation of a novel that had been rejected by the *Hauptverwaltung Buchhandel und Verlage*, the *Hauptverwaltung Film* acquired a considerable interest in guaranteeing the production of a film that would satisfy officials in the Central Committee and the juidiciary. In this way the film became something of a test case for the ability of the *Hauptverwaltung Film* to manage projects dealing with politically sensitive issues, which helps to explain why film administrators did not halt work on the film even after the changes made in the script version of 2 March 1965 were widely criticised as insufficient.

A lengthy *Hauptverwaltung Film* report dated 4 October 1965 and commissioned by the *Abteilung Kultur* addressed this issue in unusually explicit language. In the document, Günter Witt warned that requiring too many changes could lead to the view that the *Hauptverwaltung Film* was out to ruin what had been an outstanding film. According to Witt, an outright ban 'would also stifle the necessary discussion of the actual problems [...] The focus of the discussion would then be the administrative act and not the ideological and artistic issues surrounding the film.'[28] Witt recommended renewed meetings between the Studio and his office and commissioned a final position paper, to be submitted jointly by the studio director, Maetzig, and the film's producer, specifically addressing the reservations of the *Hauptverwaltung Film*. While the film would never make it to the theatres, *Das Kaninchen bin ich* was finally licensed by Witt on 26 October 1965 under the condition of three further changes, all of which bore on aspects related to the representation of the judiciary.

The Representation of Legal Issues in
Das Kaninchen bin ich

Questions of justice and the law surrounding the *Rechts-pflegebeschluß* are at the core of the conflicts that structure the narrative of *Das Kaninchen bin ich*, and the effort to shape these issues was the object of the extended negotiations sketched out in the previous section. Despite the complexity of this process, a comparison between the script versions of 12 December 1964 and 3 March 1965 – separated as they are by initial consultations between the DEFA Studio and legal and film officials – provides a convenient gauge of the influence of the judiciary on the film's representation of GDR justice.

Briefly, *Das Kaninchen bin ich* relates the story of the ill-fated relationship between Maria Morzeck, a young woman who has just completed her secondary schooling, and Paul Deister, the zealous judge who has condemned her brother Dieter to an inordinately severe prison sentence in an effort to impress his superiors and further his legal career. As the narrative unfolds, Dieter's case becomes the occasion for a comparison with a second offence involving the fisherman Grambow, whose slanderous outburst against the army is witnessed by Paul and Maria. To Maria's disbelief, Grambow is not brought to trial as her brother had been for a presumably comparable crime only a few years before. Despite Paul's insistence that Grambow's case be brought to a proper trial, the local mayor arranges for the matter to be settled in a public forum, where it is resolved that the fisherman be required to perform one hundred hours of community service. Thereafter Maria's frustration and probing questions lead to a break with Paul, whose tangled excursions on the nature of law and justice and whose feeble defence of his ruling in the trial against her brother convince her of his lack of character.

In both versions of the script, the circumstances of Dieter's trial provide the point of departure for later developments. Introduced by a short scene in which Maria must ask the school director for a day off to visit her imprisoned brother in Brandenburg, the court scene takes the form of a flashback that begins with Maria and her aunt entering the courtroom, where they observe the opening of the proceedings before being odered to leave by Paul Deister, the presiding judge. First signs of concessions to the pressures of legal officials to improve the image of the judiciary can already be discerned in this brief scene preceding Dieter's trial. In the December 1964 script the prosecution requests that the public be excluded from the proceedings in the interest of protecting 'state secrets' – a request that is incomprehensible to Maria, who doesn't even know what her brother has actually done. The March 1965 version on the other hand refers rather less ominously to 'national security'.[29]

More significant than this subtle change of timbre in the 1965 script is a shift of time frame in the following scenes that relocated Dieter's trial to the period after the 1961 *Rechtspflegebeschluß*. This temporal displacement was accompanied by a marked reduction in the severity of the offence with which he was charged and a change in the legal paragraphs applied. Thus whereas the earlier script had Paul Deister open the case against Maria's brother on 18 September 1959 with the charge of 'sedition and premeditated agitation,' the March 1965 script had rescheduled the trial for 18 June 1961 and mercifully reduced Dieter's charge to simple 'agitation'.[30] A glance at the 1957 Penal Law Amendment ('Strafrechtergänzungsgesetz') suggests why this was an important distinction.[31] As per §19, Judge Deister had acted strictly but within the bounds of the law in imposing a five-year prison sentence in the December 1965 script. Governing especially grievous offences involving planned or premeditated actions, Section 3 of this paragraph placed no upper limit on prison terms. 'Sedition', according to §20, Sections 1 and 2, would already have justified a prison term of up to two years. In the revised script of March 1965, censorial clemency led to a two-year reduction in Dieter's prison sentence; §20 was dropped from the charge altogether.

The point of this juggling act regarding a crime to which neither script dedicated a single shot was the way in which it reorganised the relationship between Dieter's trial and that of Grambow. Situating Dieter's crime after the first *Rechtspflegebeschluß* of 30 January 1961 eroded its role in motivating the disparate treatments of the two affairs. In the revised script the legal reforms associated with the resolution could no longer be solely credited with the more lenient treatment enjoyed by Grambow. From the perspective of the film-makers this economical abridgement of the first script would have left the principal dramatic conflicts largely intact while diffusing the official critique that the plot turned too much on the interpretation of the *Rechtspflegebeschluß* as an abrupt change of legal policy. The Grambow sequence prompted more complex changes in the course of revisions on the December 1964 script. Here, too, legal officials had objected to what was in effect the script's all-too-literal appropriation of the *Rechtspflegebeschluß*. The changes made on this scene all aimed at mediating a representation of justice that would allow the affirmation of legal reforms without fundamentally calling into question past judicial practices. Viewed as interpreters of judicial policy, director Maetzig and his film team found themselves in a predicament not unlike that faced by legal administrators as they tried to construct an acceptable rendition of the Grambow problematic.

Grambow's transgression takes place at the local bar near Paul's weekend cottage, where Maria has spent several summer weeks to cure a minor ailment. During the course of a visit from Paul, the local fisherman Grambow makes a drunken public appearance in which he insults the army as a 'gang of pigs' and shows disrespect toward a drowned petty officer whose body has been found earlier that day. The scene ends in a brawl and Paul's request that the responsible police official be summoned. Up to this point the two scripts coincide in all essentials: when it turns out that the police official is on another call, Paul proposes ringing the district office – advice that the mayor ignores in favour of expelling Grambow from the bar by the seat of his pants.

It was the handling of Grambow's case in the following scenes 68-78 that raised some of the most weighty objections among the legal officials who became involved in the film project. Attempting to contain its liberal impetus, Tord Riemann of the *Abteilung Staats- und Rechtsfragen* insisted, '[T]he *Rechtspflegebeschluß* by no means justifies the treatment of the case of Grambow as it is to be depicted in the film.'[32] In the script version of 12 December, the young mayor visits Paul on the evening of Grambow's outburst. During the course of a dialogue overheard and interrupted by Maria, the mayor tries unsuccessfully to enlist Paul's support in his plan to schedule a public meeting – nothing less than one of the 'conflict committees' instituted by the *Rechtspflegebeschluß* – to arrive at a decision regarding Grambow's slander of the army. Impervious to the mayor's appeal to changed times, 'From one comrade to another: nowadays we don't take such things quite so seriously, do we?', Paul vehemently defends the hard line: 'Since you asked me as a comrade, than I'll answer as one: the *Rechtspflegebeschluß* is not a free pass for the enemy' (scene 68/shot 235). The remainder of the sequence fleshes out the contrast between the mayor's tolerant and pragmatic attitude toward Grambow and Paul's excessive ideological vigilance and dogmatism. Realising that he is not making any headway against the immovable judge, the mayor requests Paul's testimony as a witness at the meeting. The scene ends with a confrontation between Paul and Maria, for whom the comparison to her brother's trial has become unavoidable and who has become even more suspicious of Paul and the kind of justice disbursed by GDR courts.

The following scenes 69–73 depict the committee meeting itself. In addition to various townspeople, representatives of the army, and a variety of other officials are also present. Very much in the sense of the appeal to tolerance and differentiation characterising the rhetoric of legal reform, various testimonies before the committee illuminate the background to Grambow's actions. As it turns out, Grambow's libellous tirade had been the product of a number of factors, including his drunkenness and emotional distress at the horrifying sight of the drowned officer and an understandable grudge against the army for disruptive military manoeuvres that were costing his fishing brigade the entire season's catch. Tolerant partisanship characterises the meeting, which, as is revealed by an angered and shaken Maria in a later dialogue with Paul, results in a scant hundred hours of community service for Grambow.

'Paul, what is justice, really?' (scene 76/shot 287). Paul's futile attempt to answer this question is skilfully orchestrated in a subsequent sequence of four scenes at the court building in which the judge's awkward attempt to lecture on the nature of justice and the law is repeatedly interrupted. Maria finally gives up on her lover, but not before confronting him, finally, with her brother's case and the disparity between Dieter's five-year imprisonment at the Brandenburg penitentiary and Grambow's hundred hours of community service at the hands of the conflict committee. Maria: 'Was it right what you did?' (scene 78/shot 291). Trying to avoid the issue, Paul complains that the question is too abstract before replying, 'Look, some things have naturally changed since the *Rechtspflegebeschluß*.

How a law is applied, how strictly – that depends upon the given situation ...' (scene 78/shot 293). Now that he has betrayed himself as an opportunist, the stage directions call for the sound to be faded out.

The March 1965 script devotes an additional minute of dialogue to this three-scene, 310-second sequence, giving Paul greater opportunity to explain his position and changes in legal policy and averting somewhat the direct contrast between the cases of Dieter and Grambow. Whereas in the earlier version Maria provocatively asserts that her brother would have received an even lighter sentence than Grambow today – a contention to which Paul does not definitively respond – the March 1965 text avoids this equation altogether. Instead Paul expresses his doubts that the last word has been spoken in the Grambow case, thereby calling into question the finality of the verdict levied by the mayor's public forum.

Attempts such as these to recontextualise Dieter's severe sentence and to play down the role of the *Rechtspflegebeschluß* ultimately proved insufficient. *Das Kaninchen bin ich* never premièred. While the director of the *Hauptverwaltung Film* was able to license the film in late October against the wishes of the Central Committee, by November the *Rechtspflegebeschluß* had become too sensitive an issue to play such a prominent role in a feature film. Once eager to publicise its commitment to legal reform, the state ultimately preferred to stifle *Das Kaninchen bin ich* rather than to risk public debate on policies that were already being abandoned.

What is striking about the production history of *Das Kaninchen bin ich* is not the spectacle of the ban, however. Far more interesting are the circumstances of its production – the way in which film-makers and film administrators sought to mediate the fluctuating pressures of legal discourse. Bans such as that imposed on Maetzig's film would become even more infrequent throughout the course of the 1970s and 1980s as the system of film regulation became more fine-tuned. Despite the film's eventual suppression, the case of *Das Kaninchen bin ich* suggests that censorship in the GDR film industry was not simply something inflicted upon films from above, but a complex and contentious process of negotiation with historically shifting parameters. *Das Kaninchen bin ich* would not be the last film to run aground on the contradictions inherent in this process.

Notes

1. Hermann Weber has pointed in particular to the setting up of Party organizations such as the FDJ and the *Gesellschaft für Sport und Technik* (GST) that began in the late 1950s. See Hermann Weber, *Die DDR 1945–1990*, Munich 1993, pp. 48–76. Dietrich Staritz undertakes the same periodization in his *Geschichte der DDR* (revised edn.), Frankfurt, 1996, pp. 197-275.

2. The following account of the *Rechtspflegebeschluß* is indebted to Falco Werkentin's *Politische Strafjustiz in der Ära Ulbricht*, Berlin, 1995, in particular the chapter 'Strafjustiz nach dem 13. August 1961' (pp. 243–80). References in the text refer to this edition. Actual developments in the judicial sphere were of course much more complex than the following summary suggests. The initiative signalled by the first *Rechtspflegebeschluß*, for instance, was initially nullified by the harsh measures implemented immediately following 13 August 1961. The liberal course was reinstated in mid-1962 by the Politbüro resolution 'Vorlage über die Durchführung des Staatsratsbeschlusses über die weitere Entwicklung der Rechtspflege', which once again advised restraint in the application of the law and emphasised the independence of judges in the legal system (Werkentin, p. 263).

3. 'Beschluß des Staatsrates der Deutschen Demokratischen Republik über die weitere Entwicklung der Rechtspflege', *Gesetzblatt der DDR*, 2, 1961: 3–4(4). Reprinted in *Neue Justiz* 13, no. 5, 1961: 73–74. References in the text are to the *Gesetzblatt* edition. Also widely referred to as the *Rechtspflegeerlaß*.

4. Joshua Feinstein cites an October 1964 'Jurisprudence Decree' in the context of the *Das Kaninchen bin ich* project as the force behind judicial reforms. See Joshua Feinstein, 'The Triumph of the Ordinary: Depictions of Daily Life in the East German Cinema, 1956–66' (PhD Diss. Stanford University, 1995), p. 215. In fact, the 1964 dictum was an 'Amnestieerlaß' or pardon which did not refer specifically to the reforms outlined in its more significant 1961 and 1962 precursors. Notable, however, was the explicit reference to political prisoners. The author is grateful to have been able to corroborate his independent research with Feinstein's unpublished doctoral thesis. See 'Amnestieerlaß des Staatsrates der Deutschen Demokratischen Republik', *Gesetzblatt der DDR*, 13, 1964: 135–6. In Werkentin's account, this large-scale pardon of GDR prisoners – the State's latest attempt to manage prisons overflowing with perpetrators of lesser crimes – marked the beginning of the end of judicial reforms in the mid-1960s. Werkentin, p. 387.

5. Werkentin also points to the 'Staatsratsgesetz' of September 1960 as an example of the state's appeal to legality and justice (p. 245). The

Staatsrat ('State Council') was the legislative body within the *Volkskammer* ('People's Chamber') responsible for the authorisation of GDR laws.

6. The pamphlet was entitled 'Rechtspflege in der DDR in Frage und Antwort'. For insight into the production of the document, see the Ministry of Culture file [BAP(= Bundesarchiv Potsdam): DP 1 VA 2469].

7. Herbert Kern, 'Die Rechtspflege weiter vervollkommnen', *Neue Justiz* 12, no. 16, 1962: 361–4 (361).

8. Kern, 362. The text also provided the example of a youth who had been sentenced to what the author considered to be a needlessly severe prison term for attempting to leave the country illegally. The legal professional faulted the court for paying insufficient attention to the fact that the young man was a member of the SED youth organization, the FDJ, and that his actions had been neither premeditated nor prompted by political opposition to the GDR state.

9. Less polemical than the article in question, a decree issued on 4 April 1963 endorsed the spirit of the first *Rechtspflegebeschluß* and specified the new responsibilities of the judiciary. 'Erlaß des Staatsrats der Deutschen Demokratischen Republik über die grundsätzlichen Aufgaben und die Arbeitsweise der Organe der Rechtspflege', *Gesetzblatt der DDR* 3 (1963): 21–44.

10. 'Dogmatische Auffassungen in der Strafwissenschaft und -praxis überwinden!', *Neue Justiz* 14, no. 16, 1962: 425–8 (425).

11. 'Zwei Standpunkte in der Beurteilung des Films *Das Kaninchen bin ich*, 15 October 1965 [SAPMO: IV A2/906/124], p. 7.

12. Little is known about the history of this office's relationship to DEFA. Unfortunately, much of the documentation produced by the Attorney-General's Office on feature-film and television projects no longer exists due in large part to its standard procedures of thinning out its shelves every ten years or so. Other files were destroyed when the office moved out of its Berlin headquarters at Scharnhorststraße in the mid-1960s. As a consequence only older files considered 'historisch wertvoll' ('of historical significance') tend to have been preserved. The author was unable to locate any material on *Das Kaninchen bin ich* in the files of the Attorney-General's Office itself.

13. During the time that Maetzig's project was in production, for instance, the Ministry met with DEFA Studio representatives to discuss legal issues bearing on the film *Lots Weib* (*Lot's Wife*, 1965) directed by Egon Günther. The immediate cause of the Ministry's interest in the film was probably the theme of divorce raised in the film and the fact that the Ministry of Justice was in the process of drafting a code of family law. See [BAP: DP 1 VA 8288]. Cf. 'Aufgaben der Woche in der Zeit vom 25. bis 30. Oktober 1965', 22 October 1965 [BAP: DP 1 VA 8287].

14. The flow of information observed in the case of *Das Kaninchen bin ich* corroborates this assumption. A memo from Tord Riemann in the *Abteilung Staats- und Rechtsfragen* to Siegfried Wagner in the *Abteilung Kultur* relates that the former had been sent the script with the request for qualified legal review. 'Letter from Riemann to Wagner', 21 May 1965, [SAPMO: IV A2/13/3]. Although reporting between sections was routine, at this stage of research into censorship in the GDR cinema it is still difficult to say precisely what forms it took in matters of film regulation.

15. According to Herrmann Schauer, an official in the *Hauptverwaltung Film*'s Production Department (*Produktionsabteilung*), in an accountability report on his department's involvement in the filming of *Das Kaninchen bin ich* written after its banning, the director of the *Hauptverwaltung Film* was already in possession of a damning analysis of the film's literary source in the form of a report from the *Hauptverwaltung Verlage und Buchhandel* dated 15 December 1964. See 'Chronologischer Ablauf der Entstehung des Films *Das Kaninchen bin ich*', 17 January 1966 [BAP: DR 1 4313].

16. Conversely, the ban on *Das Kaninchen bin ich* had repercussions for a collection of short stories by Bieler that the *Aufbau Verlag* had planned to release under the title of *Märchen und Zeitungen*. Commenting on the story 'Rede eines Aufsehers über das Wesen des Strafvollzugs' one editor remarked, 'In a general sense, this is the idea behind *The Rabbit*: justice is a matter of interpretation. [The story is] hardly printable.' See the *Hauptverwaltung Verlage und Buchhandel* licensing information on 'Märchen und Zeitungen', handwritten notes, 15 April 1966 [BAP: DR 1 2085].

17. Also in mid-December Günter Witt, the director of the *Hauptverwaltung Film* and Hans Bentzien, Minister of Culture, met with *Hauptverwaltung Verlage und Buchhandel* officials in the matter of the film project. In the *Produktionsabteilung* account of the meeting, Witt and studio director Jochen Mückenberger vigorously supported the plan to film Bieler's novel, appealing to Maetzig's integrity and proven Party loyalty. See 'Chronologischer Ablauf der Entstehung des Films *Das Kaninchen bin ich*'.

18. A Ministry of Justice file on the judiciary's involvement in the film project provides some insight, although when interpreting such documents it is important to attend to the existence of inter-agency rivalries and attempts to disclaim responsibility after the film was finally banned in November 1965. See 'Einflußnahme des MfJ und des GStA auf die Herstellung des Films *Das Kaninchen bin ich*' [BAP: DP 1 VA 8117].

19. Ullmann writes: 'Generally, we would like to assure you that the Ministry of Justice would be happy to serve as consultant in any projects of a similar nature, something which would certainly be

advantageous in such matters.' See 'Memo from Ullmann to the DEFA Studio', 19 January 1965 [BAP: DP 1 VA 8117], p. 1.

20. See 'Memo from Ullmann to Schreier, 27 January 1965 [BAP: DP 1 VA 8117], p. 1.

21. It is worth noting that Riemann and his colleague were both involved in the production of the public relations brochure on GDR jurisprudence mentioned in the preceding section and thus likely to be particularly sensitive to issues surrounding the *Rechtspflegebeschluß*. They met with the *Abteilung Staats- und Rechtsfragen* to discuss the brochure on at least one occasion. See the 'Memo', 13 November 1964 [BAP: DP 1 VA 1904], p. 1. See also n. 6 above.

22. 'Aktenvermerk', 28 January 1965 [BAP: DP 1 VA 8117], p. 1.

23. 'Aktennotiz', 17 February 1965 [BAP: DP 1 VA 8117], p. 1.

24. 'Expertise', 19 May 1965 [BAP: DP 1 VA 8117], p. 2. At the bottom of the document, Ullmann made a note that Deputy Attorney-General Wendland was dissatisfied with the second script draft as well. 'Wartburg' refers to the 'luxury' class automobile of domestic production.

25. See 'Memo from Riemann to Wagner', 21 May 1965 [SAPMO IV A2/13/3], p. 1. In addition, Riemann reported that Wendland had not been consulted again following the meeting as had been agreed upon and that the Minister of Justice had also contacted him on the Section's measures regarding the project. A personal acquaintance of director Maetzig, Benjamin may have played a mediating role in the discussion surrounding the film project. A notice filed in late June 1965 suggests that Benjamin had agreed to talk to Maetzig on behalf of the Central Committee should problems with the script continue. See 'Memo', 29 June 1965 [BAP: DP 1 VA 8117], p. 1.

26. The repeal of the film's licence is recorded in 'Der ideologische Führungsplan der *Hauptverwaltung Film* des Ministeriums für Kultur', 27 November 1965 [SAPMO: IV A2/906/60], p. 1.

27. See report of 15 December 1965 [SAPMO: IV A2/13/3], p. 3. This was also the critique of an *Abteilung Kultur* position paper on the film from mid-October. See 'Zwei Standpunkte in der Beurteilung des Films *Das Kaninchen bin ich*', 15 October 1965 [SAPMO: IV A2/906/124].

28. See 'Probleme des Gegenwartsschaffens im DEFA-Spielfilm 1965/66', 4 October 1965 [SAPMO: IV A2/906/60], p. 33. The detailed document was submitted to the Central Committee for review along with a lengthy appendix of materials pertaining to the film.

29. Cf. scene 13/shot 35 in the 12 December 1964 script and the corresponding scene 9/shot 23 in the 3 March 1965 script [BAP: DR 117 DB 262, vols. 2-3]. Scene numbers in the text refer to these sources. The script of the film – together with the script of *Denk bloß nicht, ich heule* (*Just Don't Think I'm Crying*, 1965) and excerpts from discussions on both films – is available in *Prädikat: besonders schädlich. 'Das*

Kaninchen bin ich' und *'Denk bloß nicht ich heule'*, ed. Christiane Mückenberger, Berlin, 1990.

30. These are my translations of the terms 'Staatsverleumdung und planmäßige Hetze' and 'staatsgefährdende Hetze' respectively.

31. The scripts refer to this law when Dieter's sentence is revealed at the end of the sequence. 'Gesetz zur Ergänzung des Strafgesetzbuches - Strafrechtergänzungsgesetz', *Gesetzblatt der DDR*, 78, 1957: 643–7.

§19 Subversive Propaganda and Agitation

(1) Anyone who
1. glorifies or propagates fascism or militarism against other peoples or races,
2. agitates against or threatens with force the GDR, its institutions, social organisations, or citizens on the basis of membership in a state institution or social organisation shall be sentenced to a prison term of no less than three months. Attempted subversion or agitation is punishable by law.

(2) The same shall apply to producers, suppliers, or distributors of written or other material of such subversive content.

(3) In severe cases, in particular when the offence is perpetrated at the behest of persons or groups named in §14 [a paragraph governing espionage] or in premeditated fashion, the sentence shall be prolonged imprisonment ('Zuchthaus')

§20 Sedition

Anyone who
1. publicly defames or distorts the measures or activities of state or social institutions,

2. publicly defames or disparages a citizen due to state or social activities or to participation in state or social activities, shall be subject to a prison sentence of up to two years.

32. Report of 15 December 1965 [SAPMO: IV A2/13/3], p. 3.

❖ *Chapter 10* ❖

PATHS OF DISCOVERY: THE FILMS OF KONRAD WOLF

Anthony S. Coulson

In his relatively short working life as a director, Konrad Wolf produced thirteen feature films and several films for TV. His first feature film, *Einmal ist keinmal* (*Once Is Never*), a light comedy for which Wolf was by temperament hardly well suited, was completed in 1955, and his last, *SOLO SUNNY* in 1980. His productions are by no means fragments of one great confession, but they are closely related as the work of a man personally marked by the Nazi dictatorship and later wholeheartedly dedicated to the cause of the young East German state. Wolf was eight years old when his family was driven into exile, only returning as a soldier in the Soviet army in 1945, a fluent Russian speaker for whom Moscow was home. After a difficult period of readjustment to his native nationality and language, he committed himself to the building of a Communist society and culture in East Germany. His growing reputation as a film-maker in Germany and abroad, together with his exemplary record as a soldier and socialist and the high esteem in which he was held by colleagues and friends, qualified him eminently for the office of president of the GDR's *Akademie der Künste* (Academy of Arts), a function he performed conscientiously from 1965 until his death.

The urgency of the struggle to reclaim Germany, first territorially, and then spiritually, from fascism, and the earnestness of his commitment as a creative artist and state functionary to social debate and progress under Communism, inform Wolf's work from first to last. Broadly, his films can be divided by their historical subject matter into four main groupings: first, those such as *Lissy* (1957) and *Professor Mamlock* (1961) portraying the rise of National Socialism before the war; second, those dealing with the war itself, including the only East German film directly relating to the genocide of the Jews, *Sterne* (*Stars*, 1959), which won a prize at the 1959 Cannes Film Festival, and the two films based on Wolf's own war experience, *Ich war neunzehn* (*I Was Nineteen*, 1968) and *Mama, ich lebe* (*Mother, I'm Alive*, 1977). A third group, of later films, addresses the social and political role of the artist in society: *Goya oder Der arge Weg zur Erkenntnis* (*Goya or The Hard Road to Understanding*, 1971) and *Der nackte Mann auf dem Sportplatz* (*The Naked Man on the Playing Field*, 1974), together with two episodes of a TV series on the folk singer Ernst Busch, which proved in the event to be Wolf's last productions. Finally, from *Sonnensucher* (*Sun-Seekers*, 1958) to *Der geteilte Himmel* (*The Divided Heaven*, 1964) and *SOLO SUNNY* (1980) there are the films which take up contemporary social and political issues and the general conditions of life in the GDR.

Perhaps the one dominant concern in all of these groupings is that indicated in the subtitle of the Goya film – 'the hard road to understanding' – along which the central characters learn to reassess themselves and their place in society, a process of searching and reflecting which forms the core of Wolf's conception of the social and political issues he projects onto the screen. Time and again his films raise questions of perception and awareness, and of the material and mental barriers that obstruct them. We see his protagonists steeped in false values or misled by the force of circumstances, learning, though perhaps only partially, to face and correct their mistakes. Or there are those who are confronted with dilemmas and complexities, moral or political doubts, who may succeed, to a certain degree, in rethinking identities and strategies of survival. In this sense Wolf's films can be seen to illustrate paths of exploration and discovery, social and political in their goals, but charted out in portrayals of individuals whose lives ultimately affirm a commitment to open-mindedness and change. In demonstrating their will to see and understand what lies before them, and the courage to set their course accordingly, these characters speak for an ideal which itself comes to maturity in the visual language of Wolf's later work: the ideal of enlightenment through the art of cinema, the critical engagement of the spectator through the interaction of the formal structures of text and image.

I wish to examine two films from the middle period of Wolf's output: first, *Professor Mamlock*, the drama of a Jewish professional and intellectual at the end of the Weimar Republic who learns, too late, to recognise his enemies; and second, *Ich war neunzehn*, a study of Germany at war, of the experience of national consciousness and personal identity. Both focus on one of Wolf's central themes, the rise and fall of National Socialism, but provide contrasting views of their protagonists' progress along their individual paths of discovery, a contrast which reflects the transition in Wolf's own filmic language from what, in the 1950s, is fundamentally an eloquent rhetoric of persuasion, in the service of a strongly held political and social creed, to the reflections of a voice of exploration which speaks across doctrinal frontiers and points the way, in the late 1960s, for the emergence of a new German cinema, in both East and West.

Professor Mamlock, which Konrad Wolf and Karl Georg Egel adapted from Friedrich Wolf's 1933 play of the same name, is one of two films in Wolf's earlier output which portray the rise of National Socialism in the last phase of the Weimar Republic. Both *Professor Mamlock* and *Lissy* are concerned less with Hitlerism itself than with the strength of its appeal to the German people, and, above all, with the weakness, blindness or corruption of those who might have resisted it. Both films portray error, confusion and conversion – the point where the main protagonists discover the path which leads them away from complicity and towards reconciliation with themselves and their own inherent integrity. The two films address opposite ends of the social scale. In the first, Lissy is a girl from a working-class family who is drawn away from her roots and social conscience through loyalty to her *petit-bourgeois* husband and the desperation of the circumstances into which they, with their infant child, are plunged by the Weimar crisis. Lissy, her husband, and her ne'er-do-well brother Paul are all seen as vulnerable figures, just seeking to escape the humiliations inflicted upon them. While the husband gradually succumbs to temptation, and for him success and privilege drown out all doubt, Lissy herself is still able to recognise the mounting injustices, even though the moment of decision only comes for her when she learns the truth of her brother's murder by his fellow Nazis. Those friends she could have turned to for support are already betrayed, but now at least she is prepared to follow her conscience and step out alone. With the title figure of the later film, Wolf turns to circles which enjoy the highest status and greatest influence in Weimar society. Mamlock is seemingly untouched by the turmoil and hardships of the time. Yet he, too, proves vulnerable, and eventually stands, and dies, alone. Friedrich Wolf's play, already filmed in Moscow in 1936, provided his son with the model of a Jewish family, fully assimi-lated into German upper-class society and its culture, in which the father falls a victim to persecution and the son joins the resistance. Whereas the play and first film lay emphasis, as to be expected in the 1930s, on the cause of opposition to the Third Reich, it is characteristic of Wolf's film, seen in the context of the evolution of his work, that it focuses on the processes of self-deception and enlightenment in the central character.

In both *Lissy* and *Professor Mamlock*, Wolf leaves no doubt as to what his own ideological position is. The voice-over narrator who finally approves Lissy's choice of a difficult but honest path is echoed by Mamlock's dying blessing of the way chosen by his Communist son. And in case we are still unsure about our moral and political imperatives, we are reminded by a final caption passing over the profile of Mamlock's death-mask, the words he himself has just enunciated at the last moment of decision for all the characters: 'There is no greater crime than refusing to fight when the situation demands.' One might well ask about the crimes of those who made the fight so necessary, but there is no doubt left in this, and other earlier films by Wolf, about the identity of those who have taken up the struggle, and where their path will lead. More than *Lissy*, *Professor Mamlock* is also at times overloaded with the abstrac-tion and pathos of the debates which defined the political and social conflict in the original play. However, in focussing on the figure of Mamlock, and his progress towards understanding, the film often succeeds in going beyond these static positions. What stands between him and recognition of the reality of National Socialism is not, as with Lissy and her kind, vulnera-bility to economic forces, but Mamlock's own misplaced sense of invulnerability: his unquestioning confidence in the security of his profession and reputation as a leading surgeon, his trust in the social élite who are his friends, guests and patients, his belief in the supremacy of reason and science, and, above all, his faith in the universal values of German humanist culture. Initially, there is no place in all he represents for any sense of the threat that faces him and his family. While it follows the basic plot of the play, Wolf's portrayal concentrates on the gradual erosion of resistance to a new consciousness in his central character, whose advance is seen to emerge out of the ongoing interaction, captured in the film's narrative structure, between Mamlock's world, his creed and his culture, and the forces ranged against him.

From the beginning, the film explores for the spectator those interrelationships which Mamlock has chosen to ignore. As it does, it anticipates his changing experience, as he, too, comes to share in our reading of those connections. The burden of Wolf's ideological commitment, eager to pass judgement on his character and his times, certainly remains evident, but it is at least partially offset by the multi-dimensionality of perception embedded in the film's audio-visual montage. The interplay of perspectives embodies a principle of open-mindedness which is the prerequisite for Mamlock's transformation. At the same time the cinematic breaking down of the barriers behind which he has entrenched himself also represents in itself an important element of imaginative insight in the film that counteracts its explicit political intention. Where the character's dogmatic stance is subverted, the spectator also acquires a degree of critical freedom towards the fiction as a whole, including Wolf's own favoured reading of his tale.

The linking of the perspectives of spectator and central figure is introduced in the very first shot of the film in a way which immediately draws our attention to what Mamlock excludes from his vision. In close-up he speaks directly into the camera: 'You're weighed down with worry ... Will there be another war, after the last mass slaughter?' It is as if we were being drawn directly into the fiction and as if Mamlock had adopted our perception of the danger of war. But then the camera tracks back to take in the wider scene, and we return to the role of observers. Mamlock is talking to guests, on New Year's Eve 1932–3. As he continues, he also withdraws from the insight he had appeared to share: 'But there's no cause for despair.' The chorus of Beethoven's Ninth breaks in, and he assures his listeners that reason will prevail over barbarism. We are faced with the calm confidence of the bourgeois enjoying the pleasures of the festivities on the eve of catastrophe. The remaining dialogue serves to introduce the figures of Mamlock's inner circle, and to anchor the Professor firmly in the values of German conservative tradition and culture. The power of the spirit over the political excesses of Left and Right is evoked, while the camera pans the pictures, on the wall, of Mamlock's past, including the commemorative war-plaque that reappears at the end of the film, when his world has collapsed in ruins: 'The Fatherland thanks its heroes.'

Having introduced that world, Wolf immediately turns to the other players that will determine its future. In two scenes, each framed by a brief return to the party, and at first seemingly unconnected, we meet the Communists and the Nazis. Mamlock's son Rolf meets a fugitive worker at the station to lead him to a safe house. Overhead and long shots stress the danger and secrecy of the encounter. The source of the danger is then identified in the second scene: we look in at the window of a pub crowded with celebrating military and brown shirts. Then, prominent in the foreground, a truck-load of SA men moves off. Back at Mamlock's house, all wait for midnight with their glasses poised, but the mother glances down anxiously at one glass left standing: Rolf's. The following rapid montage sequence fuses the three groups of protagonists into one. As the SA gang attacks Rolf and comrades in the street, matching cross-cutting between the fighting and Mamlock's celebrations visualises how closely these worlds belong together, while underlining the indifference and complacency that bar the Professor from sharing our insight. As the glasses chink, a knife flashes; as the men struggle, the couples dance; as the police baton beats on the door behind which Rolf and friend have taken refuge, hands conduct the gramophone record. The Blue Danube alternates with the sound of explosions, fireworks which anticipate future gunfire.

At home and in the hospital Mamlock resists this identification of events within and outside his familiar world, rejecting both the Communist commitment of his son and the strident jargon of the National Socialist sympathisers on his staff: 'No politics please – just doctors and patients, patients and doctors', he insists. The Communist wounded in the street fight is treated strictly as a patient. He is taken to task for the irresponsibility of his political activities, but it is Mamlock who bends the rules and keeps the cause of injury a secret from the authorities. Mamlock sees in this no challenge to the law he reveres or any kind of political gesture, but the following shots suggest otherwise: in double exposure we see images of the subsequent development

of the affair under the shadow of a superimposed newspaper
picture of the Führer-to-be, an image which fills the screen. The
issue is put to Mamlock directly by his Communist patient in
their last consultation: he, the Professor, is the patient, and the
danger that threatens him and the nation is the 'cancer of
fascism'. Again it is Wolf's shifting of narrative perspectives
which turns the rhetorical phrase into a sudden insight into
dimensions still hidden from Mamlock. We cut straight from his
patient's challenge and the look of bafflement on the
Professor's face to the half-disbelieving words of his financier
friend Schneider: 'What did you say?!' he exclaims, answering
the telephone, and we can hear the surprise is not altogether an
unpleasant one for him. The cause, it soon transpires, is the
news of the Reichstag fire, and he is quick to profit nicely from
the new government's anti-Semitism. Soon after, the exchange
between the Communist and the uncomprehending Mamlock
is matched by the argument between Rolf and sister Ruth,
sitting framed in identical positions over the radio, which is
broadcasting Goebbels's speech on the fire, the Nazi 'provocation' predicted by the Communist at the hospital. The debate
between brother and sister offers a parallel commentary on the
father's response to events.

In fact, the Reichstag fire becomes the turning-point for
Mamlock and his family (as well as for Lissy, in the earlier film).
The daughter still identifies, we are told, with 'all that is unpro-
letarian, spiritual and preserving'. Soon, she is to be driven in a
panic from school by chants of 'Jews out!' and the grotesquely
distorted faces of tormentors which swirl around in a wild
hand-camera sequence. But by then the process of discovery
has already begun for Mamlock himself, and he, too, is
confronted with the masks of a society he had never recognised. His financier friend advises him to take leave, and
against the crescendo of a Hitler-speech in the background,
Mamlock finds his own wife is infected, albeit only momen-
tarily, with the racialist jargon enveloping them. Shocked,
Mamlock withdraws into the gloom of his house. As he closes
the blinds, the noise of frantic crowds, hailing their Führer, is
suddenly cut off. The Professor returns to his spiritual suste-
nance. A gramophone record spins, and the sound of
Beethoven's Ninth again fills the room. He listens in calm solitude, the camera fixed on his face. Then the close-up dissolves

into the image of the radio speaker, and the news of the measures of the new government penetrates his refuge. The image of the loudspeaker dissolves into the record, then his face, and back again. The music and announcements continue in parallel, until the news reaches the decree banning Jews from the professions. The gramophone record and radio seem to merge into one, as the needle sticks on the word 'prohibited' ('untersagt'). The culture by which Mamlock has lived will no longer secure him against Nazi persecution: Beethoven's Ninth belongs to the world that they now have in their grip.

Defiantly, Mamlock returns to the hospital to reclaim the place denied him. In the name of his old creed, he smashes the portrait of Hitler now hanging in his office, the voice-over ironically reminding us, and him, 'just doctors and patients, patients and doctors'. But the long hospital corridor along which he was accustomed to march, assured of his unquestioned authority, is now the scene of his fall, and we see him, with the same long shot, disappear under SA escort. As he is paraded through the streets, the white coat of his profession is now daubed with the stigma of exclusion. When a carnival procession engulfs the small marching column, the frozen features of his face are reflected and distorted in the mockery of the masks around him, recalling the persecution that drove Ruth from school. Mamlock has no option but to see where he now stands in this society.

Mamlock's growing, though enforced, awareness of his isolation is repeatedly balanced, through ambiguities of narrative structure, against the evocation of answers that lie beyond his reach. Immediately after the attack on his daughter, we see, and hear, the name of the Jewish partner being chipped off the entrance to Schneider's bank. The financier is also no longer available, it seems, when Mamlock is defamed in the press and his wife seeks help. 'But someone must help', she says. The scene cuts to Rolf and comrades at work: 'That will help', Rolf is told, in praise of his leaflet against Nazi anti-Semitic acts, and the chipping sound is resumed – but this time it is the signal from a friend standing watch that all is still clear. Later, after his humiliation, Mamlock still insists that his son's comrades are not his, but here again match-cutting underlines the limitations of his vision. 'Are you my son?', he asks Rolf, and the answer follows an immediate cut: 'Yes, I am Rolf Mamlock', but the speaker is Rolf's Communist friend, whom we hear deceiving his captors in a sacrificial attempt to divert them from Mamlock's son. Mamlock cannot acknowledge where the real help for him and his family lies. It is perhaps predictable, then, that though he now prepares to leave the land, he allows himself to be deluded again, briefly. Schneider, who happens to want the professional attention of the man he discarded, now presents himself as the true friend in need. Once more the strains of Beethoven's chorus ring out, and the Professor marches again to the clinic. But when the conditions are made apparent, Mamlock shows that he, too, has at least learnt to resist. With that decision he excludes himself irrevocably from the world he knew. Abandoned, even denounced, by friends and colleagues, he finds the last door closed to him. Like the repeated 'prohibited' of the earlier montage, the sign over the operating theatre ceaselessly flashes 'prohibited', alternating rapidly with extreme close-ups of Mamlock's face, the mask of a man about to commit suicide.

Finally, Mamlock's transformation is presented as a renunciation of his previous self and of the society to which he belonged. But that insight comes too late to save him and his kind. It is indicative of Wolf's ideological control of his theme that his main character remains primarily the object, rather than the subject, of the process of discovery. He advances only as realities are imposed upon him. His fate is attributed, highly questionably, to his failure to fight. If Mamlock is exiled from his own world, he is also barred from the ranks of the true warriors. The lesson of his suicide is spelt out quite explicitly: he failed to find, he concedes in his dying moments, the one true path, the one taken by his son, and his own path, without the solidarity of the cause, could lead nowhere. In its conclusion Wolf's film reaffirms the political pathos of his father's play in a way that sits uncomfortably with the principle of openness and discovery which he himself has integrated into his narrative form. As yet the interplay of perspectives is employed against the central figure from a position of authority located outside the fiction, rather than permeating the relationship of spectator and screen fiction in a way that calls for interpretation rather than assent. The camera may discern what Mamlock refuses to see, but Wolf's cinema has not yet learnt to subvert its own certainties. *Professor Mamlock* is the last of his propagandistic melodramas, and marks a stage in his work at which his films are beginning to advance towards critical maturity. It anticipates, as yet tentatively and unsuccessfully, an openness of reflection that will eventually escape the confines of doctrinal presuppositions.

Between *Professor Mamlock* and *Ich war neunzehn* lies the adaptation of Christa Wolf's novel *Der geteilte Himmel* (*The Divided Heaven*). The choice of the literary source confirms Konrad Wolf's willingness to experiment with narrative techniques in the quest to discover a filmic language that could articulate what he saw as the social and psychological complexities of his theme and the issues it raised for GDR society: 'the usual kind of film dramatisation', he commented at the time, referring to the option of a single, chronological narrative line, would have produced 'a story that was very superficial, artificial, and remote from reality'.[1] Later, it is true, Wolf came to doubt whether his experiment had been entirely successful, and considered 'that in looking for an original film structure which would do justice to the structure of Christa Wolf's novella we got bogged down in unresolved formal problems'.[2] Against this, one critic has persuasively argued that this film represents a 'breakthrough' in Wolf's cinema, leading to a 'much freer, associative handling of time and space', in comparison with the 'complicated' montage passages of *Lissy* and *Professor Mamlock*.[3] Crucially, even where the density of narrative structure in *Der geteilte Himmel* may suggest an over-rigid search for equivalence to the literary model, the multi-perspectivism shared by both book and film embraces, for the first time in Konrad Wolf's work, the totality of his fiction. Rather than steer his narrative towards preconceived norms, Wolf permits it to unfold without judgmental interventions or declarations: the path of discovery upon which his heroine Rita embarks leads back, with its closing voice-over and final shot, to its starting-point. Rita returns to familiar terrain and her life in the GDR, but there is little suggestion that the issues have been resolved or that this vote of confidence means more than making the best of the future.

Three years later, in his first 'autobiographical' film devoted to the war, a subject where one might imagine that the strength of his political convictions and the harrowing memory of his own and his adopted homeland's confrontation with Nazi Germany would have militated against critical openness of mind, Wolf's portrayal is structured as an exploration in which the goal can only emerge out of the uncertain distance through ongoing reflection upon a plurality of fragments of perception and experience. For the generation of 1967, *Ich war neunzehn* looks back in time to recall and record Germany's past, and forward, from that past, to question what it might become in the future. At the same time, advancing into the Germany of 1945 with its young hero, the film reaches out in space to open up ever-changing perspectives on this unknown land and its people, where each new encounter both explains and confuses what the last has brought to light.[4]

Scripted by Wolfgang Kohlhaase, *Ich war neunzehn* is partly based on the war diary Wolf kept, against orders, during the campaign in Germany in 1945. Clearly, the film contains a significant autobiographical element, but it is also much more than a self-portrayal. In the context of the chaotic and monstrous events of the time, the film examines the possibilities of perception and understanding for one young man, Gregor, who could be any, but finds himself in a singular situation, mediating, in a way he cannot fully anticipate or comprehend, between two peoples at war. In the film, he is torn between the land he is fighting for, the only home he is conscious of, and the unknown land of his origins. This sense of a divided self is even reflected in his attitude to language itself: his mother tongue, now seemingly a voice of barbarism, is also the only language in which decency and humanity can be restored. The issue of the ambivalence of the German language he speaks, and the culture it stands for, is raised at several points in the film. Vadim, the young Russian officer in Gregor's unit, whose intention is to return to Leningrad and teach the German literature he reveres, asks Kurt, a German they have liberated from Brandenburg prison: 'How can I explain ... Goethe and Auschwitz ... two German names ... two names in one and the same language?' 'It's my language, too', the German replies. Wolf's film never lets that paradox remain just a conceptual puzzle. It lies embedded in the sounds and images of this Germany that meets Gregor as the Russians advance, experiences which pose questions relating not only to the land and how it is to be understood, but to himself and his own situation *vis-à-vis* its language and culture. His very role in this war commits him inescapably to the German language: the voice of a propaganda unit whose task is to mediate with the enemy, to persuade them of the folly of further resistance. The film opens and closes with the sight and sound of the loud-

speaker van in which Gregor's unit travels. It remains, throughout the film, a physical symbol of his hesitant, problematic
'dialogue' with the Germans. Throughout the campaign he
acts as an interpreter. Repeatedly he is asked where he, a
German in Russian uniform, stands, how many there are like
him, when he was last 'home', or whether even, 'identified' by
a German from his birthplace, he does not remember people
from his early childhood in Germany. In one encounter, a
blind and helpless German soldier takes him for a comrade,
and Gregor acts as if he is. And in one sense he is what his voice
makes him here: the cigarette and company he offers acknowledge the deeper bond between them, whatever uniform they
wear. At the same time, their dialogue reminds us sharply why
they are in uniform and what the consequences have been.
Told by Gregor that the tobacco comes from the Caucasus, the
blinded German says that he, too, was there, and adds, pathetically: 'We've seen a lot, comrade.' The ambivalence of this one
encounter is characteristic of the reflective tone adopted
throughout the film in its portrayal of the bizarre and tragic
contradictions of Germany in 1945.

These beginnings of Gregor's dialogue with Germany are
also a meeting, and coming to terms, with himself, both where
he is moved by a feeling of common humanity or solidarity with
the victims of Nazism, and where he is repelled by the savagery
and mindlessness of the enemy. With the opening sequence of
the film we share Gregor's view across the river Oder, looking
over into the mist towards the Germany that awaits the
invaders, the land he is about to address through the loudspeaker. The water seems placid and peaceful enough. A tango
is played on the gramophone; the music seems to harmonise
with the gentleness of the landscape before us. In the distance
a shape emerges out of the mist: a raft drifting slowly down-
stream. We cut to the face of a boy, slightly nervous. The loudspeaker calls out across the water: German soldiers should
surrender, the war is over. Suddenly we cut to a close, low-
angled shot of what is on the raft: a German soldier dangling
from a rope, and a sign that reads: 'Deserter. I sold out to the
Russians'. The call for peace is answered: the threat that
appears out of the German mist is directed at those who might
listen, but also at the speaker, who we now see is the boy,
Gregor, looking on as the raft with its macabre cargo drifts past.
From then on he is to be confronted with the paradox of the

many faces of Germany, both hostile and responsive, and the dilemma of how to relate to them.

The film is narrated as a chronicle, covering the period 10 April, the date given for the river episode, to 2 May. After the opening sequence, it falls into six sections, each headed with the date. The first section, 22 April, is introduced with a complex audio-visual montage combining documentary film of the historical offensive, juxtaposed with scenes of the propaganda unit advancing along country roads or, briefly, engaged in combat. These images are accompanied on the sound track by repetitions of the loudspeaker announcement, interrupted by the music and alternating with a voice-over – Gregor himself, recording his family's exile from Germany (matching Wolf's own experience) and his present return: 'They say that's my home', a 'home' with which he has yet to open any kind of dialogue. Almost every day, we are told, he makes the same announcement, but gunfire is the usual answer. His opening narrative concludes 'I am nineteen'.

The last section of the film takes up that title phrase and a number of the motifs introduced at the beginning, forming a frame around Gregor's journey of discovery and returning to the central questions: the nature of this Germany, its guilt and its future, and of Gregor's place in it, both now, at the time of the events, and later, as the narrator. Three weeks after the chronicle begins, remnants of German forces, led by SS troops, launch a final senseless offensive to break through the lines encircling Berlin. Again the threat materialises out of a deceptive calm. The propaganda unit, unprotected, makes a last attempt to minimise further bloodshed; they take up position at a farm, once again looking out over a quiet landscape with water. This time, the Germans respond in numbers: wounded, exhausted, all ages, they make their way over the marsh and up the hill. It seems as if peace has finally come. The silence is broken only by the scraping of spoons, as the Russians and their German prisoners eat. The SS attack that suddenly erupts, from over the water, is beaten off, but only at the cost of the life of Sascha, the commander and comrade who saved Gregor at the beginning of his tale. We see Gregor against the landscape, looking over the water, screaming at the murderers 'We'll get you yet', as if they were hidden out there in the fields. While he continues to vent his anger and grief, we cut from close-up to a frontal long shot, from across the water, and then, from the same perspective, to an extreme long shot in which Gregor has now merged into that landscape which he was berating. The voice changes to a more controlled, though still angry, threat: 'until you can't shoot any more, you criminals!' Finally, the camera moves back to the farm, to a close-up again of Gregor's face, and now he speaks quietly and sadly, the voice of his thoughts: 'until you've finally understood that it's all over'. His anger at the enemy has led him back to himself, and he himself has become part of the land he denounces. The final shot combines the recurrent images of landscape and loudspeaker van. Gregor's journey leads on. He sits on the back steps of the truck as it disappears into the dusty distance, but the final voice-over, the voice of the narrator looking back, tells us what the boy has begun to discover but will only later learn to accept: 'I am a German, I was nineteen years old.' The conflict of tenses marks the shift in consciousness, and sense of identity, that will result from his experiences.

As the title of the film suggests, Gregor's meeting with Germany is also a process of coming of age, learning to find himself as he responds to the contradictions that confront him. From the first close-ups of his face, Wolf places emphasis on the youth, innocence and vulnerability of his hero – to an extent not apparent in his own diary. We see his perplexity and embarrassment as well as his practical good sense during his twenty-four- hour elevation to the rank of Commandant of Bernau. We see his anxiety and nervousness, in contrast to Vadim, his superior, inside Spandau fortress. When called upon to propose a toast at the 1 May festivity, he can only think of his mother, to whom his thoughts return when he falls off the terrace parapet, drunk, and a voice-over dialogue with her ensues in which he imagines himself gently reproached for his naughtiness. However, Gregor's youth and cheerful naïvety serve here as the eyes through which we too experience the confusion and strangeness of the multiplicity of voices that constitute the broken Germany of 1945, voices which seem to defy interpretation or dialogue. After he is nominated Commandant, we see Gregor from above, standing alone and somewhat at a loss in the deserted square. The space around him is duplicated in his dealings with the inhabitants. A girl calls him into a house where a woman has committed suicide. The camera follows Gregor's uncomprehending gaze as he looks around the room, from the gas pipe and the feet of the corpse to the furniture, belongings and family photos on the walls: a life surrendered apparently for no reason (in his diary Wolf recorded how he intervened to save a woman from suicide). Even more startling for Gregor is the girl's despair, and he has no answer to the series of questions she fires at him as to what will become of her, leading to the inevitable: 'Are you a German? How did you get to be here?' Her underlying assumption as to where he belongs, as if fascism has no consequences, is challenged, later, in the angry dispute with a Soviet woman soldier. When asked, accusingly, why the Germans came to Russia and caused such misery, the girl can only cry 'I didn't do anything'. Gregor stands between them, trying to interpret where there is no understanding. Town officialdom assures its new masters of its goodwill by hanging out the only red flag to hand, the Japanese red sun, while the mayor, graciously putting his probable past behind him, calls for 'human understanding' ('Verständnis von Mensch zu Mensch') and offers his 'sincere cooperation' ('aufrichtige Mitarbeit') in healing the wounds of war. Other business calls for a less forthright response from the young commandant: the courteous priest who would like permission to preach; the old socialist, nominated mayor, who corrects his spelling. When Gregor leaves the town we look back with him from the rear of the truck, looking down at the girl who remains standing by the square, passing in and out of view as the truck turns, till she fades into the distance. Later the reverse tracking shot is repeated with Kurt, the ex-prisoner installed as mayor in another town, seated in the sun in the middle of an empty square. On the second occasion the image is reinforced with Ernst Busch's 'Jarama' song, from the Spanish civil war, and the implications are decidedly more positive. However, here and elsewhere the end of a passing acquaintance, a brief basis for dialogue, is signalled, and the individuals concerned are left to make their uncertain way, in their own fashion, in the new Germany, just as we see with Gregor himself, at the end.

Gregor's tale is the linking narrative, but the film works both within and outside his perspective in constructing its review of the images of Germany. When the unit reaches Sachsenhausen Gregor comments on a shot of the abandoned camp: 'We'll find the culprits ... And then what will they say?' The answer is given directly by the following clips of Soviet documentary film, in which a camp guard explains with calm expertise how the gassings and shootings took place. The sequence is intercut with shots of Gregor under a shower, one who could have been amongst the thousands of Russian prisoners we are told were murdered. Other dialogues are connected as fictive extensions of Gregor's own path of discovery. At the farm, in the last section, a young soldier boy explains how he suffered his injuries, when ordered to clear a way across Spandau Bridge for the Führer. Or there is the episode of the equally child-like hero in Spandau fortress describing, in a reproduction of a National Socialist newsreel, how he destroyed an enemy tank and was rewarded with a bar of chocolate. These tales of the abuse of youth are complemented by a portrait of the perversion of the mind: the mystifying, self-exculpating rhetoric of the philosophical landscape-designer, whose house is a mausoleum of German culture, a culture which apparently left no trace of anything resembling a moral consciousness. In his account of the historical inevitability of events, of the irresistible appeal of National Socialism, of war as an 'anthropological problem' (an 'anthropologisches Problem'), he has words for everything, but no answer to Vadim's specific question as to how he managed to live under fascism – and despise it so eloquently at the same time. His patronising eagerness to claim Gregor for the 'innate idealism' ('angeborenen Idealismus') of the German people provokes an abusive response. It is easier for Gregor's Russian comrade Vadim to believe in the land of poets and thinkers. When the two of them stand together looking out at the sun setting over the German landscape, again across an expanse of water, Vadim reverently recites Heine: 'Once I had a fine Fatherland...' ('Ich hatte einst ein schönes Vaterland ...'), but Gregor angrily refuses to identify with the mystique of *Heimat* Germany and its heritage. When the frame then broadens to take in the background, we see the reason for his particular sensitivity: they are standing, in fact, outside the walls of the concentration camp. Gregor's rejection of any such idealisation reflects his alienation from the German in himself. Yet the contradictions and confusions of his identity are inescapable encounters along his path.

Within the German establishment itself, Wolf carefully records voices which range from strident and fanatical to humane and pragmatic. There is the venom and deceitfulness of the Nazi radio broadcasts; there is the Spandau SS officer for whom a garrison without medals to pin on the breast of child heroes is a 'pig-sty', and who chooses suicide rather than join in the surrender of the fortress. We see those who surrender but, at times comically, cling to the illusion of honour and discipline, such as the section commander who requests permission to telephone his superiors and report off-duty and into captivity; or the officer who hands over his ceremonial dagger to Sascha with multiple salutes and later considers it a disgrace for a German to shoot at other Germans. There is also the contrasting figure of the elderly Swabian commander at Spandau, whose undignified descent down a rope ladder, viewed from below, is followed by his endearing readiness to capitulate, but only 'in strict accordance with the ethical and moral standards' expected of a German officer. After the adjutant is sent back up to ascertain the garrison's response to the Soviet ultimatum, Vadim, Gregor and the commander wait somewhat awkwardly, not really knowing what to say, until the German offers his fruit drops. Each is then framed, close-up, sucking solemnly. Such discreetly ironic elements suggest moments of human contact, if not dialogue. But even with those Germans who were the victims of oppression, that dialogue is still problematic. At the May Day celebration Kurt, lamed by past suffering, cannot find the words he wants to propose a toast, while a second prisoner gives vent to his rage and demands bloody revenge. At the farm, too, the film extends our vision, with Gregor, of a Germany that eludes immediate understanding. We see the unassuming kindness of the farmer and his wife, prepared to conceal the wounded boy prisoner from the Russians (though one wonders whether they would have hidden him from the SS), while our perception of the brutality of the SS attack is sharpened by the figure of the frail little girl, caught, covering her eyes, in the middle of the cross-fire. The SS are repelled with the help of Willi, a soldier from Berlin, and other prisoners, but he, too, is unable to explain to Gregor, or to himself, why he joined that last futile offensive out of the town where he belonged.

This question, like many before and to come, remains unanswered, but not forgone or forgotten. Gregor's journey continues: his chronicle, and the film itself, represent an enduring demand that this nation, individually and collectively, must account for itself. If *Ich war neunzehn* is categorised as a drama of the Second World War, it is one in which the relationship of past and present is central, and the act of recovering the past, in filmic narrative, is just as essential as the events of 1945 themselves. Engaging the past in dialogue is at the same time to build a critical historical consciousness in, and towards, the present. This alone belies the charge that in conceiving this film Wolf might have been tempted to look backwards in order to escape the dilemma of the DEFA crisis of 1966. In one sense this is indeed an autobiographical portrayal of the last days of the war and of the real experiences of those who endured it. Of this and the later film, *Mama, ich lebe*, Wolf spoke of his desire to bear witness to what might gradually slip from memory and to try to explain to new generations, the youth for whom 1945 is a school history lesson, what it actually meant to live at that time.[5] But this memoir looks forward as well as back. Its inquiry and insistence on dialogue admits a present that does not command the answers, but is learning to seek them. In contrast to *Professor Mamlock, Ich war neunzehn* persuades by committing itself fully to discovery. It does not compromise but enhances its political and moral relevance by offering a study in the perception and interpretation of a personal and national history. Following Gregor's path, it traces out for us a process of watching and listening, reflecting and distinguishing. That process, the 'hard road to understanding', is articulated in a cinematic language of exploration which is one of Konrad Wolf's, and DEFA's, most positive contributions to the fostering of a critical modern culture in Germany.

Notes

1. Konrad Wolf, '*Der geteilte Himmel*: Probleme des sozialistischen Realismus in der darstellenden Künste. Diskussionsbeitrag auf der Plenartagung der Deutschen Akademie der Künste, 30.6. 1964', in *Konrad Wolf: direkt in Kopf und Herz. Aufzeichnungen, Reden, Interviews*, ed. Aune Renk, Berlin, 1989, pp. 92–7 (p. 93).
2. Konrad Wolf, ' "Auf der Suche nach dem Lebenszentrum": Werkstattgespräch für *Film und Fernsehen*, April/Mai 1975' in Renk, *Konrad Wolf*, pp. 235–50 (p. 240).
3. Marc Silberman, 'Remembering History: The Filmmaker Konrad Wolf', *New German Critique* 49, 1990: 163–91 (178).
4. The film *Ich war 19* is the subject of an extended discussion in Marc Silberman's book *German Cinema: Texts in Context*, Detroit, 1995 (esp. 145–61). Regrettably at the time of researching this article, Silberman's excellent study had not yet been published.

5. Konrad Wolf, ' "Auf der Suche nach Deutschland": Pressegespräch, 31.1.1968', in: Renk, *Konrad Wolf,* pp. 159–61. See also: 'Von den Möglichkeiten sozialistischer Filmkunst: Reaktionen auf Mama, *ich lebe.* Rede, 3.5.1977', in Renk, *Konrad Wolf,* pp. 267–74.

✤ *Chapter 11* ✤

FROM MODELS TO MISFITS: WOMEN IN DEFA FILMS OF THE 1970s AND 1980s

Andrea Rinke

Ever since 1945, mainstream cinema in the Federal Republic has been dominated by Hollywood and its female stereotypes: the housewife, the glamorous sex-symbol and the demonised temptress. By contrast, an initial overview of DEFA films reveals an altogether different variety of female protagonists from Western images of women on the screen. Films in the GDR tended to portray their heroines at their workplace, as ordinary average people, avoiding glamorous extremes. The majority of women on screen are working mothers with one or two children, more often single than married. Throughout two decades of DEFA *Gegenwartsfilme* – films dealing with contemporary life – only three or four housewives are portrayed, suggesting that this way of life was socially unacceptable and doomed to fail as part of a relationship.

There was no explicitly feminist approach to film-making in the GDR, the official view being that women's emancipation had been successfully accomplished by achieving women's economic independence. However, there was a remarkable number of DEFA films featuring female protagonists and addressing women's issues in the 1970s and 1980s. According to Joshua Feinstein, it was the general turn towards everyday contemporary issues during those years, the focus on more concrete social realms conventionally associated with women, which favoured the female experience.[1]

Indeed, of the films in the 1970s and 1980s, a large proportion dealt with everyday life in contemporary GDR society as seen through the eyes of a female protagonist. Of the roughly ninety *Gegenwartsfilme* ('contemporary screen dramas') produced from 1972 to 1988 there are more than half with a female character at the centre of the story or a female-male relationship, as their main theme. Does this mean that GDR cinema audiences in the 1970s and 1980s were swamped with *Frauenfilme* ('women's films') in the Western, feminist sense, i.e., with consciousness-raising films about women by female directors for female spectators? The answer would appear to be no. For only a very small proportion of film directors were in fact women: of all the directors of *Gegenwartsfilme* working for DEFA between the years 1946 and 1992 (a group of roughly thirty directors on permanent contracts at any one time) only three were women: Ingrid Reschke (who died in a car accident in 1971), Iris Gusner and Evelyn Schmidt.

How was it, then, that the almost exclusively male group of directors working for DEFA became so interested in women's roles and gender relations in a state where the authorities assumed equality of the sexes to be an accomplished fact in all areas of society? What message did they aim to convey by resorting to female rather than male protagonists? In this essay I will attempt to examine these questions by giving an overview of the cinematic depiction of women in DEFA *Gegenwartsfilme* of the 1970s and 1980s and asking how they related to their audiences and to the contemporary GDR society which they aimed to represent. Three of the lesser known films have been chosen for closer analysis as representative of tendencies and patterns of developments in the portrayal of DEFA film heroines. *Bis daß der Tod euch scheidet* (*Until Death Do Us Part*, 1979) directed by Heiner Carow stands for those films which challenge the assumption that the emancipation of women in the GDR was a successfully accomplished fact and that equal rights in the home was a topic of the past. In *Unser kurzes Leben* (*Our Short Life*, 1981), directed by Lothar Warneke, the heroine is a rebel who wants to instigate changes in society from within. And in *Das Fahrrad* (*The Bicycle*, 1982) directed by Evelyn Schmidt, we are presented with an anti-heroine, a misfit who has dropped out of society.

Ideal and Reality

Following the disastrous consequences of the Eleventh Plenum of the SED's Central Committee in 1965, film-makers tended to portray women in *Gegenwartsfilme* of the late 1960s and early 1970s in terms of the ideal 'socialist personality'. These model heroines participated in the social production process, and, being highly qualified, held down prestigious jobs, (often in traditionally male domains) such as that of a university lecturer in mathematics in Ralph Kirsten's *Netzwerk* (*Network*, 1970), a director of a research project in physics in Horst Seemann's *Liebeserklärung an G.T.* (*Declaration of Love to G.T.*, 1971) or as a *Meisterin* ('Supervisor') in a mechanical engineering plant in Helmut Dziuba's *Laut und leise ist die Liebe* (*Love is Loud and Silent*, 1972). This tendency was criticised by Regine Sylvester, who pointed out that these idealised model heroines were not representative of the majority of women who were still at the lower end of the employment scale doing menial jobs: 'we should not focus on the professionally advanced and successful woman in our films when, for the majority of women, the only interesting experience of work open to them is at home in the evening – when their husbands tell them about what *they* do in *their* working lives'.[2]

In films of the later 1970s and early 1980s, the work that women did on screen tended to be a more realistic reflection of the position of female workers in GDR society. Although there were still female protagonists to be found pursuing 'exceptional' careers, there was an increasing number of DEFA heroines holding down ordinary, traditionally female, jobs such as shop assistants, cashiers, cooks, cleaners, nurses, post office clerks or teachers, as well as workers in textile or shoe combines or in manufacturing factories. Drawing upon one of Marx's well known statements about the relation of the sexes being an indicator of social advance, the film critic Hans-Rainer Mihan concludes that 'female protagonists stand for the potential for the development of human beings under socialism'.[3] Accordingly, DEFA *Frauenfilme* were perceived as providing 'snapshots of social conditions' in the GDR.

After the promising – but short-lived – shift in official policy heralded by Erich Honecker's speech declaring the absence of any taboo subjects in 1971, DEFA films started to challenge the rather simplistic view that had dominated the late 1960s, namely that once conditions in the workplace had been sorted out, happiness at home was sure to follow. In these films the heroines aimed to achieve self-fulfilment at an individual level, for instance, through a love relationship, rather than through their role in society. Often they took a critical view of the discrepancies between ideal and reality, between the new opportunities which the socialist state offered women – full-time employment, on-the-job training and staff development schemes, for instance – and the outdated attitudes which prevented men and women from making the best of such opportunities.

In Egon Günther's *Der Dritte* (*Her Third*, 1972), one of the most interesting and well-known DEFA films, the gap between the traditional concepts of gender-roles still present in GDR society and the progress that women had made on a professional level, is addressed explicitly. The main character, Margit, a mathematician with a successful career, is divorced. She has two children, each by a different partner, and is now looking for Mr Right, 'the third'. In one of the best-known scenes she complains about the discrepancy she still experiences between equality at work and the outdated role of the passive, submissive female she is expected to play in her private life: 'I am a mathematician. I work, think and feel in a manner appropriate to the technical, scientific and political developments brought about by the techno-scientific conditions of revolutionary socialism. But if I fancy a man, if I need him, if I want him, I'm almost bound to make a fool of myself if I tell him so.'

Perhaps the most dramatic film that addresses the problems that women in the GDR still experienced in their attempt to combine the new socialist role of the working woman with a harmonious marriage and happy family life is Heiner Carow's *Bis daß der Tod euch scheidet*. The film's narrative – a gripping, melodramatic story – is based on an authentic police report. Sonja and Jens are getting married and appear to be the 'ideal' couple: they have good jobs, are fun-loving and very much in love. After the birth of their child, however, Jens wants Sonja to quit her job as an assistant in a grocery shop and become a full-time wife and mother. Sonja finds it very hard to accept this, but as they do not discuss their feelings – they simply have sex and hope this will solve the problem – the conflict escalates. While Jens, a construction worker, is out of the house, Sonja secretly takes a course at home to gain additional qualifications, receives a diploma and returns to work. When Jens find out about this turn of events, he beats her up and rapes her. He fails his own exams for additional qualifications, feels inferior and takes to drink. Later he discovers that Sonja has had an abortion because of his drinking problem, and he almost kills her. Finally, when he returns drunk one evening and hits her, she watches as he accidentally drinks from a bottle of mineral water which she has been using to store bleach. He survives but has ruined his voice for life. Reflecting on her shattered dreams, Sonja cries out in bewilderment: 'How did it all happen? ... I did everything I was supposed to, but it all went wrong.' This highly emotional scene is seen by Gisela Bahr, as implicitly attributing the entire blame for the failed marriage to the wife. And she concludes that in its portrayal of a woman's struggle to achieve equality the film is biased in favour of the male protagonist.[4] In my opinion, however, both parties in these 'Scenes from a marriage – GDR style' are shown to be equally helpless in the face of their conflicting interests and equally unable to discuss their feelings. In Jens's case, however, his attitude requires a greater degree of psychological motivation from within the narrative, as it stands in stark contrast to the socialist ideal of a good marriage, as expounded by the registrar – who speaks off-camera – in the wedding ceremony with which the film begins. Both Sonja's mother and her close female friend, Billy, express their bewilderment at, and disapproval of, Jens's brutal and authoritarian behaviour, and advise Sonja to get divorced. Sonja's trades union colleague calls Jens's refusal to let Sonja go back to work anti-socialist, 'enforced slavery' and insists – despite Sonja's anxious protests – on having a serious word with the erring husband.

In the general context of an awareness of true socialist behaviour within a marriage – as outlined in one of their wedding presents, a book of advice for young families – Jens's expectations of his wife are so obviously outdated that it is necessary for the film to provide the audience with a plausible explanation for it. Thus Jens refers to his own unhappy childhood, his working mother who was never at home, and his wish that his son should not have to undergo a similar experience: 'My son is not going to be brought up by strangers!' Thus Jens's anger and violent tendencies become understandable in the light of his own family background, but are still condemned as unacceptable within the overall context of the film. Interestingly, an analysis of the audience's response to the film revealed that male viewers were more critical of Jens, whilst female members of the audience took a more understanding view of him.[5] One possible explanation is that Jens is portrayed very much as a lost little boy who desperately wants to get things right and who resorts to violence because he simply doesn't know any better. He carries a tremendous chip on his shoulder about his intellectual inferiority, which wins him the sympathy of his colleagues – and to some extent of his wife – when he fails an exam that she has passed with distinction. Again, this almost serves as an excuse for his subsequent drinking excesses and wife-beating.

Sonja's attitude to her husband is, in its own way, just as outdated as his attitude to her. She resorts to a conventionally feminine behaviour pattern of cunning and deviousness in order to avoid confrontation. Out of a misplaced sense of wifely loyalty, she excuses his drinking, rudeness, and even his beating of her by displaying a maternal understanding for his weaknesses. She is just as unable as Jens to explain her own needs verbally. The camera expresses her feelings in long close-ups of her face: it is very young, vulnerable and defiant at the same time. For instance in the scene where she is waiting for Jens to return – wearing a sexy transparent black dress in the hope of surprising and seducing him – the camera catches a whole range of emotions: from cheeky anticipation and flirtatious posing, to sheer disbelief at his drunken state, disappointment at his rudeness, brave persistence in making the best of things and, finally, resignation. Her attempt to encourage him to snap out of his self-pitying depression and to rekindle their sexual passion for each other – which was the initial basis of their relationship – fails.

At public discussions of the films, many female spectators said they welcomed the film as an opportunity to speak freely about a former taboo topic: physical and verbal abuse in the home: 'The beatings are not the worst of it. It is worse still to destroy each other with words.'[6] However, when asked whether this was a film about women's struggle for equal rights in the domestic sphere, Carow himself argued that this was not what lay at the core of the film. He wanted to address a more general issue: 'We live in a society which provides a basis for harmonious relationships, for happiness with each other and for a more liberated attitude to love. Nevertheless life is complicated. People fight with each other, they find it hard to rid themselves of old habits and out-moded attitudes which they have often inherited from their great-grandfathers, and from which they cannot escape.'[7] In this way the dramatic conflicts that arise from the struggle of women for self-fulfilment stand for the emancipation of men and women in a wider sense and for the overcoming of out-dated attitudes in the quest for genuine equality in human relationships.

Rebels and Individualists

On the one hand, DEFA films of the 1970s and 1980s presented women's changing role in order to highlight both the social advance made by women in the GDR and the conflicts they experienced as a result. On the other, film-makers used female protagonists as vehicles to allude to more general problems within society. Women were seen as less conformist than men and thus as more willing to articulate the need for change: 'Men experience far fewer difficulties in conforming to social conventions, conventions which date back to a time when men had almost all say. When women demand a change, they signal far more clearly the need for a change in society generally.'[8] In what follows I shall focus on two ways in which film heroines were used to express this general need for change within society. First, by rebelling against social conditions and promoting social change from within society, and secondly, by asserting their independence as individuals in opposition to society's norms and expectations.

An example of the first type of female protagonist is to be found in Lothar Warnecke's film, *Unser kurzes Leben* based on Brigitte Reimann's novel, *Franziska Linkerhand* (1974). Franziska, who works as an architect in a town planning department, is, given her profession, a typical example of a socialist heroine, in that her role in society involves taking an active part in creating the much-needed living space for her fellow citizens. As in many other DEFA films, the construction site is used as a metaphor for the shaping of the new socialist country. However, Franziska is also portrayed as a rebel against established rules, as a 'woman who's not prepared to compromise'.[9] In her capacity as an architect she raises a highly delicate issue, criticising the official building plan in the provincial town where she works. (In the context of the acute housing shortage in the GDR in the 1960s and 1970s and the SED's attempt to tackle the problem with a large-scale construction programme, such criticism was bound to be regarded as a direct attack on the working class and the Party leadership.) Franziska initially provokes her boss, Schafheutlin, by insisting on her vision for a more humane design for the town centre instead of the high-rise blocks stipulated in the official building plan. Ultimately, however, she has to accept defeat, for although her scheme for redeveloping the old town centre has won a prize, it is clear that it is not going to be implemented.

Despite the controversial issues raised – which resulted in Regine Kühn having to wait almost ten years before having her film script accepted by the DEFA authorities – *Unser kurzes Leben* was a success with audiences and most critics in the GDR. Indeed it is my view that the eventual acceptance of the film was, at least to some extent, the result of having chosen a female protagonist. As it was women who were expected to liberate themselves from their traditional domesticated roles, they were allowed some freedom to break new ground and make their mark in the work-force. Thus it was predominantly women who were seen to represent change and challenge in socialist society. At the same time, however, the authorities may have made allowances for female protagonists on the basis that women were still implicitly held to be the 'weaker' sex and thus represented a more harmless form of criticism. Indeed the GDR film critic Oksana Bulgakowa argues that in many *Gegenwartsfilme* of the 1970s and 1980s, female protagonists were chosen because they represented 'subversive tendencies in a more moderate form'.[10] Women could be deployed in films to address controversial social issues and articulate feelings of dissatisfaction shared by the majority of viewers.

In the case of *Unser kurzes Leben*, the central character is a very attractive young woman, who persists in banging her head against a brick wall, who poses no real threat to the prestigious government housing programme and whose older and more experienced male colleagues keep telling her in a well-meaning, but patronising tone, that she will have to have her wings clipped. Indeed the film ends with Franziska accepting the need to compromise, thereby apparently conveying the message that relinquishing idealistic dreams and confronting the limitations of the real world is part of the process of growing-up. Nonetheless, Franziska's remarkable openness, courage and single-mindedness throughout the film can also be seen as constituting a serious attempt to go beyond what is immediately feasible and to insist upon one's right to harbour dreams of a better world and to fight for their realisation. When asked why he had chosen to adapt such a long and complex novel for the cinema, Warneke replied that he had been fascinated by its main female character, Franziska, and her uncompromising idealism. As he elaborated in an interview, he saw women like Franziska as representatives of a utopian vision of a better society : 'We all have to reconcile our decisions, not only with the prevailing political contingencies, but also with the ideals of society and with a vision of the future. In this respect it is disappointing that there are so few utopian films in socialist countries expressing how we imagine that future might be.'[11]

In *Unser kurzes Leben*, as in many other DEFA films featuring female protagonists, characteristics traditionally attributed to women – the predominance of emotional rather than rational motivation – are used to criticise rigidity, conformism and stagnation in mainstream society (usually represented by men). The emphasis of these conventional gender-specific characteristics in some DEFA films has been criticised – in the light of developments in Western feminist theory – as consolidating male myths of female stereotypes. For instance, in one of the most popular and highly acclaimed DEFA films of the 1970s, Heiner Carow's *Die Legende von Paul und Paula* (*The Legend of Paul and Paula*, 1973), Paula persists in searching for self-fulfilment in love even to the point of wanting to have Paul's child despite knowing that this will result in her death. This was one of the reasons why two West German film critics, Helke Sander and Renée Schlesier dismissed the film as 'a sexist schmaltz from the GDR'.[12] However, in my view their approach is too narrow and ignores the film's socio-political context as well as the way it contrasts with previous DEFA films in which the happiness of the individual could only be achieved as a result of successful integration into the collective. Against this background *Die Legende von Paul und Paula* can be read as a radical plea for individual self-determination, diametrically opposed to the message of socialist realism. Paula's uncompromising demands are contrasted with Paul's rational self-restraint and 'sensible' outlook on life which prevent him, at least to begin with, from committing himself to his future beloved:

Paul: With you it's all or nothing.
Paula: So what?
Paul: What about one's responsibilities. Nobody can simply go on doing what he wants forever – there comes a time ...
Paula: But what about one's own happiness?
Paul: That's fine, so long as it doesn't interfere with others.

Throughout the film, the audience's sympathy is with the female protagonist, Paula, on account of her spontaneous enjoyment of life and her capacity to immerse herself completely in her relationship. Whereas in *Unser kurzes Leben,* Franziska attempts to change society from within and rebels against social stagnation and opportunism, Paula seeks individual self-fulfilment in spite of, and with no regard for, the expectations and restrictions of society.

Probably the most well-known female protagonist of this type is Sunny, played by Renate Krößner in the film *SOLO SUNNY* (1980) by Wolfgang Kohlhaase and Konrad Wolf. Sunny's aspirations to be taken seriously as an artist and become a star, together with her bohemian lifestyle, glamorous make-up, stylish dress and provocative manner, make her stand out from the mediocrity of her provincial philistine audience and backyard neighbourhood. When she is treated with suspicion and hostility by her neighbours, mocked by the night-club announcer and threatened with sexual harassment she does not give in. On the contrary, she asserts herself and fights back: when the neighbour who reported her to the police cleans the staircase, she gets her own back by 'accidentally' stepping on her hand; when the night-club announcer insults her in public by announcing her to the audience as 'a new, up-and coming talent, no longer quite so new', she refuses to perform and calls him a 'wanker' ('Eckenpinkler'); when a man in a bar provokes her and finishes her drink without asking, she retaliates, calmly removing his glasses, breaking them and then putting them back in his pocket; and when a drunk fellow-musician from the band tries to rape her, she hits him on the head with her shoe.

In the course of the film almost all men are shown in a generally unsympathetic light: they are either aggressive macho figures such as the saxophonist, Norbert, arrogant bullies such as the night-club announcer or pathetically pig-headed suitors such as the taxi-driver, Harry. The other (male) members of the band are either cowards, unwilling to stand up for Sunny when she is fired, or hypocrites such as the band-leader, Hubert, who lives an adulterous double life. Like Sonja, Franziska, Paula and the majority of other DEFA heroines, Sunny cannot find a male partner who is her equal – not even the lover of her own choosing, the philosopher, Ralph. For eventually he proves to be a social drop-out who has withdrawn from life, love and true feelings and taken refuge in bitter self-pity and frustration. Throughout the film Sunny prepares herself for a big solo performance on stage, searching for the right lyrics for a melody she likes. This solo performance also symbolises her quest for a role in life that is truly hers, a place in society where she is recognised as an individual in her own right. On a personal level, too, she needs to feel that she is someone uniquely special for the man she loves. For a brief period, it seems as though Ralph might fulfil this need, especially as he agrees to write the lyrics to the melody of her solo song. However, he casually betrays her with another girl, an affair which he regards as meaningless: 'no offence meant', he tells her. Sunny is so deeply hurt by his casual attitude and by the shock of realising that she is not irreplaceable in Ralph's feelings that she gives in to an irrational outburst and plans to kill him. Once again, the portrayal of emotional strength and vitality in a woman goes hand in hand with an inability (or unwillingness) to rationalise and express her feelings verbally. Sunny does not reflect and discuss conflicts: instead she experiences them intensely, responding with immediacy and passion. Nonetheless, her naïve, impulsive, and non-verbal approach to conflicts is portrayed as a positive female quality which has the potential to bring about change and improvement in society.

Throughout the film, moments of casual cruelty, insensitivity and indifference between men and women are shown to be symptomatic of a dangerous form of social alienation. As the director, Konrad Wolf was to comment: 'In my view, the fact that people now regard the spread of casual brutality within relationships as something normal is far more disturbing and threatening than more obvious cases of extreme violence. It is this mixture of indifference, insensitivity, selfishness that leads to catastrophe, the origins of which nobody subsequently understands'.[13] Western critics unanimously praised the film for the openness and honesty with which it portrayed a female protagonist who wanted something that was unconventional and somewhat suspect in the GDR, namely a career of her own choosing and a personality that was truly hers. In the GDR, the film triggered audience discussions which lasted for weeks and created passionate controversies amongst critics and viewers. One issue was Sunny's unconventional behaviour which some male spectators found too aggressive and unfeminine to be truly representative of GDR women. Another was the legitimacy of her demand for a solo role, the recognition of her individuality. One viewer wrote to the Berlin newspaper *Wochenpost:* 'I wonder if Sunny's personal development applies to other areas of life. Becoming a well-known soloist is something only very few people can aspire to. Nonetheless, you can still become a respected individual within the collective without necessarily having a solo role.' [14] However, the vast majority of GDR viewers wrote in with enthusiastic comments about Sunny, sympathising and identifying with the screen heroine who was later to become a cult figure for fans in Berlin, who copied her confident, sexy dress-sense down to tight jeans, high-heeled shoes and a fox-fur collar.

The Private Niche: Misfits and Drop-outs

In some DEFA films of the 1980s there was a notable shift of emphasis from portraying the heroines within their working context to an almost exclusive focus on their personal lives. Regine Sylvester suggests that the increased interest in depicting gender-relations in the home may have been a reaction to the fact that films of the late 1960s and early 1970s had primarily addressed practical issues resulting from the new role of women in full-time employment and addressed these from a sociological point of view, rather than looking at emotional problems on an individual level. [15] Oksana Bulgakowa goes a little further in her assessment of the shift of focus in the *Gegenwartsfilme* of the 1980s, claiming that the private sphere represented an intimate refuge from an otherwise strictly regimented collective life in the GDR: 'This intimate and erotic setting was exploited as a means of approaching hidden social problems.' [16] The frustrations, disappointments and dissatisfactions female protagonists expressed in the context of their personal lives could thus be seen as representative of a wider sense of disillusionment with socialist reality experienced by the majority of people. Moreover, as Marc Silberman has suggested, by drawing attention to the problems commonly experienced by women in their relationships, it became possible for film-makers to explore nihilistic attitudes and individual failure as part of the human condition, themes which socialist realism had tended to exclude.[17] As a result of this development an altogether different type of female protagonist appeared on the scene: the social misfit or drop-out ('Aussteiger'). This development is to be seen in the context of a more general shift of focus discernible in the *Gegenwartsfilme* of the 1980s whereby these films looked more closely at individuals at the margins of society in an attempt to address psychological and existential issues. For instance, the question of how individuals cope with illness, pain, depression and death was at the forefront of Lothar Warneke's controversial film *Die Beunruhigung* (*Apprehension*, 1982).

Anti-heroines and social misfits such as Nina in Herrmann Zschoche's *Bürgschaft für ein Jahr* (*On Probation*, 1981), Susanne in Evelyn Schmidt's *Das Fahrrad*, and Christine in Herrmann Zschoche's *Die Alleinseglerin* (*The Solo Sailor*, 1987) often elicited a mixed – sometimes bewildered – response on the part of GDR critics. All three women are portrayed as non-conformist individualists wrapped up in their own 'little lives'. They seem to have no ambition to be recognised or to make their mark in society and are quite content to pursue a modest degree of individual happiness in their private niche. As they are no good at expressing themselves, they are unable to represent their own interests in an appropriate way and end up having to either avoid, subvert or violate the conventions of society. Indeed Nina and Susanne even resort to deceit, theft and fraud. Like other female protagonists in DEFA films of the 1980s, they are single working mothers in unglamorous jobs which they do not enjoy. Their lifestyles appear subversive because they refuse to go along with the socialist code of conduct: they do not seek approval, help or advice from the collective at work; they show no 'team spirit' and having a successful career is not one of their priorities. Instead they seek personal fulfilment and social recognition in alternative subcultures such as bars and discos or else in total solitude.

A film which is often compared to *Bürgschaft für ein Jahr* is Evelyn Schmidt's *Das Fahrrad*, a *Gegenwartsfilm* by one of few female directors to work for DEFA. In what follows, I shall look at this film a little more closely with a view to asking whether the presence of a female director results in a different depiction of woman in GDR cinema.

Das Fahrrad shows the problems that an allegedly emancipated working woman with the benefit of state-provided childcare still has coping with love relationships and everyday life. The film portrays this ordinary life with documentary realism and in graphic detail. Susanne, an unskilled factory worker and a single mother, struggles to make ends meet. One day she cannot take her monotonous and lonely job at a metal working plant any longer and quits. It proves much harder than she expected to find another job, especially since the responsibility of bringing up her child rules out night shifts, work at weekends and travel. Her daughter falls ill and her father refuses to advance money to tide her over the crisis, all of which leads to her following the advice of her friend Mary, namely to report her bicycle as stolen and claim the insurance money. Meanwhile she has met Thomas, a successful engineer, in her local night-club. They fall in love and he persuades her to move in with him and gets her a job at his company. When her insurance fraud is discovered and she is faced with a court case she tells Thomas everything. He is confused, irritated and worried that her 'outrageous behaviour' will cast him in a poor light at work, but gradually he comes round and decides to help her. His initial reaction hurts and alienates Susanne to an extent that she gives way to a hysterical outburst and eventually leaves him. The film ends on a positive note, however, as she is determined to continue the pursuit of happiness in her own carefree way, stubbornly rejecting caution, moderation and sensibility.

In an interview, Evelyn Schmidt pointed out that she wanted to draw attention to those people who fall through the net and who lose out, to the silent minority of non-heroes ignored by society, describing the film as 'a social portrait of a woman who at the age of 30 is still dogged by bad luck, who doesn't seize the opportunities she has, who hasn't got a lot, can't do much and, above all, doesn't know what she wants'.[18] Unfortunately, Evelyn Schmidt was swimming against the tide of cultural policy at the time. In 1981, the newspaper *Neues Deutschland* had published a (presumably fake) letter by a reader under the rubric 'What I would like to see our film-makers doing', a letter some people suspected was written by Honecker himself. The author of this letter had looked at some contemporary DEFA

Gegenwartsfilme and had found them wanting: 'Where are the works of art which tell of the – let us call them – monumental achievements of building up our thriving, stable and flourishing Workers' and Peasants' State?'[19] This public rebuke was to have far-reaching consequences for subsequent film releases. *Das Fahrrad* was not advertised in the GDR and was released only for a short run in a very few cinemas. Most people in the GDR were aware of it only on account of the venomous attacks it provoked in the papers. A typical example is provided by the well-known GDR film critic, Renate Holland-Moritz, for whom Susanne is 'a screwed-up drop-out, suspicious of everyone except her obscure drinking mates in the underground disco' and who dismisses the film as 'a lame expression of grumpy social discontent'.[20]

As there was certainly nothing 'monumental' about the heroine's achievements in *Das Fahrrad*, it is hardly surprising that Evelyn Schmidt's promising career – she had worked with Konrad Wolf – was nipped in the bud. She soon fell from grace and was eventually banned from directing any more feature films for DEFA. However, the film was sold abroad eleven times and shown on West German television in July 1986 as part of a summer festival of women's films. The presenter introduced the film to West German audiences praising its well-observed details and its honest portrayal of ordinary people in the GDR.

Thomas's role in this film is, generally speaking, to act as a foil to Susanne. He is young and dynamic, a mechanical engineer who has managed to become head of department in his company by dint of hard work and obtaining a degree qualification at evening classes. When Susanne and Thomas meet for the first time in the film, their contrasting worlds and backgrounds are represented by the upper and the lower levels of a building, by light and darkness. For while Thomas's promotion is being celebrated – albeit rather stiffly – by his collective on the brightly lit ground floor of the *Kulturhaus*, Susanne has a laid-back night out with her friends in the dimly-lit discotheque in the basement. He is attracted towards this 'underworld' almost against his will and tries, in the course of the film, to draw Susanne up to his own level of propriety. Although initially portrayed as a likeable, sincere young man who is genuinely fond of Susanne and her child, his personality is a blend of Mr Sensible, the model socialist who always goes by the book, a 'knight in shining armour' who comes to the aid of damsels in distress, and 'Pygmalion', the man who expects his protégé to show her gratitude for having been rescued from the gutter by behaving in accordance with his expectations. She, however, insists on being herself, on doing things her own way, even if they do go wrong for much of the time. This is exactly the point which irritated GDR critics about this anti-heroine: why did she have no qualifications, why did she have such unreasonable expectations of happiness despite her lowly record of achievement, and why did she not at least try to follow Thomas's shining example and change her ways? According to some reviewers, such unfortunate people did not exist in the reality of socialism or were – at worst – an insignificant minority who only had themselves to blame and who certainly did not merit being portrayed in a feature film.

The inability of both Susanne and Thomas to articulate their feelings and communicate with each other is reflected in a scene which takes place during a boat trip. They sit opposite each other at an empty table indoors. The scene is totally silent and filmed with soft focus lens so that it has a blurred, dream-like quality. There are no other people to be seen, no direct sounds or music, as the couple shut out the external world and are wrapped up in their own thoughts. They neither touch nor look at each other. Susanne is slightly turned away from him towards the camera while the voice-over soundtrack allows us access to their trains of thought in parallel, interrupted, streams of consciousness. Only in their thoughts do they seem to be able to verbalise their need for each other.

Throughout the film, Susanne's relationship with her child is portrayed as loving and caring and this is the one area of her life where she does know what she wants. Raising her daughter as best she can is the priority in her life. She declines the only immediate well-paid job she is offered because this would mean leaving her daughter in a kindergarten during night shifts. She cuddles up with Jenny in bed telling her fairy tales and, when, in their final argument Thomas reproaches her, shouting 'What've you achieved up to now, tell me!', Susanne replies calmly and confidently: 'I've brought up Jenny.' And when he replies: 'Yeah, someone who'll start nicking things one day!', Susanne, cut to the quick by this insidious remark, briefly closes her eyes, swallows and says in a low, controlled voice: 'That's it.'

In *Das Fahrrad*, Evelyn Schmidt deals with three aspects of social reality which young mothers in the GDR may have had to face. She points out the bleak sides of women's lives by focusing on a single woman without any job qualifications who does not fit the official image of a confident assertive female role model and who does not live in pleasant surroundings but struggles with poverty and deprivation: 'Her life consists of monotonous work, child care and the occasional visit to a disco. This is a far cry from a happy life. And there are plenty of women who live within such constraints, who do so little.'[21] The presentation of Susanne's daily routine shows that she is not able to take advantage of those facilities which were designed to make it possible to combine motherhood with full-time employment, with the result that the pressure of having sole responsibility for her child is almost too much for her. In her home as well as at work she faces conditions which officially 'did not exist' within socialist society: poverty and alienation in the workplace.

Arguably the one aspect which does reveal a specifically female perspective on women's issues is the presentation of male and female attitudes towards bringing up children. Throughout the film Susanne is confronted with attitudes which either belittle or fail to recognise the hard work of child-raising as an achievement in itself. Thomas in particular reflects 'traditionally male' values and norms of achievement, insofar as he has difficulty empathising with other people's circumstances. This is in stark contrast to the values represented by Susanne: her loving patience with the child, her unconventional, lively behaviour with her friends and neighbours and her feelings of solidarity with a female colleague from work, a single mother with three children who does not leave her partner although he beats her.

The social system in the GDR is criticised indirectly through Susanne and Thomas's relationship. Thomas wholeheartedly believes that the state is just and offers equal opportunities to everyone. Accordingly he criticises Susanne for not making better use of such opportunities. His attitude towards Susanne mirrors that of the GDR state towards the individual, in that it is predicated on patriarchal modes of thought: Susanne is helped back on her feet and looked after, all of which makes her feel secure and comfortable for a while. When Thomas starts patronising and criticising her for being ungrateful, declaring her to be quite incapable of doing anything without his help, she realises that this imbalance of power is in fact weakening and paralysing her. Only when she realises this is she able to break free from his controlling influence.

When asked why she preferred to portray female protagonists, Evelyn Schmidt explained that it was a simple issue of identification, of being closer to women's experiences than to those of men. In addition, she wanted to speak up on behalf of women and, more generally, for the disadvantaged in society, who were still to be found even in a society which claimed to have got rid of inequality:

> Men served in the army and had opportunities to study; their reason and emotions always prompted them to do the right thing at the right time. They simply have a wider range of possibilities than women in our society. I don't think you can deny social differences, the fact that certain people have very different opportunities to develop and that some can make use of these opportunities better than others ... In my view, building up one's self-confidence is a very important issue – especially for women.[22]

In the end, the central female character in *Das Fahrrad* opts for a life as a cyclist rather than a motorist. Moving under her own steam on her bicycle, she is closer to life; for her cycling represents an intensity of experience at grass-roots level and a degree of autonomy. However, it also means a solitary journey through life and being exposed to its adversities – such as the icy spray from a lorry on a rainy day. At times cycling is also used as a metaphor for Susanne's spontaneous capacity to enjoy life's trivial moments, as we see, for instance, in the scene in which she takes her young daughter on an impulsive bike-ride. After a picnic by the river – one of the few scenes set in bright sunshine in the film – she teaches Jenny to ride the bike. This motif is taken up once again in the final scene which brings the film to a hopeful conclusion when she teaches her daughter to ride around a fountain, trying to pass on to her her own sense of autonomy, joy, and willingness to take risks. This time the daughter succeeds, much to the delight of her proud mother, who urges her on with enthusiastic cries.

Conclusion

Female protagonists in DEFA films rarely appear in the role of glamorous sex object, wicked temptress, or passive housewife dependent upon her husband. The *Gegenwartsfilme* I have discussed are *Frauenfilme* in the sense that they focus first and foremost on a female protagonist and her experiences, and address typically feminist issues such as equality in the domestic sphere, male violence against women, patronising male behaviour, and sexual harassment at work. By drawing attention to the inability of men and women to communicate with each other, all the films criticise the prevailing state of gender relations in the GDR. In the majority of them women are portrayed as emotionally stronger, morally and intellectually superior or as having a more advanced social consciousness than their men – by whom they are generally let down. This could be interpreted as a reflection of women's achievements in filling simultaneously the roles of worker, comrade, mother and lover, and the new sense of self-confidence that went with this. Women were perceived to make more rigorous demands of their partners and of life in general, all of which led to dramatic conflicts which made them appear more powerful protagonists in the cinema than their male counterparts. In a great many DEFA films there seems to be a binary opposition of male and female qualities, in which the masculine stands for external authority, the public sphere, stability and stagnation, entrapment and denial; by contrast the feminine stands for a more personal psychological reality, the private sphere, openness and spontaneity, indulgence and emotional excess. Yet even within this traditional scheme of gendered attributes, the female protagonists manage to question and qualify manifestations of institutionalised power where they confront them. On the surface it might appear that the female protagonists in DEFA films are fighting a losing battle and have to face defeat at some point in their lives. Nevertheless they come across as strong, resilient women, and were regarded as individuals with whom their viewers could identify. They fight for their ideals and dreams – against all odds – and they air their views passionately.

After the *Wende*, at a film seminar in Berlin on DEFA *Frauenfilme*, a number of female participants from the West criticised the DEFA heroines for being unrealistic puppet-figures who – whenever they were knocked down – always came bouncing back up again. But it is my view that these female protagonists were portrayed as resilient, determined and indestructible in order to make important points about where things were going wrong in GDR society and to point the way forward to a utopian vision of a better future. And it is this quest for real equality in relationships that are genuinely humane that is reflected in the themes of breaking out, starting afresh and searching for a truly meaningful existence in these films.

Notes

1. Joshua Feinstein, 'The Triumph of the Ordinary: Depictions of Daily Life in the East German Cinema: 1956–1966'(PhD Diss., Stanford University, 1995), p. 205.
2. Regine Sylvester, 'Filmfrauen: Suche nach neuen Konturen', *Sonntag*, 1975, no. 25 (22 June).
3. Hans-Rainer Mihan, 'Sabine, Sunny, Nina und der Zuschauer: Gedanken zum Gegenwartsspielfilm der DEFA', *Film und Fernsehen* 10, no. 8, 1982: 9–12 (12).
4. Gisela Bahr, 'Film and Consciousness: The Depiction of Women in East German Movies', in *Gender and German Cinema: Feminist Interventions*, vol. 1, ed. Sandra Frieden, Richard W. McCormick, Vibeke Petersen and Laurie Melissa Vogelsang, Oxford, 1993, pp. 125–140 (p. 132).
5. Ibid., p. 134.
6. Dieter Wolf, 'Die Kunst miteinander zu reden: Bis daß der Tod euch scheidet im Gespräch', *Film und Fernsehen* 7, no. 11, 1979: 9–10 (9).
7. See *Für Dich*, 30 June 1978.
8. Konrad Wolf, Wolfgang Kohlhaase and Klaus Wischnewski, 'Was heißt denn "happy end …"': ein Gespräch über *SOLO SUNNY*', in *Film und Fernsehen* 8, no. 1, 1980: 9–15 (15).
9. ' "Eine junge Frau von heute zwischen Ideal und Wirklichkeit": Interview mit Lothar Warneke zu seinem neuen Film *Unser kurzes Leben*', *Die Union* (Dresden), 19 January 1981.
10. Oksana Bulgakowa, 'Die Rebellion im Rock', in *Außerhalb von Mittendrin: Literatur/Film*, ed. Annette C. Eckert, Berlin, 1991, pp. 98–102 (p. 98).
11. *Die Union* (Dresden), 19 January 1981.
12. Helke Sander and Renée Schlesier, 'die Legende von Paul und Paula: eine frauenverachtende schnulze aus der ddr', *Frauen und Film* 2, 1974: 8–47.
13. Wolf, Kohlaase and Wischnewski, 13.
14. Reader's letter from Ernst Reimann (Karl-Marx-Stadt) to *Wochenpost* (Berlin), 7 March 1980.
15. Regine Sylvester, 'Film und Wirklichkeit: einige Gedanken zu Frauengestalten in neueren Filmen der DEFA und des Fernsehens

der DDR', in *Emanzipation der Frau: Wirklichkeit und Illusion*, ed. Margarete Schmidt (= *Aus Theorie und Praxis des Films* – Sonderheft 1975), Potsdam, 1975, pp. 91–108 (p. 97).

16. Bulgakowa, 98.
17. Marc Silberman, 'Narrating gender in the GDR: Herrmann Zschoche's *Bürgschaft für ein Jahr* (1981)', *The Germanic Review* 66, no. 1, 1991 [Special issue on German film, ed. Richard Murphy]: 25–33.
18. *Filmspiegel*, 1982, no. 13: 20.
19. Allegedly a reader's letter by 'Hubert Vater' in *Neues Deutschland*, 17 November 1981.
20. *Eulenspiegel*, 27 August 1982.
21. 'Kino-Eule', *Filmspiegel*, 1982, no. 13: 20.
22. Ibid.

❖ *Chapter 12* ❖

THE CONCEPT OF 'HEIMAT-GDR' IN DEFA FEATURE FILMS

Harry Blunk

In the book *Vom Sinn unseres Lebens* (*Life's Purpose*)[1] which young people in the GDR received at their *Jugendweihe* – a ceremony in which fourteen-year olds were formally welcomed into the adult world – the chapter entitled 'The GDR – our Socialist Fatherland' begins with the words:

> We call the patch of the earth on which we were born, grew up and have our home, our *Heimat* ('homeland'). For the most part we think of it as a beautiful place. When we are far away, we miss it: this is called being homesick. However, we do not always regard our homeland as identical with our *Vaterland* ('fatherland'). They are only one and the same thing in a society in which we feel cared for, in which we can learn, in which we can earn our daily bread, in which we have a say in matters relating to it and the state, as citizens with equal rights, in which there is peace; in short, a society in which we are happy to live. In this sense, the German Democratic Republic is not merely our *Heimat* but also our *Vaterland*. Accordingly we call the GDR our socialist *Vaterland*. Because in our Republic under the leadership of the working class and its Marxist-Leninist Party we have policies that are for the good of the people, and that is why it is a real Vaterland for working people, a country which is worth living in and fighting for.[2]

Apart from the strongly persuasive use of language what is striking about this text is the way in which it differentiates between the concepts of *Heimat* and *Vaterland*. The cultural-political dictionary of the GDR offers an even more precise distinction:

> Working-class ideology distinguishes between *Heimat* and *Vaterland*. *Vaterland* is the term used to describe the socio-cultural milieu in its

entirety, a socio-political totality which functions as a battle-field, as the battle-ground for the historic mission of the working classes. Thus the feeling of *Heimat* is not to be equated with, or mistaken for patriotism ... In the GDR the citizens' feelings of *Heimat* are bound up with their knowledge of history, with the spirit of socialist internationalism and with socialist civic awareness. Feelings of *Heimat* are an important factor in the creation of a socialist society.[3]

Günther Lange, the GDR's specialist on the theory of *Heimat*, emphasises another aspect to this distinction between the two concepts:

Let us get to the heart of the matter: the *Vaterland* is a form of socialisation in which *indirect* social relations are the determining factor, because the process of production permeates the whole of society. In the more immediate sense of *Heimat*, which is a less extended form of socialisation, social relations exist in a more *direct* form. They are based on direct personal contact and are reproduced in it.[4]

The texts I have quoted testify to the high expectations placed on *Heimat* and *Vaterland*, and what would have to be achieved if a huge discrepancy between theory and practice was to be avoided. That there was such a discrepancy in many respects cannot be denied. How was it to be overcome? How could such expectations be reconciled with the brute facts of the sheer provincialism of the small nation state called the GDR, the travel restrictions under which most of its citizens had to live, the attempts, both successful and otherwise, to flee the country and the huge number of applications to emigrate to the West?

Citizens of the GDR were encouraged to develop an awareness of their problematic homeland in a variety of ways: in nursery school on excursions into the countryside and during classes in singing, drawing and painting; at senior school in *Heimatkunde* (lessons in local history and geography); in pioneer camps and on holiday in particularly attractive parts of the country such as Thuringia and Brandenburg or the Baltic coast. The task of winning the hearts and minds of the populace for *Heimat* and *Vaterland* was seen primarily as that of the artistic media. And a closer look at the feature film industry – which saw its official function as essentially that of educating the general public – reveals the range of images used to capture the concepts of *Heimat* and *Vaterland* at different times and in a variety of cultural-political contexts.

The first productions filmed in 1946 and in the years immediately after the war focused (quite understandably) on the
destruction of 'Heimat Germany' and constitute a kind of
horrific stock-taking. Ruined buildings – filmed Expressionist-
style against the light and with the use of low-camera angles so
that they seem to tower up against the sky like grim, terrifying
memorials – assume a role no less important than the guilt-
ridden and poverty-stricken human beings portrayed in
Wolfgang Staudte's *Die Mörder sind unter uns* (*The Murderers Are
Among Us*, 1946). And in Gerhard Lamprecht's *Irgendwo in
Berlin* (*Somewhere in Berlin*, 1946) a similar role is played by the
mountains of rubble, among which the surviving children play
at 'war' because they have not learned anything else, all of
which leads in turn to yet more appalling misery. The authentic
settings of these films in the bombed and shattered towns and
cities of Germany make them documents of horror and extend
their scope of reference far beyond the film narrative itself.
Indeed it was only some years later that it seems to have been
possible to achieve a degree of distance from the initial shock
and to approach the subject matter in a more analytical
manner, as for instance in Staudte's film *Rotation* (1949) which
portrayed the apolitical attitude of many Germans during the
period of National Socialism as a pre-condition of the moral
catastrophe and ultimately bitter finale.

Slatan Dudow made the first DEFA film to embody an unam-
biguously socialist perspective, *Unser täglich Brot* (*Our Daily
Bread*) in the year 1949, the same year in which the GDR was
founded. It was a simple epic tale based on the everyday life of
a Berlin family in which the fate of the protagonists reflects the
development of post-war Germany. In the poverty of the post-
war years various relatives (both close and distant), who have
been rendered homeless by the war, live together out of necessity in the flat of the accountant, Webers. Initially it is the basic
problems – food and the overcrowding in the flat – that lead to
quarrels round the family table. These assume an ideological
character when Webers's son Ernst – who has been bombed
out, and has brought his family to stay with his father – rebels
against the bourgeois attitudes of the family. Although
desperate for employment, Webers senior will not even
consider joining his son in the task of rebuilding the factory
where he had once worked as an accountant and which has
now been taken over by the State. Webers feels that he has been

proved right when his younger son, Harry – in contrast to his elder brother Ernst – reveals evidence of material success. Unbeknown to his gullible father, however, his success has come about through black market deals in the western sectors of the city. Blind to the causes of this post-war reality and its future, Webers does not notice the gradual moral decline of his favourite son Harry, and fails to value the honesty and dependability of his other son, Ernst. As a result, the family, which survived the war intact, falls apart.

In its portrayal of the declining fortunes of a family in its post-war homeland, Dudow's film highlights the different ideological positions which underlined approaches to the new beginning in economic and political affairs. These ideologically opposed positions are evident in a number of films – particularly those made in the 1950s – which deal with the divided Fatherland. Nonetheless, the films made immediately after the Film Conference in 1952 are marred by an over-rigid application of the aesthetics of 'socialist realism', a defect which is all too apparent in the black-and-white characterisation of the protagonists and the crude appeal to allegedly 'typical' patterns of behaviour. By contrast, the so-called 'Berlin-Films' made in the mid- to late-1950s – which stylistically owe much to Italian neorealism – represent a considerable advance on these films. But despite the authenticity of the settings and the manifold variations in the presentation of the conflicts the characters experience, the basic message in these films is still the same, namely that Western influences are liable to lead the (predominantly youthful) protagonists astray and that only by living in the Eastern sector of the city will they have the chance to develop their careers and lead a fulfilled personal life. This ideological underpinning is clearly discernible in films like *Alarm im Zirkus* (*Circus Alarm*, 1953), *Eine Berliner Romanze* (*A Berlin Romance*, 1956), *Berlin, Ecke Schönhauser* (*Berlin – Schönhauser Corner*, 1957) by Gerhard Klein and Wolfgang Kohlhaase – both of which are analysed in some detail elsewhere in this volume by Horst Claus – and in Heiner Carow's film *Sheriff Teddy* (1957).

Heimat in the sense of 'the good society', 'the better fatherland' , is directly evoked through the symbolic resonance of the words 'going home' which we hear at the end of *Eine Berliner Romanze*. In the final scene, a group of young men – all of them out of work and little prospect of a fulfilled life – are hanging around in a square in West Berlin. One of them has tried his luck in Hamburg and failed. Now he wants to try Australia. While they talk, Uschi – Hans's girlfriend from East Berlin – comes up to the group and invites him back to her place:

1st Youth: […]	Why did you go there in the first place?
2nd Youth: […]	Hamburg was just an experiment. But now I've found something really wild: Australia. I'm off there in a month.
Hans:	They are just waiting for you, I bet.
2nd Youth:	An Australian company is even paying my fare.
3rd Youth:	You're kidding!
Hans:	What would I do in Australia?
2nd Youth:	Moses wants to get away from here too.
3rd Youth:	There's nothing going on here any more. Just another couple of months and then: 'Up, down!' and a smart American uniform.
Hans:	I'd rather go crazy than wear a uniform like that.
1st Youth:	Haven't you got over her yet, then?
3rd Youth:	There's no point in having a girl from the East.
Hans:	How do you mean, no point?
3rd Youth:	With the situation today. One of these days they won't let you over.
Hans:	If I really want to see her, I'll get there, believe me!
1st Youth:	Want to see a fairy?
3rd Youth:	Hans!
Uschi:	Would you like to come home with me? They said I was to invite you.
Hans:	I should come home with you?
Uschi:	I love you.
Voice-over:	(*off camera – final shot*) Well, now they are a real couple. One of thousands in Berlin. Or, as we say, they are going together. And together they will find a place, Uschi and Hans, a place in our life here, where there is work, where there are battles to be won, where there is love.

Thus a sense of *Heimat* is inevitably present in films where the action takes place on home territory, and appears quite naturally as a backdrop against which the characters play out their roles.[5] And when handled well it is often hard to determine whether or not the film contains a latent ideological agenda. For instance, the 'Berlin-Filme' referred to above promote the notion of *Heimat* only insofar as they articulate a generally warm feeling towards the socialist *Vaterland*. In every other respect the urban milieu is presented in a starkly realistic manner: streets, meeting places, railway sidings, backyards are significant in their own right rather than there to convey an ideological message.

This was no longer the case in many of the films made in the 1960s. Frequent references of a propagandist nature are to be found in those films made in the years between the Eleventh Plenum in 1965 and Honecker's take-over of power from Ulbricht in 1971. The disciplinary measures to which many writers and film-makers were subjected, the requirement that they conform both to the ideological demands of the Party and adhere to a rigid interpretation of socialist-realist aesthetics led to many films containing scenes which were obviously only there in order to communicate a particularly positive image of the visual appearance of the GDR.

Such scenes appear relatively frequently also in later films, the reason for this being the educational function attributed to film in the GDR. Most of these scenes consist of camera impressions of the capital, Berlin – almost always filmed in brilliant sunshine – and in particular the Alexanderplatz with its television tower and clock, the ministries, the Palast der Republik – as well as of other large cities in the GDR, where 'tours of the city' or visits to famous buildings, museums and cultural monuments are integrated into the action of the film. An extreme example of this tendency is to be found in the television film, *Du und icke und Berlin* (*You, Me and Berlin*, 1977), for it presents the city almost entirely in the above manner: 'Berlin, how we have changed you and above all, how quickly!' Other DEFA productions, such as Kurt Maetzig's *Januskopf* (*Janus Head*, 1972), Siegfried Kühn's *Im Spannungsfeld* (*In the Field of Tension*, 1970) displayed a more subtle approach. Indeed, when analysing the semantic function of such sequences, we have to be cautious in respect of individual cases. For instance in Roland Gräf's *Märkische Forschungen* (*Exploring the Brandenburg Marches*, 1982) we see the Berlin cathedral and the façade of the Palace Hotel filmed with a very low-angled camera mounted in a moving car. This is done not in order to promote the GDR's capital city, but on the contrary, it is an ironic device, designed to convey the village school-teacher's emotional state as he encounters both the famous professor and the city itself with high hopes of embarking on a prestigious academic career there.

The filming of huge new building complexes was another favourite technique used to convey an impression of the GDR's size and efficiency. Occasionally this resulted in pathos verging on the ridiculous. In Ralph Kirsten's film about industry, *Netzwerk* (*Network*, 1970), the wife of an engineer gives an account of her move to the city. 'When towards morning the flares appeared on the horizon, I woke the children ... I told them, there is the city. This is where your new home is going to be. We are going to live in one of those big, bright houses.' The great height of the new block of flats is brought into dramatic focus when later on the engineer's small daughter climbs into an open window and nearly falls out. The camera looks down at the street below as she cries 'Just look how high we are'. The train journey through the night is intended to create the impression of huge distances in the GDR, as is the remark made by one of the heroes in another film – *Ete und Ali* (*Ete and Ali*, 1985), directed by Peter Kahane – namely that he had got around a lot when doing his national service, travelling 'all the way from one end of the Republic to the other!', as he puts it.

The notion that technological progress in the GDR was not incompatible with the preservation of nature and natural beauty is another key theme in a number of DEFA films. With this in mind I want to look in some detail at one particular sequence from the film *Weil ich dich liebe* (*Because I Love You*, 1970), directed by Helmet Brandis and Hans Kratzert, to show how mini 'advertising spots', designed to promote the concept of *Heimat*-GDR as a natural paradise, were slipped into the overall narrative structure of the film.[6] As is well known, the function of advertising is to sell a product, to 'find a taker for it'. Accordingly, although advertising may begin by presenting a realistic image of the product, it concentrates above all on reminding the potential 'customer' of its beneficial – rather than negative – aspects. This process is evident in the following sequence from *Weil ich dich liebe* which takes place 'beside a lake in Mecklenburg' and consists of twelve shots lasting a total of 82 seconds (Duration 81.5 secs.). The sequence runs as follows:

1. Eva and Gerd in a rowing-boat. Eva is standing, Gerd is rowing. Eva speaks to Gerd and sits down.

2. Eva's face, smiling. She is speaking to Gerd, pointing out something to him with a gesture of the hand (low-angle shot).

3. Gerd's face, smiling. He turns (wide-angle shot).

4. Swans taking off from the reeds at the edge of the lake (pan to the left), one single swan flying, landing on the water (long pan to the right, following the bird's flight).

5. A tern, flying over a fishing net which has been spread out to dry between several posts.

6. A pair of storks in a nest (low-angle shot).

7. Fruit trees in blossom (close-up).

8. Heads of lambs and sheep (high-angle shot).

9. Oyster-catcher sitting on the post of a willow fence.

10. Seagulls circling (low-angle shot).

11. Eva and Gerd by the sea, beside a breakwater of natural stones, teasing each other; Gerd pursuing Eva (pan to the left), pulling her down on the sand, kissing her.

12. Eva and Gerd (seen from behind), with their arms round each other, walking towards the sea which is glowing in the sunset (zoom out).

Here it is clear how the image of Mecklenburg – and rural life in general – is being presented through the use of techniques appropriate to advertising. The images of the landscape and animals are set within a framework of human relationships, characterised by shared experiences, mutual trust, sympathy, joy, love. These provide the background onto which the 'Mecklenburg experience' is projected in the mind of the viewer. The negative images associated with this region – 'provincial', 'boring', 'primitive', 'no cultural life', 'desolate', to say nothing of the disparaging epithet 'fish-heads' ('Fischköppe') used to refer to its inhabitants – are conspicuous by their absence. Instead we are presented with a plethora of typical landscape images – lake, sea, meadows, animals and plants – which in their turn have been especially selected for their emotional appeal (young lambs and a pair of storks!). It is virtually impossible to imagine a muddy field of turnips overrun by pigs in this sequence. The overall message is further enhanced by the length of the shots; nonetheless, it is the camera angles which convey the impression of peace and space. This is particularly evident in the final shot in which the use of the zoom lens leaves the viewer with a lasting image of wide open expanses of natural beauty.

The selective presentation of the 'Mecklenburg-experience' is also reinforced by the use of sound. During the entire scene the film's main theme tune is played very quietly in the background. The only audible sounds related to events on camera are those of the oars splashing (Shots 1–3), the swans flying (Shot 4) or the waves breaking on the shore (Shots 11–12). The conversations and teasing episodes between the couple have been blended out of the soundtrack, further proof that the scene itself does not really advance the film's plot. Indeed quite the reverse is the case: the dramatic 'action' – the couple's outing – is only really a pretext, an excuse to present the viewer with a series of rosy images of 'Mecklenburg, the natural idyll'. The emotional connotations of the images of nature draw on traditional romantic traditions in which individual animals trigger conventional emotional associations and reactions – for instance the 'sweetness of the lamb' – all of which contributes to the basic impression conveyed by the sequence and renders the film a *Heimatfilm* in the traditional sense of the term.

In the late 1970s and early 1980s the treatment of the concept *Heimat* becomes noticeably 'colder', and even the fatherland itself is frequently subjected to criticism, both open and covert. In many films the darker side of life in the GDR features prominently. The first indications of this change of mood can be discerned in the presentation of towns, villages and GDR architecture generally. The desolate appearance of vast expanses of delapidated old buildings is exploited frequently as a setting for films whose protagonists have almost nothing in common with the 'positive heroes' and 'socialist personalities' of earlier DEFA films. The gloomy stories presented in Herrmann Zschoche's *Bürgschaft für ein Jahr* (*On Probation*, 1981), and Heiner Carow's *Bis daß der Tod euch scheidet* (*Until Death Do Us Part*, 1979), take place in such urban environments. In Konrad Wolf's *SOLO SUNNY* (1979), the melancholy tristesse of the Prenzlauer Berg with its decaying streets, crumbling façades, dark doorways, filthy backyards and primitive flats is starkly felt, and if there is an element of nostalgia in the eye of the camera, it is quite incidental. Indeed, there have been suggestions[7] that in setting his film *Vorspiel* (*Prelude,* 1987) in Schönebeck – an appallingly delapidated town on the Elbe – Peter Kahane's intention was to exploit the location as a symbol of the desolate state of the GDR as a whole.

At the same time the new blocks of high-rise flats which had appeared in remarkable numbers all over the GDR are presented in a totally new light. The first rumblings of discontent regarding the GDR's housing programme are discernible as early as 1972 in Egon Günther's *Der Dritte* (*Her Third*), which was in many ways a remarkable film for its time. Here the heroine goes to the window of her flat, only to turn away with a shudder after casting a brief look at the barren evening streets, devoid of human life. Similarly, in a series of shots in his film *Die Legende von Paul und Paula* (*The Legend of Paul and Paula,* 1973), Heiner Carow contrasts, in enigmatic irony, the coldness, anonymity and sterility of the new housing conditions with the strong sense of neighbourliness, albeit at the price of a somewhat disreputable lifestyle, associated with the old buildings that were gradually being demolished. The symbolic targets of the film are really the 'old' and the 'new' society, and for this reason the film was regarded as highly controversial when compared with the 'official' version of 'Fatherland' in the GDR.

These themes are further explored in Lothar Warneke's *Unser kurzes Leben* (*Our Short Life,* 1981), a film based on Brigitte Reimann's novel *Franziska Linkerhand*. The film's heroine is a young female architect who openly rebels against the inhuman schemes of the town planners: 'You can't choose to build flats without a town. You can't have the one without the other', she shouts defiantly. She angers her colleagues – and especially her boss – by pinning up what she claims is a quote from Marx on the notice board: 'The city is civilisation's most precious invention, second only to language as a purveyor of culture' prompting the following exchange:

Boss: That's a provocation!
Franziska: Yes, and why not? A provocation can also represent an attempt to encourage, it doesn't necessarily imply a negative attitude ...
Boss: For us the term provocation has a very clear meaning.

Herrmann Zschoche's film *Insel der Schwäne* (*Swan Island,* 1983) goes even further, indeed controversially so, insofar as it appears to be encouraging those who are affected by such building policies – in this case the children living in Marzahn, a desolate high-rise suburb of Berlin – to stand up for their interests by protesting. The children pin up a declaration on the noticeboard of the block of flats: 'We don't want a playground made of concrete. We want a tunnel and some grass.' When their demands are not met they deliberately destroy the freshly-poured concrete in a spontaneous, anarchic demonstration – something unheard of in the GDR where demonstrations were only permitted when they were in support of the Party and were organised by it. Heinz Kersten quotes a remark by the scriptwriter Ulrich Plenzdorf concerning the difficulties in getting the film accepted:

> DEFA was told that the film was not in the interests of our society. Furthermore they had sought advice from leading comrades who were of the opinion that there were various aspects that were not acceptable. There were a great many of these, and the criticism was formulated very strongly. Actually these comrades should have taken the matter to court.[8]

Indeed most of the critics reacted to the film in accordance with the official line, pointing out, for instance, the changes from the original novel on which the film is based:

> The positive, sympathetic and helpful characters in Pludra's book have, in the film version, fallen victim to the wholesale rejection of typical socialist elements in the life of our society. Thus the boy Stefan, who could have been a character with whom children could have identified, has become an outsider in a world which is falling apart, which is unreal and hostile to children. A world which is not our world ... What ignorance or narrow-mindedness could have induced someone to make a film about young people in order to denigrate the very achievement that so many of them have been involved in, for instance, the building of new, modern housing estates, to portray them as a terrifying and depressing world of concrete?[9]

In a similar vein, another review comments: 'Anyone who uses a literary text to criticise those very things that give our social processes warmth and those involved in them self-confidence must expect to have questions asked about his reasons and intentions.'[10]

There were, however, some who spoke up for the film, for example, in the periodical *Film und Fernsehen*:

I cannot think of any other recent film in which new housing blocks have more accurately reflected the thoughts and feelings of their inhabitants. The film has avoided over-simplifying things into purely negative versus purely positive ... The film by Herrmann Zschoche and Ulrich Plenzdorf shows a piece of revolution, for housing construction is a necessary element in the process of social transformation. But are better housing conditions always synonymous with better living conditions? Having a flat of one's own does not always bring with it a sense of security. That depends on how we live together with our neighbours. How do we treat each other? This is what the film is asking. It is acutely observed and it pulls no punches. That is its merit. It documents a period in which great changes are taking place, in which we are adapting to better conditions, and yet await expectantly that island of the swans, on which we once awoke.[11]

The cautious tone of these remarks – 'as we are adapting to a better life' – testifies indirectly to how hypersensitive commentators had to be when dealing with uncomfortable references in films to notions of *Heimat* and *Vaterland*. Indeed the example of *Insel der Schwäne* demonstrates very clearly how uncertain people were regarding those areas which were open to critical scrutiny and those which remained taboo.

One such taboo subject and one which, in view of the pressure coming from the south of the Republic in particular, could no longer be kept under wraps, was pollution: the destruction of the *Heimat* as a result of crimes against the environment. For although the subject was alluded to repeatedly, more often than not the impact of the appalling reality was softened by the use of harmless images and words. Thus Konrad Wolf's film *Der geteilte Himmel* (*The Divided Heaven*, 1964) begins with a voice-over (the words are taken from the novel by Christa Wolf on which the film is based):

That summer the town breathed more heavily than usual. Its breath rose into the clear sky as dense smoke from a hundred factory chimneys. Suddenly we felt that there was something unusual and hard to bear about the sky. The air weighed heavy on us, and the water, this accursed water that stinks of chemicals, and had done so for as long as we can remember, tasted bitter in our mouths ...

These sentences are accompanied by a restless montage of images from the town of Halle whose central buildings, streets and squares are shown almost exclusively from an extreme camera angle. The sequence symbolises the political 'climate' just prior to the building of the Berlin Wall. But the fact is that Halle's air and water really were like that. In the context of the narration, the pollution is evoked as a familiar characteristic of the narrator's immediate *Heimat*, thereby acquiring an almost 'homely' aspect. At the same time, however, the emotional resonance of the opening voice-over has the effect of concealing the really threatening aspects of industrial pollution from view. In a similar vein, the television film, *Broddi* (1975) uses skilful photography to imbue the desolate and barren craters left behind by open-cast mining with a kind of romantic beauty. And although in Rolf Losansky's film *Verdammt, ich bin erwachsen* (*Damn It, I'm Grown-up*, 1975), the huge excavators and bulldozers which destroy the central character's lake paradise and eject him from his adolescent dream into the harsh world of the grown-ups function as symbols of destruction, they do so primarily in a psychological – rather than ecological – sense.

It is not until the appearance of Roland Gräf's film *Bankett für Achilles* (*Banquet for Achilles*, 1975) that the seriousness of the situation is fully exposed. Here in the midst of the chemical landscape around Bitterfeld people working their allotments use strange contraptions to protect their plants against the polluted air and experiment with techniques of cross-fertilisation in order to breed flowers which can thrive in this hostile environment. But as one gardening enthusiast puts it:

> It's all going to die, anyway. Just look at the gardens; nothing grows there anymore. Sure, they have gardens, but gardens without trees. They have to buy their fruit from the supermarket. Even the fish in the tanks are dying. I tell you, one day wood will be as valuable as ivory, and leather, real leather, will be something only the élite will be able to wear – presidents and pop-singers.

It was only possible to tackle this topic with such openness in the mid-1970s, during a relatively liberal phase. But even at this time *Bankett für Achilles* was an exception in its portrayal of environmental problems. Indeed just how at odds this kind of treatment of the theme was from the official version is made clear in the following extract – published as early as 1973 – from Günther Lange's study of *Heimat*:

> In socialist literature we find an eloquent expression of respect for that second, humanised nature, which has been transformed by human hand from a mere natural landscape into a cultural landscape. Valentin Katajev writes in an essay: 'I do not love wild nature. An unnavigated sea terrifies me. Dark woods and lonely mountains make me sad. Nature is only beautiful if it reflects the active presence of people, of the builder who transforms nature with the power of his reason and his unbending will. The steamer on the open sea. A lighthouse on the rocky shore. A mountaineer climbing Ebrus. A highway cutting across the Taiga. A dam taming a river. A cotton plantation. A green, cultivated landscape. A canal in the desert. For me that is truly beautiful nature. Nature is the most conservative element of our country. We have fundamentally changed Nature with the building of communism – we have made it serve us.' To an ever greater extent human beings are influencing their – potentially – infinitely great natural environment. In doing so human qualities are objectified within it: capabilities, needs, objectives ... As a result, the natural environment, which man has transformed into his *Heimat* is – as Marx said of industry – the 'open book of human qualities, of human psychology in sensual form ...' Thus one can say that basically *Heimat* is nothing other than the human genus itself, the material manifestation of its subjectivity.[12]

Elsewhere in his book Lange writes – and here is referring specifically to the GDR:

> From now on the repair and prevention of the damage inflicted on our environment by capitalist over-exploitation of natural resources will become a task which can be completed by our society. The shaping and care of the countryside, the protection of endangered buildings, the conservation, care and improvement of the soil, the use and protection of the waters and the forests, the reduction in air pollution, the abatement of noise harmful to our health, and safe methods of waste disposal are matters regulated by law. The implementation of these measures will still require some time, but they can no longer be hindered by the interests of private ownership.[13]

Another problematic topic for DEFA film-makers was the provincial character of GDR life, a problem that was inevitably exacerbated by the size of the country and the travel restrictions to which its citizens were subjected after the building of the Berlin Wall in 1961. A number of films made in the late 1960s and early 1970s attempt to get round the problem by

portraying the GDR as a centre of 'proletarian internationalism'. Thus in films such as *Netzwerk, Im Spannungsfeld,
Januskopf, Zeit zu leben, (Time to Live,* 1969), and *Der Dritte,* we see
shots of Africans and Asians mingling in GDR society at parties,
lectures and political meetings, though often their presence is
striking precisely because it appears so arbitrary and unmoti-
vated. Nonetheless, the impression conveyed is one of the GDR
as a 'fatherland of the international working class' and cham-
pion of Third World countries fighting for their liberation.

The frustrations arising from restrictions on travel to the
West, together with the feeling of being shut in in what was,
geographically speaking, a very small country, were, inevitably,
difficult subjects for DEFA film-makers. In order to slip such
topics past the censors, it was often necessary to resort to
complex verbal allusions. Thus in Herrmann Zschoche's *Glück
im Hinterhaus* (*Happiness in the Backyard,* 1979), a librarian
spends a weekend with his young lover in a tiny village:

He: Well, here we are in Nennhausen. What now?
She: Well, nothing. But wouldn't it be a terrible thought, to die without
ever having visited Nennhausen?
He: You've got a nerve! Paris, yes, or New Orleans!
She: But if I have never been to Nennhausen, then I have only myself to
blame.

In another film by Zschoche, *Und nächstes Jahr am Balaton* (*And
Next Year at Lake Balaton,* 1980), young people talk about their
holiday plans: they want to hitch-hike to the Bulgarian Black
Sea coast. One of them quotes an absent friend: 'Andy says, you
can dive there like in the Mediterranean.' Another: 'Andy must
know what it is like.' More controversially still, the film contains
a sequence showing the humiliating treatment of a young East
German at the frontier by the Bulgarian passport control compared to the politeness shown to his Dutch girl companion.

Not surprisingly, the question of those who turned their back
on the GDR, an issue which might have been exploited to question the GDR's claim to be the 'socialist *Vaterland*', either
does not appear in DEFA films at all or is dealt with in accordance with official policy. I do not know of a single film in
which the subject of legal emigration from the GDR is
mentioned; leaving the country illegally ('Republikflucht') is
occasionally referred to, but the reasons why people were

prepared to abandon their country for ever – running considerable risks in the process – were without exception explained in terms of the weak characters of the individuals concerned rather than the inhospitable nature of the GDR. Thus, in *Der geteilte Himmel*, Manfred goes to the West because he cannot overcome his 'bourgeois' attitudes and because he was unable to tolerate a professional set-back in his career. In *Der Dritte*, the blind man flees to West Berlin because he has embezzled money from the union's account. In Erwin Stranka's *Die Stunde der Töchter* (*The Daughters' Hour*, 1981) a successful surgeon fails to return from a conference in the West, abandoning his wife in the GDR. In Roland Gräf's *Die Flucht* (*The Flight*, 1977), Dr Schmith, senior physician in the post-natal clinic of a women's hospital, fails to get his superiors to support an application for a research project designed to achieve a decrease in the mortality rate in premature babies. So he decides to leave the GDR in order to accept a highly paid post in a hospital in the Federal Republic.

Films made by former GDR film-makers in the Federal Republic cannot really be referred to as examples of GDR cinema. However, if they are set in the GDR it seems justifiable to include them in a discussion of this kind as an interesting special case. They are interesting because they are enduring documents of this *Heimat*. The fact than many of those who left the GDR continued to make it the subject of their art, is, I think, not without significance. We seem to be confronted here with a kind of ambivalent 'homesickness'. On the one hand they could at last criticise conditions in the 'socialist *Vaterland*' without fear of censorship, even in highly sensitive matters, as for instance Reiner Kunze in the film *Die wunderbaren Jahre* (*The Wonderful Years*, 1979). On the other hand, their feeling for the atmosphere of everyday life in the GDR, which was never matched by directors who had always lived in the Federal Republic, reveals the strength of their continuing involvement with their former *Heimat*.

By way of conclusion, I would like to refer to two sequences from a remarkable film which was first shown immediately after unification in January 1990, *Die Architekten* (*The Architects*, 1990), directed by Peter Kahane and written by Thomas Knauf. The film records how a group of not-so-young architects put forward their ideas and designs for a major, innovative new housing project and shows their growing frustration as their proposals are gradually blocked and come to nothing. Off-screen a well-known song from the Pioneers' song book sung by a children's choir is accompanied by a montage of images which take the viewer rapidly along the Berlin Wall, then through desolate, tree-less streets of delapidated old buildings, across a motorway which seems to lead straight into a huge wall of concrete, as a new high-rise block of flats towers up in front of the camera, huge and threatening. The choir sings:

> Our *Heimat* is not just towns and villages
>   our *Heimat* is all the trees in the wood.
> Our *Heimat* is the grass in the meadow, the corn in the field
>   and the birds in the air and the animals of the earth
>   and the fish in the river are our *Heimat*.
> And we love our beautiful *Heimat* and we protect it
>   because it belongs to the people, because it belongs to our people.

In a café the young wife of the architect who is in charge of the project tearfully explains to her husband why she has decided to leave him. She has fallen in love with a Swiss member of the team and wants to accompany him to his *Heimat*:

If you don't believe me when I say that I love Klaus, then at least believe me when I tell you that I can't live here any longer ... I am now thirty-five, I have lived half my life already; what have I experienced? Nothing. There is more to life than what we have here, more than this endless everyday routine. Our love has been destroyed by it and you haven't even noticed ... It's not about sex, it's not about physical things, about food, sleep, drink, none of that is a problem here. It's about other things. Call it surprise or variety. There's nothing that I can feel pleasantly surprised about anymore. I go to the supermarket and realise that for years everything has remained the same. The only surprise is when I suddenly find there's no longer a shortage of UHT-milk but of onions instead and that I have to spend even more time running around to find a single pair of children's trousers and that they have become even more expensive ... But, why should I live here? Just because I was born here? I need more. I want to find myself again. At work, in the way people relate to me, and how I can relate to others. I can't find myself anywhere any more ... You know exactly what a psychotherapist can achieve: nothing at all, zero! Of course I have achieved something. Quite often. But I can't pretend that I haven't had bad experiences. Seeing problems everywhere, in the clinic, for example, that's not what's bad; what's bad is that I can't change anything ... Hope! I simply haven't the time to hope for something new.

(*Translated from the German by Margaret Vallance*)

Notes

1. *Vom Sinn unseres Lebens*, Berlin, 1983.
2. Ibid., pp. 143–4.
3. *Kulturpolitisches Wörterbuch*, Berlin, 1978, p. 263.
4. Günther Lange, *Heimat: Realität und Aufgabe*, Berlin, 1973, p. 62.
5. The strong sense of regional identity, which operated at many different levels, and quickly developed in the GDR, was the result of forceful official promotion in the 1980s. However, with the exception of the 'Berlin-Filme', it found little expression in DEFA films, for example in the use of dialect, in the emphasis on and presentation of 'territorial' and local traditions, customs and particular regional characteristics. This was because of the centralised organisation of the film industry and the need for it to cater for the expectations of the country as a whole.
6. Harry Blunk, *Die DDR in ihren Spielfilmen* (2nd edn.), Munich, 1987, pp. 192–4.
7. Private communication with the director.
8. See 'H.D.', 'Eine Insel im Häusermeer?', *Film und Fernsehen* 11, no. 5, 1983: 5–6 (5).
9. Horst Knietsch, 'Verstellte Sicht auf unsere Wirklichkeit', *Neues Deutschland*, 4 May 1983.
10. Hans Eggert, 'Ein DEFA-Film auf der Schattenseite', *Junge Welt*, May 1983.
11. 'Eine Insel im Häusermeer?': 5.
12. Lange, pp. 86–7.
13. Ibid., p. 77.

❖ *Chapter 13* ❖

THE RE-EVALUATION OF GOETHE AND THE CLASSICAL TRADITION IN THE FILMS OF EGON GÜNTHER AND SIEGFRIED KÜHN

Daniela Berghahn

In the wake of Erich Honecker's declarations at the Eighth Congress of the SED and the Fourth Plenum of the Central Committee in 1971 that 'there can be no taboo subjects as far as art and literature are concerned',[1] the genre of the *Gegenwartsfilm* (films with a contemporary subject matter) – which had been so vehemently attacked at the Eleventh Plenum of the Central Committee in December 1965 – flourished once again. The 1970s witnessed the production of major box-office hits such as Egon Günther's *Der Dritte* (*Her Third*, 1972) and *Die Schlüssel* (*The Keys*, 1974), and Heiner Carow's *Die Legende von Paul und Paula* (*The Legend of Paul and Paula*, 1973). Even Konrad Wolf's hitherto banned film, *Sonnensucher* (*Sun-Seekers*, 1958) was released in 1972. While the preponderance of *Gegenwartsfilme* which cast a realistic light upon the often conflicting relationship between the individual and society is indicative of the liberal political climate that prevailed at least at the beginning of the decade, the sudden surge of DEFA films in the 1970s drawing on the works of authors from the classical period – the so-called *Erbefilme* – is less readily explained. Between the years 1971 and 1980, no fewer than eight such films were made by DEFA. That is more than during any other decade. Only the 1950s witnessed a comparable interest in the literary works and writers of the classical and early realist periods.

This essay attempts to explore the factors that contributed to DEFA's strong interest in the pre-socialist cultural traditions in the 1970s, and, by looking in detail at three examples of such period adaptations, to analyse the specific cultural and ideological functions fulfilled by these *Erbefilme*.

As the appropriation of cultural and literary traditions played a much more prominent role in the cultural politics of the GDR than in the Federal Republic and was perceived to be an important aspect in shaping the nation's identity, anniversaries of writers, painters and composers were usually celebrated with much pomp and circumstance. The DEFA studios contributed to the staging of such centrally organised celebrations by producing appropriate films. For instance, *Die Wahlverwandtschaften* (*Elective Affinities*, 1974), pays homage to the 225th anniversary of Goethe's birth; *Lotte in Weimar*, made in 1975, commemorates both Thomas Mann's hundredth birthday and the one thousandth anniversary of the city of Weimar. Yet the various jubilees alone cannot account for the surge of period dramas and films dealing with literary figures that occurrred during the 1970s. Portraits of artists – such as Konrad Wolf's *Goya* (1971), Horst Seemann's *Beethoven – Tage aus einem Leben* (*Beethoven – Days from a Life*, 1976) and Lothar Warnecke's Büchner portrait, *Addio, piccola mia* (1979) were not motivated by anniversaries, nor were the two adaptations of Romantic literary texts, *Aus dem Leben eines Taugenichts* (*Excerpts From the Life of a Good-for-Nothing*) and *Elixiere des Teufels* (*The Devil's Elixirs*) both of which had their première in 1973. Celino Bleiweiß's and Ralf Kirsten's Romanticism-films in particular reflect the influence of the debate concerning the reception of the traditional literary canon ('Erbedebatte') and its radical reassessment in the 1970s.

During the early 1970s, questions revolving around the appropriation of this canon were high on the cultural-political agenda. In 1969, the East German periodical *Weimarer Beiträge* organised a round-table discussion on the problems of a socialist reception of works of art from a previous epoch which ushered in a wide-ranging and controversial debate as is documented in the vast number of colloquia and articles on the topic published in *Weimarer Beiträge* and in another journal, *Sinn und Form*. Until that time, the reception of the classical literary canon had been governed by a sense of continuity between the humanistic ideals of socialism and the bourgeois cultural tradition whereby it was the task of socialism 'to put the great ideals which Goethe expounded in his writings and his life into practice through the socialist workers' movement'.[2] However, with the demise of this view in the early 1970s, the utopian burgeois humanism of Weimar Classicism ceased to be the model for socialist literature. The new cultural agenda emphasised a discontinuity between the classical bourgeois tradition and the new, different ideals of socialist culture. Hand in hand with this revised view of the German literary tradition went a critical reappraisal of those movements which had been hitherto marginalised, notably Romanticism. Indeed the rising interest in the Romantics was also associated with a more general thematic shift which focused on the conflicting needs of the individual and society – a conflict which becomes most apparent in the artist's role in society. The DEFA artist biographies mentioned above and those which were to follow during the next decades, such as Herrman Zschoche's *Hälfte des Lebens* (*Half of a Life*, 1985) and Herwig Kipping's *Hommage à Hölderlin* (1983) or even his recent film *Novalis – Die blaue Blume* (*Novalis – The Blue Flower*, 1993) can still be seen in this context.

A major event which extended the debate around the appropriation of literary traditions to the public at large was the publication of Ulrich Plenzdorf's *Die neuen Leiden des jungen W.* (*The New Sorrows of Young W.*) – a paradigmatic text in the context of these debates[3] – and the première of the stage adaptation of the novel in 1972. Not only was the irreverent reception of Goethe's *Werther* by an adolescent drop-out seen as a desecration of the classical canon, but the text also highlights the ineffectualness of cultural policies that aimed at turning the literary canon into the intellectual property of the entire nation. Undeniably, Plenzdorf did far greater service to broaden the reception of *Werther* than the officially implemented educational initiatives. The success of *Die neuen Leiden des jungen W.* illustrates how the critical appropriation of literary works from the past – which implied the need for a continuous re-interpretation of, and adjustment to, the ever-changing requirements of a rapidly evolving socialism – could be put into practice more effectively.

The principal rationale for the contemporisation of the cultural tradition was not to ensure mass audience appeal but rather to safeguard the educational function assigned to the reception of the canon and of art generally in the GDR. With the evolution of the socialist state, the active appropriation of the classical tradition was subjected to a multitude of educational and ideological purposes, ranging from anti-fascist democratic re-education between 1945 and 1949 to the provision of an ideological basis for the construction of socialism and even an increase in productivity after 1963.[4] The critical appropriation of this tradition was thus never static: its dynamism was driven by 'the continuous endeavour [...] to utilise the cultural values of the past to solve the tasks of the present'.[5] In this educational project, film – which according to Lenin is the most important of all the arts – has a key role to play. Its mass appeal makes it a particularly effective medium for the development of a socialist consciousness. In the specific context of a film that draws on literary sources from an earlier epoch, its didactic potential is to be regarded as follows: 'The rendering of our literary canon in the cinema must be governed by the ideological perspective of the class struggle today. That is to say, the old concept of human nature can only be appropriated from the new vantage point of today's socialist understanding of human nature.'[6] Such normative aesthetics summarise succinctly the official role assigned not only to the reception of the canon, but to film in general in East German cultural politics: a crucial instrument in the project of socialist consciousness raising.

However, this is only one side of the coin – the official side – for both film and literature in the GDR were, in equal measure, the site of critical dissidence. Arguably, period dramas are particularly well suited to expressing dissident views under the pretext of contributing to the project of socialist education. This, as Harry Blunk has observed, explains the prominence of this genre during politically repressive periods:

At times when particularly restrictive cultural policies were being implemented, such as, for example, after the Eleventh Plenum of the Central Committee of the SED (December 1965) when the treatment of contemporary themes was subject to rigid regulations concerning the films' form and content, cinema adaptations of the bourgeois-realist literary canon seem to have offered a welcome escape from the officially imposed silencings [...] and ensuing conflicts. The prevalence of literary adaptations during such times seems to be rather symptomatic.[...] Thus, the appropriation of the cultural legacy becomes a tactical device in a carefully calculated strategy of artistic survival.[7]

Though by no means repressive throughout, the 1970s were a period of tremendous cultural-political vicissitudes ranging from the liberal political climate in the wake of the Eighth Congress of the SED in 1971, which inaugurated the period of 'thaw', to the more restrictive cultural policies which were reintroduced in 1973 at the Ninth Plenum of the Central Committee, a move which indicated that the spirit of 'no taboos' had rapidly become outdated. Until the end of the decade, the cultural-political climate was to remain highly volatile, culminating in the expatriation of Wolf Biermann in November 1976 and an exodus of writers to the West in 1977. By the end of the decade a reform of the penal code and currency law made it even more difficult for GDR writers to publish in the West, leading to a yet more isolated and claustrophobic atmosphere in East Germany.[8]

These vicissitudes are mirrored in the cinematic œuvre of many a DEFA film director. Egon Günther's productions during the seventies alternate between *Gegenwartsfilme,* among them the major box-office hit *Der Dritte* in 1972, which was followed by the rather more controversial *Die Schlüssel* in 1974, and a number of period dramas based on literary works and figures. More often than not these literary adaptations were, as Günther confessed 'only born out of necessity. Between each of these films I dealt with contemporary social issues of contemporary society.'[9] Indeed after the controversial reception of *Die Schlüssel,* Günther had little choice but to make such seemingly politically innocuous films as *Lotte in Weimar* and *Die Leiden des jungen Werthers* (*The Sorrows of Young Werther,* 1976).[10] Siegfried Kühn's career with DEFA testifies to a similarly chequered history which reflects the unpredictable cultural climate. Coinciding with the Ninth Plenum of the Central Committee in June 1973, for example, Kühn's *Das zweite Leben des Friedrich Wilhelm Georg Platow* (*The Second Life of Friedrich Wilhelm Georg Platow*) came out. It met with disapproval on the grounds of allegedly misrepresenting the working class. Though not banned, the film was released with a low public profile: it was shown in just a few studio cinemas, received no reviews in the press and was banned from export.[11] The next film Kühn made was a period drama, a cinematic adaptation of Goethe's novel *Die Wahlverwandtschaften.*[12]

The following analysis of the 'Goethe-films' will examine the extent to which they fulfil their officially ascribed function of raising socialist consciousness while at the same time exploiting the specific opportunities for camouflaged ideological criticism which films based on canonical works of literature afford. In order to establish the ideological thrust of these films, it is necessary to focus on those scenes which constitute significant divergences not only from the blueprint of the original literary text but, more importantly, from the orthodox Marxist-Leninist interpretation of those texts. If we proceed on the basis that a film adaptation 'is a product of the culture that created it and thus an expression of the ideological forces operative in that culture at a specific historical moment',[13] the tensions which exist between the ideologically endorsed reception of the text and the deliberate deviations from the official reading are of crucial interest insofar as they provide clues to the affirmative or dissident ideology embedded in the cinematic adaptation. In other words, the key parameter by which the culturally affirmative character of the 'Goethe-films' is measured is the extent to which they conform to the Marxist interpretation of the literary texts on which they are based. Conversely, any deviations from this reception deserve particular attention as they are likely to be signposts of ideological dissent.

Lotte in Weimar (1975)

Assuming the guise of a costume drama, Egon Günther's film adaptation of Thomas Mann's novel *Lotte in Weimar* constructs a discourse which oscillates between apparent conformity and covert criticism. A comparison of the correspondences and differences between the images of Goethe depicted by Mann in 1939 and Günther in 1975 reveals how these multiply refracted images relate to Goethe's role as the most revered proponent of the classical literary tradition in the GDR. As both Thomas Mann and Egon Günther project certain aspects of their own socio-political situation onto Goethe, the images they render do not purport to be historically accurate but are in equal measure a reflection of the cultural and political conditions under which Mann and Günther created these images. Thomas Mann's approach to Goethe is, at least to some extent, coloured by the specific historical situation of Germany in the 1930s. In *Lotte in Weimar*, which Mann wrote in exile, Goethe becomes his creator's mouthpiece voicing the latter's indictment of developments in Nazi Germany. Egon Günther's appraisal of Goethe is similarly anachronistic. It is indebted to the pro-Romantic spirit which prevailed among many writers and intellectuals in the GDR during the 1970s and which in many instances went hand in hand with an 'anti-Goethe' tendency.[14]

In order to convey this critical image of Goethe, Günther did not have to invent anything that was not already contained in Thomas Mann's text; he merely had to omit certain crucial scenes. Günther cuts Goethe down to size by the almost complete omission of chapter seven, or rather as Mann terms it, 'The Seventh Chapter'. The centrality of this chapter in the novel is marked by the use of the definite article which singles it out from the other eight. If one reads *Lotte in Weimar* in the light of Mann's own remarks, the 'The Seventh Chapter' would seem to stand for Thomas Mann's sense of rapture, his 'unio mystica' with the creative genius he so loved and admired, whereas the remaining chapters enunciate more or less explicitly 'the malice and irony in which this love is cloaked'.[15] It is the pivotal chapter, in which Mann attempts to give a 'character sketch of Goethe, indeed, of the man of genius *per se*',[16] and in which he explores the question: what constitutes artistic genius?

In the film adaptation of the novel, the focus clearly lies elsewhere: Günther is less interested in the poet of genius himself than in the 'Goethe-cult' that surrounds him. It is thus only logical that the film assigns far greater importance to such scenes which render variously refracted images of Goethe, who, in a series of conversations, is presented from the vantage point of his Weimar circle and his erstwhile beloved, Lotte. These conversations between Lotte and Goethe's famulus Riemer, his son August and Adele Schopenhauer take up more than three quarters of the film, indicating Günther's primary concern: the cinematic adaptation of *Lotte in Weimar* investigates the process of idolisation and myth-making – only in order to totally demystify the elaborately constructed image, when finally the genius himself appears in the banquet scene towards the end of the film.

The prominence assigned to those aspects involving the personality cult has tempted critics from the West to interpret Günther's film as a political parable attacking this phenomenon in socialist society.[17] However, this reading seems somewhat foreshortened: with Stalin's death in 1953, the worst manifestations of the cult of personality in socialist states were over and this theme was of no particular topical relevance any more in the 1970s. It would seem that Günther's criticism is more subtle and has to be read against the backdrop of the radical reassessment of the appropriation of the traditional literary canon, in particular the renewed interest in Romanticism. The reappraisal of the Romantics, who had been hitherto marginalised and who had been labelled as pessimistic, pathological and sick, had negative implications for the image of Goethe.[18] What texts of the 1970s, such as de Bruyn's *Leben des Jean Paul Friedrich Richter* (*The life of Jean Paul Friedrich Richter*) Kunert's *Pamphlet für K.* (*Pamphlet for K.*), Gerhard Wolf's *Der arme Hölderlin* (*Poor Hölderlin*) and Christa Wolf's *Kein Ort. Nirgends.* (*No Place on Earth*) all have in common is that they aim to redress the balance between the absolutised Weimar classicists, notably the cult figure Goethe, and the hitherto denigrated Romantics. Goethe is presented as insensitive to and intolerant of artistic talent that differs from his own. Moreover, he is exposed as exploiting his privileged position in Weimar by using his power to either foster or stifle the creativity of less well-established poets. Given that the authors of the seventies saw their own role as artists in GDR society reflected in the sufferings of their Romantic predecessors, certain correspondences between the powerful Weimar poet and the cultural functionaries of the SED cannot be entirely dismissed. Moreover, these texts expose Goethe as someone who did not translate the ideals of his writings into reality: in short, they dismantle the humanistic ideal which Goethe represented.

While on one level Günther's portrayal of Goethe seems to subscribe to the officially endorsed view, by presenting him as the most revered poet, worshipped by the whole of Weimar, on another level, Günther follows the anti-Goethe spirit which prevailed in the literary reception of Romanticisim by questioning whether Goethe deserves this esteem. Significantly, Günther chooses not to show the all-rounded personality ('der ganze Mensch'), the humanistic ideal which Goethe represents: by not portraying the supreme artist, he leaves out that side of Goethe's character which merits respect and admiration and which redeems his darker sides – his need to dominate and even to inflict a certain degree of impairment upon those close to him, especially his son August. Having suppressed the individuality of others around him to such an extent that they merely echo his own words – as is illustrated in the long dinner scene – Goethe's authority and greatness are uncontested because he is surrounded by slaves, as he rightly observes quoting Frederick the Great's words 'I am tired of ruling over slaves' ('Ich bin es müde über Sklaven zu herrschen'). In other words, Goethe who is upheld in the GDR as the embodiment of the humanistic ideal is presented by Günther as a narcissistic egomaniac, whose humanity is impaired and who fails in the human sphere. In this way, Günther calls the legitimacy of Goethe as a role model into question. Rather than being a political parable of the socialist cult of personality, Günther's film can be read as a parable of the hypocrisy underlying the project of raising the socialist consciousness by implying that this project is bound to fail if its role models are less than perfect themselves. That this attack is directed not so much at the historical figure Goethe but rather at what he represents in the context of the GDR becomes evident during the banquet scene. While Goethe keeps pontificating in a long almost uninterrupted monologue, the camera pans to – and focuses on – a decoration on his chest establishing a rather tenuous associative link between the pompous educator Goethe and high-ranking officials in the contemporary GDR. The topical thrust of Günther's implicit criticism is further underscored by the anachronistic opening sequence of the film which shows cars instead of coaches against the scenic backdrop of Weimar – a device which hints at the contemporary relevance of the film's message.[19] It obliquely comments upon the hypocritical relationship between the proclaimed objectives of raising a socialist consciousness and its actual outcomes: while pretending to promote the development of the well-educated and all-rounded individual, it actually breeds a nation of slaves, of impaired individuals, who only parrot their supreme educator's words and never dare to voice their own opinions. Through the almost grotesque portrayal of the entourage of slaves that gather round Goethe's dinner table Günther passes a harsh but hidden verdict on the constrictiveness and hypocrisy of the GDR.

Die Leiden des jungen Werthers (1976)

In his next film, *Die Leiden des jungen Werthers*, Günther adopts the same strategy: by choosing a text that is clearly recognisable as an integral part of the traditional literary canon and by following the tenets of the Marxist reading of Goethe's text, he succeeds in constructing a persuasive camouflage of complicity which affords him the freedom to intersperse the film with subtle ambiguities which obliquely hint at a hidden agenda.

Following Georg Lukács' interpretation of *Werther* from 1936, Marxist literary historians argue that *Werther* continues the progressive tradition of the Enlightenment in a more radical form. Contrary to the bourgeois reception, Werther is not seen as an extreme individualist whose inwardness, emotional absolutism and desire for a totality of existence determine his tragedy. In Marxist criticism, Werther assumes an entirely different role: he is a bourgeois intellectual in the progressive tradition of the Enlightenment, a precursor of the French Revolution who thereby contributes to the 'necessary historical progression from feudal society via bourgeois society to a classless society'.[20] His malaise is attributed to the class differences and the restrictions of humanity which they entail.

Egon Günther's *Werther* film, based on a script written by Helga Schütz, fully subscribes to the Marxist reading of Goethe's *Werther* by emphasising the social rather than the emotional factors leading to his self-destruction. It is therefore only logical that the film consistently deflects from the emotional intensity and subjectivity of Goethe's epistolary novel. Instead of attempting to emulate the subjectivity and sense of inner turmoil conveyed in the novel, the film employs a number of distantiation devices which pay tribute to Brecht's dictum that 'the spectator must not be misled along the path of empathy' if he or she is to transcend the limited private world of emotions and to penetrate the more comprehensive social conflict underlying Werther's tragedy.[21] Consistent with this approach, the film precludes simple audience identification by interrupting the dramatised events both by drawing attention to the process of mediation as well as by interspersing the film with sequences which stand in stark contrast to the predomi-nantly realistic visual style. For example, the enactment of Werther's grotesquely exaggerated fantasy about Albert's sudden death at the dinner table or the grimace of his own face which stares at him from a mirror deliberately undercut any tendency towards a purely naturalistic viewing. The somewhat enigmatic use of colour filters, such as a shocking bright green

in the mirror scene, is anything but a stylistic self-effacement in
the realist tradition. The same holds true for the film's
language in that the realistic mode of plainly spoken dialogue
alternates with the heightened poetic diction of interspersed
verbatim quotes from the epistolary novel which are predominantly delivered as voice-over monologues.

In addition, the film's structure which renders the events
that lead to Werther's suicide retrospectively accentuates
Günther's analytic rather than empathetic approach. The
opening scene which shows Werther's friend Wilhelm hand
over his letters to a publisher, raising the question 'Was it
merely his unhappy love affair or was it everything taken
together?', programmatically invites the spectator to participate in the intellectual enquiry of the causes of Werther's
death. The answer which Günther's cinematic adaptation gives
is unequivocal: Werther's suicide is determined by the destruc-
tiveness of the social conditions rather than by the insoluble
conflict of his love for Lotte.

The casting and characterisation of the central figure recon-
firm that Werther's sorrows are not primarily of a romantic
origin, since neither Lotte nor Werther display any significant
emotional depth or passion. Lotte, played by the boyish and
brash Katharina Thalbach, even rejects any expressions of
Werther's romantic sensibility outright. In one scene, for
example, he quotes from Goethe's novel, confessing enthusiastically: 'When choosing Waldheim for my country walks, I
would never have guessed that it would be so close to heaven',
which prompts Lotte to burst out indignantly: 'My God! Stop it,
will you!' The stylistic montage – which juxtaposes eighteenth-
century poetic style and contempory casual usage, coupled
with occasional traces of Katharina Thalbach's Berlin accent –
underlines the dual temporal perspective which this film
adopts in approaching the past from a historical and contemporary vantage point.

On the historical level, Werther is depicted as a 'crucified
Prometheus' ('ein gekreuzigter Prometheus') – a reading
which was originally proposed by Goethe's contemporary
Lenz – and was subsequently adopted as the appropriate one
in GDR literary history since it was felt to emphasise the
novel's social function.[22] Günther translates the secularised
symbol into a complex visual leitmotif which combines the
motifs of the cross and crucifixion with that of blood and the

colour red, which is the colour of the letters in which the film's title appears.

The most explicit reference to a secularised form of crucifixion occurs in a scene early on in the film which shows a craftsman hammer a nail into the palm of a wooden Christ figure on a cross. The next shot focuses in a close-up on the palm of the craftsman into which the clergyman, who commissioned the Christ figure, counts some coins – the pay for the craftsman's work. The cross is then carried away by the artisan and some servants while the clergyman follows. The scene – which has no corresponding passage in Goethe's text – reverberates with ambiguities: on the one hand it alludes to Judas's betrayal of Jesus and the pieces of silver he received, on the other hand, it hints at the division of labour and the class differences and unwholesome restrictions of humanity they entail. Significantly, this scene marks the beginning of Werther's sojourn in Waldheim, suggesting that what appears to be a rural idyll 'is in fact everyday life set against the background of the crucified figure. Werther is mistaken in his assumption that this world stands in marked opposition to bourgeois life, since it is actually part of the bourgeois world itself. Experiencing this is one of the main causes of Werther's sufferings.'[23] The motif of the crucifixion is more unequivocally associated with Werther's sufferings and social misery in a scene which follows a long discussion between Albert and Werther about the ethics of suicide. Werther, who has borrowed Albert's pistols, provokingly puts the weapon to his head and compares the act of suicide to a rebellion through which a people tries to liberate itself from the unendurable yoke of its oppressive tyrant. In this defence of suicide, Werther already alludes to the rationale which is to motivate his own resolve later on. Through a visual reference to the crucifixion motif – Werther grabs a pair of scissors and pretends to drive them like a nail through his hand, whereupon he assumes the position of the crucified Christ, or rather a 'crucified Prometheus', leaning against the wall of Albert's study – the social dimension of Werther's suicide is futher underscored.

Linked with the motif of the cross and Jesus's stigma is the image of blood: culminating in the image of Werther's fatal wound, the blood motif functions as a visual metaphor which joins together two scenes which reveal the inhumanity inherent in a class-ridden society. To emphasise this aspect, the film grotesquely exaggerates Werther's exclusion from a *soirée* at the court of the legate where he has taken up employment. In the book, Werther only finds out on the following day that some of the aristocratic guests were offended by his presence, which was deemed inappropriate for people of their social rank. Though hurt, he finds solace in reading Homer. In the film, the court scene is elaborated in great detail: representatives of the feudal society appear like grotesque masks reminiscent of Fellini's satirical portraits of society. Werther is not only excluded and ignored, he is asked to leave. This act of humiliation is followed by an act of violence, when one of the courtiers pretends to embrace the departing Werther, but actually grabs hold of Werther's face and rubs it against the medals of his uniform so that Werther finally escapes mutilated and bleeding profusely. The inhumanity of the court society is exposed by a sequence of shots which contrast the uncaring attitude of the guests with the caring affection they bestow on the pedigree dogs which, ironically, are considered to befit this illustrious social circle.[24]

The dissonant music which accompanies Werther's ejection from the soirée functions as an acoustic leitmotif, commenting, as it were, upon scenes which expose social conflict and inhumanity, such as the cruel persecution and humiliation of the farm-labourer, Reinhard, through a raging mob, or Werther's crossing of the St. Gotthart Pass carried on the back of another man. Although in Goethe's time it was not uncommon to hire a professional 'porter', from today's vantage point – and, as stated earlier, the film constantly oscillates between a historical and a contemporary perspective – the social tensions underlying the opening scene reverberate all too painfully. The image of Werther on the back of the porter makes this scene an emblem of exploitation, of the humiliated inflicting humiliation onto those lower down the social hierarchy. Consistent with the film's message, it is only logical that similarly dissonant sounds precede the fatal shot which marks Werther's suicide, thus interpreting it as an act of social rebellion.

Given the emphasis placed on the social dimension of *Werther*, it would seem that Günther's adaptation is entirely faithful, if not to Goethe's text then even more so to the Marxist reading of Goethe's novel. In order to emphasise the progressive socialist spirit which Marxism sees inscribed in the text, Günther even added a number of scenes – such as the mountain crossing,[25] the artisan's completion of the wooden cross, and the mutilation at the legation. Werther is a 'crucified Prometheus' because the social conditions preclude him from channelling his creative energies in a meaningful way. Even the dual temporal perspective of the film could be ascribed to the orthodox notion that any creative appropriation of the literature of the past must reflect the 'prevailing stage of development of Marxist-Leninist consciousness' in order to reach the 'more enlightened understanding of the present'.[26]

In an interview which Günther gave to the *Berliner Zeitung* in 1976, he emphasised the orthodox ideological perspective of his film adaptation of *Die Leiden des jungen Werthers* by pointing out that he had been committed to the idea of class struggle since 'the history of past struggles, in particular of class struggles, can teach us a great deal'.[27] While rejecting the notion that history repeats itself, he nevertheless endorses the view that we continuously learn from history, because of the 'recurrent patterns which we can uncover'.[28]

Not surprisingly, in the politically tense atmosphere of 1976, Günther could not be more explicit about the laws underlying historical processes, but after unification he revealed in what way the attack levied at the social conditions of eighteenth-century feudal society was at the same time targeted at the conditions surrounding him. In an interview with the *Sächsische Zeitung* in 1995 Günther explains that the grotesquely exaggerated scenes at the legation were intended as a historical analogy parodying 'the machinations of functionaries, [...] the grotesque way of going about things and the prevailing servility in so many areas of life' which he saw as existing in the GDR during the 1970s.[29] The analogy between the decadent feudal society and the functionaries in the East German bureaucracy is not all that obvious, yet as film reviews from 1976 testify, the public in the GDR was quick to pick up the hidden message which Günther was trying to get across. One film critic, for instance, attributes Werther's tragic failure to his unwillingness 'to succumb to the subservience and hypocrisy of the court'.[30]

That hypocrisy and the associated spirit of subservience are indeed the principal targets of Günther's camouflaged criticism becomes particularly evident in the film's final scene. Whereas in the novel both Albert and Lotte find themselves in a state of shock as a result of Werther's death, in the film Albert continues with business as usual. He seems to be almost relieved to have got rid of the trouble-maker Werther in order to be able to continue, undisturbed, with his pedantic office routine. The relevance of this deviation from the original text did not go unnoticed by reviewers and was recognised as a subversive subtext. One review implied that it is 'well-behaved, pragmatic citizens' like Albert who take on the role of 'reliable civil servants' in the GDR.[31]

The fact that Albert is intended to represent the bureaucrat *par excellence*, the spirit of law and order and subservience which is required to succeed and survive in the bureaucratic apparatus of the GDR, is underlined by the aforementioned device of stylistic montage: certain phrases which Albert uses in the film are blatant anachronisms which make little sense in the historical context but invite the audience to take an associative leap into the present. For example, in one scene Albert reinforces the need for law and order by using the ambiguous words, 'the very basis of the state would collapse if everyone were to think like that'. Similar incongruities occur in the chancellery at the legation and in Albert's office: one of the pedants at the legation pontificates about neat handwriting and advocates the use of a ruler to ensure straight lines and uniformity. But it would appear that it is more than the neatness of documents that is at stake, as the remark of Werther's superior at the legation suggests: 'We cannot allow people to do just as they please.' Similarly, Albert's pedantic reiteration of the difference between the words 'appearance' ('Schein') and 'swine' ('Schwein') can be read as an allusion to the world of appearances, that is to say, to the hypocrisy that Günther saw as characteristic of GDR bureaucracy, whilst the word 'Schwein' might be read as a condemning verdict on conformists and inhumane philistines like Albert who fulfil their duty regardless.

Die Wahlverwandschaften (1974)

Despite the official occasion – the 225th anniversary of Goethe's birth – which prompted the making of the film adaptation of Goethe's novel *Die Wahlverwandtschaften* (1809) in 1974, the scriptwriter/director couple, Regine and Siegfried Kühn, were reluctant to create a historically remote period drama. Instead, they were keen to stress the contemporary relevance of Goethe's highly symbolic novel about marriage and adultery. The Kühns perceived the topicality of Goethe's novel to lie both in the personal and the political sphere: the marriage problem and the isolated existence of the four protagonists who live out – to use the director's own words – 'an apparently idyllic existence on an island removed from space and time, quite apart from society and history'.[32] In order to highlight 'what is interesting, problematic and exemplary for us today',[33] the Kühns altered the original text by omitting certain minor events, reducing the complexity of character portrayal and simplifying the discursive structure of the novel. At the same time they reduced the number of symbols of Goethe's text and intensified the evocative potential of just some of its spatial and visual symbols.

Although remaining by and large faithful to Goethe's rendering of marital and spiritual adultery, the Kühns made a number of significant changes which can be attributed to their intention to contemporise and politicise the message of their film adaptation. In the novel, the marriage of Eduard and Charlotte and their bucolic existence are initially presented in a positive light. Yet the very first scenes of the film which sketch the couple's everyday life together emphasise the underlying tensions of the bond which makes the retreat from society to celebrate their love together appear like a rather questionable experiment. Its failure is precipitated the moment Ottilie arrives, when the emotionally weak basis of the marriage pales against the natural vigour and vitality of the strong attraction which develops between Eduard and the young woman. Unlike in the novel, where this new bond finds its symmetrical correspondance in the 'elective affinity' between Charlotte and the Captain, the film plays down the emotional strength of this relationship. Charlotte's half-hearted, dispassionate confession to the Captain, 'I could spend my life with you', suggests that she lacks the capacity for genuine love, while the use of the subjunctive indicates that she is scared of turning a possibility into a reality. Therefore, in the film her act of renunciation in order to save her marriage is less an expression of an admirable power of self-sacrifice, strength of character and moral integrity than indicative of the half-heartedness that governs all her actions. This aspect of Charlotte's character is conveyed indirectly, mainly through the use of spatial symbols. When the Captain inspects the estate he observes that Charlotte's attempts at landscape gardening mirror her character: 'On the whole, the park is wonderful. The path, however, is flawed. Just as arduously as Charlotte struggles uphill through the rocks, so she now tortures everyone she leads uphill, so to speak. It is impossible to walk side by side, but even walking behind one another is difficult.' The Captain's perceptive observation is reminiscent of an ambiguous comment which Regine Kühn made in an interview about the film, when she said: 'Human beings should not grow content with the situation in which they happen to find themselves. They must break free from its constraints. Otherwise, they will never really develop, they never really live life – they merely exist'.[34] But it is precisely such change or real development that Charlotte attempts to avoid. In terms of the spatial imagery, she does not break through the rocks and stones to make the path more accessible and comfortable, instead she evades the obstacles and adapts to what is already there. The spatial analogies used by Regine Kühn in the interview as well as in the film are only a thinly veiled allusion to the socio-political situation in the GDR. This becomes more transparent, as one continues to decipher the significance of other spatial analogies used in the cinematic adaptation of *Die Wahlverwandtschaften*. Charlotte's timid attempts at landscape gardening and the claustrophobic restrictiveness of her moss hut prefigure her handling of the marriage problem and her general outlook on life: unlike Ottilie, the character of the greatest personal and moral integrity amongst the four, who has the courage not to compromise, as her programmatic statement, 'to be a complete personality in her own right and not to put up with less', reveals. By contrast, Charlotte proclaims 'that one should not make undue demands of the circumstances of one's life'.

Whilst Goethe's portrayal of Charlotte is ambiguously complex and resists any clear moral judgement, the film renders a much more biased view of Charlotte: she is typecast as the embodiment of repression and stagnation. The last aspect is epitomised in the final scene of the film. After Ottilie's disappearance – and, we are to assume, death – we see the couple alone together in their mansion. Eduard, though still alive, is sitting in his room, motionless with an expressionless, mask-like face while Charlotte, summoning all her strength, is trying to rearrange the furniture to reinstate the old order which existed before Ottilie and the Captain arrived. For almost thirty seconds we watch her futile attempt to push a heavy wardrobe across the threshold, but it gets stuck; relentlessly she persists as the film fades out, capturing this emblem of stagnation.

Throughout their film, the Kühns rely on the ambiguity of spatial symbols and visual imagery to convey messages of contemporary relevance which are, on the one hand, acceptable to the watchful eyes of censors while, on the other hand, able to communicate a subtext of critical distance to the audience. The most prominent spatial symbol around which the film is constructed is that of isolation. Siegfried Kühn explains the strategy of dual coding through spatial symbolism which the Kühns employed in their adaptation of *Die Wahlverwandt-schaften* as follows:

> We had to find a contemporary interpretation which we could justify to the State and which was at the same time relevant to us. These were two quite different things. The concept we put to the bureaucrats was that one cannot live in total isolation from society, since this will end in catastrophe and, ultimately, ruin. This is certainly true. At the same time, this official interpretation, albeit in a somewhat modified form, coincided with our own views of the matter insofar as we were in fact living in a country that was totally isolated. We were completely cut off [...] you cannot imagine anything worse. Everything was isolated, both inwardly and outwardly – there was hardly any genuine human contact. And this existence, which barred any contact with the outside world, always seemed to me to be very dangerous. [...] The life on the island that the people in *Die Wahlverwandtschaften* lead is in many respects comparable to the isolated existence we lead in the GDR.[35]

In order not to draw too fine a line between the 'life on an island' in the GDR and that portrayed in the *Wahlver-wandtschaften*, the Kühns took great care to emphasise the historical remoteness of events, thus exploiting the opportunity for camouflage that such *Erbefilme* afforded.[36]

Consequently, the opening sequence of Kühn's film seems to suggest that the precarious isolation from society and history, which results in the characters' tragic dilemma, stems from the specific historical conditions of the time: in a series of abruptly edited shots the camera homes in on a formerly grand and impressive baroque manor house, gradually revealing its desolate state of decay, thereby making the setting an emblem of a historical period in decline. The uninhabitable house stands for an unaccommodating social order which has become outlived. The dissonant soundtrack that accompanies the establishing shots – reminiscent of the opening scene of Günther's *Werther* film – is suggestive of a sense of disharmony, be it social or personal, that overshadows the scene and of which the inhabitants of the mansion are apparently totally oblivious. The emphasis placed on physical decay is an alteration which the Kühns made to Goethe's idyllic setting in order to find a visual correlative for the Marxist-Leninist interpretation of *Die Wahlverwandtschaften* which attributes the tragedy, in particular the failure of Ottilie and Eduard to realise the great utopia of attaining a totality of existence through a perfect, humane love, to the inherent deformation of feudal society. As such a decaying social order does not offer any meaningful mode of existence, be it work, creative productivity or even shaping the course of history, it forces the individual to retreat into the private sphere. Similarly, in an attempt to find a solution to their ethical dilemma, the characters are thrown back upon themselves, since a social order in decline is based on the unstable premises of a moral and ethical relativity which cannot offer sufficient guidance.

Ironically – or rather, intentionally – the film mirrors and reinforces precisely this ethical dilemma which the characters in the film face by refusing to provide the audience with ethical guidance or positive solutions to the conflicts raised. Such an open ending stands in flagrant opposition to the principles of socialist realism which committed writers and film-makers to offer positive solutions for the conflicts and problems rendered. While in any *Gegenwartsfilm* such an ending would have been anathema, the historical remoteness of this adaptation of a classical work of literature gave the film-makers considerable leeway and provided them with the opportunity for ambiguity. Kühn explains: 'This was the advantage of adapting a classic literary text for the screen ... by transposing events to a different time [...] we avoided the need to provide a solution and to comment on the present and on the kind of life we are supposed to be leading'.[37] Paradoxically, the absence of a positive solution ostensibly affirms the officially endorsed view that, in the kind of society depicted in *Die Wahlverwandtschaften*, personal fulfilment and happiness are unattainable because the social order is fundamentally wrong. By withholding a positive solution an ideologically correct message was conveyed which was enough to placate the censors. At the same time, however, the openness invites potentially subversive interpretations.

How, then, is one to interpret the quotation from Goethe's journal for the benefit of Frau von Stein – 'Incidentally, I have had the opportunity to get to know a number of happy people whose happiness is due solely to the fact that they are *whole* personalities in their own right' – a quotation which is added to the film like an epitaph? Almost as an afterthought the answer to the central problem of the film – how is individual human happiness to be attained? – is given. Yet in the fictional world of the film itself even those characters, Ottilie and Eduard, who yearn to realise their individual desires and to attain a state of wholeness and happiness together, are unable to do so partly because of their own inconsistencies, partly because as individuals they are not strong enough to break all taboos imposed upon them. Hence they are doomed to either die or to persist in a state of stagnation. Due to the analogies which the film establishes between the characters' historical situation and the situation in the GDR during the 1970s, it implies that wholeness and happiness are equally unattainable in the present society. To provide a constructive solution for the attainment of happiness within the present system was impossible at that time, short of suggesting – as Regine Kühn did rather obliquely in the previously mentioned interview: 'Human beings should not grow content with the situation in which they happen to find themselves. They must break free from its constraints.'[38]

Notes

I would like to express my sincere gratitude to Hiltrud Schulz of Progress Film-Verleih in Berlin, Margaret Deriaz of the Goethe Institute London, and Seán Allan of The University of Reading, for their kind assistance in providing me with various material. Without their help, this paper would not have been possible.

1. Erich Honecker, 'Schlußwort Erich Honeckers auf der 4. Tagung des ZK der SED Dezember 1971 (Auszug)', in *Dokumente zur Kunst- , Literatur- und Kulturpolitik der SED: 1971–1974*, ed. Gisela Rüß, Stuttgart, 1976, p. 287.

2. *Manifest zur Goethefeier der deutschen Nation* (28 August 1949), cited in Wolfram Schlenker, *Das 'kulturelle Erbe' in der DDR: Gesellschaftliche Entwicklung und Kulturpolitik 1945–1965*, Stuttgart, 1977, p. 71.

3. See in particular 'Diskussion um Plenzdorf: *Die neuen Leiden des jungen W.'*, *Sinn und Form 25*, no. 1, 1973: 219–54 and 'Stimmen zu den *Neuen Leiden des jungen W.'*, *Sinn und Form*, 25, no. 4, 1973: 848–87.

4. See Schlenker, p. 162.

5. Horst Haase, Rudolf Dau, K. Kilche, 'Zur Aneignung des kulturellen Erbes in der DDR', *Weimarer Beiträge*, 30, no. 9, 1984: 1413–22 (1417).

6. Hermann E. Schauer, 'Adaptionsprobleme des literarischen Erbes', in *Sozialistisches Menschenbild und Filmkunst: Beiträge zu Kino und Fernsehn*, ed. Hartmut Albrecht, Berlin, 1970, pp. 298–314 (p. 298).

7. Harry Blunk, 'Bemerkungen zur "Erbe"-Aneignung im Spiegel des DEFA-Spielfilms', *Deutsche Studien* 25, no. 98, 1987: 155–68 (160).

8. Alexander Stephan, 'Cultural Politics in the GDR under Erich Honecker', in *The GDR under Honecker 1971–1981*, ed. Ian Wallace, (GDR Monitor Special Series, no. 1), Dundee, 1981, pp. 31–42.

9. 'Warum sind Sie so zornig, Herr Günther?', *Neue Zeit*, 23 December 1993.

10. However, even with cinematic adaptations of literature which were generally most welcome to the cultural functionaries, since they contributed to the appropriation of the traditional canon, Günther often did not fare much better: his unorthodox adaptations of texts of the literary canon, such as Johannes R. Becher's *Abschied* (*Farewell*, 1968) and Gottfried Keller's *Ursula* (1978), both caused considerable controversy. The television adaptation of *Ursula* ultimately compromised Günther to such an extent that he decided to leave and work in the Federal Republic. See Blunk, 'Bemerkungen', 164.

11. Klaus Wischnewski, 'Träumer und gewöhnliche Leute: 1966–1979', in *Das zweite Leben der Filmstadt Babelsberg: 1946–92*, ed. Ralf Schenk, Berlin 1994, pp. 212–63 (p. 251).

12. Kühn's career with DEFA continued to be difficult: having expressed his partisanship for the head of Solidarnosc, Leck Walesa, in 1980, certainly did not count in his favour; his next film *Don Juan, Karl Liebknecht Straße* (*Don Juan, Karl Liebknecht Street*, 1980) was criticised for its subjectivism; various projects he worked on were never realised; in 1982 he left the SED and was put under surveillance by the Stasi. Thereafter, Kühn was put on a series of projects which never came to fruition since in each case official approval was withheld. In order to be able to make a film at all, he finally chose another safe theme, Gottfried Keller's *Romeo und Julia auf dem Dorfe* (*A Village Romeo and Juliet*, 1984).

13. Christopher Orr, 'The Discourse of Adaptation: A Review', *Wide Angle* 6, no. 2, 1984: 72–6 (73–4).

14. See Dennis F. Mahoney, 'A Recast Goethe: Günther's *Lotte in Weimar* (1975)', in *German Film and Literature: Adaptations and Transformations*, ed. Eric Rentschler, New York, London, 1986, pp. 246–59 (p. 254).

15. Thomas Mann, 'Die Entstehung des *Doktor Faustus*', in *Gesammelte Werke*, 13 vols., Frankfurt am Main, 1960, vol. 11, p. 147; Thomas Mann, 'An Heinrich Mann, Princeton den 3. März 1940', *Briefe: 1937–1947*, 3 vols., Frankfurt am Main, 1963, vol. 2, p. 134.

16. Thomas Mann, '*Goethes Werther*', in *Gesammelte Werke*, vol. 9, p. 655.

17. Hans Drawe, 'Literatur im Film', in *Die Literatur der DDR*, ed. Hans-Jürgen Schmitt, *Hansers Sozialgeschichte der deutschen Literatur*, vol. 11, München, Wien, 1983, 187–228 (222); 'DDR-Film: Personenkult mit Popanz-Goethe', *Der Spiegel*, 3 November 1975, 172–5.

18. See Patricia Herminghouse, 'Trends in Literary Reception: Coming to Terms with Classicism: Goethe in GDR Literature of the 1970s', *German Quarterly*, 56, no. 2, 1983: 273–84; Bernd Leistner, 'Zum Goethe-Bezug in der neueren DDR-Literatur', *Weimarer Beiträge*, 23, no. 5, 1977: 86–120.

19. Such anachronistic references are not uncommon in such films: the final shots of Horst Seemann's Beethoven-biography, *Beethoven – Tage aus einem Leben* (1976), show the composer amidst busy traffic in contemporary East Berlin rather than in nineteenth-century Vienna, where the rest of the film is set. In Egon Günther's television adaptation of Keller's novella *Ursula* (1978) the topical relevance of anachronisms is only thinly veiled. Not only does the audience which is listening to Zwingli's agitating sermon wear contemporary clothes, but machine guns, pylons and a hang-glider with the inscription 'ZETKA' [= ZK, the German abbreviation for 'Central Committee'] leave the viewer in no doubt as to the political thrust of Günther's adaptation.

20. Martin Swales, *Goethe: The Sorrows of Young Werther*, Cambridge 1987, p. 102.

21. As cited by Martin Walsh, *The Brechtian Aspect of Radical Cinema*, London, 1981, p. 7.

22. J. M. R. Lenz, 'Briefe über die Moralität der *Leiden des jungen Werthers*' in: *Werke und Schriften*, 2 vols., ed. Britta Titel and Helmut Haug, vol. 1, Stuttgart, 1966, p. 396; Hans-Heinrich Reuter, 'Der gekreuzigte Prometheus: Goethes Roman *Die Leiden des jungen Werthers*', *Goethe Jahrbuch*, 89, 1972: 86–115.

23. Dieter Schiller, '*Die Leiden des jungen Werthers*', in *DEFA Filme 1976–1977: Kulturpolitik – Kunst*, ed. Betriebsakademie des VEB DEFA Studio für Spielfilme (= *Aus Theorie und Praxis des Films*; 1979, no. 2): 108–23 (116–7).

24. The ill-placed affection recurs at the end of the film which shows Albert and his clerks dedicating all their caring attention to a blos-

soming plant in their office but showing no sympathy for Werther's tragic death.

25. The mountain crossing scene in Günther's film is not entirely his own invention, as some reviewers believe, but is based on Goethe's editorial practice. Although there is no corresponding scene in *Die Leiden des jungen Werthers* Goethe included his 'Briefe aus der Schweiz', which records his own journey across the St Gotthart Pass in all later editions of Werther, as he intended the 'Briefe' to represent Werther's state of mind before he met Lotte. See Nicholas Boyle, *Goethe: The Poet and the Age* – vol. 1, *The Poetry of Desire (1749–1790)*, Oxford 1991, p. 30.
26. Schauer, 'Adaptionsprobleme', p. 311 and p. 308.
27. E. Novotny, '"So aufrichtig wie Goethe den Werther schrieb": BZ-Gespräch mit Regisseur Egon Günther', *Berliner Zeitung*, 6 August 1976.
28. Ibid.
29. '"Politischer Druck aktivierte die künstlerischen Kräfte": Im Gespräch mit Regisseur und Autor Egon Günther', *Sächsische Zeitung*, 17 Janurary 1995.
30. H. Gossing, 'Werthers Lieb und Leid', *Ostsee Zeitung*, Rostock, 12 September, 1976.
31. E. Midel, '*Die Leiden des jungen Werthers*', *Sächsisches Tageblatt*, 5 September, 1976.
32. Fred Gehler, 'Insel der Inkompletten' (interview with Siegfried Kühn), *Sonntag*, 1974, no. 34 (25 August).
33. Ibid.
34. Klaus Meyer, 'Was leicht geht, macht mich stutzig: Interview mit der Szenaristin Regine Kühn', *Kino DDR*, 8, 1974: 6–7 (6).
35. Author's tape-recorded interview with Siegfried Kühn, Berlin, December 1995.
36. Siegfried Kühn describes this camouflage technique as follows: 'film adaptations based on works from the classical literary canon offered the opportunity to express certain ideas which were not immediately obvious, ideas which the audience would understand but which would at the same time placate the cultural bureaucrats. [...] The existence on an island was a very useful concept for they had little difficulty in accepting.' (Author's interview with Siegfried Kühn).
37. Ibid.
38. See Meyer above.

✤ *Chapter 14* ✤

IDEALISM TAKES ON THE ESTABLISHMENT: SOCIAL CRITICISM IN ROLAND GRÄF'S FILM ADAPTATIONS OF *MÄRKISCHE FORSCHUNGEN* (*EXPLORING THE BRANDENBURG MARCHES*) AND *DER TANGOSPIELER* (*THE TANGO PLAYER*)

Detlef Gwosc

There has been no shortage of attempts to develop a theory of filming literary works. None of them has been successful and it seems unlikely that anyone will come up with a definitive theory in the future. For discussions of this topic have tended to suggest that – however desirable it might seem from the point of view of film producers and their companies – there is no hard and fast set of guidelines which would tell us how to transform a book into a film successfully.

The contributions of DEFA directors and script-writers to this debate were published by DEFA's Film School – the *Betriebsakademie* – at the beginning of the 1980s.[1] These indicate the wide range of views – some of them highly controversial – with which we are confronted today. And at a meeting of the GDR's *Akademie der Künste* (Academy of Arts) in East Berlin in 1964, Konrad Wolf, perhaps DEFA's most well known and respected director, offered the following comments on the process of filming a work of literature:

> In my opinion, whenever we film a work of literature, be it be a narra-
> tive work, a short story, a novel or an original film script, it is imperative

that those who interpret the work, the director, the cameraman, the actors, the composer etc. be totally committed to putting precisely *this* work onto the screen. They should not harbour any false ambitions of making it into a work of their own.[2]

There are two points which are surprising about Wolf's demand for a utterly faithful reproduction of a literary work. First, he would appear to be denying the consequences of a change of medium when a work of literature is transformed into film, and secondly – and in my view even more puzzling – the director seems to regard a literary adaptation as a substitute for reading the text rather than as the creation of an original artistic experience in its own right.[3]

The principle of adhering faithfully to the literary original was, even as recently as 1989, cited as a fundamental principle by Alfried Nehring, the man in charge of GDR TV drama: 'The film-maker must exercise self-discipline and respect the content, message, meaning and culture of the original literary text. Respecting a literary work means respecting its values. We regard this as a very important artistic virtue.'[4] We might note, in addition, that Konrad Wolf also believed there to be only one correct interpretation of a literary work for he always claimed to be searching for the 'unique key to a literary text, the only one there is'.[5] In the mid-1960s it was still perfectly acceptable to hold such views and thus to refer to interpretations of literary texts as right or wrong. Of course it was not until the mid-1980s that literary theorists began to look to theories of reception and communication to replace traditional notions of representation and mimesis. From then on the text was considered not as an entity endowed with a fixed latent meaning to be uncovered by the reader, but as the starting-point of a communicative process, as an entity which acquired meaning through the very act of interpretation.[6] If we accept these principles, then the logical consequence must be that every film adaptation of a book is the realisation of just one of a (possibly infinite) number of possible interpretations. Accordingly the audio-visual *mise-en-scène* has become itself a mode of reading.

Reception is more than the mere explication of meaning insofar as it also involves questions relating to the social function of art. Reception is a process of interpretation that draws upon our own experience of meaning and artistic needs as a framework, and is dependent on our capacity to experience, to communicate and make judgements, a capacity that is determined by social and individual influences. In short, reception is dependent on social interpretative horizons.[7] The reception of a literary text is in part crucially influenced by the historical and social context and the prevailing *Zeitgeist*. 'The reader relates the text first and foremost to the contemporary political and social structures of meaning in which he attempts to establish his own structures of meaning.'[8] Seen from this perspective it is perhaps understandable that in his film adaptation of Christoph Hein's novel *Der Tangospieler* (*The Tango Player*) made in 1989, Roland Gräf should present the material simply as a political story about people's sense of hopelessness under everyday socialism. Admittedly, this is a perfectly plausible interpretation of Hein's story. However it does only limited justice to Hein's story insofar as it remains a reading that fails to penetrate beyond the surface of the literary text. It fails to recognise what the book is really about, namely the presentation of a fatalistic attitude to the world in general.

The story revolves around the thirty-six-year-old historian Hans-Peter Dallow who, in February 1968, is released after twenty-one months in prison. He had been convicted for agreeing to play the piano accompaniment in a student cabaret, the original pianist having fallen ill. According to the prosecution, a song slandering the leaders of the GDR had been sung during the performance. All those involved in the cabaret had received the same sentence. The story begins at the point when Dallow is released from prison. A qualified historian, Dallow sets about finding alternative employment since a return to his academic career is – at least for the time being – out of the question. His attempt to work as a lorry driver ends in failure. He finally gets a temporary job as a seasonal waiter on the Baltic island of Hiddensee. Then comes the turning-point in the story: a former colleague from his institute comes to visit him on the island and asks him if he would like to return to a senior academic post in Leipzig, which has been vacated by a colleague who has been sacked due to his 'misjudgement' of events in Prague in 1968. Dallow wastes little time in making up his mind and returns to Leipzig.

The main protagonist in Hein's text is far more than a mere victim of the doctrinaire attitudes of those in power in the GDR. He is first and foremost the embodiment of a philosophical position in which the individual is always at the mercy of sinister forces. Those whose lives have never strayed from the straight and narrow are – as in Dallow's case too – suddenly compelled to embark upon a labyrinthine detour: 'Prison was an unforeseen interruption in the steady, monotonous flow of his existence' (*TS*, 110).[9] That this philosophical aspect of the novel is not dealt with in the film – which has as its main theme Dallow's personal (though perfectly understandable) bitterness at the injustice he has suffered – compels us to take a critical view of Gräf's adaptation. In the director's defence, it might be pointed out that his reading of Hein's story – which fails to go beyond the surface structure of the text – was heavily influenced (and perhaps even determined) by the prevailing political climate when the book was published and when the film was being planned.[10] However, such an explanation for the limitations of Gräf's reading of the text seems questionable on two grounds. First, ever since the great success of Christoph Hein's novel *Der fremde Freund* (*The Distant Lover*) in 1982 – a novel published in the Federal Republic under the title *Drachenblut* (*Dragon's Blood*) – it should have been obvious to anyone that all Hein's characters embody a highly provocative tendency which extends beyond the limits of their individualism. This is something to be borne in mind when approaching *Der Tangospieler*.

Writing in the *Süddeutsche Zeitung*, Michael Althen comments that *Der Tangospieler* is an important film, 'which shows how people conform in a political system'.[11] It would appear, then, that the director had achieved what he set out to do, for Gräf had claimed that *Der Tangospieler* was about 'the extent to which one must adapt and make compromises'.[12] In another interview Gräf maintained that through the character of Dallow he wanted to hold up to the audience a mirror image of itself: Dallow is one of those people who, against their better judgement, and in the face of all the bad experiences they have had, end up making compromises.[13] However, this is not made clear in Gräf's portrayal of Dallow in the film. For Dallow certainly does not appear as someone who is prepared to conform. When Dallow finally obtains a university post – a more senior post than that he held prior to his arrest – this is not the result of underhand dealings on his part. Indeed quite the reverse, for in spite of the persistent pressure of the Stasi – represented in the film by the characters Müller and Schulze – he rigorously declines all their offers in this respect. Dallow's appointment to a more senior post at his former institute is – for him – just as unexpected as the prison sentence he had received two years earlier. Just as then he had been asked whether he could stand in for the sick piano player, now he is asked whether he would accept a senior post which has suddenly become vacant. The fact that Dallow accepts the offer has nothing to do with a desire to conform but rather with the sense of satisfaction he feels. For right to the end, Dallow has always regarded himself as innocent: 'I was only the tango player', he is heard to say repeatedly (*TS*, 136–7). He has no need to think over the offer of the lectureship (*TS*, 203); for him it is a kind of compensation for the injustice he has suffered through his imprisonment and the interruption in his career.

Gräf's film provoked a number of contradictory interpretations; an editor of the *Neue Ruhr-Zeitung* after seeing the film at its première at the 1991 Berlin Film Festival dismissed it as 'the right film at the wrong time' because 'the hero's problems with the Stasi and the East German judicial system … had for West German observers merely the somewhat shallow charm afforded by glimpses into a rather exotic world'.[14] The fault must surely lie with the director, who, in a rather pale imitation of the literary text, limited his adaptation to the biography of a GDR citizen, Peter Dallow, between his release from prison and his return to the academic world. Accordingly, Gräf is mistaken if he believes that his portrayal of Dallow as 'an example of GDR conformism' has done justice to Hein's fictional character.[15]

Hein's novel – once described as a 'parable of imprisonment'[16] – does far more than merely expose the 'mechanisms of life in the GDR', as reviewers pointed out when the film was shown on German television.[17] Its thought-provoking claim that individuals are constantly exposed to, and at the mercy of, arbitrary, threatening forces, has a general validity irrespective of any specific social, political or historical context.[18] The crucial event occurs somewhere in the middle of the book. One evening Dallow happens to find himself in a pub frequented by gardening enthusiasts. There he becomes acquainted with a couple who try to draw him into conversation. The husband, who happens to be a pipe-layer, reads nothing but the works of the philosopher Arthur Schopenhauer, since in his view, 'You'll find it all in there' (*TS*, 91). When Dallow asks him what he has learned from reading Schopenhauer, he replies: 'I have learned that the straight path is the labyrinth' (*TS*, 92). Dallow, who had been on the point of leaving, 'wished them good night once more and left the pub. He went ... straight home. A few yards from his street he had to step off the pavement as it had been dug up. A deep hole had been cordoned off with poles and red-and-white-striped tape. Dallow tried to peer down into the black hole. A labyrinth, he thought, that is a remarkable philosophy for a pipe-layer' (*TS*, 92). In Hein's novel Dallow is living proof of the validity of this way of looking at the world.[19] For the historian never really abandons his academic career, either in thought or deed, 'since he has grasped one thing, namely that the world runs according to an absurd system of rules'.[20]

Roland Gräf, who once declared quite categorically that he was not interested in making a film adaptation of a literary work, but simply a film in its own right,[21] should have been more consistent – as he had originally intended[22] – in his treatment of the literary text. Either he should have stuck more closely to the book and its key scenes or he should have diverged more clearly from the text. Had he done the latter, he might, for example, have changed the ending. Various possibilities come to mind: Dallow might have rejected the offer with the result that an outsider gets the lectureship; or, after a frustrating time working on Hiddensee, Dallow might have agreed to collaborate with the Stasi – and be offered another lectureship at the university; the story might have been extended so as to show Dallow becoming a conformist during his subsequent academic career. However, Gräf, by adhering rigidly to the ending of the novel without presenting the key scenes that are essential to explain it, has failed to do justice to the potential meaning of the text.

West German critics accused the director of not being critical enough in his portrayal of the GDR. 'Gräf's treatment of the subject ... is so tentative that you would think he still had Comrade Mielke [the head of the GDR State Security Services] looking over his shoulder at the set.'[23] Even *Neues Deutschland*, the newspaper which was once the central organ of the SED, and which has remained a socialist daily paper since the political *Wende* in the GDR, expressed visible surprise at the film's mildness, a quality which was not to be found in the novel on

which it was based.[24] It was Oksana Bulgakowa who put it most
aptly in the *taz:*

> The novel is detached and grotesque. The film is saturated with melan-
> choly, nostalgia and whining self-pity. Gräf does not convey the
> grotesque nature of his subject matter ..., he shows understanding for
> the system. The literary metaphors are reduced to details of everyday
> life, the clownish Stasi pair Müller-Schulze have lost their incisiveness
> and seem stale, infantile, unthreatening.[25]

The film, the review continues, 'lets everybody off the hook –
the former bosses, the poor idiots in the Stasi, the defenceless
intellectuals'.[26] In the light of this, Gräf can hardly have been
surprised to find himself accused of contributing to the white-
washing of socialism in the GDR. For at the end, Dallow comes
through his ordeal relatively unscathed and has advanced his
career. Despite being sent to prison on political grounds,
Dallow is promoted within a short space of time to a prestigious
position in higher education; neither his threats to the judge,
nor his refusal to collaborate with the Stasi appear to have any
repercussions. It seems as though Gräf is trying to show that
under socialism even former rebels were given the chance to
redeem themselves. The film's tameness is really puzzling.[27]
Alfred Holighaus adds:

> *Der Tangospieler* resembles a folksy trip down memory lane to a time in
> the past when things were particularly hard in the GDR. The film does
> not deal sufficiently harshly with the former State, with its lackeys and
> fellow-travellers. It looks as though Gräf made the film for reasons of
> nostalgia and not out of the need to tell a compelling story. A strange
> theme at a time like this.[28]

Gräf's indecisiveness, his reluctance – as he himself admitted –
to pass judgement on the GDR in *Der Tangospieler*[29] rendered
the film in the end 'honourable but harmless'.[30] At best the
film is a statement about the absurdity of political justice in the
GDR (which was well-known before the *Wende*). This failure can
only be explained by the political situation at the time the
film was being made, namely the socio-political transformation
that began to take place in the autumn of 1989 and which gathered momentum with incredible speed in the GDR. This
turn of events led to a strong sense of insecurity among a
section of the population which had itself helped to initiate this

transformation, namely the critical intellectuals, a group which included artists and academics. In addition to the large number of writers there were some DEFA directors. Even if these intellectuals, who, in their work, had often enough dealt with the 'whispering imperfections' of their society, were geared to a change in conditions in East Germany, they certainly were not aiming at a total renunciation of socialism. What the majority rejected was the Stalinist bureaucratic form of socialism that affected their everyday lives. The reforms they hoped for were aimed at creating a democratic version of socialism. What they wanted was a reformed GDR. The hope of realising such a plan was articulated most powerfully at the great demonstration at the Alexanderplatz in Berlin on 4 November 1989 and documented in the *Aufruf für unser Land* (*Appeal for our Country*) that was issued a short time later.

During that historic period of dramatic change at the end of 1989, the intellectuals were under the illusion that the population as a whole shared this aim. The people however did not want any more experiments with socialism. As we all know, the slogan which accompanied the peaceful revolution 'Wir sind das Volk' ('We are the people') quickly changed to 'Wir sind ein Volk' ('We are one people'). Thus the way was prepared for the political unification of Germany. This situation caught many of the formerly critical intellectuals unawares and unprepared, causing widespread insecurity, prompting many to ask themselves whether they had for decades been clinging to an illusion and had dedicated their whole lives to a false premise. For many writers (particularly those with an international reputation, such as Christa Wolf for example) this process of introspection led to a deep personal crisis, one which expressed itself by, amongst other things, a long break in creative activity. Volker Braun explains the silence of the literati in a poem in which he claims that many were ashamed of 'their way of writing which exuded the odour of the state which is being fed into the shredder'.[31] At any rate, it was impossible for most artists in the period immediately after the demise of the GDR to condemn totally the system they once lived under.

When asked whether *Der Tangospieler* represented his judgement on the GDR, Roland Gräf replied in a similar vein:

> It was not, for the very reason that I developed the idea for the film at a time when the GDR still existed. Although anyone with the slightest

sense of reality had long since realised that the GDR could no longer continue to exist in its present form. Hein's book focused on the changes that were necessary – at least that is how I understood it – and the film was supposed to point in that direction: a different kind of socialism, the kind that had been suppressed in Hungary in 1956 and in Prague in 1968. Judgement – I don't like the term at all. It suggests that I am someone who wants to judge others. But I don't want to do that. For as long as I can remember I was myself involved, right in the thick of things, one way or another.[32]

Gräf believed that he could only remain true to himself by fore-going cruder, more simplistic tones when making his cinematic assessment of the GDR in *Der Tangospieler*. That is a laudable aim. However, the consequence for the director was that he made Hein's grotesquerie into a psychological story, deter-mined by its environment,[33] in the centre of which stands a figure whom Gräf wants to hold up as a mirror to people.[34] 'What I found fascinating was ... the character with his strange mixture of idealism, good will and opportunism. It explains why things happened here like this for forty years, how it happened. [...] If you accept this Dallow it means that you cannot exonerate yourself.'[35]

Hans-Peter Dallow is – as portrayed by Gräf – neither the prototype of the rebel nor of the opportunist. He is naïve to a considerable degree, in that he believes in a kind of higher justice. This is an attitude he shares with a character in *Märkische Forschungen* (*Exploring the Brandenburg Marches*, 1982) Ernst Pötzsch, the village schoolteacher who has the temerity to question the authority of a famous literary academic. Dallow and Pötzsch, as different as they may be in other respects, are both naïve figures who challenge the establishment and are put in their place by it.

In marked contrast to *Der Tangospieler*, which did little credit to GDR cinematography,[36] Gräf's *Märkische Forschungen* was in the best tradition of DEFA film-making: it was relevant to social reality, well acted, and politically committed.[37] *Märkische Forschungen* is a more successful film adaptation because it is far truer to the spirit of the original text. As Gräf put it: 'With *Märkische Forschungen* I tried to remain faithful to the literary text by making a kind of film adaptation which does homage to the author.'[38]

Made in 1982, the film *Märkische Forschungen* is based on Günter de Bruyn's 1979 novel of the same name. It tells the story of the rediscovery of a hitherto neglected and forgotten writer and journalist, Max von Schwedenow, by the historian, Professor Winfried Menzel. Menzel writes a six-hundred-page book about Schwedenow, in which he portrays him as a 'Jacobin of the Marches' thereby incorporating him into the GDR's progressive national tradition with a view to holding him up as an exemplary figure. Menzel appears to be the only Schwedenow expert in the GDR, until he chances to meet, in the sandy Marches of Brandenburg, not far from his poet's birthplace, the village teacher and amateur historian, Ernst Pötsch, who turns out to have an equally profound knowledge of the forgotten poet. Plans are forged for a joint project, a friendship begins to develop. A friendship, to be sure, that is based on very different motives; in Pötsch's case it is inspired by a boundless admiration, in the case of Menzel, on the other hand, from the very beginning personal liking and interest is mixed with deliberate calculation: he is checking out Pötsch as a potential colleague.

At the end of the story Menzel and Pötsch are embittered opponents. The cause of this is provided by the zealous schoolmaster. Driven by the joy of discovery and the desire to prove himself worthy of the professor, Pötsch discovers that Max von Schwedenow was in reality called Max von Massow and that in his old age he had recanted the radicalism of his youth. Pötsch's research reveals that the 'Jacobin of the Marches' did not die a hero's death at the battle of Lützow in 1813 – as Menzel had assumed – in fact, he did not die until seven years later, by which time he had become a dyed-in-the-wool reactionary. This discovery, were it to be published, would undermine Menzel's book which is based on the myth of a heroic life. From this point on, Menzel – who is more concerned with his personal prestige than in finding out the truth – takes on Pötsch, obstructing his career development in the process, in order to preserve his memorial to Schwedenow (which at the same time is a memorial to himself). Right up to the very end Pötsch never fully grasps Menzel's motives and continues searching for proof with which to convince the professor of the truth. Gräf's film is an impressive adaptation of the story which many (including de Bruyn) had considered to be unfilmable.[39] He portrays the 'unequal duel'[40] between the famous professor of literature and the unknown village schoolmaster as a modern-day battle between David and Goliath. The film critics were unanimous in their praise, referring to the film as 'one of DEFA's rare successes' [41] as 'a thoroughly consistent film, one of the best that DEFA has produced over the last ten years' [42] and as 'an enigmatically cheerful movie'.[43]

Gräf's 'brilliant contemporary satire'[44] became, not surprisingly, one of the favourite films of GDR intellectuals at the time.[45] For, according to Gräf's interpretation of his own work, the film tells the 'story of a man who finds out the truth but cannot make it public'.[46] This of course described the situation of many intellectuals in the GDR, who, like Pötsch, were in many different ways desperately and hopelessly fighting for the truth. Pötsch, the unworldly schoolmaster obsessed with his work, may not have represented someone with whom they could identify totally, but they did share the same experiences: the forlorn battle against the monopoly of the authorities – there is only one 'central' literary institute, only one 'authorised' publisher, only one expert 'competent' to read the script. In view of the lack of a democratic distribution of power, and the non-existence of a critical public as a counterbalance, this represented an implosion factor of the first order.

When the film was shown on West German television in the autumn of 1984, Michael Stone wrote in the *Tagesspiegel* that he was deeply impressed by it: 'Never before have I seen such an apt, witty and yet deeply sad summing-up of the German situation than in the GDR film *Märkische Forschungen.*' [47]

There were hardly any unfavourable reviews of the film in the media, not even in the GDR, apart from the obligatory objections in *Neues Deutschland* to non-rosy presentations of reality, in which Horst Knietzsch expressed his deep regret that the film had failed to overcome the book's sense of resignation, its one-sided view of society:

> So here too Pötsch, the seeker after truth, remains in the end just an endearing eccentric, the type of melancholy idealist who is hopelessly outmatched by the massive self-assurance of a man like Menzel. The opportunity was missed for making Pötsch into a character with whom the audience can identify. Problems in our lives cannot be overcome by treating everything purely with critical irony, by keeping everything at arm's length.[48]

What is revealing about this review is that it shows quite clearly that the concept of the positive hero – conceived as an instrument of cultural policy in the 1950s, based on a simplistic, causal understanding of the function of art – was still alive in the minds of the Party bosses in the GDR.

In view of this background, the assessment of the film in *Junge Welt*, which after all was the central organ of the FDJ youth movement, comes as something of a surprise. Raymond Stolze begins his review with a quote from Bertolt Brecht's play *Life of Galileo*: '*The little monk*: But don't you think that the truth will get through without us, so long as it's true? *Galilei*: No, no, no. The only truth that gets through will be what we force through.' The reviewer has recognised, rightly, that Gräf's film is only superficially about an abstract academic argument, only superficially about a poet of the Marches,[49] pointing out that the film is really about the prospects for truth – historical truth – in the GDR. According to Stolze, Gräf is concerned with 'formulating an important question about our reality: how can we help to establish the truth in the interests of social progress in our everyday lives?'[50] In actual fact *Märkische Forschungen* represents a highly complex game about truth, the search for truth, the finding of the truth, about the value of truth.[51] Furthermore, the discourse about a bygone poet does not merely raise the question as to the truth in relation to a specific subject, the academic object of enquiry also operates at a general level; it can be transferred and applied to other areas of life.[52] *Märkische Forschungen* is therefore a film which aims quite specifically at investigating the present[53] by raising the question of the morality and responsibility of the individual in a socialist society.

When Horst Knietzsch expresses his unease at the book and the film, and his regret that Pötsch does not succeed in standing up to Menzel's dominating manner, this is not for aesthetic-artistic reasons, but rather for political ones: the portrayal of the helplessness of the individual when confronted with the power of the state, as represented by Menzel, was not an acceptable subject. Or at least, as it had already been made public, not one to be approved of. The claim that the individual, even though he be in possession of the truth, cannot receive justice, did not fit in with the ideological image of the socialism that was claimed to exist by the GDR authorities.

In view of this background it was surprising that neither de Bruyn's book, which aroused admiration both in the East and the West, nor Gräf's film were subjected to any state interference, and passed the GDR censors without problems. Dennis Tate's conclusion – that the GDR authorities regarded themselves as the real historians and thus tolerated someone taking a swipe at the academic historian[54] – seems highly plausible. Or put another way: the GDR leaders did not realise that the figure of Menzel was meant to represent themselves, and the system they stood for.

As many critics have pointed out, Roland Gräf stuck closely to the narrative form of the literary text and de Bruyn's characterisation. It was generally acknowledged, quite correctly, that the director had done justice to the complexity of the subject matter by his use of linear narrative style, a straight-forward dramaturgy and an expressive use of language: 'With sensitivity, with a sharp eye for detail and poetic imagery, the director makes realistic portrayal of background serve his purpose, for instance when he contrasts the rural life of the teacher with that of the professor in his mansion, with his opulent meals and grand parties.'[55]

Nonetheless, Gräf extended the film's social horizons beyond those of the literary text.[56] This was possible because the director was able to find acceptable visual solutions to problems that arose from the not uncomplicated procedure of creating a film out of the book. 'Gräf has succeeded in conveying de Bruyn's biting irony on screen' remarked one critic.[57] An example of this is provided by the final scene which is more shocking in its effect than in the book. We see Pötsch, not only robbed of his academic career, but also unable to return to schoolteaching, now earning his living as a tractor driver, searching through the ruins of a house in the hope of finding the irrefutable evidence which will prove his thesis. And the scene which takes place at the Berlin Wall also has a powerful impact:

> It must look highly suspicious when the teacher, in his search for the grave of the man who combined being a poet of liberty and a censor for the authorities, turns up close to the frontier between the sectors of East and West Berlin, asking for admittance to the cemetery which is in the no-go area of the border. In response to the question put to him by the armed guard, as to which organisation had authorised his research, he replies that he is acting on his own behalf. For this one moment the film focuses on the authority of the State. But this one moment is sufficient to indicate that the conflict between the self-centred, politically conformist university professor and the selfless amateur historian

reflects the structure of the entire system. Clearly we find ourselves in a system which sets no value on the individualist who fights his own battles.[58]

The fact that the film is essentially an extended – but probing – dialogue between the unequally matched Pötsch and Menzel hardly suffices to explain how it was that Gräf should have succeeded in turning his film into a more meaningful and cohesive work of art than the book on which it is based.[59] For if viewers are to appreciate the film's specific charm, they need to become complicit in its structure, in this instance its language.[60] The viewer is confronted with this language right from the very first scene in which the chance meeting between Menzel and Pötsch takes place. It strikes us as an artificial language, excessive and pointed, subtle and antiquated. Gräf has 'incorporated the literary language into the film, at first one cannot believe one's ears, and then it gradually becomes a pleasure to listen to: the timbre, the dignity of the formalities, long-forgotten, melodious words – the characters handle each other with kid gloves, on the surface.'[61]

They may appear to treat each other in a friendly manner, on a superficial level, but when the chips are down Menzel and Pötsch confront each other as implacable opponents. It is like a clash between two opposite poles. In a nutshell: 'Pötsch is moved by opinions, Menzel by intentions. This is the difference between them.'[62] Writing in *Filmspiegel*, Günter Agde describes the characters as follows: 'Menzel's primary concern is to enhance and consolidate his own reputation. To this end he is prepared to bend the truth about the poet, in spite of what he knows, with an untroubled dogmatism. Pötsch, on the other hand, is concerned solely with the truth. He is totally incapable of any kind of opportunism and thus becomes a zealot, dedicated to the cause, to the point of self-sacrifice.'[63]

When Pötsch confronts Menzel with his Massow theory the professor does not allow himself to be troubled by any doubts:

He is not too concerned about the truth and has no intention of allowing his beautiful, smooth, rounded and simple image of Schwedenow to be spoiled. The main thing is for the basic outlines to look all right and the troublesome details can be safely ignored. [...] And Menzel has the power to make sure that he and his view prevail by withdrawing grace and favour from his annoying, stubborn adversary. Pötsch's career is over before it has even begun.[64]

Menzel makes it quite clear to Pötsch what he cares about when
the two adversaries come across each other at a public lecture
under the auspices of the Urania Society at which the forgotten
poet is to be introduced. As Menzel says to Pötsch:

> You care about a phantom that you ... call the truth. I care about much
> more: about whether to be or not to be in academic life and in the eyes
> of posterity. I have secured myself a place of honour in the history of
> historians by securing a place of honour for Schwedenow. My hair has
> gone grey in the process and now you come from your village and want
> – in all innocence, I'm quite sure – to ruin everything. You must see,
> surely, that I will use any means in my power to stop you.[65]

Part of the tragedy is that while Menzel goes about ruthlessly
destroying his 'rival', Pötsch continues to believe in the
professor's integrity. He proves to be incapable of seeing
through Menzel's manipulative behaviour – after all, Menzel
had been about to give him a job in his department, offering
him the chance of a highly desirable academic career. At the
end of the film we see Pötsch still searching for a hundred-year-
old tile, carrying an inscription that would provide irrefutable
evidence for the truth of his thesis.

The film is, of course, not really about the figure of the
Brandenburg poet. The Schwedenow story merely provides a
pretext for a discussion about morality and human behaviour.
And yet this very political film is using Schwedenow as a case
study to inform us about the way in which people in the GDR at
the end of the 1970s handled their traditions and their
heritage, and what premises they used. For its part the GDR
was re-discovering its cultural heritage and was trying to enlist
figures like Luther and Friedrich II as allies for its own political
ends. The fact that this kind of exploitation of its historical
heritage was not always successful can be seen by looking at the
reception of various historical figures in the GDR. The dramatist Claus Hammel found material for satire here, for instance,
in his play *Die Preußen kommen* (*The Prussians are Coming*) first
performed in 1981, which takes a satirical look at the problems
encountered when attempts were made to integrate Luther
and Old Fritz into the socialist interpretation of history. A
typical feature of the way in which the historical heritage was
treated at the time was the suppression of parts of individual
biographies if these did not fit in with the progressive image

desired by the authorities. What was lacking in the GDR at that time – and what de Bruyn and Gräf were both demanding – was a more honest approach to the past.

An excerpt from a novel by Jürgen Borchert, *Die Papiere meiner Tante* (*My Aunt's Papers*) published in 1984 is an illustration of the one-track-mindedness with which people were constantly on the look-out for progressive features and were prepared to suppress aspects that did not fit the picture. This is the story of two brothers who are going through the papers of their aunt after her death and take the opportunity to do a bit of research into their family history. In view of the extremely disparate family that comes to light, the first-person narrator, one of the two brothers, asks himself, in relation to his family background:

> Where did I come from? What was 'my' tradition? The East Prussian peasants who were direct descendents of serfs? My aunt with her unswerving monarchism and her absolute honesty? My father, who was in turn a young shop-assistant, became unemployed, then a member of the NSDAP, a soldier, a prisoner of war and an apolitical office worker ? What must I delete from my family history in order to have and to be able to show a desirable past? What did people see in me when they asked me, and above all, what was I supposed to say? 'My father was in the Nazi party' – 'my ancestors were serfs' – 'I come from the lower middle class'. It is all true and nothing can be taken back. And when I look at my grandfather's five children one by one, I see that they were all linked to their background, each in their own way, and each had sought to find a way for themselves of coping with their life and their time: Marthe hung a picture of Old Fritz on the wall and locked herself away. Minna became a nun and abandoned the outside world. Anna didn't care about anything as long as she had enough to smoke. Fritz put a bullet through his brains, and Karl joined the Brownshirts.[66]

This résumé by the narrator of the wide political spectrum of his family is a clear rejection of the selective procedure that was practised in the GDR: 'And taken altogether: that was my, that was our background.'[67] This kind of honest approach to the whole life of a historical figure is what Menzel is incapable of and his attitude stands here for the GDR's treatment of the past.

In its social and political critique *Märkische Forschungen* is sharper and more penetrating than *Der Tangospieler*, which was written nine years later. Gräf has managed to find a convincing way of conveying de Bruyn's reserved narrative style and the writer's rigorous refusal to put a gloss on reality. The DEFA director has done a great service to the critical examination of the contemporary reality of the GDR by provoking a discussion about whether the dictatorial leaders of the GDR wanted only servile conformists and no independent spirits.

In the *Frankfurter Allgemeine*, Sibylle Wirsing accuses de Bruyn and Gräf of having paid for this provocation with the appalling price of a loss of credibility:

> You allow the village scholar to hope that he can get his own back on the dictatorial Berlin boss with help from the West, that he could publish the truth about the alleged Jacobin of the Marches in the other Germany. But instead of getting his own back on the professor he falls from the frying pan into the fire. At any rate the book and the film imply that over in the West a publication would be unthinkable in which the Karlsbad censorship decisions were looked upon critically. So we have the discussion at the edge of the cornfield during which the village schoolmaster employed by a socialist state is informed by the emissary from the West [Professor Lepetit from Brunswick – D.G.] that without Metternich's strict policy there would have been no intellectual freedom in Germany. In the end the only recourse for the German conscience without a *Heimat* is to collapse into quiet despair.[68]

It is possible that this scene was intended by de Bruyn and Gräf as a deliberate piece of German-German provocation. However, there are two other aspects which provide a more convincing explanation of its function. (In the novel Lepetit communicates his reservations to Pötsch by post.) First, de Bruyn and Gräf could not, for dramaturgical reasons, in view of Pötsch's tragedy, use more than one West German publisher to turn down the manuscript. The fact that this would inevitably convey a distorted image of the West German publishing scene was something that would simply have to be accepted. Secondly, both author and director, with their *de facto* denial of a pluralist publishing scene in West Germany, were sending a message to the East German Party leaders which could be construed as signalling that there was still a willingness to engage in dialogue. Clearly at the beginning of the 1980s, de Bruyn and Gräf did not want the GDR to disappear, but with *Märkische Forschungen* they were demanding the reform of a political system which had rigidified over the decades. The biography of Professor Menzel, referred to on his fiftieth birthday, and by the professor himself in a speech directed at Pötsch in his study, supports this interpretation. Menzel, it becomes clear, was not always as he presents himself today. Somewhere along the way certain ideals and virtues have fallen by the wayside. What Menzel has become over the years is a reflection of what the GDR system has become : complacent and self-satisfied. This is what Gräf had to say about what fascinated him about the novel, *Märkische Forschungen*, and what inspired him to turn it into a film:

> Of course the character of Pötsch interested me very much – how he appears, naïve, obsessed, consistent to the point of obstinacy. Qualities which in my opinion are essential, not only if we are to uncover new possibilities, but also if we are to have a creative relationship with the world. Above all they are essential if we have to defend what we have discovered against pressures, which come from both within and without.
>
> Then Menzel fascinated me, this man who was once a lively, critical individual, but who somewhere along the line became a fossil, caring more about his reputation than about true knowledge. I was also fascinated by the relationship between the two, which brings out the question of power and the abuse of power.
>
> However, philosophical points fascinate me just as much, such as our relationship to history, which in de Bruyn's text means our relationship with the truth.
>
> Another thing that fascinated me was that the story requires movement. That for me is its main impetus: it attacks what is static, in the philosophical as in the social sense. Social development can only be imagined as a permanent process of change.[69]

Thus *Märkische Forschungen* is far more than the story of a man who is fanatical about the truth being destroyed by an ambitious careerist. The film is rather a complex discourse about two different characters and attitudes in everyday socialism. What appears on the surface as an argument between two academics is in actual fact a story which tells of the complicated, two-faced nature of reality, of the tricky temptation to use power in a dangerously one-sided way for one's own, selfish, trivial and harmful ends. The film offers 'material which can be used to support both sides in the constant struggle between intellectuals and the abuse of power'.[70]

Märkische Forschungen is – as Gräf rightly points out – 'the story of a man who finds the truth and cannot bring it to light'.[71] Thus the film was a powerful and effective piece of social criticism at the beginning of the 1980s, as a review in *Forum* testifies:

One enjoys the irony as much as one is shattered ultimately by the degree of human ignorance that is shown, or astonished by the consequences of Pötsch's naïvety. We wish that Pötsch could manage to break out of the stranglehold of his futile, obstinate belief that he can manage without the help of anyone else. But the audience doesn't leave the cinema feeling cast down![72]

(*Translated from the German by Margaret Vallance*)

Notes

1. Christoph Prochnow (ed.), *Thema: Literaturverfilmungen* (=*Aus Theorie und Praxis des Films*; 1983, no. 2), Potsdam, 1983.
2. '*Der geteilte Himmel*: Probleme des sozialistischen Realismus in der darstellenden Künste. Diskussionsbeitrag auf der Plenartagung der Deutschen Akademie der Künste, 30. 6. 1964', in *Konrad Wolf: direkt in Kopf und Herz. Aufzeichnungen, Reden, Interviews*, ed. Aune Renk, Berlin, 1989, pp. 92–7 (p. 92).
3. Alfred Estermann expresses totally the opposite view to that of Wolf at about the same time: 'It is certainly not the task of a film to "retell" a literary text. It should aim at creating an independent work. [...] A film should primarily be an original experience, not a reworked substitute for reading.' Alfred Estermann, *Die Verfilmung literarischer Werke*, Bonn, 1965, p. 4.
4. 'Gespräch mit Alfried Nehring' in *Neues Deutschland*, 4/5 February 1989. Nehring had expressed similar opinions in an earlier conversation: 'In our film adaptations our first principle is that of faithfulness to the work – not to be understood as the linear transmission of the ideas of the prose author in relation to the dialogues or scenes, but in relation to the truth of his work, to its moral content ...'. See Alfried Nehring, *Berliner Zeitung*, 16/17 April 1988.
5. Renk, *Konrad Wolf*, p. 92.
6. See the remarks by Ursula Heukenkampf in this context in her discussion article, 'Gibt es richtige und falsche Interpretationen?', *Zeitschrift für Germanistik* 6, no. 4, 1985: 415–22.
7. See Michael Franz, *Wahrheit in der Kunst: Neue Überlegungen zu einem alten Thema*, Berlin and Weimar, 1984, p. 300.
8. Ibid.
9. Quotations taken from Christoph Hein, *Der Tangospieler*, Berlin and Weimar, 1989, hereafter referred to in the text as TS. (Page numbers refer to the original German; translations are by Margaret Vallance.)

10. It should be remembered that Hein's book was published at a particularly tense moment in GDR politics. Factors causing resentment in the population included the organisation and running of the local government elections in May 1989, which, as was later confirmed, were manipulated. Gräf's film, on the other hand, was made during the turbulent times in the aftermath of the *Wende* in the GDR, at a time when there was intense interest in the crimes of the Stasi as well as in the arbitrary use of power in the GDR.

11. See Michael Althen, *Süddeutsche Zeitung*, 22 February 1991.

12. See Roland Gräf, *taz* (Eastern edn.), 20 February 1991.

13. See Roland Gräf, *Filmspiegel*, 1991, no. 5.

14. See *Neue Ruhr-Zeitung*, 19 February 1991.

15. See Roland Gräf in an interview with Horst Knietzsch in *Neues Deutschland* (Berlin edn.), 7 July 1990.

16. See Iris Denneler, *Der Tagesspiegel*, 7 May 1989.

17. See *Leipziger Volkszeitung*, 9 July 1993.

18. See also my review of the novel, 'Vorführung einer labyrinthischen Sicht', in *National-Zeitung* (Berlin), 3 July 1989. More recent interpretations have failed to take this aspect into account. See Michael Schenk, *Fortschritts-und Modernitätskritik in der DDR-Literatur: Prosatexte der achtziger Jahre*, Tübingen, 1995, pp. 168-201. Christl Kiewitz, *Der stumme Schrei. Krise und Kritik der sozialistischen Intelligenz im Werk Christoph Heins*, Tübingen, 1995, pp. 235–65.

19. See Gwosc, 'Vorführung einer labyrinthischen Sicht'.

20. See Oksana Bulgakowa, *taz* (Eastern edn.), 18 February 1991.

21. See Roland Gräf's response in Prochnow, *Literaturverfilmungen*, p. 24.

22. Immediately after the end of the filming Gräf admitted in a conversation: 'When I read the text I had another character in mind. I did not particularly like Hein's "tango player". True, I had completely accepted the literary character but initially I was not keen on making a film about such a "minor hero". I discussed this with Christoph Hein because I wanted to give the character a different interpretation; I wanted to make Dallow more involved. I wanted to make Dallow – and I have to smile about this today – into a man who feels impelled to attack the structures of society.' In *Neues Deutschland* (Berlin edn.), 7 July 1990.

23. Wolfram Schütte, *Frankfurter Rundschau*, 21 February 1991.

24. Birgit Galle, *Neues Deutschland* (Berlin Edition), 4 March 1991.

25. Bulgakowa, *taz*. Other film critics also refer to the Müller/Schulze Stasi duo as appearing unreal and comic, rather like Laurel and Hardy. See Torsten Wahl, *Volksstimme*, (Magdeburg), 11 March 1991.

26. Ibid.

27. See Alfred Holighaus in *Berlinale-Tip*, 1991, no. 4.

28. Ibid.

29. See Roland Gräf in conversation with Axel Geiss in *Filmspiegel*, 1991, no. 5. In an interview for the *taz* (Eastern edn.) Gräf commented:

'*Der Tangospieler* was never intended to be a political judgement on the GDR. What interested me were the GDR taboos that Hein touches on in his book: that there were political prisoners in the GDR, that when you came out of prison you were asked to work for the Stasi, and Prague '68'. See *taz* (Eastern edn.), 20 February 1991.

30. See Holighaus, *Berlinale-Tip*, 1991, no. 4.
31. See Volker Braun, *Schreiben im Schredder*, Frankfurt am Main, 1996, p. 164.
32. Gräf, *Filmspiegel*, 1991, no. 5.
33. See Bulgakowa, *taz* (Eastern edition), 18 February 1991.
34. See Gräf, *Filmspiegel*, 1991, no. 5.
35. Roland Gräf, as quoted by Fred Gehler in ' "… nur ein Tangospieler": Roland Gräf's Verfilmung der Erzählung von Christoph Hein', *Film und Fernsehen* 19, no. 2, 1991: 6–7 (7).
36. See Schütte, *Frankfurter Rundschau*, 21 February 1991.
37. Klaus Wischnewski makes this same point – in my view incorrectly – in respect of *Der Tangospieler*. See *Weltbühne*, 19 March 1991.
38. See Roland Gräf's response in Prochnow, *Literaturverfilmungen*, 92.
39. See the correspondence between Günter de Bruyn and Roland Gräf, 'Briefwechsel mit Günter de Bruyn' in *Roland Gräf: Gedanken beim Filmemachen: eine Dokumentation*, ed. Ugla Gräf and Rolf Richter (= *Aus Theorie und Praxis des Films*, 1987, no. 4): 82–8.
40. See Raymund Stolze, *Junge Welt*, 4 May 1982.
41. See *Thüringische Landeszeitung*, 4 May 1982.
42. See *Thüringer Tageblatt*, 11 May 1982.
43. See Heinz Kersten, *Der Tagesspiegel*, 30 May 1982.
44. See Klaus Baschleben, *National-Zeitung* (Berlin), 7 May 1982.
45. See Dieter Wiedemann and Hans Lohmann, 'Der DEFA-Spielfilm zwischen Anpassung und Protest', *Zeitschrift für Literaturwissenschaft und Linguistik* 21, no. 82, 1991: 38–51 (49).
46. Roland Gräf as quoted by Hans-Dieter Tok in *Leipziger Volkszeitung*, 4 May 1982.
47. Michael Stone, *Der Tagesspiegel*, 2 November 1984.
48. Horst Knietzsch, *Neues Deutschland*, 12 May 1982.
49. See Gisela Buhrig, *Die Union*, 3 April 1982.
50. Stolze, *Junge Welt*, 4 May 1982.
51. See Günter Sobe, *Berliner Zeitung*, 4 May 1982.
52. See Helmut Ullrich, *Neue Zeit*, 22 April 1982.
53. Ibid.
54. See Dennis Tate, ' "Natürlich ein politisches Buch": *Märkische Forschungen* im historischen Kontext der Honecker-Ära', in *Text und Kritik* 127: *Günter de Bruyn*, ed. Heinz Ludwig Arnold, Munich, 1995, pp. 84–91.
55. See *Thüringische Landeszeitung*, 4 May 1982.
56. See Stolze, *Junge Welt*, 4 May 1982.
57. *Thüringische Landeszeitung*, 4 May 1982.

58. Sybille Wirsing, *Frankfurter Allgemeine*, 8 April 1983.
59. See Sobe, *Berliner Zeitung*, 4 May 1982.
60. See Günter Agde, *Filmspiegel*, 1982, no.10.
61. Regine Sylvester, *Lausitzer Rundschau*, 21 April 1983.
62. Sobe, *Berliner Zeitung*, 4 May 1982.
63. Agde, *Filmspiegel*, 1982, no.10.
64. Ullrich, *Neue Zeit*, 22 April 1982.
65. Günter de Bruyn, *Märkische Forschungen: Erzählung für Freunde der Literaturgeschichte*, 4th edn., Halle, Leipzig, 1982, p. 153.
66. Jürgen Borchert, *Die Papiere meiner Tante: Roman*, Halle, Leipzig, 1984, p. 137.
67. Ibid.
68. Wirsing, *Frankfurter Allgemeine*, 8 April 1983.
69. Prochnow, *Literaturverfilmungen*, 26.
70. See Michael Pantenius, *Liberal-Demokratische Zeitung*, 6 May 1982.
71. Roland Gräf as quoted in *Volksstimme*, 20 May 1982.
72. Ulrike Bresch, *Forum*, 1982, no. 9.

✤ Chapter 15 ✤

THE DOCUMENTARY WORK OF JÜRGEN BÖTTCHER: A RETROSPECTIVE

Richard Kilborn

Documentary has never enjoyed the same degree of popularity as feature film, and this is as true of documentary production in the former GDR as it is of the Federal Republic. At the same time, however, it is also the case that well-known East German documentarists such as Jürgen Böttcher enjoyed certain advantages over their West German counterparts which should not be underestimated. Generally speaking, makers of film documentaries in the East – in spite of the strict censorship which determined all aspects of media activity there – had relatively favourable working conditions. There were excellent training facilities and, once they had made the grade, GDR documentarists could rely on a degree of technical and logistical support which was the envy of many film-makers in the West. Not only were they mostly able to film using 35mm, they also had the luxury of not having to complete their projects at break-neck speed. (Extensive and unhurried research is often an important prerequisite of the successful documentary.)

Documentary production in the East can be contrasted with that in the West in another respect. In the Federal Republic documentary has become increasingly dependent on funding from television, to the extent that made-for-the-cinema documentaries have become virtually extinct. In countries such as the erstwhile GDR, the support given to film-making in the shape of the state-owned company DEFA enabled a comparatively healthy tradition of documentary film-making to be maintained. This is not to say that support for DEFA film documentarists came with no strings attached. They were of course required to toe the Party line just like all those working for any

Richard Kilborn

State institution. It did mean, however, that DEFA film-makers had, in relative terms, significantly more creative opportunities than their comrades in television. As one commentator has observed:

> Television reporting served the policy needs of the SED in the informational field. By contrast, those working for the DEFA documentary studios – which even in the 1950s employed a large number of people – had considerable opportunity for free artistic expression. Compared with television, which dutifully conformed to Party wishes, the DEFA organisation (founded in 1946) gained the reputation of being a place which offered creative opportunities for self-confident, critically-minded directors and production teams.[1]

Documentarists have always considered themselves, to a greater or lesser degree, to be chroniclers of the contemporary world. Accordingly, their work acquires historical significance, in so far as it provides a chronicle-like account of individual occurrences or events. At the same time, however, a documentary is always something more than quasi-scientific reportage. Documentaries are what individual film-makers *make* of events and situations. Each documentarist has a particular angle on what he or she presents, and as such there is a distinct authorial component in every documentary account. This is not to suggest that film-makers indulge in wilful, imaginative embroidering of events. It is to say, however, that documentarists leave their personal imprint on what they produce. In the words of one critic:

> Documentarists do not simply reproduce reality, but are engaged in processing, heightening and interpreting the real. Documentarists are also 'auteurs'. As such they can be distinguished by their own personal style, not only in the way they favour certain types of shot, but also by how they edit together these shots and by the manner in which they approach their documentary subjects. They are able to create their own cosmos, which – though based on reality – may be markedly different from, even be in direct opposition to, the reality we know.[2]

Jürgen Böttcher himself has always been well aware of this subjective aspect of documentary. For him each work carries with it traces of its making, as well as reproducing certain contours of that part of the world on which the camera has been trained. And as he astutely observes, documentaries are in this sense multidimensional works:

Documentaries have many more dimensions than some critics expect. They claim to be authentic and at the same time they are a poetic means of expresion. They are objective and at the same time much more subjective than most feature films. We look down on Tbilisi, at a particular time, in a particular light. Even the smell is distinctive. Is that not mysterious?[3]

These reflections on the function of documentary also provide some explanation of why Böttcher quite often ran foul of East German cultural bureaucrats. If something is 'mysterious', as he suggests, it also means that it might be capable of more than one interpretation. If this is the case, then it clearly throws some doubt on the work's potential as a propagandist vehicle. Propaganda has to be much more one-dimensional to achieve its persuasive aim. This may well explain why no small number of Böttcher's works did not receive the censors' blessing. His understanding of documentary's basic function was very different from theirs. The bureaucrats were interested more in what they saw as documentary's potential social effects, whereas Jürgen Böttcher was more concerned to underline documentary's capacity to move viewers in ways which permitted them occasionally to read between the lines of what was being depicted at the denotative level.

Böttcher: A Biographical Sketch

Jürgen Böttcher was born in 1931 in Strawalde, in the region of Ober-Lausitz, in the south-eastern corner of what was to become the GDR. He was the third child of a teacher whom the Nazis pensioned off in 1937. As so often with members of Böttcher's generation, the experience of war marked him deeply, to the extent that – as he confided in an interview with the author – he regards the paintings and the documentaries he produced over a thirty-year period largely as an act of atonement. After the war he became politically active on the left. He joined the Communist Party and also began to study the work of Brecht, together with the films of the great Soviet filmmakers, in particular those of Dovzhenko and Eisenstein.

In the aftermath of the war Böttcher also began to develop his own talent as an artist. In his own words:

At the age of sixteen I began to take an intensive interest in drawing and painting. That was shortly after the period of war and destruction which proved so challenging for me, as for so many members of my generation.[4]

From 1949 to 1953 he studied at art school in Dresden. He was clearly quite a talented artist and much of his later documentary work bears witness to his earlier art training. He was, however, more than a little resistant to official Party doctrine about the function of art in a socialist society and it was not long before he was involved in disputes with cultural officials. He was, for instance, castigated for producing paintings and drawings which were considered too dark, too experimental, too unpredictable – in short, work which deviated from the officially prescribed norms. Sensing that his further progress as a painter could be seriously impaired, he decided to try his hand at a new form of expressive activity: film-making.

From 1955 to 1960, Böttcher studied at the *Hochschule für Film und Fernsehen*, the film school in Potsdam-Babelsberg, where he acquired the tools of the documentarist's trade. During this time his imagination seems to have been especially stirred by the Italian neorealists. He always makes a point of stressing in interviews that films like Rossellini's *Rome: Open City* (1945) and Visconti's *Terra Trema* (1948) had a particular influence on him, as well as the Soviet film-makers referred to above. From 1961 onwards he was a full-time employee of the DEFA documentary and newsreel studio. Right from the outset he was drawn to making films about workers and their lives. In this respect it has sometimes been suggested that it was fortuitous that his own priorities fell so harmoniously in line with those of the 'Workers' and Peasants' State'! In his own words:

Even when still at school I knew I wanted to make films about workers. And even today I'm very aware of what tough lives they lead. This is why I'm always trying to discover more about where these people get their strength from. Also what conditions make it possible for them to carry out the work which keeps them together.[5]

Much of Böttcher's work bears witness to this desire to chronicle the lives of individuals in their working environment. Much later in his career, however, as he reflects back on what he had set out to achieve in his work, he recognises that in certain important respects these chronicles throw important light on his own attitudes and aspirations, especially on his film-making activities. Capturing aspects of the lives of normal, unheroic individuals thus becomes a kind of metaphor for his work as a documentarist:

> Obviously there are reasons why I always feel drawn to the people who are doing tough, dirty jobs – jobs where people are normally inconspicuous. This activity has a lot in common with our own work as film-makers. What is the explanation for this? It's partly to do with my own personal biography, I'm sure, but it's also something which many members of my generation have experienced. The roots lie there. A film acquires a special truthfulness and depth the more it has to do with the most radical experiences of one's own life.[6]

Böttcher's documentary œuvre, the series of documentaries for which he is best remembered, is in many ways a realisation of what he outlines above, an emotional and intellectual commitment to revealing important truths about the lives of unsung heroes in factories or elsewhere in the workplace. In this respect his work represents a kind of homage to working people. Beyond this, however, he also regards film as having the potential to capture some of those hidden, mysterious aspects of life. To the extent that documentary is able to convey the unique qualities of individual personality and to evoke the resonance or spirit of particular places, it is in his view an art form with almost magical properties. As he puts it:

> The task which I feel that documentary has to fulfil is – in the most profound sense – to reveal something of the magical qualities of life. It's a question of finding appropriate images ... Documentary, as I understand it, is one of the most magical art forms, by means of which one is able to conjure up the real. It represents a seismographic account of the here and now. Feature film on the other hand represents something that has passed. Documentary film is immediate and can draw creatively on the magic of the world, on the myths of everyday life.[7]

Böttcher's Career as a Documentarist

Jürgen Böttcher began his documentary career on quite a controversial note in that his first film *Drei von vielen* (*Three of Many*, 1961), a short and seemingly innocent documentary about three of his painter friends, was banned. The film was to a large extent made up of re-enactments, but what cultural officials took particular exception to was the sight of a barefooted worker sitting in a rocking chair. Although the ban was doubtless a severe jolt to his confidence, it may in other respects have been quite salutary in that it made clear to him that even a slight deviation from the norm could almost be met with unqualified hostility.[8] As he commented:

> It was the first film in the GDR which set its sights on the personal and private sphere. People hated the film so much that it was banned without further ado.[9]

It may have been partly for this reason that a year later in 1962 he came up with a film better calculated to appeal and to which even cultural officials would not take exception. *Ofenbauer* (*Furnace Builders*, 1962) is a short film which we in the West would probably call an industrial documentary. It depicts a group of workers shifting a massive blast furnace into position. Although not particularly adulatory in its tone, the film clearly fits in with GDR establishment thinking on the role of the artist in a socialist society. Not surprisingly therefore Böttcher was given the green light to proceed with further projects.

It was from now on that Böttcher began to develop a mode of documentary which bears his particular authorial imprint. In *Stars* (1963) he set up his cameras in the quality control division of a light-bulb factory. The 'stars' of the film are the women who work there. The role of the film maker is not simply to document the activity of a group of workers not usually singled out for eulogising treatment, even in a socialist documentary. It is rather to reveal something of the underlying attitudes of the women to the mind-numbing tasks they are called on to perform. To these ends Böttcher gets the 'stars' of his film to voice their own opinions straight to camera rather than have these reported through the filtering device of a narrator-commentator. Capturing synchronised sound in this way was no easy task in the early 1960s, since GDR documentarists did not yet have access to the light-weight recording equipment which was beginning to be available in the West. Although the sound recording techniques which he employs in *Stars* are, by contemporary standards, still relatively crude, they do reveal his commitment to achieving a high level of authenticity in his documentaries. At the same time, there was more to this than simply aiming for a high degree of verisimilitude. In getting the women to describe in their own words what it was like for them, Böttcher not only pays them the respect due to all working individuals, he also avoids falling into the conventional trap of merely mythologising the workplace. His aim is rather to get the women to tell it 'as it really is'. As he remarks:

> I wanted people to see that these women – like many others of their kind – are all worthy of being loved. I wanted quite consciously to contrast them with those generally accepted ideas of beauty which are all too often extolled.[10]

For the next two decades Böttcher was to refine these observational techniques to the point in the late 1980s when he was generally accepted as the GDR's leading documentarist. It is always invidious to pick out the most representative works of any artist, but the documentaries for which he will probably be best remembered are *Der Sekretär* (*The Secretary*, 1967), *Wäscherinnen* (*Washerwomen*, 1972), *Martha* (1978) and *Rangierer* (*Shunters*, 1984). All these films are marked by certain common features. First and foremost there is the attempt to tell simple truths, to get behind the façade, to bring to our attention the lives and voices of those who do not usually get heard. (This in itself quite often brought him into conflict with State officials, when the sentiments voiced by ordinary people were sometimes capable of misinterpretation.) Nevertheless, the key aspect of Böttcher's documentary technique has always been to communicate through his films the unique quality of lived experience. Indeed in all the interviews he has given over the last two decades it is noticeable that he constantly reiterates his desire to attain the greatest measure of authenticity and honesty in his documentaries. He has also always clung to the belief that his films provide a particularly telling portrayal of life as it was really lived. As he put it when he was invited to talk about his films to members of the Bundestag Commission of Investigation on the GDR in May 1993:

> These are really very representative DDR films dealing with so-called everyday life in the GDR or depicting working practices and conditions there.[11]

Style and Approach

The nub of Böttcher's documentary approach, as revealed in
films such as *Wäscherinnen, Stars and Martha,* has always been to
home in on individuals, usually within their workplace environment, and to give them space and opportunity to speak for
themselves. Whilst it is possible to see this method as Böttcher's
contribution to a style of film-making which had an important
impact on the documentary tradition in the GDR, one can also
see it in the context of wider developments in the field of documentary. There were, namely, from the 1960s onwards, clear
signs elsewhere in Europe and in the United States that documentarists were becoming increasingly dissatisfied with earlier
techniques of presentation.[12] There was a widespread desire to
develop new modes which would address the audience in
different ways from hitherto. (This same desire gave special
impetus to the development of the new light-weight equipment, which observational documentarists in the West were
increasingly able to exploit.) Thus, whilst it is possible in one
respect to agree with Böttcher that his documentaries are
archetypal GDR films, the same works can be seen as fitting in
with wider developments. Further credence is given to this idea
when one considers that, from the mid-1970s, he enjoyed
growing international recognition in documentary circles. His
work was screened and discussed at a number of international
festivals, culminating in a major retrospective at the Edinburgh
Film Festival in 1988.

Part of Böttcher's success as a documentarist is attributable
to his determination to create a style which bore his distinctive
authorial imprint. One of the factors which contributed to this
style is his ability to develop a good working relationship with
his documentary subjects. Consequently, in all his best work,
his protagonists display a naturalness which often belies the
presence of camera operator(s) and sound recordist(s). This
naturalness is in no way contrived and has much to do with the
trust that subjects feel they are able to invest in him and his
team. It is in this respect no coincidence that he has always
been implacably opposed to any form of secret filming. His
method has been to do everything in his power not to be an
obtrusive presence and never to use his camera as a dissecting
instrument, as if he were an investigative journalist. It is not so
much that Böttcher is never prepared to intervene (sometimes

you do hear him asking questions from behind the camera). When he does this, however, it is always in the spirit of genuine inquiry and never with the intention of tempting his subject into unguarded statements.

Böttcher's documentary method is closely connected to his choice of subject matter. His favoured subjects are ordinary people in workaday situations. It is for this reason that most of his most representative work tends to take the form of individual or group portraits – *Stars, Wäscherinnen, Martha, Rangierer* – once again calling to mind his initial training as a painter. *Martha* is the portrait of a *Trümmerfrau*, one of the women who in the immediate aftermath of the war sorted rubble in the ruins of devastated cities. Even more poignantly, however, Martha has continued to sort rubble for thirty or more years until the day comes when she finally has to retire. The film offers its audience a series of quietly observed scenes in which Martha goes about her sorting business, sometimes alone, sometimes in the presence of her much younger colleagues. The film is without commentary and moves forward at a pace and in a manner which constantly invite the viewer to reach their own conclusions about what it is that is being represented. To what extent, for example, is Martha's struggle typical or representative of many other lives in this socialist state? Or is it rather that she is telling us something about the indefatigable human spirit triumphing over adversity? Or, yet again, can the film be read as a commentary on the process of documentary making itself, since quite often in the almost hour-long film we are made aware of the perspective from which events are being viewed and the manner in which the camera eye is capturing actions and movements within the confines of Martha's world?

In a not dissimilar manner *Rangierer* records activity and movement within another working environment, this time in a railway marshalling yard on the outskirts of Dresden. Whereas in *Martha*, the emphasis is frequently on the warm glow of a distinctive, loveable personality, the focus in *Rangierer* has noticeably changed. No longer do we home in on the individual workers, the eponymous shunters, but we view their activities from the middle-distance, with shots linked in such a way that they seem to become part of some elaborate, ritualised game.[13] It is indeed almost as if the movements and actions captured on film have been transformed into the formal rhythms of the film. As one commentator has observed:

> Language (in this film) is reduced to individual signals; it becomes pure noise. The images reveal the elementary rituals of life. The everday routines of life continue. The shunters marshal their trains.[14]

The noticeable 'taciturnity' of *Rangierer* leads us to make a more general point about Böttcher's documentary development. There is a marked progression in his work from early documentaries, where external commentary is still quite prominent, to later ones in which commentary has been wholly abandoned. When he began his career in the 1960s, the accepted practice, or even requirement, was that each documentary be supplied with an explanatory commentary. This was primarily to ensure that any account of GDR reality be presented in such a way as to allow no scope for false interpretation. Böttcher always considered such commentaries to be highly dubious and with the benefit of hindsight (after unification) his criticism took on a still sharper edge:

> As soon as explanations were required, the censors and the authorities intervened. You always had to dress things up verbally. You always had to regulate things – and it was absolutely horrible.[15]

As his own work shows, in the course of time Böttcher became far less prepared to compromise on the issue of commentaries. Whilst accepting that on occasions a certain amount of initial explanation might be necessary, he comes out quite strongly against what he terms 'an inflationary element in language and in speaking'.[16] He is also of the belief that an all-too wordy documentary can have the detrimental effect of drawing the audience's attention away from the 'messages' contained in the images themselves. His primary ambition as a documentary artist therefore has been to integrate the images and sounds of the natural and social world into what becomes in effect a painterly composition. As he notes:

> Film reproduces far more than words. Far more than any other medium film can capture original tones which can be very meaningful, even if we don't understand the actual language being used. Language is like music, when one is not just interested in seeking after what is clearly articulated in words; when one is fascinated by sound alone.[17]

Böttcher's Relations with the GDR

No retrospective of any GDR film-maker would be complete without at least a brief consideration of their relations to the state in which they were nurtured and with which many had such a problematical relationship. Like many of his contemporaries, Böttcher found it difficult to reconcile his strong socialist beliefs with his experience of living in an often repressive system. He remained throughout his career, however, dedicated to producing work which he hoped would provide a telling account of that same world.

The problems which he encountered with GDR officialdom are nowhere better illustrated than in his one failed attempt to produce a fictional work. The making of the film, which had the working title *Jahrgang 45 (Born in 1945*, 1966)] followed the censor's rejection of two of his previous documentaries.[18] Böttcher clearly thought he might be able to overcome some of these difficulties by producing a fictional work which would, however, have a distinctly documentary feel about it. The making of the film coincided, however, with the now infamous Eleventh Plenum in 1965 at which any project which even mildly deviated from the prescribed norms was condemned. Further work on *Jahrgang 45* had to be abandoned, and Jürgen Böttcher was left feeling suitably devastated and embittered.[19] As so often in these cases, it is difficult in retrospect to understand why the film attracted such opprobrium. To us it seems merely to tell a relatively innocent tale about a young couple – Al and Li – living in the Prenzlauer Berg district of Berlin and going through a difficult patch in their relationship. To the GDR Ministry of Culture at the time, however, the film was regarded as a travesty of all that the GDR was supposed to stand for. In the words of the Ministry official:

> In this film we meet a group of young people in a milieu which is very far from being typical of the conditions which prevail in our state. We are not doing justice to our young people, if we only portray them as individuals beset with doubts and uncertainties.[20]

After the banning of *Jahrgang 45*, Böttcher was almost tempted to abandon film-making altogether. Matters were also not made any easier for him in that, as was customary with 'deviant' GDR artists, he was required by his paymasters to atone for his waywardness. In his case the requirement was that he become involved in a number of manifestly non-controversial projects to show that he had rid himself of any dangerously dissident tendencies. Böttcher refers to these projects as 'punishment exercises' ('Strafarbeiten'). In practice this meant producing run-of-the-mill accounts of official meetings, gatherings of workers and other Party-sanctioned events.

Following these early set-backs, it is not surprising that Böttcher took some time to establish his documentary credentials. In the course of the later 1960s and 1970s, however, he gradually acquired the reputation as the GDR's leading documentarist and also began to exert an increasing influence on the up-and-coming generations of documentary film-makers in the GDR.[21] With the collapse of the GDR, however, his enthusiasm for the making of documentaries also waned and he chose this moment to step down from the documentary stage. It is, of course, not without a certain irony that he chose to end his documentary career – and to return to his first love: painting – just when it might have appeared that new opportunities were opening up. Indeed, like many established GDR artists, he was well aware that the conditions of capitalist production under which he would have to work in the new post-communist era would not be particularly conducive to his style of documentary work. Better therefore to accept that a chapter of his life had closed than to take up arms in what would inevitably prove to be an unequal struggle.

Before stepping down, Jürgen Böttcher made just one more documentary – *Die Mauer* (*The Wall*, 1990) – which in some ways can be read both as a commentary on his relations with the GDR and a reflection on the role of the film-maker within such a society. At one level *Die Mauer* can be interpreted as a moving account of a GDR citizen (Böttcher himself) coming to terms with a dramatic turning-point in the country's fortunes. To an equal degree, however, the film can also be seen as an extended self-reflective account of documentary's role in chronicling the ebb and flow of history. Nowhere is this latter point better illustrated than in those sections of the film where he arranges for documentary footage of significant events in Cold War history to be projected onto what remains of the grim surface of the Wall. In this way *Die Mauer* incorporates both a valedictory statement on Böttcher's part and a challenge to the viewers to reflect on the process(es) by which history itself is represented and the manner in which meanings are generated from such accounts.

Assessing Böttcher's Documentary Achievement

No one has ever claimed that Böttcher made polemical films. (For this we can perhaps be grateful.) Neither can his documentaries be considered oppositional in the normal sense of the word. Nevertheless, for the perceptive members of the GDR audience, the works undoubtedly contain many subtle pointers to some of the internal contradictions in GDR society.[22] As Böttcher put it when he addressed members of the Bundestag commission who were enquiring into the role played by culture in the former GDR:

> I knew that I could never get involved in any far-reaching critical examination. That's never been my concern. What I've wanted to produce are a series of honest and nuanced reflections, so that – from these individual fragments – you can get some idea about how things are. What I've always wanted to know was: Where do these workers get their strength from, in spite of all the miserable things they've had to endure?[23]

Knowing that he would not be able to make critical films as such, Böttcher persisted – in spite of regular set-backs – in focusing his gaze on those members of GDR society who he felt were in danger of not being properly represented. Reducing it to a simple formulation, the documentaries which he produced are in many ways deeply subjective. As he explains:

> Actually I've always wanted to make films about people who I like and admire, people who I would like to commend to others. The main theme of my work has been getting to know people. What I have is a yearning to get to know certain groups of people.[24]

There remains the question of how Böttcher's films were actually received by indigenous audiences. It almost goes without saying that these quietly reflective documentaries did not have wide popular appeal. They did on the other hand acquire the status of works which, in quite significant ways, pushed forward the boundaries of documentary expression. This was in itself no mean achievement, given the constraints under which all film-makers in the GDR had to operate.

When assessing the films' impact, one should also never underestimate the importance of the fact that they were primarily conceived for screening in the cinema, even though many have subsequently been shown on television. This brings us back to the point I touched on earlier, namely the different opportunities afforded to documentarists according to whether they were operating in the area of film or of television. In the very early years of the GDR, film had been the principal medium through which propagandist messages had been channelled. Consequently DEFA documentary films frequently had to function as propaganda vehicles, leaving very little scope for experiment or for alternative ways of looking at the world. With the coming of television, however, this situation began gradually to change. Television quickly acquired the main responsibility for public information and ideological education.[25] This is not to suggest that film documentarists working for DEFA were now able to produce radical critiques as and when they pleased, but it did lead to a slight shift of emphasis. Relatively speaking, film was from now on not subject to quite the same intense scrutiny as it had been hitherto. It would of course be wrong to speak of liberalisation. It would be more appropriate to talk of occasional windows of opportunity opening up in the later 1970s and early 1980s, as new cultural and media policies were promulgated from within the Party.

Critics will continue to speculate on how exactly changes in media policy determined what could or could not be made. An equally important consideration is the type of knowledge and frames of reference which cinema audiences themselves deployed when viewing a Böttcher documentary. It is of course notoriously difficult to obtain accurate information which could provide an answer to this question. There is some evidence to suggest, however, that the response to his documentaries depended more than with many other films on the establishment of a knowing relationship between audience and film-maker. Thus, audiences who gathered in the selected venues where these films were shown (film clubs, university film circles and the like) developed especially sensitive antennae for picking up the true import of what was being shown or stated. In a society where the opportunities for free expression of views were radically curtailed, one quickly learned the art of reading the reality barometer.

The picture of the GDR which emerges from Böttcher's documentaries is one that is marked by contrasts and contradictions. On the one hand it might be possible to conclude from some of his individual or group portraits that GDR citizens were being given opportunities to lead lives of some contentment, in spite of their constantly being constrained by a system which was clearly unable to satisfy many of their deeper aspirations. Yet, for all these manifestations of cheerfulness and good humour in the face of adversity, his films resonate with a marked air of sadness. The latter is closely connected with what seems to be a growing awareness on his part that the political system as such could never deliver the supportive, sustaining environment which many, particularly in the early days of the GDR, had fought so hard to achieve. In the final analysis then, what his documentaries seem to point to is that growing gulf between GDR citizens' increasingly bitter experience of everyday reality and the vision of what might have been. No-one has put this better than Wilhelm Roth when he observed:

In their work Böttcher and [Volker] Koepp present us with self-confident individuals who view the world around them with critical eyes. As time went by, however, it became clear that this view could not be reconciled with the political views associated with that more 'bureaucratic' socialism which prevailed in reality. In this respect these films do not provide us with any confirmation of ways in which socialism could develop further; they are rather valedictions anticipating its demise.[26]

Notes

1. Peter Zimmermann (ed.), *Deutschlandbilder-Ost*, Konstanz, 1995, p. 9.
2. See *Abenteuer Wirklichkeit* (Booklet published by the Akademie der Künste – Abteilung Film- und Medienkunst and the press offices of the ZDF and 3sat television channels to accompany a series of GDR documentaries screened on 3sat in November and December 1989), p. 2.
3. Ibid., p. 3.
4. internationales forum des jungen films Berlin 1987, 'Filme von Jürgen Böttcher' (Programme notes and transcripts of interviews), p. 5.
5. Ibid.,p. 5 (Interview with Böttcher: 1974).
6. Ibid., p. 1 (Interview with Böttcher: 1987).
7. *Abenteuer Wirklichkeit*, p. 5.
8. The film was finally screened, some 27 years after it was made, in June 1988.

9. 'Filme von Jürgen Böttcher', 1.
10. Zimmermann, p. 162.
11. 'Kunst und Kultur in der DDR' (Transcript of the proceedings of the 35th session of the Bundestag Enquete-Kommission: 'Aufarbeitung von Geschichte und Folgen der SED-Diktatur in Deutschland'), May 1993, p. 195.
12. Direct Cinema aims at minimal intervention on the part of the documentarist, whilst Cinéma Vérité draws attention to the encounter between the film-maker and the documentary subject.
13. The fact that there is a dark, brooding quality about the film and the people appear to be 'going through the motions' has caused some critics to inquire whether *Rangierer* is a symbolic anticipation of the demise of the GDR. See Rolf Richter, *DEFA Documentary Films*, (Booklet to accompany a DEFA retrospective), Goethe-Institut (London), 1992, p. 9; Zimmermann, p. 188.
14. Richter, p. 9.
15. 'Kunst und Kultur in der DDR', 195.
16. 'Filme von Jürgen Böttcher', p. 16.
17. Jochen Wisotzki, 'Unbekannte Räume: Gespräch mit Jürgen Böttcher', *Sonntag*, 1988, no. 14.
18. *Drei von vielen* and *Barfuß und ohne Hut* (*Three of Many* and *Barefooted and Hatless*, 1964) had both been heavily criticised for not conforming to what was expected of a GDR documentarist.
19. It was only after unification that he was able to complete the postproduction work on the project, since when it has had several screenings at home and abroad.
20. Miklos Gimes, 'Ein Leben in Quarantäne', *Das Magazin*, 1990, no. 3: 21.
21. See Zimmermann, p. 173 and Richter, p. 6.
22. See Richter, p. 7.
23. 'Kunst und Kultur in der DDR', 200.
24. Wilhelm Labisch, 'Liebeserklärung an kleine Leute', *Film-korrespondenz*, 1973, no. 10: 9
25. Zimmermann, p. 15.
26. Ibid., p. 177.

Chapter 16

DOCUMENTING THE *WENDE:* THE FILMS OF ANDREAS VOIGT

Helen Hughes

Introduction: The End of the DEFA Documentary Tradition?

In the volume that came out of the 1992 conference at the Haus des Dokumentarfilms in Stuttgart on DEFA documentary film, the *Wende* is seen as potentially meaning the demise of the DEFA documentary tradition, a source of considerable regret for most of the participants. Peter Zimmermann, the editor of the volume, begins his introduction by saying, 'With the collapse of the GDR and the winding down of DEFA a significant German documentary film tradition came to an end', and he concludes it by labelling the actions of the *Treuhand* – the organisation entrusted with the privatisation of industry in the former GDR – a demolition job ('einen Kahlschlag').[1] Other contributors to the conference are not so pessimistic, although all of them recognise that the decisive factor will be those dreaded market forces. Interestingly, one of the issues at stake is the question of who will be responsible for the continuation or loss of such a film tradition – the producers, the distributors, the television networks or, perhaps, the film-makers. To the question: 'does the end of the DEFA Documentary Film Studios signify also the end of a documentary film tradition?', Bernd Burkhardt, former head of the DEFA Documentary Film Studios, states:

> These discussions in Stuttgart have shown me that the end of an institution going by the name of DEFA-Dokstudio cannot and will not mean the end of a category of film-making. In Brandenburg there are already

eleven producers who have taken on documentary and other forms of film production; in Berlin many new producers have been added to the pool. I believe it is not a question of structures and institutions. The question of whether the genre or category of film known as documentary will continue to exist or not is in the hands of the film-makers. The question is whether the film-makers will be in a position to produce documentary films under the new conditions and whether they will be prepared to do so.[2]

This question is clearly addressed to such film-makers as the subject of this article, Andreas Voigt, a documentarist trained by DEFA, who began to make his own films just as the changes in the Eastern Bloc started to be felt, and who has decided to continue to make documentary films in a politically united Germany. To point to his work is hence to some extent to answer the question put by Bernd Burkhardt. What is more, an investigation into the work of any DEFA documentarist post-1989 is bound to approach some further issues also touched on in Stuttgart, in particular by Michael Albrecht, television director of the East German broadcasting company, Ostdeutscher Rundfunk Brandenburg, and former director of GDR television, who wound up the podium discussion with another pressing question addressed to the film-makers:

On the other hand there is also the question to the film-makers: is there enough depth within the DEFA tradition to be able to continue existing trends? How valuable are these trends? Which ones should be discontinued? What are the new developments that have come about recently?[3]

In looking at Voigt's films, which clearly derive their aesthetic from DEFA, but have found their subject matter during the *Wende* and in a unified Germany, these questions are crucial, even decisive. The name DEFA has, indeed, to all intents and purposes disappeared, but has the tradition also been extinguished? I hope to demonstrate that it has not, but also to suggest that its continued existence in a new political context has highlighted the fact that many of the distinguishing features of DEFA film-making were dependent on the existence of the GDR, and its organs of propaganda in particular, and do not translate comfortably into the pluralistic media landscape of the larger Federal Republic.

Winter adé: The Relaxation of Censorship in DEFA Documentary Film-Making before 1989

The substantial body of documentary films made by German film-makers that appeared during the period bears witness to the fact that the *Wende* itself brought about a flowering of documentary film-making in Germany. Both East and West German film-makers, sometimes getting together in teams to provide multiple perspectives, shot footage of the events in the GDR between 7 October 1989 and 3 October 1990.[4] Whilst some set out to chart these historic changes systematically, others recorded events as they unfolded in late 1989 by chance rather than design. As time passes these films have become an important window on a place experiencing a historic sequence of events. While they offered to the German audiences an alternative view to that presented by television, they provided those not living in Germany at that time with a unique view of the people who were there and of the landscapes and cityscapes they inhabited. With the benefit of hindsight they are also becoming windows of a different kind for the people who were there, a record of chances taken and missed. Together with recorded television broadcasts they have become a means of measuring the distance between then and now, as well as documents charting and explaining the development of public opinion. As documentary films they are evidence of the enduring impulse to want to record and see events unfolding in terms of the long-term effects on communities and individuals, not only as news.

This body of documentation is, however, also about a change in political conditions which made it possible for film-makers who had worked in the GDR to make the kind of films which they had not been able to make before, focusing, for example, on dissenters, demonstrators, outsiders and, by 1991, a new wave of discontented youth and neo-fascists. It should also be remembered that the *Wende* brought about a situation where DEFA film-makers found themselves making films about events which also affected their own lives directly and profoundly, not least to the extent that they were to lose their job security.

The films by Voigt that I shall be looking at chart the gradual disappearance of DEFA as a production company: *Alfred* (1987) was Voigt's diploma submission for the Babelsberg film school and funded by East German television; *Leipzig im Herbst* (*Leipzig in Autumn*, 1989) was made by the DEFA-Studio für Dokumentarfilm still operating within DEFA; *Letztes Jahr Titanic* (*Last Year Titanic*, 1991) was subsidised after monetary union by the Federal government and produced by the DEFA-Studio für Dokumentarfilm GmbH while it was operating under the *Treuhand*, as was *Grenzland – eine Reise* (*Borderlands*, 1992). *Glaube, Liebe, Hoffnung* (*Faith, Hope and Charity*, 1994) was a co-production between A Jour Film and the latest leanest version of DEFA, dok Film Babelsberg, all that was left once the Berlin studio had been sold to the Kirch group. Voigt's most recent films are no longer DEFA films, just films made by a former DEFA employee: *Ostpreußenland* (*Tales of East Prussia*, 1995) was produced by Löprich & Schlösser and *Mr Behrmann – Leben Traum Tod* (*Mr Behrmann – Life, Dreams and Death*, 1995), was financed by television. These films thus cover the final period of DEFA and pose the question of whether a new East-West documentary aesthetic might come out of its demise.

Born in 1953, Voigt belongs to a younger generation of documentary film-makers deeply influenced by the works of film-makers such as Jürgen Böttcher, Winfried Junge, and Volker Koepp, and by an atmosphere of documentary film-making which was not fundamentally opposed to the socialist system, but which attempted to use its relative freedom (in comparison with GDR television at least) to encourage reform from within. It was the younger film-makers, however, who attempted and, before 1987, usually failed to shift the focus of the subject matter to include political dissenters, lawbreakers, and discontented youth. Their efforts in this direction had rarely made it further than the planning stage until with *Winter adé* (*Winter Adieu*, 1988) Helke Misselwitz lifted the lid by making a film of interviews with women in the GDR, who, in their attempts to coordinate working lives with family lives in a country obviously suffering severe economic hardship, did not match the official picture of workers in a progressive socialist society. The women interviewed were open about the disappointments in their lives and in the lives of the people around them. Misselwitz is thus openly critical in the subject matter of her film, and *Winter adé* represented a significant step forward from the DEFA documentary film of the seventies and early eighties, which would be accelerated by the *Wende*.

From contemporary responses it is clear that this film came as a great relief to a whole generation of film-makers who before *perestroika* had been deeply frustrated by the fact that the politicians of the GDR appeared incapable of trusting them with the task of making topical, relevant documentary films. The frustrations experienced by this generation are captured in a fascinating and tragic collection of materials, *DEFA NOVA nach wie vor?*, put together by a contemporary of Voigt's, Dietmar Hochmuth, and containing letters, interviews, filmographies of realised and unrealised, screened and unscreened films, and a poignant manifesto written by the new generation that was never proclaimed.[5] The 'new-wave-that-never-was' was thwarted not only by the fear of political dissent in the party, but also by the increasing need to cut back on the cost of an expensively run studio system with salaried staff. The DEFA film-makers who were to record the events of the *Wende* were as frustrated by political and economic stagnation as the people they interviewed on the streets and in the factories. *Perestroika* and the *Wende* represented, however, both the chance to realise cherished film projects that had been suppressed, and a rapid change in circumstances that completely changed the picture and made many cherished projects – for both documentary and fiction film-makers – obsolete almost overnight.

Alfred, Voigt's diploma film, realised with the help of Heiner Carow and produced with money for television, became the first student-film to encounter political opposition from the party and yet be released for restricted screenings. As was customary when films were deemed politically unacceptable, Voigt was requested to re-edit the material leaving out certain scenes. He refused and the film was withheld. The fact that Voigt's film became the first case when a compromise was found for rebellious student film-making was noted and approved by the *Nachwuchsgruppe*, a group of young film-makers lobbying for change within DEFA. The case also prompted them to call for a new concept of copyright in the GDR. The compromise saw to it that although *Alfred* was not to be broadcast, it could be shown in film clubs, which were very active in the GDR and keen to show documentary films. It was awarded the film clubs' prize for best documentary film and was also invited to be shown at the Oberhausen Film Festival.

Already suspect as the portrait of a worker who had been expelled from the party, despite being an anti-fascist activist during the war, two scenes in *Alfred* caused particular problems. The first was a scene in which a group of women sit and complain about their working conditions, a highly characteristic sequence for the new wave of DEFA documentaries in the eighties and a scene which has since also become characteristic of Voigt's films in general. In the case of *Alfred*, however, it is extremely difficult to see any justification for the scene being included at this point in the film. While in the case of *Winter adé* it could be argued that a film about women in the GDR was justified in allowing women to talk about their working conditions, in *Alfred* – a portrait of a worker perceived as a dissident – such a scene appeared considerably more inflammatory. Another aspect of the film which caused problems was the sequence of shots of a freight train moving through the industrial landscape of Leipzig, the city where Alfred Florstedt, the subject of the film, had lived. Coming directly after an interviewee's comment that Alfred, as an anarchist, had called his friends in the party 'Linienkommunisten' – party-line communists, with the implication of narrow-minded and dogmatic obedience – the sight of the train moving between derelict sites can be interpreted straightforwardly as a negative comment on the development of socialism in the GDR. Voigt himself, however, sees these inserted shots as interpretable on many levels, just as Böttcher's documentary *Rangierer* (*Shunters*, 1984), which may have been an influence on Voigt here, retains an ambiguity which allows the shunters to represent both the glory of a complex system of connections and the horror of an anonymous unseen structure.

The fact that Voigt was given a contract as a director of the DEFA-Studios für Dokumentarfilme is categorical proof that times were changing. During the early and mid-eighties barely any film-makers had been given full contracts. This trend was confirmed by the fact that after the *Kulturabkommen* ('Cultural Agreement') between the GDR and the FRG in 1988 a budget was created for two films to be made by young film-makers in DEFA for transmission by the West German channel ZDF in the 'Kleines Fernsehspiel' slot – an opportunity for the frustrated young generation who, by this time, were decidedly thin on the ground. One of these was made by Voigt, *Leute mit Landschaft* (*People with Landscape*, 1988).

Leipzig im Herbst – Documenting the *Wende*

As a documentary film-maker, however, Voigt first became
widely and indeed internationally known for the collective
DEFA documentation of events in Leipzig between 16 October
and 13 November 1989. Characterised simply as 'material' and
produced by the DEFA-Studio für Dokumentarfilm Gruppe
'dokument', the film was shown under the title *Leipzig im Herbst*
at the 32nd Leipzig Festival of Documentary and Short Films in
November 1989.[6] The film material of the changes as recorded
in *Leipzig im Herbst* begins on 16 October, some days after the
counter-demonstrations all over the GDR around the 7 October,
the fortieth anniversary of the founding of the GDR – demonstrations during which violent clashes broke out between the
demonstrators and the state security forces. 'None of us was
there with a camera at the time', explains a text at the beginning
of *Leipzig im Herbst.* 'We were not able to be there. It was not
until 16 October that colleagues from DEFA Documentary film
began working on a film project. The following material is part
of a total of 11 hours that several teams shot in Leipzig, Berlin
and Dresden.'

During the interim period the film-makers had been
attending the National Documentary Film Festival in Neubrandenburg on 8 October, during which the events had been
discussed, in particular the behaviour of the police towards the
demonstrators. In an interview Voigt describes the decision to
document what was happening thus:

On the Monday I went to the studio to the acting studio director. The
studio director himself was ill. He was always ill when something had to
be decided. I sat down and said, 'Look, we have to get going and start
filming, because things are happening out there on the streets. If things
are happening in this country then we ought actually to document it.'
The situation was actually quite simple. So he said, 'Yes, you're right.
What should we do?' Of course, everyone was unsure of themselves. In
his case, he was acting in an official capacity for this studio. But on the
other hand he was of course a human being like everyone else, and he
realised that something was happening. He wasn't one of those
orthodox idiots, one of those blockheads like some of the others. He
saw that a decision had to be made, and, having thought about it,
decided that the situation was not actually that risky. If everything
turned out differently we could take the material, stick it in a safe and it
would be more fodder for the archive. And nothing more would come

of it. So then I sat down at the typewriter and typed out in triplicate that Colleague So-and-So gave authorisation to film material for the purposes of documentation. We put a big stamp at the bottom and the studio director Fritz Seidl signed it and we drove off in our studio van, Sebastian, me and a camera assistant, Thomas, and started to make *Leipzig im Herbst*.[7]

The most remarkable feature of *Leipzig im Herbst* is its sense of calm given the momentousness of the events it was recording, a feature that has often been commented upon. It is almost as if the steady gaze of the 35mm camera of the DEFA Documentary Film Studios wished to assert its ability, through its long takes and its patient and persistent interviews with people on the street, to penetrate to the essence of what was happening. We encounter people at work, sweeping the streets or in the factories, police officers and their superiors, the local parish priests. The decision was to film the reactions of the demonstrators first of all, then the street sweepers and the people at work, with the scenes with state authorities as a counterpoint signifying the fact that the struggle was between the people on the street and the state officials, those above and those below.[8]

Having decided to go to the demonstrators, the group then had the experience of being the first DEFA film-makers, the first from the GDR media, to film their own people demonstrating on the streets. As such they were not too certain of what the reaction would be.

Images on film of those very early stages – there aren't many film images from that very early period. The film begins with one such. It was a mad situation. On the first day we were a little worried about how the demonstrators would react when they saw us coming with our camera. It was a 35mm film camera, not like one of these tiny Hi-8 camcorder-thingies. And we also had enormous DEFA stickers stuck on the left and right of this great black monstrosity so that everyone could immediately recognise who it was. And then something incredible happened. It was the first time that anyone, let's say, that any of us, of the demonstrators, people from our own country, our own media, had come to deal with the problems. Not cameras from the West but our own people. And that was an amazing scene. They saw us. It was impossible to move. There were of course tens of thousands of people on the street and we were completely stuck. And when they saw us, all at once a corridor formed. It was like the parting of the waves. A corridor appeared for us and for the camera, Thomas on the right, and me on the left. The three of us went through this corridor and that is how the film begins. And then this amazing coincidence at the end of the passage. 30m or so along there is a poster with 'press freedom' on it. When they saw that we were from the East, they gave out this extraordinary cheer and that is the beginning of the film.[9]

The question: 'We are from the DEFA Studio for Documentary Films. Can we ask you why you taking part in this demonstration and what it means for you?' is not only the trigger to bring out the responses of the demonstrators, but an enactment of one of the basic rights that the crowd is demonstrating for. One demonstrator states that the discussion, the change in mood, the process of glasnost, has to be made visible, public. The demonstrations are a means of guaranteeing that the mood of the people is indeed visible. The active participation of the camera in this process is what links it with the 'black films' in some of the Eastern Bloc countries such as Poland and Hungary in the fifties, and the *cinéma-vérité* film-making of the sixties.[10] Indeed, the process of interviewing people on the demonstrations, the streetcleaners clearing away all the posters, visiting the new information centre for *Neues Forum*, all the while asking for people's opinions and for explanations from the officials, has the feel of a film actively engaged in the process it is observing.

Letztes Jahr Titanic – Documenting the Aftermath

The *Wende* itself thus provided Voigt both with subject matter and the unexpected opportunity to become known as a DEFA film-maker, enabling him to continue to make films after the unification of Germany and, subsequently, after DEFA had been wound down. Soon after the screening of *Leipzig im Herbst* he began to collect material to chart the lives of people encountered while making the film through all the events up to and beyond the unification of Germany. Planning to begin in December 1989 and end in December 1990, the crew did not, of course, know in advance what would happen during the protracted shoot of *Letztes Jahr Titanic*.

As the train draws into Leipzig station at the beginning of the film, a montage of sounds taken from the demonstrations prefigures the sequence of events due to unfold during the year, beginning with the chant 'We're staying here', followed by

'Germany, one fatherland' and ending with the carnival song 'Leipzig nights are long, they take a while to get going, but when they do, they do'. The carnival spirit takes over in the editing of the film, when images typical of the GDR documentary film – a barmaid ordering more beer and furnace workers adding more coal – are followed by a customer in a bar interviewing another customer with an imaginary microphone in the form of a banana. Such self-conscious moments occur periodically throughout the film. Other customers in the bar complain that the team has been filming for hours and hours and has never come to ask them any questions. People on the street request that the camera be switched off – the cameraman obliges, but the sound continues to run. A woman confessing her involvement with the Stasi explains that she hasn't yet told her children. Towards the end of the film the film-makers are asked about how the year has gone for them. 'We're being shut down', they reply, referring to the sale of the DEFA studios. The scene is followed by a shot of the Wintergarten cinema in Leipzig, named, appropriately enough, after the venue for the first German film-screening in 1895. 'Film only becomes really exciting in the cinema' reads a poster. Inside, the cinema is completely derelict.

These self-conscious moments do not dominate the film, however. They are one part of a volatile political situation which was swiftly abandoning measured debate in favour of hasty action. While *Leipzig im Herbst* is a film in which people express their political opinions, *Letztes Jahr Titanic* is more about people's personal feelings about the course of events and about their personal decision to stay or to leave. As such they become inevitably more individualised, more reflective, but also more passive and, paradoxically, more like the interviewees that populate DEFA documentary films made before Autumn 1989 such as Volker Koepp's *Mädchen in Wittstock* or Misselwitz's *Winter adé* discussed above. The principal question in the film – how does the future look? – is patently a difficult one to answer, although the reply is usually that it is getting better. Many of the interviewees plan to leave, while those who remain wait and see as the demonstrations become more and more focused on the issue of German unification.

Although the film includes a wide spectrum of society, three individuals in particular turn it into a reflection on the deterioration of the fabric of East German society that began to take place after the *Wende*: a journalist, a skinhead and a teenager. Not only economic uncertainty, but also social insecurity characterise the experience of these three people whose pronouncements on their experiences contribute substantially to the success of the film as a record of rapid change. The journalist, whom we meet on a train and then revisit in her office, articulates the urge to bear witness to, to confess, and to analyse the psychological, social and philosophical forces which kept the SED in power and the GDR in existence for forty years. Speaking about the conflict between party discipline and conscience, she speaks of the relatively small pressure that was enough to keep people down. The sobriety of the journalist's analysis in response to her own question 'When should we have begun to realise?', together with her own confession of involvement with the Stasi, is representative of the soul-searching that many were going through in the situation post-1989. The apparent contradictions in Leipzig youth culture are found in the life-decisions of 'Papa' the skinhead who tells of his vow to 'go to war' against the neo-fascists in Leipzig. He is shown putting on a record and listening to Mozart – music he has got to know along with thousands of others through the American cult film *Amadeus* – before he explains his resentment about being made to feel afraid and his subsequent decision to arm himself and join in the violence. His statement, 'I'm for human rights', and his thoughts about 'solidarity' are followed up in his efforts to learn to help an injured worker become independent. Sensing a paradox in the sight of a violent youth being taught to assist a disabled man in hospital, Voigt asks Papa how he reconciles gang-fighting with social work. Papa's comment that his racist enemies are not human beings but monsters gives his views a logic that in all probability accords with popular opinion, making it extremely difficult to see the young man as a villain. Similarly sympathetically portrayed is the young woman who cries on the night of currency reform, a member of a less decisive group of young people than Papa, for whom the *Wende* signifies a chaos coming from some uncontrollable force outside. 'What will be, will be' is their answer to the film-maker's questions about the future – an unexpected response from a young generation witnessing such momentous events in their country's history. In the closing scenes of the film the group is practising shooting and the young woman, seeing unification as the cause of escalating violence, finds conforming to the new society by getting a haircut and dressing more conventionally a price she is reluctant to pay for the changes to her city.

The portraits of these three new citizens of the Federal Republic are in many ways a continuation of the techniques of pre-*Wende* film-making, in which the person and their environment are shown to be inseparable. In the context of the 'Unification train', as it has been called, the interviews constitute a form of opposition which is to test the new spirit of dialogue and democracy.[11]

Letztes Jahr Titanic was a film for which Voigt was awarded the Adolf Grimme prize. The film did not garner universal approval, however. During the podium discussion at the end of the conference in Stuttgart Voigt spoke about getting the film shown on German television:

> When my film *Letztes Jahr Titanic* was ready, I rushed off saying to myself: 'Right, now the film has to get shown on TV' – because I think TV is the decisive medium for documentary film even if it is shot on 35mm. So, off I went and tried my luck, and found myself sitting in a screening with a TV programmer for a large West German television company. He wrote me a letter in which he said 'Dear Mr So-and-so, I have seen your film. I find it terrible. It is so sad, and it seems it was all much worse in the GDR than I had even imagined it to be already. But this is dreadful. Couldn't you do something more positive?' I met him later and said to him: 'You know, that is what they used to ask in the East: "Couldn't you do something positive?"' And then I said something that he really did take badly: 'You know, to be honest, I always thought actually that TV programmers in the West weren't all that different from those in the East.' Since then we haven't spoken to each other. But the story wasn't over yet, which is, of course, the advantage of the federal system. There are, thank goodness, a few other TV companies which you can approach, and with one of them it worked. I went to the SFB [the Berlin radio and TV station] and someone liked it. I should add something, however, that might throw some light on how it works with documentary film on television. My film was not accepted by the documentary film programmers, but by the feature film department. It is all a matter of the length of the broadcasting slot and things like that. However, up until now it has worked out for me from project to project, and there isn't really any other way it could work. We'll just have to see how long it lasts.[12]

Grenzland – eine Reise: The Shifting of Borders in DEFA Documentary Film

Voigt's first post-unification film *Grenzland – eine Reise,* is probably his best-known and has been broadcast repeatedly on
German television. It focuses on the new border between
Germany and Poland, and contains interviews with Germans
and Poles living on both sides of the newly contentious Oder-
Neisse border. Although the border was a hotly debated issue
following some infelicitous remarks by Helmut Kohl, the
region itself seems to have been overlooked by the *Wende,*
which for some interviewees was nothing more than a distant
media event. Indeed some of the people interviewed in the
film are not even clear about what the new Germany is
called, suggesting the German Democratic Federal Republic
('Deutsche Demokratische Bundesrepublik') as a possibility.
Grenzland – eine Reise is at times a very attractive film, moving
back and forth across the river through remote rural landscapes which contrast sharply with the dreary, run-down city of
Guben on which the film also focuses. The film as a whole is
characterised by a slow pace, patience with its subjects and a
marked bias towards the Poles, who are portrayed as gentle
philosophers, in stark contrast to the West Germans, who come
across as interested primarily in property and money. The film
is very much a reflection of, as well as on, a period during
which massive economic restructuring created insecurity for
almost everyone. The scepticism about the disappearance of
borders is clearly stated at the opening to the film, 'Not all
borders disappeared with the fall of the Wall' – a melancholy
thesis which is, however, to some extent dispelled by the
tenacity of the interviewees.[13]

What is interesting about *Grenzland – eine Reise,* as well as the
third Leipzig film, *Glaube, Liebe, Hoffnung* and Voigt's most
recent film *Ostpreussenland,* is their approach, which seeks
contact with people in relation to specific issues – borders, neo-
fascism and people driven out of their homes ('Heimatvertrie-
bene') respectively – setting them up before the camera to
speak without a framework of explicit authorial comment or
obtrusive questioning. It is an approach which within the
conditions of DEFA film-making before the *Wende* relied on a
dialectical relationship between an image projected by the official organs of state propaganda and a very different lived

reality. Films which conspicuously omitted the propaganda message while showing images of people at work could be read, not necessarily as oppositional, but at least as critical.

Perhaps the most important question facing Voigt and his colleagues is whether the same approach works in a context where the lines of opposition are not so easily drawn, where there is no readily definable official line to measure yourself against. To what extent can interviews with people met by the wayside and followed for a short time themselves be distorting? *Glaube, Liebe, Hoffung*, the third part of a Leipzig trilogy, returned to the city to follow up a group of young skinheads, some politically extreme left-wing, some on the far right. It was heavily criticised, on the one hand, as a film which gave undesirable views a public forum and highly praised, on the other, as a film which provided important insights into the real lives behind the headlines.

The genesis of *Glaube, Liebe, Hoffnung* gives some pointers to the problems that confront DEFA film-makers in the newly united Germany. Made in 35mm, it is in one respect an answer to those who feared that the high quality of such documentary film-making would be lost in the new funding structures. Exploiting the special light of the city, it is also consistent as the third part of a trilogy of films using black and white. However, it is this very high contrast, black-and-white camerawork, shot by the acclaimed Sebastian Richter, that itself becomes problematic despite, or perhaps because of, its avoidance of the flamboyant pluralism of the 1990s. The high quality of DEFA documentary film-making suddenly lays itself open to criticism for being itself decorative, mannered, even anachronistic. More importantly, it is the beauty of the images depicting self-confessed neo-fascists preening themselves that is easily misinterpreted. The exquisite photography cannot help but lend stature and solemnity to the extremists it portrays. These criticisms pose important questions to documentary film-makers about modes of representation in a new context.

Glaube, Liebe, Hoffnung also illustrates a further dilemma confronting the post-DEFA documentary. Against the background of a plurality of political positions, opinions and voices, a refusal to take sides can smack of indifference or indecision where before the *Wende* the absence of comment could be read as a clear position in and of itself. Even the focus on the working class, a consistent feature of DEFA documentaries preserved by Voigt, Koepp, Junge and others after the *Wende*, can seem very limiting and partial. In the case of *Glaube, Liebe, Hoffnung* commentators noted with disquiet the absence of victims of racial attacks in the picture, and in *Ostpreussenland* the total absence of decision-makers, politicians and the like gave the impression that the local inhabitants were the victims of mysterious and unfathomable machinations.

It is perhaps worth bearing in mind that issues of this kind are almost as old as documentary film itself, and were at the core of the heated *cinéma-vérité* debates in Europe and America in the early sixties, as predominantly leftist, new-wave film-makers attempted to define and respond to the limits of authenticity and objectivity in documentary film. Jean Rouch's and Edgar Morin's famous *Chronique d'un été* of 1961 is perhaps the keenest response to the documentarists' crisis of conscience.

Rouch's and Morin's film is an essay about how to find out about how people really live, to uncover what motivates them, and find out whether they are happy. Voigt's stock questions, 'How do you see the future? What are your dreams?' are clearly related to this tradition of documentary film-making. In *Chronique d'un été*, however, the questions are framed by the story of the documentarists themselves, Rouch and Morin, and the way in which they set up the brand-new experiment in *cinéma-vérité*, which does not run as expected. Viewing their own contributions on-screen in a group at the end of the film, the young people interviewed fail to respond to each other and the issues – the war in Algeria, race relations in France, memories of the Jewish holocaust, the passivity of French workers, the private individual despair of isolation and loneliness – as the film-makers feel they should. Instead they react to the roving microphone in the street, the interviews, the conversations, group discussion and staged reconstruction with a mixture of unease, embarrassment, aggression and philosophical distance. This result is by no means a matter of indifference to the film-makers, who agonise over the lack of sympathetic engagement in the young participants. Their comments, as Morin points out in his despair at the end, point to the crisis as one of authenticity. Smoking heavily, he expresses the significance of the results as follows:

It means we've reached a stage where we question a truth when it's not an everyday truth. We've gone beyond it. When sincerity is a bit more than life-size it's called ham or else exhibitionism. And that's the basic problem. If they are thought actors or exhibitionists, our film's a failure. But I am certain in my mind that they are neither of these things. [...] This film, unlike normal cinema, reintroduces us to life. People react as they do in life. They're not guided, nor is the audience. We don't say, this man's good, another wicked, or nice, or clever. So, the audience is bewildered by the people they actually meet. It feels implicated, but would prefer not to be.

Mr Behrmann – Leben Traum Tod. Conclusion

In response to criticisms of partiality and aestheticism in *Glaube, Liebe, Hoffung,* Voigt in interview stated a position in relation to documentary realism which places his film-making within a tradition which is sceptical about objectivity whilst asserting the value of documentary as a means of providing insights – if only partial ones – into the lives of ordinary people. Black and white versus colour, subjective reporting in documentary film versus the espousal of balance in television journalism, the documentary film-maker as the collector of stories – these issues, fundamental to documentary film-making, were debated in the GDR following screenings of *cinéma-vérité* films of Chris Marker (*Le joli mai*), Jürgen Böttcher (*Stars*) and others at the Leipzig Documentary Film Festival in 1963 and left a lasting impression on DEFA documentaries.[14] For Voigt, an admirer of Jean Rouch in particular, these issues remain crucially important today:

Colour automatically creates a certain naturalism, and naturalism in documentary film is something that I cannot stand. It is something which is very far from my personal taste, because it isn't reality which I am experiencing. Film is an image, it is a very subjective image.

Fassbinder once came up with a very neat saying, a decisive one for film-making, 'You don't experiment with a point of view ('Einstellung'), you have one.' This marvellous German word *Einstellung* with its double meaning. On the one hand it refers to the frame, to the composition of the image, and on the other to the point of view, to one's own particular standpoint. And that is what it is all about. I am someone who is living his own life and has had his own experiences in life, and I believe there is no such thing as an objective image.

And journalism, too, is always in the end a highly subjective thing. Of course we make completely different films, we are not journalists – that is very obvious in this film. It is for this reason that I don't feel compelled to be balanced. I don't have to show that in addition to this social factor there are twenty-five other ones and how they all balance each other out.

All I do is tell people's stories, which are of course subjective stories, but in their very subjectivity they are also relevant, they are a sample taken from a particular social situation.[15]

The inclusion of explicit, verbalised self-reflection in documentary films – in the manner of Marker and Rouch – never became part of the DEFA documentary film-making tradition, although in 1990 Thomas Heise saw it as a possible way forward for ex-DEFA film-makers after the *Wende*:

If we want to make documentary films, claiming to record what is happening at the moment in this country, we must not exclude ourselves from the process when it comes to evaluating our own work in relation to our history. It is high time that we made the history of our own past activities our theme, and perhaps our only chance to make our future work meaningful.[16]

Voigt's concentration on the present, in particular on the victims of political and economic restructuring in Europe, however, can be read as an affirmation of the original anthropological aspirations of *cinéma-vérité*, whilst avoiding the excesses of introspection which it later engendered. By focusing on the provincial East Germans side-stepped, robbed of employment and impoverished by the *Wende* in *Grenzland – eine Reise*, by examining the fate of discontented youth in *Glaube, Liebe, Hoffnung*, and the plight of East Prussians in *Ostpreussenland*, Voigt has drawn attention to neglected areas of discontent and given a voice to those ignored or not deemed newsworthy by the majority of the media.

In his most recent film, *Mr Behrmann – Leben Traum Tod*, made for German television (produced by Tele Potsdam and commissioned by ZDF, 3sat and MDR), Voigt has continued this valuable work in Britain, giving a voice to a remarkable victim of National Socialism, the Lithuanian Jew, Josef Behrmann, who moved to London shortly after the war. Voigt's portrait film is in the form of an extended interview, filmed in Behrmann's flat in St John's Wood. This is a film which is

programmatically partial and emphatically subjective, a portrait of an unconventional, psychologically disturbed outsider,
unmediated by authorial comment. Intriguingly it is also a film
which conforms to many of the principles of the early DEFA
anti-fascist film, documenting the life of a man who grew up in
Nazi concentration camps, managed to survive, and spent the
rest of his life suffering the mental torture of having been so
close to death for so long. A deeply moving montage of
encounters with a man who was both terrifying and pitiful, the
film is convincing proof that the DEFA documentary spirit is
thankfully anything but dead.

Notes

1. Peter Zimmermann (ed.), *Deutschlandbilder Ost: Dokumentarfilme der DEFA von der Nachkriegszeit bis zur Wiedervereinigung*, Konstanz, 1995, p. 9.
2. Ibid., p. 222.
3. Ibid., p. 242.
4. For an overview of documentary films produced during this period see Martin Brady and Helen Hughes, 'German Film after the *Wende*', in *The New Germany: Social, Political and Cultural Challenges of Unification*, ed. Derek Lewis and John R. P. McKenzie, Exeter, 1995, pp. 279–85. See also Marc Silberman, 'Post-Wall Documentaries: New Images from a New Germany', *Cinema Journal* 33, no. 2, 1994: 21–41.
5. Dietmar Hochmuth (ed.) *DEFA NOVA – nach wie vor? Versuch einer Spurensicherung*, Berlin, 1993.
6. For a report on the remarkably swift appearance at the festival of documentary films about the *Wende* see Wilhelm Roth, 'Programmänderung Leipzig 1989', *epd Film* 7, no. 1, 1990: 3–5.
7. Interview with Andreas Voigt, London, 2 July 1995.
8. The intention was expressed in the same interview.
9. Ibid.
10. See Erik Barnouw, *Documentary: A History of the Non-Fiction Film*, 2nd revised edn., New York and Oxford, 1993, pp. 262–8.
11. For an analysis of the media response to the *Wende* which traces the gathering of momentum towards German unification see *After the Wall*, ed. Geoffrey Nowell-Smith and Tana Wollen, London, 1991.
12. Zimmermann, pp. 235–6.
13. This statement is also the first in the publicity material to the film, which continues, 'One border, which also lies nearby, became even

more marked. New wealth, arrogance, a newly united people, the nostalgic gaze across to a former homeland.'

14. Günter Jordan and Ralf Schenk (eds), *Schwarzweiß und Farbe: DEFA-Dokumentarfilme 1946–92*, Berlin, 1996, pp. 124–5 and p. 373.
15. Interview with Andreas Voigt, London, 2 July 1995.
16. Thomas Heise, in a letter entitled 'Ein Vorschlag' dated Berlin, 4 July, 1990, cited in Hochmuth, p. 192.

ABOUT THE CONTRIBUTORS

Seán Allan teaches German and film at the University of Warwick. His principal research interests are German drama and literature of the nineteenth century and German cinema. He is the author of *The Plays of Heinrich von Kleist: Ideals and Illusions* (Cambridge, 1996).

Daniela Berghahn teaches German and film at Oxford Brookes University. Her research interests focus on post-war German cinema. She has published a number of articles on *Literaturverfilmungen* and is the author of *Raumdarstellung im englischen Roman der Moderne* (Frankfurt am Main, 1989).

Harry Blunk taught and researched at the Gesamteuropäisches Studienwerk in Vlotho. His specialist area of research was East German cinema. He published numerous articles on DEFA and edited (together with Dirk Jungnickel) *Filmland DDR: ein Reader zu Geschichte, Funktion und Wirkung der DEFA* (Cologne, 1990). He is the author of *Die DDR in ihren Spielfilmen* (Munich, 1984).

Martin Brady is a film historian, translator and artist. He wrote his doctoral thesis on Jean-Marie Straub and Daniele Huillet's adaptions of Heinrich Böll's fiction, and taught film and literature at King's College London from 1986 to 1995. He has published on the history of German film, the New German Cinema and Paul Celan. His current research interests include Brechtian cinema, experimental film, and Arnold Schönberg.

Barton Byg teaches German and film at the University of Massachusetts Amherst where he is co-founder of the Interdepartmental Program in Film Studies. He is the director of the DEFA Film Library at Amherst and has published widely on cinema in both the East and West. He is the author or *Landscapes of*

Resistance: The German Films of Danièle Huillet and Jean-Marie Straub (Berkeley and Los Angeles, 1995).

Horst Claus teaches Film and German at the University of the West of England, Bristol. His recent publications include articles on Carl Zuckmayer's work for the film industry and analyses of Ufa policy in the early 1930s. He is co-author of *Reclams Lexikon des deutschen Films* (Stuttgart, 1995).

Anthony Coulson teaches German in the School of Applied Language and Intercultural Studies, Dublin City University. He has published articles on German cinema from the 1920s to the 1990s, and on German literature of the nineteenth century. He is editor of *Crossing Thresholds: Exiles and Migrants in European Culture and Society* (Brighton, 1997).

Detlef Gwosc teaches and researches at the Hochschule für Film und Fernsehen 'Konrad Wolf' in Potsdam-Babelsberg. His research interests include German literature of the modern period, *Trivialliteratur*, and the impact of new media. He is the author of numerous reviews and essays on film and literature.

Helen Hughes teaches German language, literature and film at the University of Surrey. Her research interests include the history of German and Austrian film, in particular experimental and documentary film. She has published on the Austrian writer Thomas Bernhard and the Austrian feminist film-maker and artist Valie Export, as well as on developments in film in Germany since 1989.

Richard Kilborn teaches film and media studies at the University of Stirling. He is also a member of the Stirling Media Research Institute. He has published works on the process of adaptation – *The Multi-Media Melting Pot* (London, 1987), on television drama – *Television Soaps* (London, 1992), and on documentary – *An Introduction to Television Documentary: Confronting Reality* (Manchester, 1997). He has a particular interest in the media of post-communist states.

Wolfgang Kohlhaase lives and works as a script-writer in Berlin. He has written numerous scripts for DEFA and worked with the directors Gerhard Klein and Konrad Wolf. The films in which he was involved include *Alarm im Zirkus* (1954), *Berlin – Ecke Schönhauser* (1957), *Der Fall Gleiwitz* (1961), *Berlin um die Ecke*

(1965), *Der nackte Mann auf dem Sportplatz* (1974) and *SOLO SUNNY* (1981).

Karen Ruoff Kramer is the director of the Stanford University Berlin Program. She is a specialist in German Cultural Studies. She has published poetry in both English and German and is the author of *The Politics of Discourse: Third Thoughts on New Subjectivity* (New York, 1993).

Christiane Mückenberger taught at the Hochschule für Film und Fernsehen in Potsdam-Babelsberg until being forced to resign in the wake of the Eleventh Plenum. She was reappointed in 1975. From 1990 to 1994 she was the director of the International Festival of Documentary and Animated Films in Leipzig. She has published numerous articles on the history of DEFA. She is the co-author of '*Sie sehen selbst, Sie hören selbst ...*': *Die DEFA von ihren Anfängen bis 1949* (Marburg, 1994).

Andrea Rinke teaches German language, literature and film at Kingston University. Her research interests are in the field of contemporary German history, Gender Studies and Media Studies. She has published a number of articles on women in German television and East German cinema.

John Sandford is Professor of German Studies and Director of the Centre for East German Studies at the University of Reading. His principal research interests are in the field of German film and mass media, and GDR politics. He is the author of *The New German Cinema* (London, 1980), and is editor of the *Encyclopedia of Contemporary German Culture*.

Stefan Soldovieri is an Assistant Professor in the Graduate Program in German Literature, Culture, and Theory at the University of Toronto. His publications include articles on the Cold War and the science fiction film, DEFA and popular cinema, and Bertolt Brecht's experiments with photography and poetry.

Rosemary Stott teaches German at London Guildhall University. She specialises in Film Studies and has carried out extensive research on DEFA film, and interest she developed during study periods in the GDR during the eighties. The research for the article in this volume was completed when she was a guest lecturer at the Hochschule für Film und Fernsehen 'Konrad Wolf' in Potsdam-Babelsberg in 1992-3.

APPENDIX: RESEARCH SOURCES FOR EAST GERMAN CINEMA

This appendix does not claim to be exhaustive, but lists those centres of research in both Europe and the USA which are likely to provide the best starting points for those interested in further research in this field.

(a) GERMANY

Progress Film-Verleih GmbH

Progress Film-Verleih is the German company handling the world-wide distribution rights for DEFA films. Their web-site contains a list of the entire DEFA output and can be searched using a wide variety of different categories.

Progress Film-Verleih GmbH   Tel: + 49 (0) 30 24003-0
Burgstraße 27   Fax: + 49 (0) 30 24003-459
D-10178 Berlin   www.progress-film.de

Hochschule für Film und Fernsehen, Potsdam-Babelsberg

The library of the Hochschule für Film und Fernsehen, Potsdam-Babelsberg contains a wide range of publications on DEFA and is one of the most accessible sources in Germany for film scripts.

Hochschule für Film und Fernsehen
(all departments)   Tel: + 49 (0) 331 7469-0
Karl-Marx-Straße 33/34   Fax: + 49 (0) 331 7469-202
D-14482 Potsdam-Babelsberg   www.hff-potsdam.de

Hochschulbibliothek
Hochschule für Film und Fernsehen
Potsdam   Tel: + 49 (0) 331 7469-441
Rosa-Luxemburg-Straße 24   Fax: + 49 (0) 331 7469-444
D-14482 Potsdam-Babelsberg   www.bibl.hff-potsdam.de

(On-line select bibliography of DEFA material at:
www.bibl.hff-potsdam.de/defa50)

Bundesarchiv (Berlin)

Essential for viewing rare GDR (and other) films unavailable on video. There is a charge for viewing films and since the facilities are in heavy demand, it is essential to write to the archive several weeks in advance.

Bundesarchiv (Abteilung Filmarchiv)
Postfach 31 06 67   Tel: + 49 (0) 30 8681-1
Fehrbelliner Platz 3,   Fax: + 49 (0) 30 8681-310
D-10707 Berlin   www.bundesarchiv.de

The following archive also contains documents relating to GDR political and cultural policy. Again it is essential to contact the archive first to arrange a visit.

Bundesarchiv
(Abteilung Deutsches Reich und DDR
sowie Stiftung der Parteien und
Massenorganisationen der DDR)
Postfach 450 569   Tel: + 49 (0) 30 84350-0
Fickensteinallee 63   Fax + 49 (0) 30 84350-246 or 8330-695
D-12205 Berlin   www.bundesarchiv.de

Carl von Ossietsky-Universität, Oldenburg

One of the most active centres for research into East German cinema is to be found at the Arbeitsstelle DEFA-Filme als Quellen zur Politik und Kultur der DDR at the Carl von Ossietsky-Universität, Oldenburg. The *Mediathek* there has a wide range of film material and publications on DEFA.

Arbeitsstelle DEFA-Filme als
Quellen zur Politik und Kultur der DDR
B 3 Institute für
  Politikvissenschaft II
Ammerländer
  Heerstraße 114-118
D-26111 Oldenburg

Tel: + 49 (0) 441 798-2177
Fax: + 49 (0) 441 970-6180
email: defa@uni-oldenburg.de
www.uni-oldenburg.de/defa

DEFA - STIFTUNG

The complete DEFA catalog is available on the website of the DEFA-Stiftung.

DEFA - STIFTUNG
Chausseestraße 103
10115 Berlin

Tel: + 49 (0)30 2 46 56 21 01
Fax:: + 49 (0)30 2 46 56 21 49
email: info@defa-stiftung.de
www.defa-stiftung.de

(b) UK

The University of Reading

The Centre for East German Studies (based in the Department of German Studies of the University of Reading) has become a focal point for research into East German Cinema in the UK.

The Centre for East German Studies
Dept. of German Studies
The University of Reading
Whiteknights, PO Box 218
Reading, RG6 6AA

Tel: + 44 (0) 118 931-8331
Fax: + 44 (0) 118 931-8333
email: german@reading.ac.uk
www.reading.ac.uk/german

(c) USA

The University of Massachusetts, Amherst

The DEFA Film Library, set up by Prof. Barton Byg, has substantial holdings of film material and publications relating to DEFA. The DEFA film library also handles the non-commercial circulation of DEFA prints, videos, and DVDs in the United States and Canada.

DEFA Film Library
Dept. of Germanic Languages and Literatures
504 Herter Hall
Box 33925
University of Massachusetts
 Amherst
Amherst, MA 01003-3925

Tel: + 1 413 545-6681
Fax: + 1 413 545-6995
email: defa@german.umass.edu
www.umass.edu/defa

ICESTORM International, Inc., Quincy (MA), USA
ICESTORM Entertainment GmbH, Berlin, Germany

Both companies are independent video distributors and hold the world-wide rights for all home entertainment media encompassing the entire DEFA film studios productions. They have already released a number of DEFA films on video and DVD (in both NTSC and PAL formats) in German and with English subtitles and/or English voice-over.

ICESTORM International, Inc.
90 Quincy Shore Drive #317
Quincy, MA 02171-2916

email: stone@icestorm.de
www.icestorm-video.com

ICESTORM Entertainment GmbH
Hauptstrasse 159
10827 Berlin
Germany

tel: +49 (0) 30 78 09 58 10
fax: + 49 (0) 30 78 09 58 70
email: info@icestorm.de
www.icestorm.de

SELECT BIBLIOGRAPHY

Abusch, Alexander. 'Aktuelle Probleme und Aufgaben unserer sozialistischen Filmkunst: Referat der Konferenz des VEB DEFA Studio für Spielfilme und des Ministeriums für Kultur der DDR' in *Deutsche Filmkunst* 6, no. 9 (1958): 261–70.

——. 'Die Konferenz führte uns vorwärts', *Deutsche Filmkunst* 6, no. 11 (1958): 373–6.

Adorno, Theodor W. 'On the Question "What is German?"', *New German Critique* 36 (1985): 121–31.

Agde, Günter. *Kurt Maetzig – Filmarbeit: Gespräche, Reden, Schriften.* Berlin, 1987.

——. (ed.). *Kahlschlag – Das 11. Plenum der SED 1965: Studien und Dokumente.* Berlin, 1991.

Albrecht, Hartmut (ed.). *Sozialistisches Menschenbild und Filmkunst: Beiträge zu Kino und Fernsehen.* Berlin, 1970.

Arnold, Heinz Ludwig (ed.). *Text und Kritik* 127: *Günter de Bruyn.* Munich, 1995.

Bahr, Gisela. 'Film and Consciousness: the Depiction of Women in East German Movies' in: Sandra Frieden, Richard W. McCormick, Vibeke R. Petersen and Laurie Melissa Vogelsang (eds). *Gender and German Cinema: Feminist Interventions,* 2 vols. Oxford, 1993, vol. 1, pp. 125–40.

Bahro, Rudolf. *Die Alternative.* Cologne, 1977.

Barnouw, Erik. *Documentary: A History of the Non-Fiction Film.* New York, Oxford, 1993.

Bartram, Graham, and Waine, Anthony (eds). *Culture and Society in the GDR* (GDR Monitor Special Series, no. 2), 1984.

Becher, Johannes R. *Deutsches Bekenntnis: Drei Reden zur deutschen Erneuerung.* Berlin, 1945.

Becker, Wieland. '"Hoffnungen, Illusionen, Einsichten": Klaus Wischnewski im Gespräch mit Wieland Becker', *Film und Fernsehen* 18, no. 6 (1990): 35–9.

Biermann, Wolf. *Klartexte im Getümmel. 13 Jahre im Westen. Von der Ausbürgerung bis zur November-Revolution.* Cologne, 1990.

Blauert, Ellen, (ed.). *Vier Filmerzählungen nach bekannten DEFA-Filmen: 'Die Mörder sind unter uns', 'Ehe im Schatten', 'Die Buntkarierten', 'Rotation'.* Berlin, 1969.

Blunk, Harry. 'Bemerkungen zur "Erbe"–Aneignung im Spiegel des DEFA-Spielfilms', *Deutsche Studien*, 25, no. 98 (1987): 155–68.

———. *Die DDR in ihren Spielfilmen.* Munich, 1987.

Blunk, Harry and Jungnickel, Dirk (eds). *Filmland DDR: Ein Reader zu Geschichte, Funktion und Wirkung der DEFA.* Cologne, 1990.

Bock, Hans-Michael (ed.). *Cinegraph: Lexikon zum deutschsprachigen Film.* Hamburg and Munich, 1984 *et seq.*

Borchert, Jürgen. *Die Papiere meiner Tante: Roman.* Halle and Leipzig, 1984.

Boyle, Nicholas. *Goethe: The Poet and the Age – Vol. 1: The Poetry of Desire (1749–1790).* Oxford, 1991.

Brady, Martin, and Hughes, Helen. 'German Film after the *Wende*', in Derek Lewis and John R. P. McKenzie (eds). *The New Germany: Social, Political and Cultural Challenges of Unification.* Exeter, 1995, pp. 279-85.

Brandes, Ute (ed.). *Zwischen gestern und morgen: Schriftstellerinnen der DDR aus amerikanischer Sicht.* Berlin, 1992.

Braun, Volker. *Schreiben im Schredder.* Frankfurt am Main, 1996.

Brecht, Bertolt. *Journals 1934–1955* (ed. John Willett, trans. Hugh Rorrison). London, 1993.

———. *Poems: 1913–1956* (ed. John Willett and Ralph Manheim with the co-operation of Erich Fried). London, 1976.

Bruyn, Günter de. *Märkische Forschungen: Erzählung für Freunde der Literaturgeschichte.* Halle and Leipzig, 1982.

Bulgakowa, Oksana. 'Die Rebellion im Rock', in Annette C. Eckert (ed.). *Außerhalb von Mittendrin: Literatur/Film.* Berlin, 1991, pp. 98–102.

Byg, Barton. 'Geschichte, Trauer und weibliche Identität im Film: "Hiroshima mon amour" und "Der geteilte Himmel." ' in Ute Brandes (ed.). *Zwischen gestern und morgen: Schriftstellerinnen der DDR aus amerikanischer Sicht.* Berlin (1992): 95–112.

Carow, Heiner. 'Es ist Zeit, über das Kino nachzudenken', *Film und Fernsehen* 4, no. 2 (1976): 12–16.

———. 'Zwischenbilanz', *Film und Fernsehen* 5, no. 4 (1977): 5–9.

———. 'Zwischenbilanz', *Film und Fernsehen* 5, no. 5 (1977): 10–13.

Dalichow, Bärbel. 'Heimat-Filme der DEFA?', *Film und Fernsehen* 20, no. 6 (1992): 55–61.

Deleuze, Gilles, and Guattari, Félix. *Franz Kafka: Toward a Minor Literature* (trans. Dana Polan). Minneapolis, 1986.

Dennis, Mike. *GDR Politics, Economics and Society*. London, 1988.

Dimitroff, Georgi. *Ausgewählte Werke*, 3 vols. Sofia, 1976.

Drawe, Hans. 'Literatur im Film', in Hans Jürgen Schmitt (ed.). *Die Literatur der DDR: Hansers Sozialgeschichte der deutschen Literatur*, Vol. XI. Munich and Vienna, 1983, pp. 187–228.

Eckert, Annette C. (ed.). *Außerhalb von Mittendrin: Literatur/Film*. Berlin, 1991.

Eisler, Hans and Adorno, Theodor. *Composing for the Films*. New York, 1947.

Elsaesser, Thomas. *New German Cinema: A History*. New Brunswick, NJ, 1989.

Estermann, Alfred. *Die Verfilmung literarischer Werke*. Bonn, 1965.

Fehrenbach, Heidi. *Cinema and Democratizing Germany: Reconstructing National Identity after Hitler*. Durham NC, 1995.

Feinstein, Joshua. 'The Triumph of the Ordinary: Depictions of Daily Life in the East German Cinema, 1956–66.' (PhD Diss., Stanford University, 1995).

Foth, Jörg. 'Forever Young' in Harry Blunk and Dirk Jungnickel (eds). *Filmland DDR: Ein Reader zu Geschichte, Funktion und Wirkung der DEFA*. Cologne, 1990, 95–106.

Franz, Michael. *Wahrheit in der Kunst: Neue Überlegungen zu einem alten Thema*. Berlin and Weimar, 1984.

Gehler, Fred. 'Machen und Machen lassen: Auskünfte von Heiner Carow. Notiert von Fred Gehler nach Gesprächen mit Heiner Carow', *Film und Fernsehen* 18, no. 2, 1990: 7–8.

———. ' "... nur ein Tangospieler": Roland Gräf's Verfilmung der Erzählung von Christoph Hein', *Film und Fernsehen* 19, no. 2, 1991: 6–7.

Gehler, Fred and Kasten, Ulrich. ' "Wir hätten auch Aurora heißen können": mit Kurt Maetzig sprachen Fred Gehler und Ulrich Kasten' in *Film und Fernsehen* 2, no. 8 (1974): 10–14.

Geisler, Ursula. 'Untersuchung des DEFA-Films *Eine Berliner Romanze*: Die inhaltlichen Schwächen werden durch die spezifisch filmischen Mittel verdeckt'. (Diplomarbeit, Hochschule für Film und Fernsehen 'Konrad Wolf', 1957).

Geiss, Axel. 'Frank Beyer – Menschen in ihrer Zeit: Interview mit Axel Geiss', *Film und Fernsehen* 18, no. 8, 1990: 10–13.

Gersch, Wolfgang. 'Film in der DDR' in Wolfgang Jacobsen, Anton Kaes and Hans Helmut Prinzler (eds). *Geschichte des deutschen Films*. Stuttgart and Weimar, 1993, 323–64.

Gledhill, Christine (ed.). *Home Is where the Heart Is: Studies in Melodrama and the Women's Film*. London, 1987.

Goulding, Daniel J. (ed.). *Post New Wave Cinema in the Soviet Union and Eastern Europe*. Bloomington, 1989.

Gräf, Ugla, and Richter, Rolf (eds). *Roland Gräf: Gedanken beim Filmemachen: eine Dokumentation*. (= *Aus Theorie und Praxis des Films*, 1987, no. 4), Potsdam, 1987.

Gransow, Volker. *Kulturpolitk in der DDR*. Berlin, 1975.

Gregor, Ulrich. 'Konrad Wolf: Auf der Suche nach der Heimat', in Peter. W. Jansen and Wolfram Schütte (eds). *Film in der DDR*. (Reihe Film 13). Munich and Vienna, 1977, pp. 77–98.

Haase, Horst, Dau, Rudolf, and Kilche, K. 'Zur Aneignung des kulturellen Erbes in der DDR', *Weimarer Beiträge*, 30, no. 9 (1984): 1413–22.

Hasenberg, Peter, and Thull, Martin (eds). *Filme in der DDR 1987–90*. Cologne, 1991.

Heimann, Thomas. DEFA, *Künstler und SED-Kulturpolitik –Verständnis von Kulturpolitik und Filmproduktion in der SBZ/DDR 1945 bis 1959*. Berlin, 1994.

Hein, Christoph. *Der Tangospieler*. Berlin and Weimar,1989.

Heinze, Dieter and Hoffmann, Ludwig (eds). *Konrad Wolf im Dialog: Künstler und Politik*. Berlin, 1985.

Herlinghaus, Hermann (ed.). *Lothar Warneke: Film ist eine Art zu leben. Eine Dokumentation*. (= *Aus Theorie und Praxis des Films*, 1982, no. 3), Potsdam, 1982.

Herlinghaus, Rolf. 'Wie lebendig ist Geschichte? Kurt Maetzig, Konrad Wolf, Lothar Warneke und Rolf Herlinghaus im Gespräch', *Film und Fernsehen* 8, no.1 (1980): 3–8, and no. 7 (1980): 3–7.

Herminghouse, Patricia. 'Trends in Literary Reception: Coming to Terms with Classicism. Goethe in GDR Literature of the 1970s', *German Quarterly* 56, no. 2 (1983): 273–84.

Heukenkampf, Ursula. 'Gibt es richtige und falsche Interpretationen?', *Zeitschrift für Germanistik*, 6, no. 4 (1985): 415–22.

Hindemith, Bettina. 'Der DEFA-Spielfilm und seine Kritik: Probleme und Tendenzen', in Harry Blunk and Dirk Jungnickel (eds). *Filmland DDR: Ein Reader zu Geschichte, Funktion und Wirkung der DEFA.* Cologne, 1990, pp. 27–46.

Hochmuth, Dietmar (ed.). *DEFA NOVA* ——— *nach wie vor? Versuch einer Spurensicherung.* Berlin, 1993.

Hoff, Peter, and Wiedemann, Dieter (eds). *Der DEFA Spielfilm in den 80er Jahren – Chancen für die 90er?* Berlin, 1992.

Ihering, Herbert. *Theater der produktiven Widersprüche.* Berlin and Weimar, 1967.

Jacobi, Reinhold and Janssen, Herbert (eds). *Filme in der DDR: 1945–86.* Cologne, 1987.

Jansen, Peter W. and Schütte, Wolfram (eds). *Filme in der DDR,* Reihe Film 13. Cologne, 1977.

Jarmatz, Klaus, Barck, Simone and Dietzel, Peter (eds). *Exil in der UdSSR.* Leipzig, 1979.

Jordan, Günter, and Schenk, Ralf (eds). *Schwarzweiß und Farbe: DEFA-Dokumentarfilm 1946–92.* Berlin, 1996.

Jüngling, Irina. 'Jugend in den fünfziger Jahren und ihre Widerspiegelung in den Spielfilm "Die Halbstarken" und "Berlin – Ecke Schönhauser": Ein analytischer Vergleich.' (Diplomarbeit, Hochschule für Film und Fernsehen 'Konrad Wolf', 1994).

Kaes, Anton. *From Hitler to Heimat: The Return of History as Film.* Cambridge MA, 1989.

Kern, Herbert. 'Die Rechtspflege weiter vervollkommnen', *Neue Justiz* 12, no. 16 (1962): 361–4.

Kiewitz, Christl. *Der stumme Schrei. Krise und Kritik der sozialistischen Intelligenz im Werk Christoph Heins.* Tübingen, 1995.

Klauß, Cornelia. 'Ein analytischer Vergleich der "Berlin-Filme" und der "Blaulicht"-Reihe hinsichtlich der Auffindung von Realismuskriterien für den sozialistischen Kriminalfilm.' (Diplomarbeit, Hochschule für Film und Fernsehen 'Konrad Wolf', 1986).

Klein, Gerhard. 'Das Große im Kleinen spiegeln', *Deutsche Filmkunst* 6, no. 10 (1958): 300–1.

Knabe, Hubertus, (ed.). *Aufbruch in eine andere DDR.* Hamburg, 1989.

Koch, Gertrud. 'On the disappearance of the dead among the living: the Holocaust and the Confusion of Identities in the Films of Konrad Wolf', *New German Critique* 60 (1993): 57–75.

König, Hannelore, Wiedemann Dieter, and Wolf, Lothar (eds). *Zwischen Bluejeans und Blauhemden: Jugendfilm in Ost und West.* Berlin, 1995.

Kohlhaase, Wolfgang. 'Das Neue in neuen Formen gestalten' *Deutsche Filmkunst* 6, no. 10 (1958): 298–300.

——— 'Gegenwartsthematik', *Deutsche Filmkunst* 6, no. 11 (1958): 367–8.

——— 'Filmqualifizierte Schriftsteller – nicht nur Stofflieferanten', *Deutsche Filmkunst* 9, no. 8 (1961): 270–3.

——— 'Wolfgang Kohlhaase, Konrad Wolf und Klaus Wischnewski. Ein Gespräch über SOLO SUNNY: Was heißt denn "happy end"?', *Film und Fernsehen* 8, no. 1 (1980): 9–15.

Kohlhaase, Wolfgang and Kubisch, Hans. *Alarm im Zirkus – Literarisches Szenarium zu einem Kriminalfilm.* Berlin, 1954.

Kohlhaase, Wolfgang and Klein, Gerhard. *Eine Berliner Romanze.* Berlin, 1956.

Kreimeier, Klaus. '*Germania, anno zero: Eine Momentaufnahme*', *epd film* 12, no. 6 (1995): 17-25.

Küchenmeister, Claus. 'Ein neuer und guter Weg – Zum DEFA-Film "Eine Berliner Romanze"', *Deutsche Filmkunst* 4, no. 6 (1956): 176-7.

Lange, Günther. *Heimat: Realität und Aufgabe.* Berlin, 1973.

Leistner, Bernd. 'Zum Goethe-Bezug in der neueren DDR-Literatur' in *Weimarer Beiträge* 23, no. 5 (1977): 86–120.

Lenz, J. M. R. 'Briefe über die Moralität der *Leiden des jungen Werthers*' in Britta Titel, Helmut Haug (eds). *Werke und Schriften*, 2 vols. Stuttgart, 1966.

Leo, Annette. 'Der hippokratische Eid auf die Wahrheit oder Der Traum vom wirklichen Journalismus' in Hubertus Knabe (ed.). *Aufbruch in eine andere DDR.* Hamburg, 1989, pp. 83–9.

Leonhardt, Sigrun. 'Testing the Borders: East German Film between Individualism and Social Commitment' in Daniel J. Goulding (ed.). *Post New Wave Cinema in the Soviet Union and Eastern Europe.* Bloomington, 1989, pp. 51–101.

Loewenstein, Joseph, and Tatlock, Lynne. 'The Marshall Plan at the Movies: Marlene Dietrich and her Incarnations', *The German Quarterly* 65, nos. 3–4 (1992): 429–42.

Ludz, Peter. C. et al. (eds). *DDR Handbuch*. Cologne, 1985.

Mahoney, Dennis. F. 'A recast Goethe: *Günther's Lotte in Weimar* (1975)' in Eric Rentschler (ed.). *German Film and Literature: Adaptations and Transformations*. New York and London, 1986, pp. 249–59.

Mann, Thomas. *Gesammelte Werke*, 13 vols. Frankfurt am Main, 1960.

—— *Briefe*, 3 vols. Frankfurt am Main, 1963.

Maetzig, Kurt. 'Kino für mündige Zuschauer', *Film und Fernsehen* 8, no. 10, 1980: 4–7.

Meyer, Klaus. 'Was leicht geht, macht mich stutzig: Interview mit Szenaristin Regine Kühn', *Kino DDR* 8, (1974): 6–7.

Mihan, Angelika. 'Eine Stiluntersuchung der "Berlin-Filme". (Diplomarbeit, Hochschule für Film und Fernsehen 'Konrad Wolf', 1978).

Mihan, Hans-Rainer. 'Sabine, Sunny, Nina und der Zuschauer: Gedanken zum Gegenwartssfilmspielfilm der DEFA', *Film und Fernsehen* 10, no. 8 (1982): 9–12.

Mückenberger, Christiane (ed.). *Zur DEFA-Geschichte: Spielfilme 1946 – 1949: eine Dokumentation. Studentenarbeiten des I. Studienjahres der Fachrichtung Film- und Fernsehwissenschaft* (Hochschule für Film und Fernsehen der DDR: Reihe Information, nos.3/4/5/6). Potsdam, 1976.

Mückenberger, Christiane (ed.). *Prädikat: besonders schädlich. 'Das Kaninchen bin ich' und 'Denk bloß nicht ich heule'.* Berlin, 1990.

Mückenberger, Christiane, and Jordan, Günter. *'Sie sehen selbst, Sie hören selbst …': Die DEFA von ihren Anfängen bis 1949*. Marburg, 1994.

Nowell-Smith, Geoffrey, and Wollen, Tana (eds). *After the Wall.* London, 1991.

Orr, Christopher. 'The Discourse of Adaptation: A Review', *Wide Angle*, 6, no. 2 (1984): 72–6.

Pflaum, Hans Günther, and Prinzler, Hans Helmut (eds). *Film in der Bundesrepublik Deutschland.* Bonn, 1993.

Poiger, Uta. *Taming the Wild West: American Popular Culture and the Cold War Battles over East and West German Identities, 1949–1961.* (PhD Diss., Brown University, 1995).

Prochnow, Christoph (ed.). *Thema: Literaturverfilmungen.* (= *Aus Theorie und Praxis des Films*, 1983, no. 2). Potsdam, 1983.

Raupach, Rudi. 'Wachsende Anforderungen der Jugend an die Filmproduktion', *Deutsche Filmkunst* 6, no. 11 (1958): 350–1.

Reimann, Paul (ed.). *Kafka aus Prager Sicht 1963*. Prague, 1965.

Renk, Aune (ed.). Konrad Wolf. *Direkt in Kopf und Herz. Aufzeichnungen, Reden, Interviews*. Berlin, 1989.

Rentschler, Eric (ed.). *German Film and Literature: Adaptations and Transformations*. New York and London, 1986.

——. *West German Film-makers on Film: Visions and Voices*. New York and London, 1988.

Reuter, Hans Heinrich. 'Der gekreuzigte Prometheus: Goethes Roman "Die Leiden des jungen Werthers" ', *Goethe-Jahrbuch*, 89 (1972): 86–115.

Richter, Rolf (ed.). DEFA: Spielfilm, *Regisseure und ihre Kritiker*. Berlin, 1981–1983.

Rosen, Philip. 'History, Textuality, Nation: Kracauer, Burch, and Some Problems in the Study of National Cinemas', *Iris 2*, no. 2 (1984): 69–84.

Roth, Wilhelm. 'Programmänderung Leipzig 1989', *epd Film 7*, no.1 (1990): 3–5.

Rüß, Gisela (ed.). *Dokumente zur Kunst-, Literatur- und Kulturpolitik der SED: 1971-1974*. Stuttgart, 1976.

Ryback, Timothy W. *Rock around the Bloc: A History of Rock Music in Eastern Europe and the Soviet Union*. New York and Oxford, 1990.

Sander, Helke and Schlesier, Renée. 'Die legende von paul und paula: eine frauenverachtende schnulze aus der ddr', *Frauen und Film 2*, (1974): 8–47.

Sartre, Jean-Paul. 'Die Abrüstung der Kultur: Rede auf dem Weltfriedenskongress in Moskau' (trans. Stephan Hermlin), *Sinn und Form* 14 (1962): 805–15.

Schauer, Hermann. E. 'Adaptionsprobleme des literarischen Erbes', in Hartmut Albrecht (ed.). *Sozialistisches Menschenbild und Filmkunst: Beiträge zu Kino und Fernsehen*. Berlin, 1970, pp. 298–314.

Schenk, Michael. *Fortschritts-und Modernitätskritik in der DDR-Literatur. Prosatexte der achtziger Jahre*. Tübingen, 1995.

Schenk, Ralf. 'Mitten im Kalten Krieg: 1950 bis 1960' in Ralf Schenk (ed.). *Das zweite Leben der Filmstadt Babelsberg: DEFA Spielfilme 1946–1992*. Berlin 1994, pp. 50–157.

——. (ed.). *Das zweite Leben der Filmstadt Babelsberg: DEFA Spielfilme 1946–1992*. Berlin, 1994.

——. *Regie: Frank Beyer*. Berlin, 1995.

Schiller, Dieter. 'Die Leiden des jungen Werthers' in *DEFA Filme 1976-1977*: Kulturpolitik – *Kunst*, ed. Betriebsakademie des VEB DEFA Studio für Spielfilme (= *Aus Theorie und Praxis des Films*, 1979, no. 2): 108–23.

Schlenker, Wolfram. *Das 'kulturelle Erbe' in der DDR: Gesellschaftliche Entwicklungen und Kulturpolitik 1945-1965*. Stuttgart, 1977.

Schmidt, Hannes. 'Kollision mit der Umwelt: zu G. Kleins Spielfilm *Berlin um die Ecke* (DEFA 1965)', *Medium 18*, no. 2 (1988): 69–70.

Schmidt, Hannes (ed.). *Werkstatterfahrungen mit Gerhard Klein – Gespräche*. (= *Aus Theorie und Praxis des Films*, 1984, no. 2).

———. 'Interview with Wolfgang Kohlhaase' in Hannes Schmidt (ed.). *Werkstatterfahrungen mit Gerhard Klein – Gespräche* (= *Aus Theorie und Praxis des Films*, 1984, no. 2), 6–44.

Schmidt, Margarete (ed.). *Emanzipation der Frau: Wirklichkeit und Illusion*. (= *Aus Theorie und Praxis des Films*, 1975, Sonderheft), Potsdam, 1975.

Schmitt, Hans Jürgen (ed.). *Die Literatur der DDR: Hansers Sozialgeschichte der deutschen Literatur*, vol. 11. Munich and Vienna, 1983.

Schönemann, Sibylle. 'Stoffentwicklung im DEFA-Studio für Spielfilme', in Harry Blunk and Dirk Jungnickel (eds). *Filmland DDR: Ein Reader zu Geschichte, Funktion und Wirkung der DEFA*. Cologne, 1990, pp. 71–82.

Silberman, Marc. 'Remembering history: The Filmmaker Konrad Wolf', *New German Critique* 49 (1990): 163–91.

———. 'Narrating Gender in the GDR: Herrmann Zschoche's *Bürgschaft für ein Jahr* (1981)', *The Germanic Review* (Special issue on German film, ed. Richard Murphy) 66, no. 1 (1991): 25–33.

———. 'Post-wall Documentaries: New Images from a New Germany', *Cinema Journal* 33, no. 2 (1994): 21–41.

———. German Cinema: *Texts in Context*. Detroit, 1995.

Staritz, Dietrich. *Geschichte der DDR*. Frankfurt am Main, 1996.

Stephan, Alexander. *Christa Wolf*. Munich, 1976.

———. 'Cultural politics in the GDR under Erich Honecker', in Ian Wallace (ed.). *The GDR under Honecker 1971–1981*. (GDR Monitor Special Series, no. 1), Dundee, 1981, pp. 31–42.

Swales, Martin. *Goethe: The Sorrows of Young Werther*. Cambridge, 1987.

Sylvester, Regine. 'Film und Wirklichkeit: einige Gedanken zu Frauengestalten in neueren Filmen der DEFA und des Fernsehens der DDR', in Margarete Schmidt (ed.), *Emanzipation der Frau: Wirklichkeit und Illusion (= Aus Theorie und Praxis des Films*, Sonderheft 1975). Potsdam, 1975, 95–108.

Szemere, Anna. 'Bandits, Heroes, the Honest, and the Misled: Exploring the Politics of Representation in the Hungarian Uprising of 1956' in Lawrence Grossberg, Cary Nelson and Paula Treichler (eds). *Cultural Studies.* New York, 1992, pp. 623–39.

Tate, Dennis. "Natürlich ein politisches Buch": *Märkische Forschungen* im historischen Kontext der Honecker-Ära', in Heinz Ludwig Arnold (ed.). *Text und Kritik 127: Günter de Bruyn.* Munich, 1995, pp. 84–91.

Voß, Margit. 'Interview mit Wolfgang Staudte für den Berliner Rundfunk, 1966' in Christiane Mückenberger (ed.). *Zur DEFA-Geschichte: Spielfilme 1946–1949: eine Dokumentation. Studentenarbeiten des I. Studienjahres der Fachrichtung Film- und Fernsehwissenschaft* (Hochschule für Film und Fernsehen der DDR: Reihe Information, nos. 3/4/5/6). Potsdam, 1976, pp. 92–105.

Wallace, Ian (ed.). *The GDR under Honecker 1971–1981* (GDR Monitor Special Series, no. 1). Dundee, 1981.

Walsh, Martin. *The Brechtian Aspect of Radical Cinema.* London, 1981.

Warneke, Lothar. 'Der dokumentare Spielfilm' in Hermann Herlinghaus (ed.), *Lothar Warneke: Film ist eine Art zu leben. Eine Dokumentation. (= Aus Theorie und Praxis des Films*, 1982, no. 3), Potsdam, 1982: 10–35.

Weber, Hermann. *Die DDR 1945-1990.* Munich, 1993.

———. (ed.). *DDR: Dokumente zur Geschichte der Deutschen Demokratischen Republik.* 1945–1985. Munich, 1986.

Wegener, Karl-Heinz. *Berlin im Spielfilm – Katalog.* Berlin, 1987.

Werkentin, Falco. *Politische Strafjustiz in der Ära Ulbricht.* Berlin, 1995.

Wiedemann, Dieter, and Lohmann, Hans. 'Der DEFA-Spielfilm zwischen Anpassung und Protest', *Zeitschrift für Literaturwissenschaft und Linguistik* 21, no. 82 (1991): 38–51.

Wilkening, Albert. *Geschichte der DEFA von 1945–1950: Betriebsgeschichte des VEB DEFA Studio für Spielfilme*, vol. 1. Potsdam, 1981.

———— *Die DEFA in der Etappe 1950-1953: Betriebsgeschichte des VEB DEFA Studio für Spielfilme*, vol. 2. Babelsberg, 1984.

Wischnewski, Klaus. 'Wer sind wir? *Berlin - Ecke Schönhauser'*, *Deutsche Filmkunst* 5, no. 9, 1957, 264–6.

———— 'Die Unruhe und Suche des Konrad Wolf', *Film und Fernsehen* 13, no. 9 (1985): 4–10.

———— 'Träumer und gewöhnliche Leute: 1966–1979', in Ralf Schenk (ed.). *Das zweite Leben der Filmstadt Babelsberg: 1946–92.* Berlin, 1994, pp. 212–63.

Witt, Günter. 'Von der höheren Verantwortung hängt alles ab', *Filmwissenschaftliche Mitteilungen* 5, no. 2 (1964): 251–63.

Witte, Karsten. 'Geteilte Filme: Einige Erfahrungen mit Literatur und Politik im DEFA-Film', *Film und Fernsehen* 23, no. 1 (1995): 17–19.

Wolf, Dieter. 'Die Kunst miteinander zu reden: *Bis daß der Tod euch scheidet* im Gespräch', *Film und Fernsehen* 8, no. 11 (1979): 9–10.

Wolf, Konrad. '*Der geteilte Himmel*: Probleme des sozialistischen Realismus in der darstellenden Künste. Diskussionsbeitrag auf der Plenartagung der Deutschen Akademie der Künste, 30. 6. 1964', in Aune Renk (ed.). *Konrad Wolf: direkt in Kopf und Herz. Aufzeichnungen, Reden, Interviews.*, Berlin, 1989, pp. 92–7.

————. '"Auf der Suche nach Deutschland": Pressegespräch, 31.1.1968', in Aune Renk (ed.). *Konrad Wolf: direkt in Kopf und Herz. Aufzeichnungen, Reden, Interviews*, Berlin, 1989, pp. 159–61.

————.'"Auf der Suche nach dem Lebenszentrum": Werkstattgespräch für *Film und Fernsehen*, April/Mai 1975' in Aune Renk (ed.). *Konrad Wolf: direkt in Kopf und Herz. Aufzeichnungen, Reden, Interviews*, Berlin, 1989, pp. 235–50.

————. '"Von den Möglichkeiten sozialistischer Filmkunst": Reaktionen *auf Mama, ich lebe*. Rede, 3.5.1977', in Aune Renk (ed.). *Konrad Wolf: direkt in Kopf und Herz. Aufzeichnungen, Reden, Interviews.* Berlin, 1989, pp. 267–74.

Zenker, Helga. 'Berlin – Ecke Schönhauser: Vergleichende Analyse zwischen Drehbuch und Film.' (Diplomarbeit, Hochschule für Film und Fernsehen 'Konrad Wolf', 1958).

Ziewer, Christian. 'Last Words for Wolfgang Staudte (1984)' in Eric Rentschler (ed.), *West German Film-makers on Film: Visions and Voices.* New York and London, 1988, pp. 118–20.

Zimmermann, Peter (ed.). *Deutschlandbilder-Ost: Dokumentarfilme der DEFA von der Nachkriegszeit bis zur Wiedervereinigung* Konstanz, 1995.

INDEX

Abschied (Farewell), 14, 242 n10
Abschied von gestern (Yesterday Girl), 36
Abusch, Alexander, 10, 27, 110
Ackermann, Anton, 4, 88–89
Addio, piccola mia, 16, 223
Adenauer, Konrad, 87
Adorno, T.W., 25, 37–38
Affaire Blum (The Blum Affair), 27, 62–63
Aktion J. (Operation J.), 38
Alarm im Zirkus (Circus Alarm), 9–10, 32, 94, 96–68, 100, 101, 107, 122, 207, 208–209
Albrecht, Michael, 284
Alfred, 285–86, 287–88
All Quiet on the Western Front, 34
Alle meine Mädchen (All My Girls), 16
Alleinseglerin, Die (The Solo Sailor), 195
Andersen, Thom, 33
Andriyevsky, Alexander, 6
Anton der Zauberer (Anton, the Magician), 25
Antonov, Leonid, 6
Apachen, 40 n12
Apitz, Bruno, 73–74
Architekten, Die (The Architects), 18, 219–21
Arme Hölderlin, Der (Poor Hölderlin), 229
Ärztinnen (Women Doctors), 53
Aufrecht gehen (Walking Tall), 36
Auftrag Höglers, Der (Högler's Task), 67

Augenzeuge, Der (The Eyewitness), 3, 59, 79, 80
Aus dem Leben eines Taugenichts (Excerpts from the Life of a Good-for-Nothing), 223
Avant le Déluge, 71

Baal, Karin, 99
Bahr, Gisela, 184, 187
Bahro, Rudolf, 48
Baky, Josef von, 106
Balhaus, Carl, 70
Balthoff, Alfred, 58, 62
Bankett für Achilles (Banquet for Achilles), 216
Barfuß und ohne Hut (Barefooted and Hatless), 282
Becher, Johannes, R., 59, 242 n10
Becker, Jurek, 41 n24, 74
Beethoven – Tage aus einem Leben (Beethoven – Days in a Life), 16, 223, 243 n19
Behn-Grund, Felix, 59
Beil von Wandsbek, Das (The Axe of Wandsbek), 68–69
Benedek, Laslo, 34
Benjamin, Hilde, 151, 162 n25
Bentzien, Hans, 13, 161 n17
Bergmann, Karl Hans, 3, 4, 19 n9
Bergmann, Werner, 34
Berlin – Ecke Schönhauser (Berlin – Schönhauser Corner), 9–10, 33, 93, 94, 103–110, 112, 127, 207, 208–209

Berliner Romanze, Eine (A Berlin Romance), 9–10, 33, 94, 98–103, 106, 207–209
Berlin um die Ecke (Berlin Around the Corner), 33, 71–72, 94, 110–114, 131, 133, 136–141
Best Years of Our Lives, The, 33
Besten Jahre, Die (The Best Years), 25
Beunruhigung, Die (Apprehension), 195
Beyer, Frank, 9, 11, 13, 15, 25, 29, 34, 36, 73–74, 133, 134
Biberman, Herbert, 33
Bieler, Manfred, 90, 146, 150, 161 n16
Biermann, Wolf, 15, 48, 143, 226
Biologie (Biology), 18
Bis daß der Tod euch scheidet (Until Death Do Us Part), 16, 34, 184, 186–89, 212
Bisky, Lothar, 44
Blackboard Jungle, 34, 71, 105
Bleiweiß, Celino, 223
Blue Dahlia, The, 27
Boettcher, Bud, 34
Böll, Heinrich, 89
Borchert, Jürgen, 260
Borsche, Dieter, 108
Böttcher, Jürgen, 13, 15, 133, 267–81, 286, 287, 298
Brandis, Helmut, 210
Brando, Marlon, 93, 105
Brandt, Willy, 14
Brasch, Thomas, 36, 41 n24
Braun, Volker, 15, 123
Brecht, Bertolt, 6–7, 27, 72, 82, 101, 120, 121, 132, 141, 231, 256
Brezhnev, Leonid, 85, 89
Broddi, 216
Brooks, Richard, 34, 71
Bruyn, Günter de, 229, 253–63
Büchner, Georg, 63–64, 223
Bulgakowa, Oksana, 190, 194, 251
Bürger, Annekathrin, 102, 103
Bürgermeister Anna (Mayoress Anna), 7

Bürgschaft für ein Jahr (On Probation), 195, 212
Burkhardt, Bernd, 283–84
Buntkarierten, Die (The Girls in Gingham), 31, 63, 82
Burch, Noël, 33
Busch, Ernst, 37, 165, 178

Cabinet des Doktor Caligari, Das (The Cabinet of Dr Caligari), 64
Carow, Heiner, 9, 15, 16, 18, 31, 32, 33, 34, 46, 47–54, 184, 186, 188, 191, 207, 212, 213, 222, 287
Cayatte, André, 71
Chandler, Raymond, 28
Chaplin, Charlie, 86
Chiaureli, Mikhail, 28
Chingachgook, die Große Schlange (Chingachgook, the Great Snake), 40 n12
Chronik der Anna Magdalena Bach (The Chronicle of Anna Magdalena Bach), 36
Chronique d'un été (Chronicle of a Summer), 297–98
Clurman, Harold, 37
Coming Out, 18
Coogan, Jackie, 86
Coward, Noel, 63
Crossfire, 28, 33
Cyankali, 33

Dalichow, Bärbel, 103
Davies, Terence, 34
de Mille, Cecil B., 28
De Sica, Vittorio, 95
Dean, James, 105
Dein unbekannter Bruder (Your Unknown Brother), 17
Denk bloß nicht, ich heule (Just Don't Think I'm Crying), 12, 73, 132, 133, 140–42
Deppe, Hans, 7
Dessau, Maxim, 17
Dessau, Paul, 121

Dietrich, Marlene, 37
Dimitroff, Georgi, 69
Dmytryk, Edward, 28, 37
Domino, 41 n24
Domröse, Angelika, 15, 36
Don Juan, Karl Liebknecht Straße
(Don Juan, Karl Liebknecht
Street), 242 n12
Dörrie, Doris, 25
Dr. med Sommer II (Dr Sommer II),
15
DrehOrt Berlin (Location Berlin), 36
Drei von vielen (Three of Many), 271
Dritte, Der (Her Third), 15, 31, 37,
186, 213, 218, 219, 222, 226
Du und icke und Berlin (You, Me and
Berlin), 209
Dudow, Slatan, 11, 19 n1, 25, 28,
33, 34, 38, 48, 101, 206–207
Dutschke, Rudi, 36
Dymschitz, Alexander, 2, 27, 60
Dziuba, Helmut, 34, 185

Egel, Karl Georg, 166
Ehe im Schatten (Marriage in the
Shadow), 30, 61–62, 65, 79, 81,
82, 83
Einer trage des anderen Last (Bear Ye
One Another's Burdens), 18
Einmal ist keinmal (Once Is Never),
164
Eisler, Hanns, 34, 37, 38, 82 121
Elixiere des Teufels, Die (The Devil's
Elixirs), 223
Elsaesser, Thomas, 25
Emil und die Detektive (Emil and the
Detectives), 33, 100
Engel aus Eisen (Iron Angel), 41 n24
Engel, Erich, 27, 38, 63, 83
Erhard, Ludwig, 89
Ernst Thälmann – Sohn seiner Klasse
(Ernst Thälmann – Son of the
Working Class), 9, 40 n11, 70,
83–84
Ernst Thälmann – Führer seiner
Klasse (Ernst Thälmann –
Leader of the Working Class), 9,
40 n11, 70, 83–84
Estermann, Alfred, 263, n3
Ete und Ali, 210
Eyck, Peter van, 60, 75 n4

Fahrrad, Das (The Bicycle), 184,
195–200
Fall Gleiwitz, Der (The Gleiwitz
Affair), 11, 34
Fall of Berlin, The (Padeniye Berlina),
28
Fassbinder, Rainer Werner, 31, 37
Feinstein, Joshua, 136, 159 n4, 183
Fischer, Adolf, 2, 19n1
Flucht, Die (The Flight), 219
Ford, John, 22, 29, 37
Foth, Jörg, 17, 18
Frank, Lloyd, 63
Freies Land (A Free Country), 3
Frühling braucht Zeit, Der (Spring
Takes Its Time), 13, 133,
138–39, 143, 144
Frühlingssinfonie (Spring Symphony),
36
Frühreifen, Die (The Precocious Ones),
106
Frauenschicksale (Fates of Women), 38
Fünf Patronenhülsen (Five
Cartridges), 11, 29, 37

Geheimakten Solvay (The Secret Files of
Solvay), 67
Gentlemen's Agreement, 28, 33
Gerassimov, Sergei, 28
Germania anno zero, 32, 36, 95,
101
Geschonneck, Erwin, 58, 69
Geschwader Fledermaus (Bat
Squadron), 38
Geteilte Himmel, Der (Divided
Heaven), 11, 31, 34, 37, 165,
173, 215–16, 219
Glaube, Liebe, Hoffnung (Faith, Hope
and Charity), 286, 295, 296–97,
298, 299

Glück im Hinterhaus (Happiness in the Backyard), 218
Gniffke, Erich, 4
Goethe, Johann Wolfgang von, 222–24, 226–41, 242 n14, 243 n17, 243 n18, 243 n25, 244 n27
Golde, Gerd, 18
Golem, wie er in die Welt kam, Der (The Golem), 19 n1
Gorbachev, Mikhail, 18
Gorky, Maixim, 120
Gottschalk, Joachim, 62, 79, 80–81
Göthe, Wolf, 101, 109
Goya oder der arge Weg der Erkenntnis (Goya or The Hard Road to Understanding), 16, 165, 223
Granovsky, Alexis, 37
Grapes of Wrath, The, 37
Gräf, Roland, 12, 15, 17, 49, 209, 216, 219, 245–63
Grenzland – eine Reise (Borderlands), 286, 295–96, 299
Groschopp, Richard, 40 n12
Großmann, Lothar, 17
Grote, Heinz, 44
Grünsteinvariante, Die (The Grünstein Variation), 36
Gudzuhn, Jörg, 36
Günther, Egon, 14, 15, 16, 18, 31, 133, 160 n13, 186, 213, 222, 226, 227–32, 234–35, 242 n10, 243 n19, 243 n25
Gusner, Iris, 16, 184

Haacker, Carl, 2–3, 19 n1
Hager, Kurt, 17, 43, 89–90
Halbstarken, Die (The Hooligans), 71, 99, 106
Hälfte des Lebens (Half of a Life), 224
Hammel, Claus, 259
Hangmen Also Die, 27, 37
Harbich, Milo, 3
Harlan, Veit, 65, 68
Harnack, Arvid, 69
Harnack, Falk, 58, 69

Hauptmann Florian von der Mühle (Captain Florian of the Mill), 14
Hauptmann von Köln, Der (The Captain of Cologne), 25
Heartfield, John, 121
Heimat, 80
Hein, Christoph, 247–53
Heise, Thomas, 299
Hellberg, Martin, 67
Herlinghaus, Hermann, 48
Herrmann, Joachim, 43
Heymann, Stefan, 7
Heynowski, Walter, 38
Heym, Stefan, 48
Himmel über Berlin, Der (Wings of Desire), 36
Hindenburg, Paul von, 84
Hiroshima mon amour, 34
Hitler, Adolf, 28, 78, 84, 86–87, 120
Hitlerjunge Quex (Hitler Youth Quex), 97, 110
Hochmuth, Dietmar, 17, 287
Hoffmann, Jutta, 15, 36
Hollaender, Friedrich, 37
Holland-Moritz, Renate, 53, 197
Hommage à Hölderlin, 224
Honecker, Erich, 12–13, 14–15, 46, 89, 103, 196, 209, 222
Honecker, Margot, 97
Höntsch, Andreas, 18
Huston, John, 28
Hut, Der (The Hat), 18

Ich klage an (J'accuse), 30
Ich war 19 (I Was Nineteen), 14, 29, 74, 165, 173–81
Ihering, Herbert, 63
Insel der Schwäne (Swan Island), 45–46, 74–75, 214–15
Im Spannungsfeld (In the Field of Tension), 209, 218
Irgendwo in Berlin (Somewhere in Berlin), 3, 33, 206
Ivens, Joris, 37

Jadup und Boel, 17, 34, 50, 55
Jahrgang 45 (Born in 1945), 13, 15, 133, 143–44, 277
Jakob der Lügner (Jacob the Liar), 13, 15, 34, 41 n24, 74
Janka, Walter, 6, 20 n14
Januskopf (Janus Head), 209, 218
Jarmusch, Jim, 37
Joli mai, le, 298
Jud Süß (Jew Süss), 65, 68
Junge, Winfried, 286
Jürschik, Rudolf, 18
Jutzi, Piel, 33, 38

Kafka, Franz, 22
Kahane, Peter, 17, 210, 213, 219
Kalatozov, Mikhail, 35
Kameradschaft (Comradeship), 33
Kaninchen bin ich, Das (I Am the Rabbit), 12, 13, 14, 31, 80, 84, 85, 89, 133, 143, 146–63
Kann, Michael, 17
Karbid und Sauerampfer (Carbide and Sorrel), 11, 25
Karl, Günter, 151–52
Karla, 72, 133, 140–41
Kazan, Elia, 28, 33, 34
Kästner, Erich, 33, 100
Keilson, Grete, 6
Keller, Gottfried, 242 n10, 243 n19.
Kid, The, 86
Kipping, Herwig, 18, 224
Kirsten, Ralph, 9, 185, 210, 223
Klaren, Georg, 3, 63–64
Klein, Gerhard, 9, 11, 32, 33, 34, 72, 93–116, 123, 128, 129, 130, 133, 207
Klering, Hans, 2, 19 n1
Kluge, Alexander, 36
Knef, Hildegard, 61
Knietzsch, Horst, 45, 46, 102, 103, 109, 255
Koepp, Volker, 281, 286, 292

Kohlhaase, Wolfgang, 32, 33, 35, 36, 72, 93–116, 117–130, 174, 192, 207
Kolditz, Gottfried, 40 n12
Kolonne Strupp (The Strupp Convoy), 3
Komsomolsk, 28
Kramer, Stanley, 34
Kratzert, Hans, 210
Krenz, Egon, 18
Krößner, Renate, 192
Krug, Manfred, 15, 36, 37
Khrushchev, Nikita, 85
Kuckucks, Die (The Cuckoos), 7
Kuhle Wampe, 33, 37, 101
Kühn, Regine, 190, 236, 238, 239, 241, 244 n36
Kühn, Siegfried, 30, 209, 222, 226, 236–41, 242 n12, 244 n36
Kunert, Günter, 229
Kunze, Reiner, 219
Kurella, Alfred, 27

Lamprecht, Gerhard, 3, 33, 100, 206
Land hinter dem Regenbogen, Das (The Land Over the Rainbow), 18
Lang, Fritz, 27, 28, 37, 64
Lange, Günther, 205, 217
Laut und leise ist die Liebe (Love Is Loud and Silent), 185
Lauter, Hans, 7–8
Leben des Jean Paul Friedrich Richter (The Life of Jean Paul Friedrich Richter), 229
Leben mit Uwe (Living with Uwe), 15
Legende von Paul und Paula, Die (The Legend of Paul and Paula), 15, 31, 191–92, 213, 222
Leiden des jungen Werthers, Die (The Sorrows of Young Werther), 16, 224, 226, 230, 231–36
Leipzig im Herbst (Leipzig in Autumn), 286, 287–91, 292
Lem, Stanislav, 80

Index

Lenin, Vladimir Ilich, 48, 225
Letztes Jahr Titanic (Last Year Titanic), 286, 291–94
Leute mit Flügeln (People with Wings), 29
Leute mit Landschaft (People with Landscape), 287
Liebeneiner, Wolfgang, 30
Liebeserklärung an G.T. (Declaration of Love to G.T.), 185
Liebling – Kreuzberg, 37, 41 n24
Lied der Matrosen, Das (The Sailors' Song), 80
Lied vom Leben, Das (The Song of Life), 37
Lindemann, Alfred, 2–3, 4, 5–6
Lissy, 30, 31, 34, 73, 164, 167, 173
Losansky, Rolf, 216
Lösche, Alexander, 6
Losey, Joseph, 37
Lots Weib (Lot's Wife), 160 n13
Lotte in Weimar, 16, 223, 227–29
Lotz, Karl Heinz, 17, 18
Luderer, Wolfgang, 14
Lukács, Georg, 120

Mach, Josef, 14, 40 n12
Mädchen auf dem Brett, Das (The Girl on the Springboard), 80
Mädchen in Wittstock (Girls in Wittstock), 292
Mäde, Hans Dieter, 17, 18
Madonna, 37
Maetzig, Kurt, 2–3, 6, 9, 12, 14, 19 n1, 19 n9, 28, 30, 31, 38, 49–50, 54, 58, 62, 63, 66–67, 68, 70, 77–92, 133, 146, 151–53, 156, 158, 160 n13, 161, n17, 162 n25, 209
Maltese Falcon, The, 28
Mann gegen Mann (Man against Man), 79
Mama, ich lebe (Mother, I'm Alive), 53, 165, 181
Man Who Shot Liberty Valence, The, 29

Mann, Thomas, 223, 227, 228
Marker, Chris, 298, 299
Märkische Forschungen (Exploring the Brandenburg Marches), 17, 209, 245–63
Marshall, George, 27
Martha, 273, 274, 275
Marx, Karl, 142, 185
Mauer, Die (The Wall), 278
Meier, Otto, 4
Meine Freundin Sybille (My Friend Sybille), 14
Meißner, Wilhelm, 6
Metropolis, 28, 64
Mich dürstet (I'm Thirsty), 70
Mihan, Hans-Rainer, 185
Milestone, Lewis, 34
Misselwitz, Helke, 286, 292
Mondi, Bruno, 65
Mörder sind unter uns, Die (The Murderers Are among Us), 1, 3, 27, 28, 32, 59–61, 206
Morin, Edgar, 297–98
Mr Behrmann – Leben Traum Tod (Mr Behrmann – Life, Dreams and Death), 286, 298, 299–300
Mückenberger, Jochen, 14, 161 n17
Müller, Hans, 7
Mueller-Stahl, Armin, 15, 36, 37
Mutter Krausens Fahrt ins Glück (Mother Krause's Journey to Happiness), 33

Nackt unter Wölfen (Naked among Wolves), 34, 73–74
Nackte Mann auf dem Sportplatz, Der (The Naked Man on the Playing Field), 16, 165
Nehring, Alfred, 246
Netzeband, Günter, 43
Netzwerk (Network), 185, 210, 218
Night on Earth, 37
Novalis – die blaue Blume (Novalis – The Blue Flower), 224

– 325 –

Nuit et brouillard (Night and Fog), 34, 38

Odets, Clifford, 37
Ofenbauer, Die (The Blast Furnace Engineers), 272
On the Waterfront, 33, 93
Opus III, 37
Ost, Günter, 12
Ostpreußenland (Tales of East Prussia), 286, 295, 297, 299

Pabst, G.W. 33, 38
Passagier – Welcome to Germany, Der (The Passenger – Welcome to Germany), 41 n24
Pete Roleum and His Cousins, 37
Petzold, Konrad, 9
Pewas, Peter, 3
Piscator, Erwin, 19 n1
Plenzdorf, Ulrich, 12, 15, 35, 75, 224
Polizeiruf 110 (Emergency 110), 150
Professor Mamlock, 11, 164, 167–73
P.S., 49

Rangierer (Shunters), 273, 275, 276, 282, 287
Rat der Götter, Der (Council of the Gods), 38, 66–67, 77–82, 86–88, 91
Ray, Nicholas, 34
Rebel without a Cause, 34, 99, 105
Red Hollywood, 33
ReDuPers (The All-round Reduced Personality), 36
Reidemeister, Helga, 36
Reimann, Brigitte, 189
Reisch, Günter, 25, 30, 74
Reitz, Edgar, 80
Renoir, Jean, 37
Reschke, Ingrid, 15, 184
Resnais, Alain, 34
Riemann, Tord, 152, 156, 161 n14, 162 n21, 162 n25
Ritt, Martin, 34

Rodenberg, Hans, 8
Roman einer jungen Ehe (Story of a Marriage), 68
Romeo und Julia auf dem Dorfe (A Village Romeo and Juliet), 242 n12
Rossellini, Roberto, 32, 33, 36, 95, 101
Rotation, 64, 206
Rouche, Jean, 297, 298, 299
Rücker, Günther, 25, 30, 35, 74
Rückwärts laufen kann ich auch (I Can Run Backwards As Well), 18
Russen kommen, Die (The Russians Are Coming), 34
Ruttmann, Walter, 37

Sabine Wulff, 16, 31, 34
Sägebrecht, Marianne, 37
Sales, John, 34
Salt of the Earth, 33
Sander, Helke, 36, 191
Sartre, Jean-Paul, 22
Sasuly, Richard, 77–78, 81, 86–87
Schall, Ekkehard, 105
Schamoni, Peter, 36
Schauspielerin, Die (The Actress), 30
Schenk, Ralf, 19 n22
Schiller, Willy, 2–3, 19 n1
Schlösser und Katen (Castles and Cottages), 28, 31, 80, 81, 83–84, 90
Schlüssel, Die (The Keys), 15, 31, 222, 226
Schmidt, Evelyn, 16, 18, 184, 195–200
Schubert, Helga, 35
Schulze-Mittendorf, Walter, 64
Schütz, Helga, 12, 31, 35, 231
Schygulla, Hanna, 37
Schwab, Sepp, 6, 7, 8, 9, 96
Schweigende Stern, Der (The Silent Star), 80
Schweikart, Hans, 80
Searchers, The, 29

Seemann, Horst, 16, 53, 185, 223, 243 n19
Seghers, Anna, 120–21
Sehnsucht der Veronika Voss, Die (Veronika Voss), 37
Seitensprung (Escapade), 16
Sekretär, Der (The Secretary), 273
Sheriff Teddy, 33, 207
Sie nannten ihn Amigo (They Called Him Amigo), 33
Silberman, Marc, 181 n4, 195
Simon, Rainer, 15, 17, 34, 50
Sinclair, Upton, 120
Sirk, Douglas, 22, 30, 37
Söhne der großen Bärin, Die (The Sons of the Great She-Bear), 14, 40 n12
SOLO SUNNY, 16, 31, 33, 49, 55, 123, 126–27, 130, 164, 165, 192–94, 212
Sonderbare Liebe, Eine (A Strange Kind of Love), 50
Sonnensucher (Sun-Seekers), 15, 29, 31, 165, 222
Spiegel, Sam, 34
Springer, Axel, 108
Spur der Steine (Traces of the Stones), 13, 25, 29, 37, 131, 133, 136–37, 142, 144
Spur des Falken (The Falcon's Trail), 40 n12
Staatsanwalt hat das Wort, Der (The Public Prosecutor Has the Floor), 150
Stagecoach, 29
Stahnke, Günter, 12, 133
Stalin, Joseph, 9, 89, 228
Staritz, Dietrich, 159 n1
Stars, 272, 274, 275
Stärker als die Nacht (Stronger than the Night), 28
Staudte, Wolfgang, 1, 3, 25, 27, 28, 32, 38, 39, 59–61, 64, 83, 206
Stein, 18
Sterne (Stars), 73, 165

Stunde der Töchter, Die (The Daughters' Hour), 219
Stranka, Erwin, 16, 31, 34, 219
Straß, Der (Synthetic Ice), 18
Straub/Huillet (Jean-Marie Straub and Danièle Huillet), 36
Sukowa, Barbara, 37
Sylvester, Regine, 185, 194

Tangospieler, Der (The Tango Player), 245–63
Tate, Dennis, 257
Teufelskreis, Der (Vicious Circle), 70
Thalbach, Katharina, 15, 36, 232
Thälmann, Ernst, 79, 83–84
Thate, Hilmar, 15, 36, 37
Thorndike, Andrew, 38
Tintner, Hans, 33
Trauberg, Ilja, 4, 6
Tressler, Georg, 71, 106
Tulpanov, Sergei, 2, 3, 60

Ulbricht, Walter, 14, 85, 89–90, 209
Und deine Liebe auch (And Your Love Too), 11
Und nächstes Jahr am Balaton (And Next Year at Lake Balaton), 218
Union Pacific, 28
Unser kurzes Leben (Our Short Life), 16, 49, 184, 189–92, 213
Unser täglich Brot (Our Daily Bread), 34, 38, 206–207
Untertan, Der (The Kaiser's Lackey), 25
Ursula, 242 n10, 243 n19

Verdammt, ich bin erwachsen (Damn It, I'm Grown-up), 216
Vergeßt mir meine Traudel nicht (Don't Forget my Traudel), 80
Verlobte, Die (The Fiancée), 30, 74
Vogel, Frank, 11, 12, 73, 133
Voigt, Andreas, 283–300
Volkmann, Herbert, 2, 3, 4, 6
Vonnegut, Karl, 143

Vor den Vätern sterben die Söhne (The Sons Die before their Fathers), 41 n24
Vorspiel (Prelude), 213

Wagner, Siegfried, 152, 161 n14
Wahlverwandschaften, Die (Elective Affinities), 223, 226, 236–41
Walesa, Lech, 242 n12
Wallroth, Werner, 14
Wandel, Paul, 2–3, 4
Wangenheim, Gustav von, 4, 58, 67
Warm, Hermann, 64
Warneke, Lothar, 15, 16, 18, 49, 50, 184, 189–91, 195, 213, 223
Wäscherinnen (Washerwomen), 273, 274, 275
Wayne, John, 29
Weber, Hermann, 159 n1
Weil ich dich liebe (Because I Love You), 210–12
Weiß, Ulrich, 17
Wenders, Wim, 36
Wendland, Günter, 152, 162 n24, 162 n25
Wenn du groß bist, lieber Adam (When You're Grown Up, Dear Adam), 133, 136
Werkentin, Falco, 147, 159 n2, 160 n4, 160 n5
Wexley, John, 27
Wicki, Bernhard, 36
Wild One, The, 34, 105
Wilder, Billy, 33, 123
Wilhelm Pieck, 38

Wilkening, Alfred, 6, 7, 8
Winter Adé (Winter Adieu), 285, 286, 287
Wischnewski, Klaus, 11, 12, 14, 265 n37
Witt, Günter, 13–14, 20 n30, 152–3, 161 n17
Wolf, Christa, 35, 48, 173, 215, 229, 252
Wolf, Friedrich, 3, 32, 33, 58, 88, 166, 167
Wolf, Gerhard, 229
Wolf, Konrad, 9, 11, 14, 15, 16, 29, 30, 31, 32, 34, 35, 38, 40 n15, 49, 53–55, 58, 73, 74, 123, 130, 192, 193, 197, 212, 215, 222, 223, 245–46
Wolkenstein, Alexander, 4, 6
Wood, Natalie, 99
Woyzeck, 63
Wunderbaren Jahre, Die (The Wonderful Years), 219
Wyler, William, 33

Young, Robert, 28

Zeit zu leben (Time to Live), 218
Zimmermann, Peter, 283
Zschoche, Herrmann, 12, 45, 72, 74, 133, 195, 212, 214–15, 218, 224
Zweig, Arnold, 69, 121
Zweite Leben des Friedrich Wilhelm Georg Platow, Das (The Second Life of Friedrich Wilhelm Georg Platow), 226

A Berlin Romance · The Adventures of Werner Holt · And Your Love Too · Anton the Magician · Apaches · Apprehension · The Axe of Wandsbek · Bear Ye One Another's Burdens · Berlin - Schoenhauser Corner · The Bicycle · The Blum Affair · Born in '45 · Carbide and Sorrel · Carla · Children of Golzow · Chingachgook, the Great Snake · Coming Out · Council of the Gods · DEFA Animation No.1 · The Destinies of Women · The Devil's Three Golden Hairs · Ete and Ali · Five Cartridges · The Gleiwitz Case · The Golden Goose · Her Third · Hot Summer · I Was Nineteen · Intrigue and Love · Jacob the Liar · Just Don't Think I'll Cry · The Kaiser's Lackey · The Legend of Paul and Paula · Look at this City · The Marriage of Figaro · Minna von Barnhelm · The Murderers Are Among Us · On the Sunny Side · Our Daily Bread · The Rabbit Is Me · Rotation· Rumpelstiltskin · The Singing, Ringing Tree · Snow White · Solo Sunny · Somewhere in Berlin · The Sons of Great Bear · The Story of a Young Couple · The Story of Little Mook · Sun Seekers · Trace of Stones · Tzar and Carpenter · Under the Pear Tree · Until Death Do Us Part · The Wall · Wozzeck

East German Films 1946–1990
Film and Video Distribution: Outreach · Teaching · Research

DEFA Film Library
University of Massachusetts Amherst
www.umass.edu/defa · defa@german.umass.edu